IMPORTANT LANDMARKS

HAWAII

1	Beecroft Plantation—Kohala
2	*Hamakua Mill
3	Kailua (at Kailua Kona)
4	Kohala
5	Kona
6	*Kukaiau Mill
6	*Kukaiau Plantation
7	*Kukaiau Ranch
8	*Laupahoehoe
9	Niulii
10	Niulii Mill
11	*Paauhau
12	*Honokaa Sugar Co.
13	Union Mill—Puehaehu
14	Waiakea Mill
15	Honohina
16	Hakalau Plantation
17	Kamuela
18	*Aamano Plantation (next to Hamakua Plantation)
19	Hawi
20	Pepeekeo
22	*Kaiwiki Sugar Co. (Ookala Plantation)
22	*Ookala Plantation
23	Mohukona Point/Kohala
24	Waimea Grazing Co.
25	*Waipio Valley

*Now incorporated as part of Theo H. Davies & Co., Ltd. activities.

THEO. H. DAVIES & C º L™

FOUNDED 1845

Companies on Hawaii, today

HAWAII

25	Hawaiian Irrigation Co.
7	Kukaiau Ranch
26	TheoDavies Euromotors
27	Atlas Electric
27	Hawaiian Fluid Power
27	Pacific Machinery
27	TheoDavies Tire Co.
28	Hilo Iron Works
29	TheoDavies Hamakua Sugar Co.
30	Kawaihae Terminals

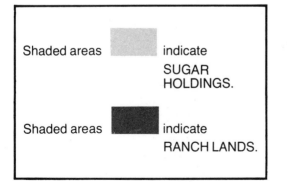

Shaded areas ▢ indicate SUGAR HOLDINGS.

Shaded areas ▮ indicate RANCH LANDS.

DAVIES

The Inside Story of a British-American Family in the Pacific and Its Business Enterprises

Theophilus Harris Davies, the founder of the company and father of the clan. Circa 1870s.

DAVIES

The Inside Story of a British-American Family in the Pacific and Its Business Enterprises

Edwin P. Hoyt

TOPGALLANT PUBLISHING CO., LTD.

Honolulu, Hawaii

1983

Library of Congress Cataloging in Publication Data Number
applied for:

Hoyt, Edwin P.

  Davies: The Inside Story of a British-American Family in
the Pacific and Its Business Enterprises.
    1. Hoyt, Edwin P.

ISBN 0-914916-57-2 Paperback
0-914916-58-0 Hardcover

Manufactured in the United States of America

 Published by
TOPGALLANT PUBLISHING CO., LTD.
845 Mission Lane
Honolulu, Hawaii 96813

CONTENTS

*Hard cover only

Preface

Theo H. Davies & Co., Ltd. has always been something of a mystery in Hawaii. From time to time writers have published histories of the islands' business and cultural life, and many of them have dealt with the Big Five, the major companies that so long dominated the islands. But in all this, Theo H. Davies & Co., Ltd. is scarcely mentioned, even when the Big Five are discussed. Volumes have been written on Castle & Cooke, Amfac, C. Brewer, and Alexander & Baldwin, but not on Theo Davies.

The reason for the void is not very complex. Among all the trading companies (that is how four of the Big Five started) Theo Davies alone was, for over a hundred years, dominated by a single family. Even at the end in 1973, when the company was sold to Jardine, Matheson of Hong Kong, the Davies family controlled thirty per cent of the stock. A Davies was chairman of the board of directors. It had nearly always been thus, and the second and third generations of the Davies family, being reticent Englishmen had never sought publicity or fame in the way that their American counterparts did.

Another reason for the mystery surrounding Theo Davies was the nature of the organization. The founder came to Hawaii and created the fortune. His sons superintended its growth. His grandsons came to carry on the tradition. But each of these men was a loyal and confirmed

Englishman, and only one of them ever seriously considered deserting England and coming to live in America forever. How they lived and worked, what they accomplished, and why in the end the Theo H. Davies & Co., Ltd. passed from the control of the Davies family is the subject of this book.

DAVIES

*The Inside Story of a British-
American Family in the Pacific
and Its Business Enterprises*

The Rev. Theophilus C. Davies, circa 1860.

Chapter One

THE VOYAGE OF THE
QUATRE BRAS

L*ate on the morning of November 14, 1856,* the Dutch barque *Quatre Bras* was making ready for sea in Liverpool harbor. Her master, Captain Bondix, was carrying cargo bound for San Francisco. He had agreed to take a passenger from the trading firm of R.C. Janion of Liverpool, bound for Honolulu, where the Janion company had its major sales outlet.[1]* When the passenger appeared on Princes' Pier and descended into the captain's gig along with his father, he was found to be an unprepossessing beardless youth of 22, slightly under medium height (5 feet 7 inches), so fleshless that the three tars who manned the gig could have taken odds that a moderate gale would blow him overboard.

The young man was Theophilus Harris Davies, and he was heading for San Francisco, and then Honolulu to repair a business career that had begun badly in a Manchester counting house.[2] The unknown, savage Sandwich Islands, as Hawaii was then called, seemed to offer an opportunity equal to the one that had slipped away from him on his native shore.

Theo H. Davies had been born in a suburb of Stourbridge, Staffordshire, on January 4, 1834, the eldest son of five children of a poor Congregational minister.[3] His grandfather, Emanuel, had more than a competence in the family seat of Llanover, Monmouthshire, supported by

---

*All references are listed beginning on page 443.

Lady Llanover, a fiercely independent Welsh woman who maintained the independent Llanover Chapel, and for 44 years kept the Rev. Emanuel Davies as her pastor. But after Theo's father, Theophilus, had been educated at Axminster Theological College, he had to make his own way. After holding two temporary pastorates, he was called to the Independent Chapel at Ludlow, where the living was miserable. The Rev. Theophilus Davies supported his growing family largely by keeping a school on the side,[4] and it was here that his son Theo H. was educated. The father must have been a good teacher, at least of grammar and English, because Theo H. all his life exhibited a distinctly literary turn of mind. As a teacher of mathematics and the ways of men, the Rev. Mr. Davies seemed on weaker ground, for when Theo H. left school at 17 and went out into the world he was schooled in religious matters, but miserably unready for a counting house.

He was hired by Henry Beecroft Jackson, a Manchester merchant who married into the Davies family. It was only proper for businessmen to take care of the families of the clergy, and so young Davies, no matter how inept, was to have his chance. He began work in the Jackson counting house just after Christmas, 1850. Within six months Henry Beecroft Jackson knew his young charge was a failure. Theo H. could not adjust his figures properly. The other clerks were openly scornful of him; he read the Bible too much, he did not drink or chase after shopgirls, and he shared none of the others' after-hours interests. For six years Davies labored in this arid vineyard, his peers laughing behind his back at his obtuseness. He was removed from his high stool at the ledgers and made a shipping clerk, where he could not ruin the balances. It was lucky for him; while the other clerks became expert at addition, Theo H. Davies learned to tell a full keg of nails from a short one and a perfect bolt of cloth from one with slipped warp, although in his wretchedness it seemed hard to understand for what purpose the Lord gave him this education.[5]

The purpose emerged in the early autumn of 1856, when R. C. Janion came up from Liverpool to see his friend and business associate, Henry Jackson, whom he knew from his old associations with Jackson's relatives, the Starkeys, who had started Janion in business. Janion said he needed a

bright young man to send out to Hawaii to work for William H. Green, the
Honolulu manager of the firm of Janion, Green & Company. The trouble
was, he indicated, that most young men these days seemed to lack ambition. They preferred the security of the counting house to the opportunity
of the unexplored.

"The very post for Theophilus, if only he had the pluck to take it,"
exclaimed Henry Beecroft Jackson.[6]

At that moment, young Theophilus was passing by the office, and Mr.
Jackson's tones had been strong enough to attract attention. Theo heard
and said to himself that, whatever new job they were discussing, he would
take the post if it were offered him.

He was not surprised then, a few minutes later, to be summoned to the
office of his employer. Janion wasted no time. He pointed to a set of
samples of Manchester cloth.

"Which of these would you send out to a savage foreign market?"

Theophilus looked and made his selection of cotton prints.

The Liverpool merchant nodded and smiled. "That's just right, my
boy. You have done very well."

Jackson looked at Janion, and then spoke.

"Theophilus, Mr. Janion wants a clerk for his firm in Honolulu. Will
you take the post?"[7]

"Yes," said Theo Davies, with no hesitation. And that was the word that
had brought him to this parting with his father on the deck of the *Quatre
Bras* on this chilly November morning. He would sail to San Francisco,
then transfer to a ship bound for the Sandwich Islands, and spend five
years as articled clerk to the firm of Janion and Green.

A clasp of hands, a hard swallow to quiet the lump in his throat, and
his father stepped down the ladder into the little boat. As the three sailors
turned the bow to the shore, the Rev. Mr. Davies sat on the thwart, waving
and smiling and growing smaller by the minute. Theo H. Davies stood
at the rail, gazing at the gig till it reached the land and his father emerged,
waved for the last time from the pier, and turned to go. How long would it
really be before he saw that departing figure once more?[8]

R.C. Janion

James Starkey

He emerged from the misery of reverie to see the ship's crew making last-minute preparations for sea. He was conscious of the clatter. The crew of the *Quatre Bras* had been largely recruited in the Dutch East Indies — Malays — and they worked to sea shanties that Davies had never heard before: "such a noise . . . unearthly groans."

Soon they were picked up by a tug and hauled out past the breakwater to the sea, the tug streaming its black smoke straight into the faces of all aboard the *Quatre Bras*. Then the tow was slipped, the sails set, and the barque was under way, bound for the Bay of Biscay, the South Atlantic, and eventually the Pacific shore of North America. The little barque took on a new action, rolling heavily in the quartering sea and pitching slightly in the current. Theo looked up; the mainmast was going 'round and 'round. For weeks family and friends had warned Theo H. that he would be seasick. He was not to worry; it happened to everyone, they said, and proceeded into accounts of their own first voyages with all the miseries made humorous by time. So Theo *knew* he was going to be seasick, and told the captain. Captain Bondix laughed.

William L. Green   Charles Reed Bishop

"Did you have plenty of ham and eggs for breakfast?" he asked innocently.

Theo H. rushed for the rail, and made it just in time. [9]

He was standing there, contemplating the depths of the gray water, when a cabin boy came up, sent by the captain, to ask if the passenger cared for any dinner. Theo took one anguished look at the messenger and turned back to the rail.

By evening he announced that he was prepared to enjoy the voyage. That night after the pilot left the ship, Theo climbed into his bunk and slept as soundly as he had ever done in his life, so deeply that he did not even notice the increased tossing of the ship as she entered a storm. Next morning as they moved through the St. George channel, the mate told him the captain had been up all night. The weather that Saturday was cold, rainy, and the sea was rough, but by evening they were out of the channel and in the greater quiet of the open sea. Theo said he was feeling much better, although he still did not have any desire to eat; a scrap of biscuit assured him that it would be wiser to try nothing more. It was Sunday

Port of Honolulu—1857.
Drawn from nature on stone by G.H. Burgess, 1861.
Courtesy Hawaii State Archives.

morning before he drank even a cup of tea. Sick? Of course he had not been sick; just a little weak and giddy. Wrapped up in his great sea cloak, he went on deck to sit at the stern on the edge of the cabin skylight and look down into the water. His father had given him portraits of all the family and three letters to read on board. Now he brought the letters out, and as he read he looked back at the low-lying shadow that was his native land, and in his imagination he was in church with them this Sabbath morning, and he no longer felt alone. So much better was his mood that he put aside one letter, from his sister Maggie, to read the following Sunday for the comfort he knew it would bring.[10]

He would not admit that he was sick, no matter how much Captain Bondix or the mate laughed at him. The mate said he must write home that he had not stirred from his cabin for two full days, but indignantly Theo refused. He was not sick, he insisted. Still, on Monday he slept until nine o'clock, and then did not go to breakfast or even on deck because it was raining. He stayed in his berth and read and dozed all day. A little of Dickens' *Sketches by Boz* was all he could manage; his head was not up to any concentration.

He ate dinner that day without enthusiasm.

The sea was strong but the wind was weak, the *Quatre Bras* made only four nautical miles an hour that day, and she pitched and tossed like a cork. Theo H. Davies wedged himself into the bunk, feet against the raised side of the two-and-a-half-foot-wide bunk, and his back against the wall. That way he spent the rough night.

But on the fifth day he awoke hungry and full of vigor. After breakfast he set to reading Ovid, but was distracted by the passing of a ship bound homeward. This incident prompted Theo to write a letter, just in case they stopped another ship which would deliver it. Next day they were in the Bay of Biscay, and the weather was rough. They were making nine knots, but when they passed another ship there was no chance to lower a boat and they had to be satisfied with an exchange of signals.[11]

Theo Davies' loneliness and homesickness were vanishing, however, prompted by a healthy interest in the world about him. He saw his first porpoises and gazed out with fascination as they passed three wrecks, one after the other. One was dismasted and reminded him of pictures he had seen in the *Illustrated London News*. Another was even odder: standing quite erect, completely under water, masts and rigging clearly visible. After a week aboard the *Quatre Bras* he was writing learnedly of the winds: "S.E. by S. & not from E.S.E. . . ." and bragging that with a good breeze *Quatre Bras* could make 200 miles a day. In a letter to his sister he described his tiny cabin with a little bravado. He was the sailor now, whose complaint was that perhaps he ate "too many pickled herrings for breakfast."

He observed the people around him with a shrewd eye—the young Dutch steward "whose mildness of demeanor is rendered more mild, by a certain oiliness which oozes out of his complexion . . ."; the captain, who invariably took gin and bitters at one-thirty for his stomach—and what a "stowmach" it was, said Theo; and the Malays, whom he discovered to be Javanese. He was much taken by one of them, Ba-wa, "the shortest, stoutest, youngest, and drollest looking of the troop."[12] He watched their dances. He roved about the ship, observing the crew at work. He read. He pondered his God's works and the universe and he kept the Sabbath by reading in his Bible and from James' *Christian Charity,* a going-away present from one of his sisters.

As a God-fearing youth he was much concerned with the loose habits of the crew. The captain took no notice of the Sabbath, except that the men were freed from all but essential work that day. He asked the captain why, and when told that Sunday was fixed only because "it is the custom," he was upset and vowed to try to work "with Christian dignity" among the members of the crew. He spent hours writing letters to all his friends and family, letters that would be surely posted at San Francisco if not before. He kept a daily diary of his activities and his thoughts.

Early in December they reached the warm waters of the South Atlantic and he saw his first flying fish—"average size of a herring . . . their motion . . . very much like a covey of partridges rising . . ." His reflections teetered between contemplation of the present and the past; one moment he was writing in his diary about the character of the oily steward, who turned out to be a "low German" rather than a Dutchman, and the next about the great Salt-and-Butter fair at Ludlow, which came to mind on its December 6 anniversary, and about his childhood and his mother, dead seven years before he sailed.[13]

He came to love Sundays:

" . . . it is *my* day; & now when I get to my solitary—no not solitary—worship, all seem to understand it, and leave me uninterrupted. Not solitary—when I pray, I know that many of God's people are bowing before his throne, & their prayers rise to Heaven, & mingle with mine as they ascend—when I lift up to God the voice of praise, I almost hear the refrain of many songs borne across the still sea on the breeze which blows so softly from my English Fatherland & the same God as He showers down blessings on His people there, lets them fall too on my head . . ."[14]

He was an intensely loyal, intensely reverent young Englishman, moving out into the far lands to earn his fortune, but not forgetting for a moment where his heart and home lay.

Chapter Two

THE NEW WORLD BECKONS

Even in the confined quarters of the *Quatre Bras,* young Theo H. Davies was subjected to a broader taste of the world than he had ever known in all his twenty-two years. On December 8, the ship was parallel with Sierra Leone, at a distance of 2,000 miles, and he found it hard to believe that he, Theo H. Davies, was "poking about this planet like a wandering Jew." The captain laughed at his young passenger's Calvinist ideas about drink and card playing, and one day they got into a discussion about dancing.

"Everything was given for enjoyment," said the old hedonist. "You don't suppose our legs were only made for us to walk with? No, they are to dance upon, too."[1]

Young Davies was shocked, but impressed enough that he jotted down the captain's remark as a "novel idea."

The voyage agreed with him in more ways than one. He gained weight; he had boarded the ship at a scrawny 120 pounds, but as they crossed the equator he was weighed and had gained half a stone (seven pounds). He began to exhibit a sense of humor, and wrote in his diary a long essay about rats, and fleas which he said threatened every member of his body. "If I find myself vanishing rapidly, I shall tie ten labels to my toes, so that whoever gets the last bits of me will have hanging out of their mouths tablets—'Sacred to the memory of the big toe of Theophilus

Harris Davies, which were barbarously slew & eat per bearer' . . ."[2] Christmas brought a profuse outburst of poignant memories to his pen: ". . . I floated away my wishes to dear old England, the stronghold of Christmas . . ." and he managed to make believe he was home at the festive table even as the steward fed them a dinner of boiled ham, boiled potatoes, boiled peas, boiled rice, parsley sauce, raw pickles and baked prune tart. On January 4 he was solemn: ". . . it is a day of many anniversaries . . . my birthday—the anniversary of my first being received as a member of Christ's Church on earth & of my first partaking of the sacred ordinance of the Lord's supper, besides being the first Sabbath of the first year of my foreign life . . . Should it not be a solemn day?" He, who had never tasted alcohol in his life, was constantly urged by the captain and mate to take a little port, or a little gin for his health. He refused to drink port with them, but he did drink small amounts of gin and water, finally admitting that he suffered dreadfully from seasickness every time they hit rough weather. Here at the outset of his exile, one of his Calvinist strictures had been tested—and dented.

Alcohol, he found, did have its uses. By January he wrote that he had taken a glass of brandy and water before bed to guard against the cold: "I think I am quite justified in this . . . if I could get milk or gruel or proper tea or coffee, I should prefer them, but in default I shall not hesitate to take spirits . . ."[3] He had pledged to his father that he would not use liquor in any form, but already he had made the decision that circumstances altered cases. The world of Theophilus Harris Davies was growing broader every day, the rough food and the fresh air agreed with him. He continued to gain weight as well as experience, and by the time the ship was off the coast of California he weighed in at 138 pounds. He was still often preoccupied with thoughts of home: his mother's birthday had fallen on February 24, and he recalled the happy celebrations of the past. But his diary was filled with accounts of the captain's harpooning of a bonito and his own growth of a mustache and sideburns to add dignity to his 23 years. Already he was studying the captain's books and charts, to learn about Hawaii, his new home. He learned with some dismay that the island of Oahu was 40 miles long and 20 miles wide. "I think of five years repose in the buzzum of the Pacific on 40 by 20! I have set it down that Oahu is a parish, and Kamehameha IV is H. M. The Beadle. My reason for endeavoring to keep under my ideas of the nature of my new abode is the very plausible one: 'blessed is he that expecteth nothing, for he shall not be disappointed.' "[4]

Theo H. Davies was beginning to have some very definite ideas about Hawaii and the Americans there. Janion had given him several copies of *The Pacific Commercial Advertiser,* and he was not much impressed with the quality of the journalism. "The editor," he wrote, "seems to me the very essence of an American democratic newspaper Editor, with an insufferable amount of bombast . . ." He was eager to be getting on, but still homesick; on March 7 he noted that he had been sixteen weeks abroad with never the sound of a proper English voice to welcome him, and he was lonely in his English tastes and habits. But he knew that he was changing already: "I leave England almost a boy—I shall return a man." His dreams alternated; one moment he was thinking about the fresh crisp spring mornings of England with "perfumed primroses and violets twinkling with the dew," and the next of the flower garden he would have in Honolulu. Then, suddenly the white cliffs of California loomed up and they were entering the Golden Gate. The pilot came aboard and brought them in to anchor, and Theo H. Davies was soon ashore in the new land.[5]

San Francisco in 1857 was a rough place, a small port made suddenly large by the 1848 discovery of gold at Sutter's Creek up the Sacramento River, and California a state of the American union for just seven years. Davies landed on a plank street run down across the marsh to the bay, and he moved up dusty streets through the wooden fronts of the city buildings to the establishment of White & Wilson, the Janion agents in San Francisco. He was expecting letters there, but there were none, to his disappointment. Wilson got him a two-week guest card at the Union Club and found him a room at the Tehama House. He met several other Englishmen and soon had settled in comfortably, taking his meals at the Union Club dining room, at a long table divided into an American end and an English end. The British consul presided over the English end. Young Davies was immediately struck by the difference between American and English manners and ideas. He was a little queasy about Americans, but some of this feeling was dispelled by excellent treatment in San Francisco. One American, George Ward, approached him *without an introduction,* but he could hardly take offense, because Ward offered to take him to the Mercantile Library Association and enter his name for a month. But on the streets he found the smoking, chewing, and spitting of San Franciscans "disgusting," and he was shocked to see every public room of every building "teeming with spittoons."

He had left England expecting the worst, having read of a wild jumble of dirty houses filled with foreign scum, with a murder at every other street corner. Instead he found the Union Club's cuisine equal to any he had ever known (which was probably not saying much), and he was surprised to see large blocks of stores, with shops "equal to England's." But the people were garishly dressed to his taste; the men had too many rings and the women wore too many layers of clothes. True to his background, Theo Davies spent much of his San Francisco stay in churches. He visited six different churches, Episcopal, Presbyterian, and Congregational. He went to Sunday-school meetings and prayer meetings. He visited Mission Dolores and heard tales of the vigilantes who had brought order out of chaos a few years before his time. He had a brief meeting with Humphrey Griffith, one of his cousins who had come to live and practice law in Sacramento, and then he was on board the American clipper *Yankee* on his way to the Sandwich Islands.[6]

Davies made friends among the passengers, and some valuable contacts. The only woman aboard was Miss Judd, daughter of Dr. Gerritt P. Judd, who had been Kamehameha III's Minister of Finance and had accompanied the king on a visit to England. He also met Maurice C. Monsarratt of Honolulu, a Britisher born but a Hawaiian citizen, and an auctioneer in Honolulu. Young Davies found Monsarratt amusing and debonair. They argued with the others amiably on the voyage across the Pacific, becalmed half the time, over the respective merits of England and America, with Davies and two compatriots extolling the English government and way of life. Davies did not much care for Americans, he found: "I have not met with one person except my own countrymen who come up to my ideas of 'well bred.' " The Americans, as he had feared, were a coarse lot, and he had some qualms about his future for the next five years.[7]

But the voyage was pleasant enough, in spite of his critical appraisals. At six o'clock every morning one of the *kanaka* boys (the native name for Sandwich Islanders, he informed his family) rang an immense bell all around the cabin, and at seven the breakfast bell rang. The first sitting usually consisted of the captain, Miss Judd, a Spaniard, Mr. Monsarratt, and Davies. After breakfast they wandered about, talked, and read; Davies was just then reading Abbott's *Life of Napoleon*. They dined at noon and then went on deck, walking to digest the heavy meal. Tea came at five o'clock, although the Americans called it supper, and then as darkness fell, he, Miss Judd, and Mr. Richard sang "glees," while the rest of them played cards for money. Theo Davies was a popular young man because he had his guitar with him and could play any number of songs. So the days passed, and Davies even grew used to the card-playing although he was not at all inclined to join the gamblers. Then, on May 6, when he awakened they were in sight of land, first Koko Head and then Diamond Head, the extinct volcanoes, and then the groves of coconut trees along Waikiki beach. They rounded Diamond Head and Honolulu came into view, dropping down from Nuuanu valley with its clumps of dazzling white balconied houses.

Soon they were approaching the harbor, surrounded by canoes full of Hawaiian men and women who had been fishing until the ship came in. Most of the men were dressed in shirts and trousers but some wore only the *malo,* a three-inch strip of cloth. The American Congregationalist missionaries, who had come to Hawaii a quarter century earlier had worked diligently to clothe the natives, the women in long high-necked Mother Hubbard dresses (known locally as *mu'umu'u*) and the men in European style. They had already been largely successful in Oahu, but there were holdouts who insisted that the old Hawaiian ways were best, in spite of the power of the foreigners.

A steamer came out as the *Yankee* neared the entrance to the coral reef that surrounds Honolulu harbor, and a pilot came aboard while the steamer took the sailing ship in tow. As the ship anchored, other white men also came out in small boats and boarded. Davies was introduced to Mr. Fishbrooke, the bookkeeper of R.C. Janion & Company, and Fishbrooke took him ashore.[8]

The wharf was lined with natives in brightly colored clothing but Theo H. Davies scarcely saw them; he was busily chattering to Fishbrooke about his voyage and looking about him to find the store where he would work. Soon they were there, in the store on Kaahumanu Street which was obviously the largest and finest establishment on the street. (Later Theo Davies would learn that it was the most important trading company in the islands.) There he met the manager, Mr. Green, who greeted him enthusiastically, wearing neither coat nor waistcoat. Mr. Green, he soon discovered, was a man of many parts; he was author of a book of geology, *Vestiges of the Molten Globe,* and a farmer, as well as a trader. Green had come to Hawaii from Valparaiso, Chile, where his father had been a partner in Green, Nelson & Co., but he was an Englishman. Davies learned some of these facts that day. He would learn much more later. The conversation was not long; Fishbrooke was waiting. He then took the new member of the firm back to the waterfront to secure a landing permit from the king's harbormaster. Taking two horses they rode up the Nuuanu Valley, so the new clerk might see the house where he would live. It was Robert Janion's old house, now tumbledown and full of mildew, but it had a beautiful view of the town below and the ships in harbor, Punchbowl Hill's fort on their left, and the watery taro patches down below along the brook called Nuuanu River.

They returned to the wharf, and the Hawaiian harbormaster first said there was no need to examine the young man's luggage; but when it was landed and he saw there were dozens of boxes, he insisted as a matter of dignity that he must open at least one. Young Theo Davies, not used to the sensitivities of native officials in a land already dominated by white foreigners, was more than a little annoyed as he stripped off rope and canvas covering, and unlocked a box for the harbormaster to investigate. Honor satisfied, he was then allowed to bring his possessions ashore and was officially a member of the Hawaiian community. The new life had begun.

(Left) Robert W. Holt, one of the "old misers," immigrated from Warwickshire to Boston where he married Miss Agnes Jones, a daughter of Boston merchant Owen Jones. Jones was also the father of Mary, who was married to Captain John Dominis. Holt and Dominis were closely associated in business. When Holt's first wife died, he was influenced by Dominis to migrate to Hawaii. He joined the shipping firm of Robinson & Company and ultimately married Robinson's eldest daughter, Caroline Tauati.

(Right) James Robinson, another of the "old misers," settled before 1820 in Hawaii, after being shipwrecked northwest of Oahu. He married a Tahitian Lady of high rank (the mother of Caroline). After her death he married a third time, an alii Rebecca Prever and produced a large family of children who became famous later in the island history: Mrs. Victoria Ward, Mrs. Mary Foster, Mrs. W. H. Allen and Mrs. Rebecca McWayne, were Robinson's daughters from the Prever marriage.

There is little known of "Bobby" Lawrence, third of the "old misers," nor is there a photograph to be found of him.

William A. Aldrich (photo page 45) founded, with Charles R. Bishop (photo page 7), the First Hawaiian Bank, known then as Bishop and Aldrich. Aldrich married Miss Elizabeth Holt, the surviving child of R.W. Holt's first marriage. Bishop and Aldrich were loaned $25,000.00 by R.W. Holt in 1858.

The "old misers" were connected with some of the most important business activities of their time. They were pioneer industrialists of Hawaii.

Davies' reference to the three old misers is not only lacking in dignity, but inaccurate as well. Holt, Robinson and Lawrence were active enough in the early Honolulu community and they certainly contributed enormous financial assistance to the business community over the years that followed. [See Diaries of Stephen Reynolds, and Papers of the Estate of R.W. Holt, Archives of Hawaii.]

Chapter Three

JANION, GREEN & COMPANY I

The firm that *Theo H. Davies* had come to join was little more than a dozen years old on that day when he arrived aboard the *Yankee*. It had its origins in the business of James Starkey, a Liverpool merchant, who traded around the world and had established a Honolulu trading house half a century after Captain James Cook had brought to the attention of London the existence of the Hawaiian archipelago. In 1825 his Britannic Majesty George IV appointed Richard Charlton, then the British representative in Valparaiso, to be consul in the Pacific. His area of responsibility covered most of the islands Cook had discovered, but especially the Sandwich chain and the Society Islands, which included Tahiti.[1]

Although Captain Cook was the discoverer, the Americans began the exploitation of Hawaii in the 1780s with the coming of the fur traders and whaling ships. The small British community pressed London for assistance in the form of official representation. Whitehall considered the request. Perhaps a deciding factor was the visit of King Kamehameha II to England. Hawaiian royalty had a strong feeling for England and it had been strengthened by the aggressive behavior of the American missionaries and traders who came to the islands. For one reason, England was a monarchy, which the Hawaiian *ali'i* (nobility) understood better than a republic. For another, England was then the most powerful nation in the world. Kamehameha I had incorporated the Union Jack into the Hawaiian national flag when he learned that a flag was a prerequisite of nation-hood.[2] Later kings would seek British protection for the monarchy, and Hawaii would be offered to Britain as a possession several times. Kameha-meha II (Liholiho) had taken his queen to England to see how his friends lived, and had died of measles there at Claridge's Hotel. The ship that brought the news of Richard Charlton's appointment also brought the bodies of the king and queen to Honolulu.

When James Starkey came to Honolulu, he and Charlton became good friends; both were ambitious men, and they were leaders of the English community in the unspoken struggle with the Americans for commercial dominance.[3]

Charlton managed to secure from the palace a 299-year lease signed by Kalanimoku, the royal regent, on a piece of land 127 yards by 160 yards in the heart of downtown Honolulu, on the east side of Kaahu-manu Street (now covered by Honolulu's wharves), crossing Queen Street and running to the water's edge. But the Hawaiian government refused to confirm the move and would not give Charlton good title, since the established policy of the royal government had been to allow only Hawaiian subjects to acquire land.[4]

Consul Charlton was furious, and after making all the representations he could in Honolulu, he sailed for England to pursue his claim, hoping that Her Majesty's government would insist on his "rights." In this era of colonial power the British government often intervened in the affairs of supposedly independent governments in a manner that would appear outrageous a century later, so Charlton had good reason to expect support from London.

He left the consular affairs in the hands of Alexander Simpson, an Englishman of strong imperialist sentiment, and his business affairs in the hands of Starkey.[5] Both pursued claims Charlton made against the Hawaiian government.

In the spring of 1843, Lord George Paulet arrived in Honolulu harbor with *HMS Corysfort,* a part of the British naval squadron under Admiral Sir Richard Thomas, which was stationed at Valparaiso, Chile, to oversee

British interests in the Pacific. Simpson told the tale of the mistreatment of Charlton and of other actions by the Hawaiian government that he considered to be outrages against the welfare and property of British subjects. Paulet was a precipitant man; he issued an ultimatum to the Hawaiian government, and concluded by running the Hawaiian flag down the pole in front of the old Iolani palace and running up the Union Jack. For five months Hawaii was a British colony, until Admiral Thomas arrived, sent Lord George Paulet off to sea, and restored the islands to the Hawaiian monarchy.

Charlton never came back to Hawaii. His place as consul was taken by General William Miller, a military hero from the War of 1812 and the Peruvian revolution. Meanwhile, Starkey too had gone home to England, leaving his affairs in the hands of the firm of French and Greenway, who had contracted to act as his agents in Honolulu. But French and Greenway went broke, leaving a dreadful financial tangle involving the affairs of Charlton and Starkey. They had one claim against the Hawaiian government for $11,000. Back in Liverpool, James Starkey pondered the problem. He needed a man in Honolulu if he was to settle the claims and make sure his business survived. He found the man in Robert C. Janion, who had connections in Manchester with Starkey's relation, Henry Beecroft Jackson.[6]

They talked over the prospects of Hawaii, and Robert C. Janion decided to go out to that far land as partner in the new firm of Starkey, Janion & Company. The partnership was formed in April 1845, and was to continue until September 1850. James Starkey had a third interest and his brother John Starkey had a third. Janion had a third, and a guarantee that his average share for the first two years should be at least £500 a year. They were not then precisely certain that business in Hawaii would continue to be profitable enough to maintain a partner, and they made provision that Janion might move to Mazatlan or Guaymas, Mexico, if he felt the prospects were brighter there.[7]

Honolulu had been a base for trade with the Orient, the raw unsettled coast of California, Mexico, Chile and Peru, but most important in the

1840s was the whaling trade. After the near whaling grounds of the South Atlantic were virtually exhausted, British and American whaling ships moved into the Pacific and found new waters off the coast of South America, then on the fringes of the Antarctic, and finally near Japan. The voyages, which in the 1830s had usually lasted a year or less, began to extend to two years and more, and the ships needed a waypoint for reprovisioning, and sometimes for shipment of their oil to London and America. Trading companies began to prosper, supplying the ships with everything from rum to oak boards for the cooper's barrel staves. The Hudson's Bay Company opened a branch in Honolulu. Other firms were formed, and some prospered while others failed, depending on luck and aggressiveness. One of these firms was Brinsmaid, Ladd & Company, which had offices on the *mauka* (mountain)-*ewa* (west) side of Nuuanu and Queen Streets across from the fish market and the Hudson's Bay Company. On his arrival in Honolulu, Robert Janion took a room in the Ladd store for $1,600 a year, and Starkey, Janion & Co. was in business.[8]

Such was the competition between Englishmen and Americans in these days that an American businessman, J. F. B. Marshall, noted Janion's arrival in a letter to a friend, and remarked, "I do not think we Yankees will be obliged to evacuate the islands in consequence . . ."

Janion bought a piece of the Charlton land for $10,000, built three warehouses and then undertook the sale of lots. The Hawaiian government was challenging the Charlton sale and warned both Janion and the public that the Charlton lands were not legally held by either Charlton or Janion.[9]

In the years before 1845, the Starkey firm had prospered by bringing trade goods to the islands, selling to whalers, and shipping out hides, skins, tallow, sugar and sperm oil to England. They owned several vessels based in Honolulu, including the *Tepic* and *Eleanor Chapman.* They sent goods by many more which sailed from Liverpool.

Shortly after his arrival in Honolulu in 1845, Janion wrote a report to his partners in Liverpool.[10] He was disturbed because the whaling season had been a bad one, with few ships putting in, and those reporting a scarcity of whales in the old grounds. Several captains had also reported losing whales which sank after harpooning. No one could explain this strange development, but it was most unsettling and gave Janion concern over the future of the whaling industry in the area.

Janion complained that the Starkeys had misrepresented to him the potential trading business in the islands. He estimated the yearly business he could conduct would bring in sales of $400,000. Commissions to the Starkeys in Liverpool would come to $10,000 (at 2½ percent). Operating expenses would take perhaps another $3,000. He had been hoping to make £1000 a year from the business (then about $5,000), but he did not see how he could.

The Starkeys could not have paid much attention to this complaint, for then, as always in their correspondence, Janion was manic-depressive; his next paragraphs were as optimistic as the previous ones had been pessimistic.

He had, he said, been looking about for an alternative industry that could be profitable for them. He had settled the various land and goods claims for $5,000 in cash, bills on the Hawaiian government for nearly $10,000 more, and had kept the goodwill of the Hawaiian government as well. So if something could be found to replace whaling, the climate was proper for continued and expanded trade between Liverpool and the islands. He had some trade with China, through the Jardine Matheson Co. Ltd. of Hong Kong. He had been meeting with representatives of the government and urging them to encourage capitalists to expand Hawaiian agriculture. He was particularly interested in sugar and coffee, and told his partners it had been established that both did well in the Hawaiian island climate. Sugar cane had grown wild in Hawaii as long as anyone could remember; the Rev. Hiram Bingham, who put the Hawaiian girls in Mother Hubbards, had grown sugar in the old taro fields below Punchbowl; Consul Charlton had a small sugar plantation, and there were a few crude mills on the island. The first commercial crop had been planted in 1835 at Koloa, Kauai. In 1845 sugar was brought into the Honolulu market at 2.5 cents per pound, but the demand was so great that the price shot to 6 cents a pound. As for coffee, he said the local coffee was superior in flavor to mocha, and grew "most luxuriantly."[11]

Consul Charlton had the right idea, Janion said. He had raised cattle, slaughtered and salted down beef to sell to the whalers very profitably at $14 per ton(250-gallon cask). At the moment the prospects did not seem very bright because of the attitudes of the Hawaiian government. What was needed was a sale of land, but whether or not that would come about was debatable, given the attitude of the Hawaiian government about land. The king was supported in his refusal to sell land to foreigners by his cabinet, which included such men as Dr. Gerritt Judd, Minister of Interior, and R.C. Wyllie, "a Scotch adventurer" who was Minister of Foreign Affairs, and John Ricord, whom Janion regarded as a scoundrel, as Attorney General. What Janion objected to particularly was the "ignorance and stupidity of the principal advisors to the king, who place every obstacle in the way of those seeking to expend capital and develop the resources of the country."[12]

Charlton, for example, had been forced to transfer his cattle lands to Janion so that Janion could look after them and protect them. A case had been brought in court against Charlton for trespass of his cattle on other lands.

So it was all very complicated and very unsatisfactory, and Janion felt that as matters stood the prospects were not very good for business. He accused the Starkeys of misleading him back in Liverpool.

But in spite of businessman Marshall's rude prognosis and Janion's disappointment, Starkey, Janion & Co. prospered in Hawaii. Still, the seeds of dissent had been sown. Two years after his arrival in Honolulu, Janion complained to John Starkey about "the disagreeable tone of Jim's letters."[13]

In 1847 Janion decided to take a look at San Francisco as a possible source of more business. He left his Honolulu affairs in the hands of his clerk, Mr. Faulkner, and the bookkeeper, Mr. Johnston, and sailed for California on the *Laura Anne* in November. He stayed in San Francisco two months and returned sure that even if ruin threatened in Hawaii because of the conditions there, he could prosper in California. Liverpool, he said, threatened the ruin of them all by its tactics. The Starkeys were complaining that Janion was not remitting money back fast enough for the goods shipped. He had already overremitted, he said, because the goods they were sending simply would not move that fast. For example, he had £2,000 worth of metal goods, mostly copper and lead, and there was virtually no market for it in Hawaii, where all the other trading firms had the same inventories. Janion had been lucky enough to ship most of it to California, where he had sent clerk Faulkner to open a store.[14]

Janion could not have been luckier. In January 1848, a few days after he founded the store and sailed back to Hawaii, gold was discovered at Sutter's Mill on the American River in the Sacramento valley. The population of California began to rise in geometric leaps and in a year it reached 100,000. All talk about failure stopped.

In Honolulu, Janion became a powerful figure, and his house the most important trading firm in the islands, very largely because of the San Francisco connection. He set up the *Sandwich Island News,* and employed an editor named Rockwell to manage the weekly paper. The purpose was to express the views of the foreign business community in their disputes with the Hawaiian government—and especially to press for the sale of lands to foreigners: the pressure plus that of other *haoles* (foreigners, but usually meaning Caucasian foreigners of the privileged class) brought about the Great Mahele (land distribution) of 1848. King Kamehameha III put the finishing touches on a change in Hawaii's land-tenure system that was to have a vital effect on the future of the islands.[15]

Originally, the Hawaiian chiefs controlled all the land. The major check on their power was the freedom of people to move and live elsewhere. No one owned land as such. When a noble died, his land went back to the great chief. But Kamehameha I had permitted lesser chiefs to inherit land, and that was the first change. Other kings made other grants, such as the Charlton grant, to *haoles* who wanted to build stores and warehouses, and to farm. The *haoles* treated the land as their own, and bought and sold it and leased it out, without regard for the Hawaiian concept that ultimately all the land belonged to the king. Kamehameha III had espoused this old theory. But in the 1830s Hawaii was opened to settlement by various foreigners, the French missionaries and English and German and American traders, and the government had been forced by treaties to give special land rights to some foreigners. In 1841 the king legalized various leases held by foreigners, but the *haoles* wanted more—the fee-simple title to their land. Dr. Judd was one of the most compelling advocates of land sale, and in 1848 he pushed the king into splitting up the crown lands. One half of them would thereafter be the king's private preserve; one half would be government lands to be controlled by the legislature. Some 250 chiefs became fee-simple landowners, and from that point on the *haoles* began to buy up the available lands. This economic change, plus the susceptibility of the Hawaiians to foreign disease, exemplified in the tragic deaths of Kamehameha II and his queen in London, made it inevitable that control of the kingdom would pass into the hands of the aggressive whites.[16]

By 1848, Janion was working busily in Honolulu. Having assumed charge of the Charlton lands, he was selling some of them off, but he retained his warehouse on the Charlton land that fronted on Queen Street and had access to the Charlton Wharf, and the lots adjoining up to property on Fort Street which belonged to Skinner & Company. The Great Mahele made moot the question of Charlton's legal right to hold Hawaiian land and the political quarrel over the land came to an end. Janion stayed right there on it.

In the spring of 1849, Janion wrote Charlton that he was doing a "rousing trade" in San Francisco. It must have been so, for he drew on Faulkner at San Francisco for $78,890 and referred to the $50,000 in gold dust in Faulkner's hands just then. Still, things were not going so well in Honolulu, and he was pressed for cash there.[17]

There were other complications. The Americans had sent a minister to Hawaii after signing a treaty in 1842 with the kingdom, and after that a series of American representatives moved to secure the annexation of the islands to the United States. President John Tyler announced that the United States claimed a paramount interest in Hawaii and would not allow any other nation to seek control of the kingdom. In 1849 this extension of the Monroe Doctrine was put to test when French Admiral Legoarant de Tromelin[18] sent troops ashore and occupied the public buildings of Honolulu in a dispute over the treatment of French Catholic missionaries. The United States might have taken military action, but the Paris government repudiated the admiral's action. Still, the hubbub had increased the sentiment of the American community for annexation of the islands, and this development made Janion gloomy. Five years earlier, the British commercial houses had been equal in number to the American. Now, his own house was still the most powerful of all, thanks to San Francisco gold, but the number of retail stores had increased from 32 to 75 and the vast majority of them were American.

Janion was negative about the long-range prospects when the whaling trade would fall off. Already the American ships from Nantucket and New Bedford were outnumbering the British, and naturally much of their business went to American firms in Honolulu. The great plus factor was that growing market of California which opened a whole new future for the traders. Everything that could be consumed by Americans could be sold in San Francisco at enormous profit. Even old taro patches were uprooted on the islands and wheat was planted for shipment to California.

Yet, all in all, Robert Janion was a happy man. In 1849 he married 17-year-old Domitila, the daughter of Francisco Rodriguez Vida, the Chilean consul in Honolulu, and they began to raise a family. He put away money, dreaming of the day when he would have a competence and could return to spend his life in England.[19] To speed that day, Janion went back to California and spent much of the last of 1849 and early part of 1850 there. He called for help from Liverpool, and John Jackson Starkey came to San Francisco while Janion went home to Honolulu. From the beginning Janion had disapproved of James Starkey's methods, and he quarreled anew with both brothers, who accused him almost constantly of deserting their interests for his own.

The original partnership was about to expire in September 1850, and the Starkey brothers seemed to be even more disenchanted with Janion than he was with them, for although he suggested formation of a new partnership, they wrote him that they wanted to end the relationship. John Jackson Starkey would take over the San Francisco end of the firm, and Janion in Honolulu would be on his own.[20]

John Jackson Starkey and Janion apparently made up their differences, and Starkey assured Janion that the relationship would be continued. There would be a new arrangement, however. The San Francisco firm would be separated from the Starkey-Janion partnership, and Janion and John Jackson Starkey would each have half shares. Since Janion estimated the value of the firm's real estate then at $500,000, it meant he was to have half of a very sizeable business.

The books of the old partnership were to be closed on August 31, 1850, and John Starkey set about clearing away.[21] The date set for valuing and transfer of lands was March 31, 1851, but Starkey was delayed, and on May 4, 1851, the great San Francisco fire that swept away most of the wooden buildings of the city destroyed the firm's building among them. This failure by John Starkey to keep his deadline brought new frictions between the partners. But the quarreling was made moot by events: John Jackson Starkey died; James Starkey overextended himself in Liverpool and on September 14, 1851, his assets were assigned to his creditors. That act terminated the partnership, and Janion then was on his own.

The change made it necessary for Janion to make new arrangements for a principal firm in England, which would secure the trading goods for Hawaii. That plan fitted precisely with his own yearning to return to England. He was tired of the islands; he had been astounded in California to see that butter sold for a dollar a pound, and he felt that the high California prices had begun to ruin the islands as well. A *kanaka* cook demanded—and got—$16 a month! Laborers were refusing to work for less than 75 cents a day! His living expenses had risen drastically to £700 a year![22]

The problem was to secure both the English and the Honolulu offices. Luckily, his clerk, William L. Green, had proved eminently satisfactory in the year he had worked for the firm. There were also two others, Ritson and Phillips, and a youngster named Duff "on trial." The office opened at six o'clock in the morning, and Janion and Green were there then. Phillips and Ritson came at seven-thirty, and at eight-thirty they all took time off for breakfast. Then they worked steadily until four o'clock when they had dinner. They returned to the office to finish whatever needed to be done, and if a ship was about to leave they might labor until midnight.

Green had done so well that Janion had no fear of leaving him in charge of the Honolulu office. He offered Green a three-year contract at $800, $1,000 and $1,500 a year, board and lodging, and the prospects of partnership if the arrangement worked out well. Then Janion prepared to go home to England. That year his father-in-law died in Honolulu, so Domitila had no further family ties there. Still, there were responsibilities. Foreign Minister Wyllie had asked Janion to take over the Chilean consul's duties temporarily, at least, and he did; so it was the end of 1852 before Janion could move his family from Honolulu to Liverpool, where he established his office as correspondent and purchasing agent for the Honolulu firm. (He also later established a business in Victoria, B.C., and one in Portland, Oregon.)

Green was a good manager and the business did well, with Janion doing the buying shrewdly in England. In 1855 the firm moved its Honolulu offices into new quarters in a building erected by James Robinson & Company, known as the Robinson Block, on the *makai* (ocean) side of Queen Street, opposite the end of Kaahumanu Street, near the water's edge—an area occupied in the twentieth century by the great steamer wharf and the Aloha Tower.[23]

Having seen the coming end of whaling and the San Francisco venture having gone sour, Janion turned his attention to other avenues of profit. In 1855 he secured appointment in Liverpool as agent for the Northern Assurance Company, one of Britain's largest insurance firms. The company had also acquired the Hawaii agency for Lloyds of London when the Hudson's Bay Company withdrew from Hawaii shortly after Janion's arrival.

Janion came back to Honolulu in 1855 for a brief visit, but with no

intention of remaining in the islands. He visited the new building, conferred with Green about the staff, and decided a new clerk should be sent
out from England. Then Janion went home to Liverpool, and in time
visited Henry Beecroft Jackson in Manchester. That was how young Theo
H. Davies came to arrive in Honolulu that spring morning of 1857.

Chapter Four

JANION, GREEN & COMPANY II

T*heo H. Davies slipped easily* into the routine of the life of *haole*s in Hawaii. Having just come out from England, he was lionized from the first day and deluged with introductions, and requests to call on various families. He lived in the Janion house that Green rented up Nuuanu valley, but at first took most of his meals at the British club downtown. Green lent him a horse to make the trip up and down the valley, but after the first week he declined, saying he preferred to walk for exercise. After two weeks he also found it more pleasant to board with a Mrs. Everett.[1]

He was particularly befriended by the Judds, having met Miss Judd when he travelled with her aboard the *Yankee*. Dr. Judd had fallen afoul of the foreign community until a petition was put up for his removal from office as Finance Minister, and he resigned to return to the practice of medicine.

The Judds lived in a fashion common to the respectable *haoles:* in a large house, surrounded by gardens and lawn, behind a planted row of trees, looking down on Honolulu from the side of Nuuanu valley. The family employed half a dozen *kanaka* servants to clean and garden. The Judds entertained often; the first week of Theo's Honolulu residence he attended a party at Mrs. Judd's sewing society with eighty other guests.

Six weeks after Davies' arrival, one of the Judd children died. He went to the funeral, and then, almost alone among the young *haole* community, he refused to attend a ball held aboard a French man-of-war, out of respect for the family.[2]

This sensitivity, his excellent singing voice, his guitar, and manners that were to most Americans exquisite, made Theo Davies the most popular young man in Honolulu with hostesses. They could count on his promptness. They knew he would not burn up the furniture because he did not smoke, or embarrass the party because he did not drink, and there was no young man a doting mother would trust further with the morals of her daughter, for his probity was complete.

Some of Davies' ideas about the world began to change. Mrs. Everett was a Spanish lady in her late twenties. She gave him breakfast at eight and dinner at four-thirty and sent a lunch down to Mr. Everett's store where Theo went after noon. Mr. Everett, Theo Davies discovered with some sense of shock, was "an American, but, strange to say, a gentleman for *that country.*"[3]

The Everetts gave him the run of the house, and invited him to all their parties. He could even ask guests.

The social life of the Honolulu *haole* community was carried on at a furious pace. Everett was the successor to Robert Janion as Chilean consul, and Davies' connection with the Janion firm created an immediate bond. But the community was so small that all respectable folk knew one another and saw one another frequently. Mrs. Everett took Davies to call on General Miller, consul and Her British Majesty's commissioner in Hawaii. He attended the funeral of Chief Justice W. L. Lee of the Hawaiian kingdom and had his first glimpse of the king, Kamehameha IV, and Queen Emma. The king was tall, thin, dark brown of complexion, "*very* gentlemanly in his appearance," and the queen was several shades fairer than the king, "but is becoming too stout."[4] They were approximately the same age, just a year younger than Theo H. Davies. The young merchant was interested in their dress, and in their income, which he said was $16,000 a year.

On the Fourth of July, with great reluctance, Davies attended the American Independence Day celebration at the U.S. Consulate (". . . to

think that I could ever attain such a melancholy climax of 'dispatriotism.' ")
He could excuse his breach only because Dr. George Lathrop, the consul,
was "a very nice man" and his wife one of the few ("entre nous — very few")
American *ladies* in Honolulu. Young Mr. Davies, besides his antipathy to
rebels, was a thorough young snob, and already spoiled by his hostesses.
He commented on the "large supply of marriageable feminines" in Honolulu and suggested that they were all thrown at his head by their doting
mamas.

At this particular party Davies spent most of his time with the McKibbens. Dr. McKibben lived in a big house on Beretania Street, which had
become the center of social life in the small British community. Davies felt
more at home here than anywhere else in Honolulu, including the
Everetts. The McKibbens had two daughters, the second of whom, Mary,
was the belle of Honolulu. They brought the young Englishman into their
party, and soon he was dancing and singing and laughing with the rest.[5]

As a Congregationalist, Davies should have found himself completely
at home with the American religious community. The Boston mother
church which had sent the missionaries out to Hawaii in the '20s was the
direct descendent of the Puritans who had left England's shores in the 17th
century, while the Rev. Mr. Davies' Congregationalists had remained to be
dissenters. But the missionaries were soon too much even for Davies' sometimes priggish ways. They frowned on card-playing and dancing and gai-
ety. Of them all he found most tolerable the Rev. S.C. Damon of the
Bethel Church, and soon he was singing tenor in the choir and was active in
the Sunday school there.

Two months after Davies' arrival, Hawaii was hit by one of those
strange fevers that so often ravaged the islands —they called it influenza.
It attacked foreigners as well as natives, and many people died. Churches,
schools, and stores were closed down; the Supreme Court was suspended.
The Rev. Damon, who published a monthly religious and cultural journal
called *The Friend,* suggested that the epidemic was a visitation of the Lord
on the wicked, which in his view meant nearly everyone in the community
save the missionary faction.[6]

Honolulu, as Davies observed, was "as setty and cliquey as the most misanthropical of Englishmen could desire." The major, division of *haoles* was between missionary and commercial factions. But there were also officials of various degrees, an American minister, commissioners, consuls, and the Hawaiian government. Among the business people, there was division between the high living and the sedate, with far more of the former swilling rum at parties than the latter drinking tea.

"It is a place of great dissipation, and a very low kind of dissipation . . .," Davies wrote home to his family. How shocked he must have been, immediately on his arrival in Honolulu, to learn that his amiable shipboard acquaintance, Maurice Monsarrat, was a scandalous figure. A few months before Davies' arrival, Monsarrat had gone to dinner at the palace of Prince Lot Kamehameha. They had sat up talking and drinking late, before Monsarrat said it was time to go home to his wife and family. But later still that evening, a servant came to Lot and said the *haole* was in Princess Victoria's room. Lot burst in the door, and found them there, undressed. Lot threw Monsarrat out of the palace with the warning that if he saw him again he might kill him. Monsarrat sailed hurriedly from Honolulu to San Francisco. But by April he had recovered his bravado and so was aboard the *Yankee* with Theo H. Davies. King Alexander Liholiho (Kamehameha IV) had him arrested and locked up in the Iolani Palace. Next morning Davies' new friend was taken down to the harbor and put aboard another ship, banished from Hawaii for life on pain of death.[7] Later, the king reduced the term of banishment and allowed Monsarrat to return, but by Ludlow Congregational standards, Honolulu's society was totally dissolute. The Hawaiian nobility regarded sexual intercourse with the same attitude that an Englishman regarded a kiss on the cheek. There was no stigma attached to such liaisons or the children of them. The Hawaiian line of family succession was through the female, and all children were adored and pampered by the group. But it was a society totally unlike any that the young Englishman might have dreamed about, and it would take luck and intelligence for one with his background to succeed here.

Davies was lucky enough and bright enough to live in both worlds.

The Janion company was foremost among the traders, and its employees were highly respected. Manager Green knew everyone. He was known for his work as a geologist as well as a merchant, and the book he was writing on Hawaii's volcanoes was to be regarded as the authoritative study. He was interested in everything about him, and dabbled in a dozen activities, sugar, shipping, cattle-raising, as well as scholarship. He approved of Davies on sight, apparently, and warned him at the outset that as a young man of religious background he would find much that was rough in Honolulu, but that he need not conform to ways that did not suit him. "Your convictions will be respected," Green said.[8]

Besides Green, and Davies who was to be his assistant, the Honolulu company consisted of bookkeeper Fishbrooke, a cashier, a boy, and three porters who did the carrying. The warehouse on Kaahumanu Street was bursting with goods; it had grown too small for the business, and soon something would have to be done about that. The business activity was periodic—it depended largely on the coming of the whalers, which meant about three months of intensive activity each year, and a great deal of spare time in the rest.

Theo H. Davies was an inquisitive young man, and he spent that spare time learning about the country that would be home for five years. One day he went to the Court House to watch the administration of justice and was dragooned to become a juror, because of a shortage of "honest and intelligent men" to make up a jury of 12. He wrote a long account of the entire proceeding in his diary.[9] He joined a riding party led by the French commissioner M. Perrin, and went on many happy evening rides around the Oahu countryside. He collected curios to send home to his family: shells, a canoe model, and coral; a Hawaiian language Bible for his father, jewelry from the Marquesas for his sisters, and sandalwood for them all.

In the business world, he was happier than he had ever been. He liked Mr. Green because, "He does not show superiority as Brierly, Briggs and Fred (clerks in the Jackson counting house) used to do . . ."

By the turn of the year 1858, Theo H. Davies had made himself valuable in the business. Green was, as Davies put it, "up to his moustache" in plans for a new store to handle the growing business. He leased another lot from the Hawaiian Interior Department for $325 a year, and soon loads of coral were being delivered at the corner of Kaahumanu Street by the king's men. (One of the royal perquisites was the sale of building materials to the foreigners.) By June the store was nearly finished. Theo Davies was not very pleased to learn that Green had built sleeping rooms over the warehouse, and intended that his staff should occupy them. Green, a bachelor, would live there as well, and sell or lease out the Janion Nuuanu valley house. With Green busy on plans and construction, Davies took more responsibility, and when the cashier left the firm that summer, he was given charge of the cash.

When the time came, Theo Davies balked at moving into the warehouse rooms, and went to live with Captain G. H. Luce, former commander of the brig *Tepic*, which the Starkey, Janion partnership had operated to deliver trade goods to the Pacific. Luce had retired from the sea and settled in Honolulu as a pilot after the dissolution of the old partnership. The Luces were like a second family to Theo Davies. When they moved to the beach at Waikiki for six weeks during the summer, he stayed in town with two old maids, the Misses Montgomery, but on Sundays he walked the four miles to the Luce beachhouse to dine with his friends.[10] When the Luces came back they all moved into "Little Britain," General Miller's house, which was two miles from Honolulu. The General had given up his post and gone back to Valparaiso, whence he had come to Hawaii, leaving B. T. Nicolas in charge of British interests. Generally speaking, British interests were not flourishing in the islands; between 1845 and 1856 imports from the United States had totalled $6 million, while those from England, France and all other countries came to only $5 million. Britain accounted for $2 million of this, much of it through the Janion firm. But the tale, as R.C. Janion had gloomily predicted in 1845, was told in the whaling fleets: in 1845 four English whalers had called at Honolulu, compared to 90 American. In the next twelve years, 400 European whalers had come, compared to 4400 American. There had been three British business houses: Hudson's Bay Company, Skinner, and Starkey Janion. Hudson's Bay

Company was long gone.[11]

R. C. Janion Company did a good business in fire insurance in Honolulu after the acquisition of the Northern Assurance agency. They were also favored by some of the American whalers who were working in the Pacific arctic. They went into the arctic and Okhotsk in March and came to Honolulu to ship oil and refit in September. These two times were the busy ones. As the ships came in, the crews were paid off in *lays,* each lay being a share of the cargo depending on the authority and responsibility of the man. The values had to be figured in Honolulu. Janion, Green bought the oil, or acted as agents for the shipowners, and made the payments. Then the sailors went to town to spend their money for the next few months, until whaling time came again in spring. Theo Davies quite disapproved of this whole aspect of the business:

> Meanwhile we folks ashore live merrily on the proceeds. We do not touch the dirty men's wages, but we provide for the wants of those that do. Have we not been laying up stores of flashy prints and costly silks and satins and hats and perfumes and fine English ales and the best, at least the strongest, of brandies to meet the demands of the glorious carnival? The charm shops and the dance houses are open every night, and the lights and sounds of revelry are incessant. Troops of Hawaiian maidens come from country homes to Honolulu for the carnival, and few of them ever return, but still the puzzling question is asked: 'Why do the native races perish . . . ?[12]

Theo Davies made a resolution then; he would never in his own right deal in the goods that corrupted men.

But the whaling trade was not all the trade. Two days after Theo Davies arrived in Honolulu the ships *Pearl* and *Osk* came in to coal on their way to China. The Janion Company sold coal, and Theo Davies was sent to the wharf to supervise and weigh baskets of coal loaded aboard the vessels. For two days he went down in the morning and came back at night as black with coal dust as any coolie, but when there were no ships in harbor, life was very quiet. In June 1858, Theo Davies had enough leisure to take a walking trip completely around Oahu with his friend Captain Luce.[13]

The black cloud of disaster appeared on the Hawaiian horizon in 1859. That year, off in the American state of Pennsylvania, the first oil well was drilled, and the production of kerosene (paraffin) began. In 1852, one day, W.L. Green could point to $10 million worth of whaling ships in Honolulu harbor. This meant business in many ways, not the least of them the accommodation of destitute seamen. Two years later the Janion company earned $5,000 from just that source, mostly from American ships because of Green's good connections. In 1856 sperm oil was selling at $1.60 a gallon in Hawaii, and ordinary whale oil at 75 cents a gallon. But in 1859 the price of sperm oil dropped to 90 cents and whale oil to 30 cents; such was the impact of kerosene on street and household lighting.[14] In the squeeze the new American consul, Abner Pratt, gave all his business to American firms, and Janion, Green had no more commissions to outfit and care for destitute seamen from the U.S. government.

The disaster struck just after Janion, Green had moved into its new building, and just after Green had been taken into partnership by Janion. What was to be done?

In this dark hour, fate intervened for Janion, Green & Company. Consul Nicolas had been behaving strangely for several months, disappearing for long periods of time, and making strange statements at public meetings. In February it was apparent to the British community that he was teetering on the brink of insanity and, in fact, the next month he went over the edge. He became violent and had to be restrained with ropes.

The British residents met to decide what must be done. Someone had to take over the seals and badges of the commissioner's and consul's offices. Britain must be represented at the Hawaiian court. Wills, depositions, and customs papers had to be taken care of by someone, and the needs of British merchant ships and Her Majesty's naval vessels must be met. Green's popularity in the English community and his aggressiveness won him the post by acclamation, just when he needed the source of income most. He took over the seals and archives, and wrote the Earl of Malmesbury, Secretary of State for Foreign Affairs, to report what he had done. He also sent his papers to Foreign Minister R.C. Wyllie of the Hawaiian Kingdom and received acceptance there. A month later former acting consul Nicolas was bundled aboard a British ship, still in a strait jacket, and sent home to Portsmouth, accompanied by E. S. Ruggles, an Englishman with some medical experience, and a servant. Green paid all Nicolas' doctor bills and passage and sent the account of $2,248 to the Foreign Office.[15]

Thus, William L. Green became Her Britannic Majesty's official representative in Hawaii, and the situation of Janion, Green & Company was greatly enhanced. Green henceforth occupied himself much with government business. That autumn he held a Naval Court of Inquiry and the trial, by a jury selected by him, of a British shipmaster charged with manslaughter. He had to bring a case in Admiralty regarding property saved from a wrecked British ship. He wrote to London that he had "an inordinate number of shipwrecked and destitute seamen."[16]

One reason for all this activity was the emergence of Victoria, British Columbia, as a major port of trade. Hawaii was directly on the route from England to Victoria, and even though the whaling trade was dying, more British ships touched at Honolulu than ever before.

When gold was discovered in British Columbia, Green decided to dispatch a schooner loaded with trade goods. He suggested that his young assistant might want to take charge of the cargo, and open a branch of the company there. Theo Davies was excited at the prospect until he learned that the principal articles of the trade were to be beer, wines and spirits. He backed off then, and told Green that he did not feel that he could take the responsibility for selling liquor to the Indians. Green shrugged. Then someone else would have the chance, he said. And so it was; a young man named Chapman who had no such scruples went with the cargo.[17]

But the incident left the Davies-Green relations unscarred. That year Lady Franklin, a British noblewoman, visited Hawaii and Davies persuaded Green to give a reception for her. Green agreed if Davies would do all the work, so he planned the party, sent out 400 invitations, arranged for the music, the ballroom, the food and the decorations. The party was held in the courthouse.

They had the legislative hall inside for supper, and the court room for the reception, and the clerk's room for the use of "royalty and rank."

It was a great success although the orchestra was dreadful—it seemed to consist of one piccolo and noise. (Davies had engaged a French piccolo player who promised to gather an orchestra for the occasion.) During an interval, Davies saw the first-violin player start to sneak out of the ballroom.

"Where are you going?" asked the young impresario.

"My God, Mr. Davies, I can't stay here!"[18]

Davies persuaded the first violinist to remain in the building with his second violinist. One more quadrille with the piccolo squeaking and he fired the orchestra on the spot, and brought out the violins. The evening was a success in spite of all, so much so that out of it came a romance, engagement and eventual marriage of William Green to Mary McKibben.

After the successful ball, Green thrust still more responsibility onto his young assistant, and soon gave him total authority to run the business, subject to his approval. Green was busy with his consular duties, his book, and a search for new investments.

All the traders were gloomy about the prospects in Hawaii. What was needed was something new in the way of industry and business. Guano (phosphate deposit) seemed to offer some hope, and several expeditions were sent out to find Pacific islands bearing heavy deposits. There was, of course, the marine insurance business, which was increasing as more British ships came to Hawaii. There were possibilities in the sugar business, too, Green said. Over on Kauai, Ladd & Company was operating at Lihue as agents for various sugar growers, and they had a steam-driven mill built for them by H.A. Pierce. When the mill was finished, a mechanic, O.M. Weston, was sent out from Boston with a power lathe to finish the installation. In 1851, when it was done, he opened a shop on Miller Street near Beretania in Honolulu where he milled flour and repaired equipment. One of his specialities was the manufacture of brass sugar baskets. The firm prospered, Weston began working on the invention of a sugar centrifugal machine and built a new building near the customs house.[14] The name of the firm was later changed to the Honolulu Iron Works. The flour mill was continued but became less important part of the business.

In 1859 Weston sold the Honolulu Iron Works to Thomas Hughes and went back to Boston. Part of the business was in sharpening spades and boarding knives for whalers, part was with the sugar planters, keeping the Pierce mills from Boston in operation. Green began to make loans to Hughes. He sensed the importance of the Iron Works. Green was good at this sort of activity—locating opportunities, but he was a dreamer, and most of the daily routine was left to Theo H. Davies.

The original staff continued: Fishbrooke, the bookkeeper, Gaskin, the cashier, Duncan, a general clerk, and the porters. When Theo H. Davies had the responsibility, he soon learned that Fishbrooke, although a splendid accountant, was completely unreliable. He drank, and when Green was away, as he often was on business in the outer islands those days, Fishbrooke was invariably drunk. Theo H. Davies stood it as long as he could, but eventually he had to push Green into discharging the bookkeeper. Fishbrooke sank to the depths, finally pulled together enough money to ship out for Sydney to gain a new start, but at the last Theo H. Davies heard he had drowned himself in Sydney Harbor.[20]

Green was completely careless about the accounts. All the salaries were overdrawn, Theo H. Davies discovered, except his own. He was the most frugal of young men. Aboard the *Yankee*, his chameleon friend Monsarrat had complimented him unctuously: "Davies," said the philanderer, whose peccadillo had apparently been conducted under the influence of drink, "never drink or smoke and it will save you $200, and if you have no other vice it will save you $500."[21]

Davies followed that advice. He had no vices, save perhaps a shade too high a view of his own superiority. In his first six months, Theo H. Davies had been paid a salary of $368 and a board allowance of $260. He had spent only $344, including $7.50 for bear grease for his hair (which made him the envy of the coarse old American consul Abner Pratt, who always called him George) and he had saved $284, which he left with Mr. Green at twelve per cent interest.[22] Theo Davies was on his way.

He found it hard to understand a man like Gaskin, good-hearted and steady in his work but perennially short in his cash. After Fishbrooke's departure, Davies tried to push Gaskin into righting his records, but Gaskin simply could not keep accounts straight. When the shortage reached $900, Davies had again to go to Green, and Gaskin was discharged. Duncan had the idea that he could pilfer the petty cash when Davies was put in charge. Davies called him to account, and Duncan pleaded with him not to tell Green, but Davies felt he must report the thefts and did. Duncan left Honolulu.

These departures left Theo Davies as the only English member of the staff save Green. Davies then had the responsibility for sales, cash, and the books. The firm hired local help a Señor de Sequeira (a Chilean language teacher with the manners of a count, who could not add, and Hayward (a deserter from a passing ship) who ruined Green's best horse by galloping him all over Honolulu.[23]

Theo Davies' intense periods of work were still interspersed with long holidays. In 1859 he made a trip to Hawaii.[24] The schooner *Mary* landed Davies and his guide at Kawaihae, on the barren northwest coast of the Big Island, and he rode to Waimea, where he stayed at the house of the manager of the Waimea Grazing Company, in which Janion, Green & Company had a large interest. As he rode up to a snug little house in a grove of peach trees, he was greeted by George MacFarlane, a young lad he had known in Honolulu. MacFarlane was spending his school holidays with his relative, manager Mallett and his wife. Davies slept in George's room. He took the boy with him the next day on a ride about the ranch with Mallett, and was pleased to see for the first time in Hawaii a landscape where trees were trees of the sort he knew at home; indeed he remarked on the similarity of the general countryside to England, minus the hedgerows and cornfields. The whole district was thick with cattle, wild beasts descended from the animals that Captain Vancouver left on the island when he visited there. These animals belonged to the Hawaiian Crown, but up above them the Parkers had rights to the cattle on their range, and Waimea Grazing Company had rights for five years to the cattle they could reclaim from the wild.

Davies took George MacFarlane with him for company on a horseback visit to the lava flow and then returned to Waimea for a week to enjoy a climate that was really temperate. He and George rode up Mauna Loa to pick strawberries and amused themselves in ways that were familiar to an English youth. When it came time to leave, a little sadly, he saddled up his mule and headed for his next destination, the Hamakua coast, via Ku-kuihaele, which he reached by traveling first through a skeleton forest. He was accompanied by a middle aged *Kanaka* on a white horse, a guide who did not talk, practically at all, on the way. Then they were in Mud Lane, a natural pathway that ran through the forest; it was notable because during the rainy season the ground was covered with mud so thick that the horses were often fetlock-deep in it, and strangers needed a guide to carry them safely through. Davies rode through eight miles of this morass along a narrow track, with jungle pressing in from both sides, "the intricacies of the most exaggerated quagmire that I had ever considered . . . what wonder if I felt some relief at being able to stand on the brink of the exquisite valley of Waipio . . . "[24]

He was in virtually virgin forest. "A perpendicular precipice, 500 feet high, barred our journey in that direction, and looking down I beheld the white foam girding the rocky base with its incessant roll." The scenery was truly overwhelming, but in time he grew accustomed to its lush beauty and went on down the Hamakua coast, stopping to eat his spartan lunch of bread and egg, to marvel at foliage and the dozens of streams and water-falls that coursed down to the sea. He stopped at Laupahoehoe and visited the plantation of Abel Harris & Company. Then he went on to the mission kept by the Rev. Mr. Coan at Hakalau. Captain Worth took him from Hilo to the volcanic crater of Kilauea. He spent several days in Hilo and became friends with David Lyman and Henry Alexander, the sons of two American missionaries. He kept his eyes and ears open and came back knowing a great deal about that island.

Then after six weeks, it was back to work. Janion, Green & Company's shipload of whiskey had proved satisfactorily that a business house could be opened at Victoria, and that autumn of 1859 Green took a ship for British Columbia to establish the firm properly. Davies was left then, not only as head of the office, but also as (acting) British Commissioner and Consul.

The company was always short of money. Charles Reed Bishop and William Arnold Aldrich had not yet established their bank, Bishop & Company. The only "bankers" on the island then were three old misers who operated under the name of J. Robinson and Co. They were Englishmen: Messrs. Robinson, Laurence, and Holt, and nobody knew how much money they had. What was known was that none of them ever seemed to spend a penny. They had been shipwrecked in the islands years before and had amassed money in the early days of trade. When the firm needed money, Davies would go to their offices with notes from Green. Old Laurence would take him up a rickety flight of steps to his bedroom, and there he would go over the notes one by one. Then, if it all was right, he would go into a little loft and come out with a bag of gold and count out ten-, twenty-, and fifty-dollar gold pieces. The interest rate was 1½ per cent per month.[25]

When the Bishop Bank (now the First Hawaiian Bank) was formed, one of its first borrowers was Mr. Green, who took $4,000. He needed money to finance the many enterprises to which he was committing the company. When the Honolulu Iron Works building burned down

(left) William A. Aldrich co-founder with Charles R. Bishop of the Bishop Bank, (now the First Hawaiian Bank). photo courtesy of Hawaii State Archives

on the night of December 29, 1860, with a loss of $55,000, Mr. Hughes did not know where to turn. Green recognized the opportunity and invested in the company. In two years Janion, Green & Co. were in control.

The year 1860 brought the American elections, and the disaster that overtook the United States with the election of Abraham Lincoln. Business was terrible; in the spring of 1861 the American crisis had upset everything. Janion, Green was the only house making any money, and that apparently largely because of the Canadian trade, but Janion, Green's business was off fifty per cent. The Honolulu Iron Works was prospering, building equipment for the sugar plantations that sprang up on every island. The markets were good in California and British Columbia. Green sent to San Francisco for his agents, White & Wilson, to hire a boiler maker and a moulder for the firm.[26] William Green was close to a number of people in the Hawaiian government, particularly Foreign Minister Wyllie, whom he saw often in his capacity as (acting) British commissioner and consul. For several years the government of Hawaii had been eager to establish steam navigation between the islands. In 1853 a company was organized with a 150 ton steamer named the *Akamai* that took twenty days from San Francisco. She was built for river traffic and went to pieces in the rough channels of the islands. In 1854 two steamers were brought in. One was a coal burner and coal cost so much ($30 a ton) that the boat was never used. The other made regular trips to Maui and Kauai until she was lost off Koloa in 1856. The company failed. A few years later there was talk about starting a government line, but the government did not have the money. An offer was made to grant a franchise, and in 1858, C. A. Williams agreed to buy a steamer and establish the service on an exclusive basis. But Williams quarreled with the government and nothing came of the proposal. In 1860 William Green organized the Hawaiian Steam Navigation Company, and Janion, Green & Company became agents as well as principal stockholders.[27]

Green brought the wood-burning steamer *Kilauea* to the islands and converted her to coal. She was licensed in July, 1860, and began her inter-island voyages. There was plenty of business, most of it managed by Theo

H. Davies, and the following year he and Green were talking about ordering another steamer for the trade. The Hawaiian government invested $5000 in the company's stock, which was doubly valuable because it indicated government approval. But after the initial response, the traffic fell off. In 1862, the steamship company was in debt $12,000 and Green offered to sell the government his shares for 60 cents on the dollar if the government would also take on the debt, or to buy the government interest for 40 cents on the dollar. The government refused to sell and offered Green 40 cents a share which he refused. The negotiations broke down, but the government and Janion, Green continued in ownership and Green continued to operate the line.[28]

As the year 1862 began, Theo Davies talked about going home. His five-year contract would end that spring and he had promised his father that he would come back to England. He mentioned this at the McKibben's house one evening, and next day Green came upon him at the office and asked if this report was true. When Davies affirmed it, Green told him how pleased Janion, Green was with his work and offered to re-engage him for two more years. He would be raised to £320 for the first year and £360 for the second, would be given a $500 allowance for the trip home, and be on half pay during the trip, with all other expenses paid, if he would look after the company's interests when in England. He could be gone for eight months, four in transit and four in England. At the end of the two years, perhaps there would be a partnership in the offing.[29]

In May Theo Davies said his goodbyes, with promises that he would be back soon enough, and in June he was on his way home, happy and self-satisfied as he had a right to be. The stigma of the Manchester failure had haunted him so during the five years that he had mentioned it often in letters to his father. Now he felt that it was entirely wiped out.

Chapter Five

INVITATION TO DISASTER

*T*heo H. Davies sailed for home in June, 1862, by way of Victoria, so he could have a look at the house Green had established there and get a feel for its needs and the opportunities involved. He was looking forward to the partnership that had been suggested. He was supposed to travel from San Francisco to the isthmus via the *Golden Gate*, but missed connections when he stayed in Victoria. It was a lucky miss; the *Golden Gate* was destroyed by fire, and his family in England, believing he had been aboard, were distraught until they finally heard from him.[1]

The English summer was passed in tranquility in the family gathering places. There were some embarrassing moments when he discussed religion and life with his father, for Theo had changed his ways. To "relieve biliousness," he had begun drinking, first beer and then wine at table. He was temperate now but not abstemious, and this attitude took a bit of explaining.

He had the explanation. After observing the strange habits of the American missionary group in Hawaii, Theo Davies had come to the conclusion that he would live his life according to a code of his own. He would do with pleasure those things that did not interfere with his character. The American missionaries, for example, had an absolute horror of dancing — immoral they called it — yet those same missionaries cheated and misused their servants. He would dance, and he would sing, and he would drink a little if he felt like it.[2]

Theo Davies' attitude toward the missionaries also accounted for a change that was harder for his father to understand: his switch in allegiance from Congregationalism to the Church of England.

During the first year or so of his stay in Honolulu, Theo Davies had been a full supporter of the Congregationalist minister, the Rev. Mr. Damon. He had been leader of the choir at the Bethel Church and Superintendent of the Sunday school. But in spite of his attachment to Mr. Damon, he could not but feel that the Congregationalists of Hawaii were American Congregationalists, and when a move was begun in the royal household and among British subjects to bring a bishop of the Church of England to Hawaii, Davies decided that he would become a member of that church; it was so much more English. The American dissenters were a bombastic, hypocritical lot. Just before he left for England he attended a meeting to enroll subscribers for the Anglican church and was elected secretary. The king was there and he gave $300 and a plot of land. All this had to be explained to the Rev. Mr. Davies, who listened and said nothing. His silence was indication of the disappointment he felt that his son would desert the family way, but he never raised his voice against the move.

Other than these matters, all was serene in the Davies household, and the visit was a successful and pleasant interlude. The months sped by, until early in 1863 Theo set out from home for Liverpool and visited with Janion, who suggested that Davies would be more useful in Liverpool, with his knowledge of Hawaii, and that the partnership eventually should take that form, with his return to England after a year or two. Then he sailed from Southampton to Hawaii.[3]

Many changes had occurred in the few months since Theo Davies had left the islands. Bishop Staley and two Church of England ministers had arrived. Davies quarreled with them almost immediately, particularly with the Rev. Mr. Ibbotson, who thought it outrageous that Davies would not submit to confirmation in the church because he had been confirmed as a Congregationalist. The bishop suggested that he go back to the Bethel Street church. The quarrel was amplified by Davies' remarks that the ministers were a "bunch of Griffins."[4] He objected to their high church ceremonies and the arbitrary decisions of bishop and clergy. He and Ibbotson continued to feud, leaving Davies to regret his part in bringing them out to Honolulu, and to recall the statement of an old *kamaaina* (person born of the land): "We have never had as pleasant times in Honolulu since we had the mails only twice a year around Cape Horn—ah, that was a magnificent time! Honolulu has not been the same since."

But what was really worrisome was the situation Theo Davies saw at the office. In his absence William Green had been plunging recklessly into debt, acquiring sugar lands and plantations, a greater interest in the Iron Works, and deeper involvement in the steamship business. His debts had grown and instead of remitting monies to Liverpool for goods sold, he was spending them on new investments and floating more debt.

From the standpoint of progress, William Green was years ahead of his time. Sugar was the future of the islands. The Honolulu Iron Works was becoming vital to the sugar industry. The *Kilauea* steamed from Oahu to Hawaii in less than 24 hours where it had taken four or five days for the schooners to reach the Big Island.

But coal was expensive, and the *Kilauea*'s boilers were not efficient. Green also followed a strange theory of steamship management, especially for an agent of Lloyd's: he did not carry insurance on the steamers on the theory that "they insured each other." The reason for this peculiar attitude seems to have lain in his experience with the *Kilauea*. For after Green had bought her in 1861, the ship had suffered an accident, and the insuring agents, Williams & Haven, had refused the claim.[5] The matter had been handled through the Hawaiian kingdom's Department of Interior, since the government maintained a financial interest in the company, but the claim was still refused. The government suggested that under the circumstances perhaps Janion, Green & Company could secure insurance in England. Green agreed to this course, and wrote Janion to secure $30,000 of insurance on *Kilauea* at twelve per cent. But such was his experience thereafter that he abandoned insurance on his other vessels even as he expanded operations. He apparently believed the money could be better used to put more ships in operation and increase profits to protect against losses.

The S.S. *Kilauea* moored at Honolulu Harbor, 1881 (center of photo) in the days when the sailing ships made the city a major port. Courtesy: Hawaii State Archives.

He proposed to the Hawaiian cabinet that the government put even more money into the Hawaiian Steam Navigation Company. The cabinet discussed the matter. He had asked that they buy an interest in his new steamer *Annie Laurie* and in the steam schooners *Emma Rooke* and *Nettie Merrill,* and that they buy an additional $10,000 in stock. The cabinet turned Green down on all counts.[6]

The *Kilauea,* by this time, was a liability. Her boilers were not worth repairing, and Green wanted to put something into her to get her across to China, where virtually anything that floated could be sold at a profit. But all this took capital, and he was desperately short of capital.

Many aspects of the business were better than ever. A Belfast company had just engaged Janion, Green & Co. as agency for their roofing and sheathing felt. Northern Assurance Company had just reduced its rates for fire coverage in Hawaii, and they could offer the best insurance bargains in the islands.

But other signs were not so favorable. The Hudson's Bay Company complained that Janion, Green should have remitted for collection of some accounts left in their hands years before. Boord Son & Beckwith of

London complained that they had been induced to make large consignments of liquors to an indifferent market—this was true because the
decline in whaling and the beginning of the American civil war had put
a serious crimp in the profits of the Honolulu grog shops. Piesse & Lubin,
perfumers, London, complained that Janion, Green had not settled an
old account. And there were others. There had to be, for Green was
grasping all the cash he could lay his hands on to feed the demands of too
many young businesses expanding too fast. He bought into the Lahaina
Sugar Company. He extended the investment in Honolulu Iron Works.[7]
He had a dozen schemes for long-range profits. The trouble was that they
were too long range.

Janion and Green agreed that Davies would be more valuable to the
firm in Liverpool, where he could answer questions about Honolulu. After
all, Janion had not visited the islands since 1855. It was agreed on April 1,
1864, that Davies was to have a salary of £100 each from the Honolulu and
Victoria houses, plus a commission on sales from each which he estimated would bring his annual income to over £600. And he could live in
England![8]

Davies was eager to be off. This second sojourn in Honolulu had been
far less satisfactory than the first. The state of the religious atmosphere
disturbed him, and he disapproved of Mr. Green's speculations. He had
been long enough abroad, he said. He sailed on the bark *Saymiote* on
November 22 for Victoria.[9] It was necessary that he stop there for a few
months to familiarize himself with the British Columbia business and
secure the agreement to his arrangement with Mr. Rhodes, the manager of
the Victoria office, who was also a partner. The separate firm of Janion,
Green & Rhodes had been organized to handle the British Columbia business. As it turned out, the decision against dealing in liquor had cost Davies
a partnership, and the change in events prevented him from having one at
this point. Honolulu, heavily in debt because of the new investments, was
not doing very well.

In Victoria, he found that the British Columbia gold strike had not
brought the prosperity expected, and business was "dull," but Janion,

Green & Rhodes was the most successful firm there. There also seemed to be good news from Honolulu: sugar and molasses production and sales were up, and there was talk that cotton was to be the coming crop of the islands.

From Victoria, safe in his new important position, Theo Davies had the courage to write Green in Honolulu warning about his uneasiness. He said he was worried about three accounts: Hawaiian Steam Navigation, the *Annie Laurie,* which was carried separately, and the Waimea Stock & Grazing Company, Green's most ambitious farming project. He suggested that Green either sell them off or close out at 25 cents on the dollar, and get rid of the investments—the interest alone was ruinous. Not one of these enterprises was showing a profit, and all demanded constant resupply of capital. Davies had reports from Victoria merchants who were puzzled by Green's apparent long delays in payment. Green had explained that he often took notes for the payment and was a long time collecting. But could he not discount the notes and pay up? Davies knew what Green was doing: using the notes as security on his other investments.[10]

"If a fire or any such calamity destroyed your property to a large extent it would be very hard to explain satisfactorily that the notes had been deposited against other operations," he warned. So delicate was this matter that Davies apologized several times for mentioning it; he suggested that Green might want to destroy the letter, and he would destroy the copy if requested.

Not three months later the first trouble began. The firm of Henderson and Burnaby of Victoria complained to Rhodes in March that against their August shipments to Honolulu they had received only $5,000 instead of the $8,500 due. Davies tried to protect Green with the old argument about extending credit to buyers, but Henderson and Burnaby would not accept it: they wanted to know why Green did not discount the notes as everyone else seemed to do. Even the draft they got was not payable for four months.[11] Rhodes paid them off because they threatened to stop doing business with the Honolulu house, but even Rhodes was growing suspicious, and Davies could not protect Green forever.

What Green needed, his young associate said confidently, was a good bookkeeper, and when he got back to England he would find one for Honolulu.

Theo Davies did not realize the full extent of the difficulties into which Green had plunged the Honolulu house. He had bought and bought. That spring he bought a piece of land for the Honolulu Iron Works, which took more money. Janion, Green & Co. owned half the Iron Works by this time; Thomas Hughes owned a quarter; Green's wife owned an eighth; and Mrs. Janion owned an eighth.[12] The Iron Works had enormous potential but needed to expand. To secure the capital, Green mortgaged the assets that summer to his mother, Mrs. Mary Green, for a loan of $20,000. With this capital Hughes was soon able to make machinery he advertised as "capable of taking off one ton of sugar per day." The future looked bright, if they could overcome the need for more capital. Soon Green was in even deeper, with a sugar mill at Waialua. Events moved so rapidly that Theo Davies could not keep up with them.

With four months' Victoria experience behind him, Theo Davies went home to England in April and joined the staff of R.C. Janion and Company in the Liverpool office, although for the next three years his income would derive from Hawaii and Victoria. Soon he was handling all the correspondence with Honolulu and most of that with Victoria. He traveled around England seeking business for the firm's line of ships.[13] Janion had purchased a number of sailing ships to carry his own goods to the Pacific and ameliorated the cost by shipping for such merchants as A.S. Cleghorn, Henry Dimond, and Castle & Cooke, the latter two being involved in the sugar business. Janion was cautious and conservative in his actions and grew more so as the end of the American civil war affected the English market for cotton and industrial goods. Green, in Honolulu, seemed to have gone mad. He was involved in sugar lands in Kohala and Kona as well as his previous holdings.

In the first month of 1866, affairs began to come to a head. The closing of the 1865 books had ended with the "astounding balance" of £19,000 due Liverpool from the Honolulu office. The immediate problem was the Hawaiian Steam Navigation Company. By January 1866, Green was operating Hawaiian Steam Navigation Company and General Inter-Island Navigation Company from one office. His ships included the *Kilauea*, in which the government still maintained an interest, the schooner *Onward*, which ran to Kawaihae, the *Nettie Merrill*, which ran to Lahaina, the *Alberni* which made the Hilo run, and the *Annie Laurie* which traveled from Honolulu to Waimea on Oahu and then to Koloa on Kauai.[14]

In mid-month, on her return trip from Kona to Kawaihae, the *Kilauea* was driven up on the reef in a storm. She was not seriously injured and all the passengers were taken off and sent off to Honolulu via the schooner *Kalama*. But the gale grew worse in the next few days, so bad that the captain of the *Kilauea* called for help from the *USS Lancaster* which was in Hawaii waters. The *Lancaster* started around the island, but the gale had increased so much that she could make no headway. The *Kilauea* remained on the reef, beaten by the storm.[15]

She was still on the reef on February 10 and Green had called for bids to pull her off. There were no bidders, so she was auctioned off on February 20 for $6,100 to L.L. Torbert of Honolulu, on the reef as she lay. She was, at the moment, uninsured.

On February 5, the *Annie Laurie* dragged her anchor while landing passengers at Koloa and smashed on the reef. Her wreckage was sold. As if this was not enough tragedy for one shipping line, on February 17 the *Alberni*, carrying passengers and 900 bags of rice from Honolulu to Waimea, Kauai, was cast on the reef. Captain Clark ordered the cargo jettisoned to lighten her; two days later she was hauled off by the tug *Pele*, and brought back to Honolulu leaking badly. Again, there was no insurance.[16]

On April 5, Torbert floated the *Kilauea* off the reef at high tide and found that the only basic damage to her was the destruction of her false keel. He said she would be running again in a few weeks. The next month he had her auctioned off; Walker and Allen bought her for $16,100, which gave Torbert a nice profit and must have given William Green a pain in the stomach.[17]

On July 14 the *Onward* was lost through the cowardice or incompetence of Captain Lambert's *kanaka* seamen. The *Onward* had gone onto the reef at Wahiawa in a blow, but the captain was getting her off. At the critical point, when she had swung around broadside to the surf and was heading up into the wind, one seaman panicked, dropped the main halyard, jumped overboard and swam to the shore. The sail collapsed, the ship went broadside onto the reef, and there she stuck until she broke up in the surf.[18] No insurance again.

Green wrote Janion in Liverpool about these melancholy events and asked his partner if he could not raise money in England for a reorganization of the steamship company. He proposed to form a new company and buy out the government's share of Hawaiian Steam Navigation Company. Janion replied that the whole inter-island shipping venture was a fiasco, and even if it were not, there was no chance of securing English capital just then. The fall in the price of cotton at the end of the American civil war had brought a financial crisis to London. The bank rate had jumped to ten per cent. Green would have to extricate them from this disaster of his own doing. He ought to tighten up, Janion said. This was no time to be increasing investments.[19]

Green continued in his own way. On September 29, he opened a new office and sample room in a brick building next to the old office on Kaahumanu Street. The stores were connected, and the Janion, Green & Company establishment had entrances on both Queen and Kaahumanu Streets.

This "prosperity" was apparently confirmed when Green bought the twenty-year-old steamer *Thames* for $11,000. But within six months disaster was to strike and change the fortunes of William L. Green, Robert C. Janion and, especially, of Theophilus Harris Davies.

In 1866 there were 32 sugar mills and plantations in Hawaii, and the export of the crop had risen from just over a million pounds in 1860 to nearly 18 million pounds in 1866. Janion, Green & Company's sugar ventures had come to nothing, but the company still had a foothold in the industry with its control of the Honolulu Iron Works, which manufactured virtually all the machinery used in the island sugar industry.

The Union victory in the American civil war had put an end to the enormous needs of the Union armies, and sugar in the fall of 1866 was a glut on the American market. The crisis caused Walker, Allen & Company, the biggest owner and agency, to go bankrupt, and sell off its plantations (and the *Kilauea*). A sugar refinery had been established at Honolulu, but it was closed down in the depression, and what sugar was sold in America was shipped mostly to the San Francisco & Pacific Refineries in the San Francisco Bay area of California.

Green began fighting for survival. He put the last of his steam schooners, the *Alberni,* up for sale.[20] The *Thames* was sold and went on the Honolulu-San Francisco run. Green held an enormous auction of goods in the warehouses "to close invoices," but such was the economic climate that there were few bidders and the inventory went at disastrous prices.

One of Green's more successful innovations was the procurement of labor for the sugar fields. He brought in Chinese contract laborers who agreed to work for five years at $4 a month, then sold the contracts at a handsome profit to the sugar planters. For fifteen years this had been a successful business, and there were more Chinese than white men in the islands, thousands of the laborers brought in by Janion, Green & Company. In April, when the steamer *Eastfield* arrived from Hong Kong, Green advertised that he had several hundred contracts to sell. He also advertised round-bottom Hong Kong rattan chairs, preserved ginger, preserved oranges, and spices. All this was auctioned, within a week, in Green's desperate attempts to raise cash and stave off his creditors. Melcher Company bid and bought the whole cargo from him.[21]

In June, Hackfeld & Company organized a new Inter-Island Steam Navigation Company at a meeting in their counting house. C. de Varigny, the Hawaiian Foreign Minister, was elected president; Hackfeld's H.A. Widemann was secretary; Green became treasurer; and Janion, Green got the agency for the ship (the old *Kilauea*) which Hackfeld had picked up in the wreckage of Walker, Allen & Company.[22]

This renewed involvement in shipping was very nearly the last straw for Janion. It was followed by a complaint from Henry Beecroft Jackson. For the Green investment in ranch properties at Kohala and lands at Kaalaea, an old associate, the Jackson firm of Manchester, had been persuaded to advance £10,000 credit, and Green had already overdrawn that by £200. From the cattle ranch came calls for money to buy more cattle. From Kailua Kona, where Green was involved in experimental farming, came reports that efforts to grow cane had failed, and so had an attempt to grow cotton.

Matters came to a head in March, 1867. Green was desperate, and he drew a draft for £1,200 on Henry Beecroft Jackson, who had invested in the Waimea Grazing Company on the advice of Theo H. Davies. Jackson wrote a furious letter to Janion, saying he would pay only if Janion guaranteed the draft.[23]

By this time Janion's Liverpool firm was in deadly danger from the reverberations that emanated from Honolulu. Thirty major creditors held thousands of pounds in bills and notes. Among them, one of the largest debts was to Ind Coope, the brewers, who had sent enormous consignments to Hawaii. The creditors were about to move in on R.C. Janion, which would force him into bankruptcy. To avoid this tragedy, Janion asked Theo Davies what might be done, since Davies was the knowledgeable man about Hawaiian affairs. It was obvious that Green was finished. But must Janion also be dragged under?

Chapter Six

SALVAGE OPERATION

I*n 1867 Green's financial* distress was common knowledge in Hawaii as he sold off everything he could, including a plot of 9,300 acres at Hakalau Nui, good sugar land between Laupahoehoe and Hilo, for a dollar an acre, to meet the creditors. (Even then it was valued by the government appraisers at $18,000.)[1]

Green's attempts to raise cash were only partly successful. The debts had piled up, and the English creditors descended on Janion demanding payment of thousands of pounds. Janion nearly panicked. In September 1867, in self defense he announced in England the dissolution of the partnership (Green still did not know about that). Theo H. Davies suggested that he go back to Honolulu and straighten out Janion's affairs—for a price. The price would be a partnership. Janion agreed and Davies sailed for Hawaii.[2]

Theo H. Davies stepped off the *Idaho* one January day, called on Green at the new offices, and delivered Janion's notice of dissolution of the partnership as of September 30, 1867. Green was out. He turned over all his assets, even his carriage, and the next day he moved to a dingy little office nearby to conduct his contract-labor business and try to restore his fortunes as a commission merchant and real estate agent. Within the week the official notice of the end of the partnership was published in the *Hawaii Gazette*, and just under it the announcement that Theo H. Davies was entering business as a general merchant and commission agent at the old premises of Janion, Green & Company.[3]

The advertisement of Janion, Green continued to run in the *Gazette* for Janion was still responsible for half of all that had occurred before September 30. But within a month Theo H. Davies had made arrangements to purchase all that was left of the Janion, Green imports, consisting largely of a cargo that had come in aboard the Janion steamer *Garstang.* No money changed hands; Green's share of the Janion, Green assets was turned over to Theo H. Davies for Janion. Narrowly they managed to stave off bankruptcy this way, but whether or not Janion could satisfy Ind Coope and the other creditors depended on how well young Theo Davies comported himself on his own.

When Theo H. Davies returned to the Hawaiian islands he had £2,500 and several hidden assets working for him. One of these was a direct result of his own activity. He had begun mingling with the *alii* in 1859 when he went first to Iolani Palace as a guest at a reception, wearing William Green's hat as British consul.[4] In 1860 he and Henry Dimond had made a trip to Kauai at the same time that Queen Emma was visiting there and had spent some time in her company at Hanalei.[5] In 1861 he had joined the Amateur Musical Society in an ambitious attempt to present the opera *Martha.* King Alexander Liholiho (Kamehameha IV) had directed the work as stage manager, and Queen Emma sang in the chorus. In one scene Theo H. Davies walked across the stage with the queen on his arm. Since this took six rehearsals before the performance, at the end of the performances Davies and the royal family were well acquainted.[6]

As a monarchist, Davies' approval of the kingdom was complete and noticeable among Americans, most of whom seemed openly bent on annexation of Hawaii to the United States. King Alexander Liholiho had been a strong Anglophile. He died during Theo Davies' second sojourn in Hawaii, and was succeeded by Prince Lot, the last of the Kamehamehas, who believed strongly in the rights of the monarchy (as opposed to the pressures of the Americans for universal suffrage and democracy) and who grew anti-American as the pressures were continued and increased.

Queen Emma. Consort of King Kamehameha IV who reigned from 1854 to 1863. Courtesy: Bishop Museum.

By the time that Theo Davies returned to England in 1863, an unpleasant overtone of racism had permeated the government structure, and a few months later a fist fight erupted on the floor of the legislature between white and Hawaiian members. Since most of the white citizens of the Hawaiian kingdom were American-born, the active opposition of Hawaiians was directed against Americans.[7] Theo H. Davies had the advantage in these tumultuous years of being away in England.

In his absence from Honolulu, in the early 1860s the sugar industry came of age. Before the war, much of America's sugar had been grown in the southern states, but that source was cut off. Prices rose so high that in the war years Hawaii's planters could make good profits even after paying the heavy U.S. import duty on sugar. Furthermore, Janion, Green and Rhodes established markets in Canada, and Hackfeld & Company, a German trading firm, had opened the Australian trade in sugar. Hackfeld had moved rapidly from the dying whaling trade into sugar, owning some lands, but largely as agent for the sugar plantations.

By February 1868, six months after setting up, Theo H. Davies had organized his business. George MacFarlane came looking for a job. He employed young MacFarlane now and soon hired Thomas Rain Walker, who came from England to be senior clerk. He ran a business-card announcement on the front page of the *Gazette,* along with those of Castle & Cooke, Hackfeld & Company,[8] Theo S. Heuck, and other Honolulu merchants. When he had something special to sell, he ran advertisements on the inner pages. He was the agent for Lloyd's, Northern Assurance Company (whose fire insurance business was one of his greatest assets) and the British and Foreign Marine Insurance Company.

In April, the *Robert Cowan* arrived from Victoria, bearing goods shipped him from Janion, Rhodes & Company and other merchants there.[9] Theo Davies then advertised his wares; cottons, linens, woollens, all sorts of clothing, shirts, saddlery, lace, and flags. He had Ind Coope ale and American whiskey, Lea and Perrins sauces, preserves from England, fire brick, hoop iron, sugar coolers, oilcloth, and roofing felt in his warehouse.

Half the profits earned in the business were credited to Janion's account. Davies used his own money and borrowed money to finance the business. His security for this was the half interest in the Honolulu Iron Works.

Janion, Green & Company had two other assets, the Waimea Grazing Company on Hawaii, operated on leased land, and an eighth share in the Kaalaea Sugar Plantation on Oahu. Davies sold off the Waimea farm for £3,800 and congratulated himself on the deal. He only got £3,000 for Janion's account, although the farm was carried on Green's books at £14,500, because Green owed £8,000 to the man who bought the farm.[10] But Davies was convinced the farm was a ruinous operation, based on land leased at high rentals.

Davies also arranged to sell the eighth interest in the Kaalaea Sugar Plantation to the manager. The investment was valued at £1,500 and he received £300 on account and a mortgage. But the new owner of the shares forfeited, so Janion had the £300 and the investment back again.[11]

On his own account Theo Davies began investing in sugar. In 1868 he borrowed money and bought the Onoulinui and Kailua sugar plantations on the island of Hawaii at auction for $11,500 and $5,000 respectively.

Onoulinui was a plantation located at Kailua Kona of 1,200 acres, 300 of them planted in cane, but it also raised cattle and mules. Kailua Plantation was located at Anaukea near Kona. It consisted of a thousand acres. The real future of sugar, Theo knew, could only be guaranteed if the American market were made profitable for the planters. Profitability could only be achieved by persuading the Americans to lower the tariff on Hawaiian sugar. But how could Hawaii persuade Washington? In 1867 they had failed when the American Congress rejected the reciprocity treaty. The next year, the planters asked the Hawaiian government to reopen the question and Theo H. Davies signed the petition.

In the depressed economy of Hawaii, caused by the decline in whaling and the decreased American purchase of sugar, a number of businessmen and many of the missionary group began to criticize the contract labor system under which Chinese were brought to Hawaii. In 1862 the American Congress had prohibited American citizens from carrying on the "coolie trade" in American ships. Five years later the U.S. government described the trade as "inhuman, immoral, and abhorrent." This gave the missionary moralists opportunity to fulminate against the contract labor system, and working men joined them because they feared the competition of cheap Chinese labor of contract employees who elected to remain in Hawaii when their contracts ran out.

The import of laborers was justified by the planters because the Hawaiian population was so definitely on the decline, and because planters found that Hawaiians made very poor farm hands. Since 1864, when the Planters' Society was organized, they had encouraged William Green and others to bring in a steady flow of Chinese. In the middle 1860s, editor Henry M. Whitney of the *Pacific Commercial Advertiser* began a campaign against contract labor which made him so unpopular among the planters that they tried to promote a boycott of his paper, and finally (1870) made life so unpleasant and unprofitable for him that he sold the paper.[12]

In 1869 this quarrel was in full flower. Public meetings were held on all the islands, where businessmen and civic leaders quarreled about the morality and economics of the Masters and Servants Act which legalized the contract labor system.

On the night of October 29, such a meeting was held at the Kaumaka-pili Church.[13] The missionary group was in control, and Chairman William Claude Jones spoke for a change in the law to make labor contracts unenforceable by penal terms. Hackfeld's H.A. Widemann tried to get the floor to speak for the planters, but was shouted down. J.O. Carter fulminated against the planters. Samuel Castle rose, and his age and position in the community won him a hearing. He remarked that to change the law would be to strike a heavy blow against Hawaii businessmen. The missionaries could hardly wait for him to stop so they could refute his remarks. Theo H. Davies kept trying to get recognized but was ignored repeatedly, but near the end of the meeting he did manage to get the floor.

"There are many in this building who came to this land as I did, under contract," Davies said. "The land is perhaps as much indebted to them as it is to those who came here without any contract, but . . . runaways from other lands, or adventurers seeking in a foreign country that success which was denied them in their own . . ."

So Theo H. Davies, by 1869, was thoroughly committed to the sugar industry and was already a powerful figure in that industry. He was investing in plantations and securing contracts as agent for others. In the fall of 1869 he advertised "choice sugars" available through his firm from the Kaalaea and Laia plantations.

He still had to resolve the problems of Janion, Green & Company to live up to his agreement with Robert Janion, but even in doing this, he managed to turn the task into profit for himself. For example, one day he travelled to Maui to visit Robert Hind at Wailuku. Hind owed $12,000 to Janion, Green and Davies had come to collect.

The sour expression on Davies' face as he came to the shop led Robert Hind to expect the worst. Still, he showed Davies through the shop and explained that most of the work on hand was being done to manufacture and repair sugar machinery for Alexander & Baldwin at Paia where they were going to put up a mill. (It later became the Puunene Mill.) After the inspection trip, Davies' disposition seemed to improve, and he smiled instead of frowning. He also told Hind not to worry about the debt just then,

Robert Hind

and that if he needed another $10,000 of credit, Davies would give it to him. Thus began a relationship that would secure for Davies the agency for Hind's extensive sugar holdings after he moved from Maui to the island of Hawaii. Theo H. Davies also visited the Big Island of Hawaii again. He believed the best cane lands in the islands were to be found in the Kohala district.

The Honolulu Iron Works was the most valuable of all the assets left over from the Janion, Green days, and Theo Davies knew it very well. In 1869 the iron works was doing all sorts of business besides making sugar mills. In January they built a new boiler for the tug *Pele*.[14] They offered to clean rice for planters. They would do anything they could to make a little profit, for the company was suffering. A few years earlier, Thomas Hughes had employed 200 men and kept them going at full speed to keep up with the demands of the sugar planters. But with the American market virtually gone, the number of employees was down to 25, and in 1869, Hughes sold out his interest in the company.

The purchaser was Alexander Young. He had left England in the middle 1850s with a group of colonists led by William Lidgate. They had first gone to Mazatlan but did not like Mexico and so decided to head for Hawaii. The winds were against them and they ended up on Vancouver Island, where they established a colony at what is now Port Alberni. They built a small wharf and a sawmill there. In the 1860s Lidgate and Young and their families decided to go on to Hawaii and settled at Hilo, where Young established a blacksmith shop and a small machine shop and foundry. It did not do very well, and in 1869 Young came to Honolulu and bought Hughes' shares in the Honolulu Iron Works. He paid $16,800 for

Hughes' twenty-one per cent interest, $2,000 in cash and the rest in notes.[15]

The sale established the value of the Iron Works at $80,000, the assets being the property on the site bounded by Marin, Maunakea and Queen Streets, and including all the machinery, equipment, and supplies on hand. Young rented a house and then settled in as manager of the iron works. One of the first jobs was a set of new boilers for the *S.S. Keolaa.*[16]

While this work was being done, Theo H. Davies was away in England. His success in business was now well enough assured that he could be married. He went home to marry Mary Ellen Cocking, daughter of a pharmacist in the Davies home town of Ludlow. His father no longer lived there—the elder Davies had gone to live in Theo's house in Liverpool in 1865 but the memories had not died. Before the marriage Theo H. Davies made a settlement on his bride-to-be of a house he had bought in the Nuuanu valley up above Honolulu from the Rev. Eli Corwin and christened Craigside, and a £500 insurance policy on his life with the Northern Assurance Company.[17] They sailed from Liverpool in October and returned to Honolulu aboard the *Moses Taylor* on November 25, 1870. A whole new life was beginning for them both.[18]

Chapter Seven

FORTUNE

The merchants of Hawaii were a resilient lot. After Walker and Allen went bankrupt in 1866 they picked up the pieces, rented an office near the wharf, and within two or three years were doing very well again. So, too, was William L. Green doing well. By 1870 he was back in business advertising in the newspapers to sell all sorts of merchandise, particularly whiskey and other alcoholic beverages. The liquor business had always appealed to him and been one of his most profitable lines. He also had a close connection with the Hawaiian government, and ironically, was often appointed receiver for various bankrupt firms.[1]

What Theo H. Davies thought of Green's comeback he never said. The liabilities of Janion, Green & Company hung heavy around Davies' neck, but had there been no problem neither would there have been the opportunity for Davies to take over a going business as he had done.

While back in England in 1870, Davies had negotiated a formal settlement with the 30 creditors of Janion, Green & Company, and Robert Janion had signed notes amounting to £14,000, which would be paid off in 1871, 1872 and 1873 from the sale of assets in Hawaii and Janion's half of the profits of the Theo H. Davies company.[2]

Janion began to believe he had made a bad bargain and suggested that Davies had taken advantage of him. The younger man denied it, and said that he was certain he could have done as well to come out alone and set up in business.[3] The facts do not entirely support such a suggestion;

much of Davies' success was due to the very firm foundations the insurance agencies and Honolulu Iron Works gave his business, although to say that is to take nothing away from his brilliant business maneuvering.

By 1871, the thirty-seven year old Davies was one of the most successful of Honolulu businessmen. He lived on the 12-acre estate up Nuuanu Valley and rode down to the office on Queen Street on his horse every day. The horse was stabled nearby, and at the end of the day he rode back home. Mary Ellen—Nellie he called her—was pregnant, and on September 28 their first son was born. He was christened Theophilus Clive Davies in a Church of England ceremony.

Shortly before the collapse of Janion, Green & Company, William Green had been replaced as British government representative by a full time commissioner and consul general, who came out from London. By the time Davies had returned to Honolulu in 1868, Major James Wodehouse had been given the post, but Green had maintained his tie as vice-consul, which meant he represented Britain when Wodehouse was away from Honolulu. Theo H. Davies had set about getting that post for himself, and had worked through Mrs. Wodehouse, who had taken a liking to him. She interceded with her husband, and Wodehouse arranged with the Foreign Office that Green should be terminated and Theo Davies should have the post of vice-consul.[4] He had no salary but did get the consular commissions.

"It is very useful in bringing business," Davies said as he announced proudly to Janion that he had secured the post, "and I have had a very fair amount of business."[5]

By 1871, his business was much better than fair. He held $100,000 of notes from various planters, all well secured, and $53,000 in notes for goods. The Iron Works had another $50,000 in notes for work done. The problem, as it had always been in Honolulu, was what a later generation would call cash flow. There was never enough cash to go around, and the Bishop Bank could not handle all the business. Perfectly good notes were discounted at twelve per cent, and this pained Davies so that he asked Janion to arrange, if he could, for London financing. Davies offered to put up £6,000 in notes for every £5,000 in cash.[6]

Hackfeld & Company started a bank in competition with Bishop, but this was of little use to Davies because Hackfeld & Company were his fiercest competitors in every way, as merchants, sugar agents, and in the acquisition of sugar properties. One of Davies' closest friends had worked for Hackfeld, W.H. Dimond—but he had then moved to Huntington Hopkins & Company in San Francisco. They were agents for the sale of sugar to the San Francisco refinery and the east, and for general merchandise. In the old days Janion, Green & Company had dealt with various agents and done much business in Victoria with Janion's house there. But Theo H. Davies did not like Rhodes, Janion's partner in Victoria. He refused to buy a half interest in the ship *Robert Cowan,* partly from caution, but also partly because of his antipathy to Rhodes, and he began diverting business to his friend Dimond in San Francisco.[7] Dimond also began to find cash for him with the San Francisco banks—the Bank of California and the Anglo-Californian Bank.

Janion constantly pressed Davies for remittance of cash, even when remittances were not due. For the first half of 1871 the profit of the enterprise was nearly $6,500. Ordinarily the profits would have been left in for working capital, but Janion's need was so great that Davies sent him his half. By this time, the partnership owed Davies $18,000. His security, as agreed, was half interest in the Honolulu Iron Works.

In a short time, Theo H. Davies had learned much about sugar and plantation management, largely as a result of mistakes made by W.D. Bickerton, the manager of the Kaalaea Plantation in which the partners had the one-eighth interest.[8] Henry Beecroft Jackson also had an interest in that enterprise, and Davies was his representative, which in effect made Davies the major factor in the company.

The Iron Works was doing so well that Davies knew it would be the keystone of his own position in the future. He anticipated as early as 1871 that by the time Janion's debts were paid off two years later, the partnership would owe him $30,000, but he was content, because in the Honolulu Iron Works he saw a fortune.

Janion wanted him to sell the Iron Works immediately, but Davies resisted. In 1872 the Iron Works was so profitable it paid a dividend of $16,000 which meant half to the account of Davies.[9]

Davies had established a position as a person of probity and common sense. When Major Wodehouse fell into financial difficulties by overspending, he looked to his vice-consul to bail him out and was not disappointed. Davies put the Wodehouses on a strict budget and made them keep to it. He also advanced cash for them, and trusted them to pay him later for his efforts.[10] The result was to place the Wodehouses in deep moral as well as financial debt to Davies, and to cement his position as vice-consul.

By the fall of 1872, Manager Bickerton at Kaalaea Plantation had so far failed to produce results that Davies decided he must go. This change meant Davies had to spend time on the sugar business, just when affairs of state were pressing heavily on him. The Wodehouses had gone home to England on leave that year, and Lot, who had been crowned as Kamehameha V, died in December, throwing the whole diplomatic community into an uproar since he left no heir. Whitehall had to be informed in detail, a task that took hours of Vice-Consul Davies' time, not just once, but week after week as the government crisis deepened in the competition between William C. Lunalilo and David Kalakaua, both high chiefs.[11] The male Kamehameha line had died out with Lot, so the legislature would elect the next king. In the politicking, the big powers flexed their muscles. The American minister called on Washington for a warship to come to Honolulu. Vice-Consul Davies also called for a warship when popular meetings threatened to become riots as the two Hawaiians campaigned. A straw vote held on New Year's day, 1873, showed Lunalilo as the people's choice. A week later the legislature confirmed it, and Lunalilo was crowned without incident.[12]

Although business in general in Hawaii had been poor in 1872, the Theo H. Davies business had been excellent, and the next year was the same. That year Davies paid off the last moneys due Janion's creditors. His working capital amounted to $62,000 that summer, and he had $50,000 out in loans.[13] But when the time came to settle finally with these creditors, Davies wrote disparagingly of the prospects of the Iron Works. It was certainly true that sugar was in a precarious position, with the American market virtually closed by the tariff. But already voices were being raised in Honolulu that might change this situation. Earlier, the matter of "reciprocity" had not meant much. The U.S. could get along quite well without Hawaiian sugar. But there were stirrings of imperialism in the American soul, and when Henry Whitney suggested that reciprocity of trade and a lease on Pearl Harbor for the U.S. Navy be tied together, Washington took a new interest in the plan.

Davies' final card in his long, woeful letter to the 30 creditors was to suggest that the Iron Works would net nothing if sold at auction, but that he would reluctantly accept that half share in final settlement of all the Janion company owed him for advances to the creditors.[14] Of course, he said, he would prefer to be paid off in cash, and let the creditors hold the Iron Works. The same, he said, was true of the Kaalaea Sugar Plantation.

The creditors in England had no intention of coming to Hawaii to take over the Iron Works (as Davies must have known very well). In effect, he had them over a barrel. It was true that the short-term prospects of the company were not good because of the depression in the sugar industry, but the long-range prospects were as high as any in Hawaii, and in the interim Davies was doing well in wool, insurance agencies, and shipment of sugar to Canada. His English trade really was the lesser part of his business.

As he expected, Janion and the creditors agreed that he would take over the Iron Works investment in lieu of the cash owed him for advances. He was concerned about his investments, but in 1873 the partnership made a profit of $22,000, and he was so well satisfied with events that he took his family back to England for a visit. It was a growing family, a daughter had been born to Nellie in 1873, and they lived very well. Most of the year was spent in Craigside, but for two or three months they took a beach house at Waikiki, just for the change, and moved the Chinese cook and servants down with them. Now, leaving for England, Davies rented

Craigside to Commissioner Wodehouse, left detailed instructions for his clerks Walker and MacFarlane and sailed on the *Tartar* bound for six months of glorious freedom in his beloved England.[15]

The six months were uneventful, but on his return to Honolulu he began to have trouble with clerk MacFarlane, who had involved himself deeply in the court life of old Iolani Palace and was neglecting his work at the office. At least part of Davies' reaction was from pique; he had the makings of a martinet and insisted that his employees devote their total interest to his business—more, that they keep him completely informed about even their private lives. He wrote MacFarlane a long admonitory letter, occasioned by the younger man's acceptance of a post on the executive committee of a forthcoming royal ball without asking Davies' permission, but the reason for his upset went deeper: "One thing I am compelled to do and that is establish at once an order and system in our business which do not at present exist. I want to do that and everything through you, and to feel that sometime in the future, if I want to live in England, you will have fitted yourself to take the reins . . ."[16] The date was June 8, 1875. Already Theo H. Davies had planned to quit the islands and return home as soon as his fortune was secure.

Chapter Eight

TROUBLE IN PARADISE

The unwritten agreement of partnership between Theo H. Davies and Robert C. Janion continued, and would continue until Janion's death in 1881, but the company was entirely in Davies' hands; Janion never again came to Hawaii. The staff difficulties mounted. George MacFarlane continued to disappoint Davies, but so did others. Mr. Wilder, his new manager at Kaalaea Plantation, turned out to be a drinking man, hardly a novelty in Hawaii, but Davies would have none of it. "On more than one occasion I have fancied that you talked rather at random in the evenings, but last Tuesday I could not shut my eyes to the fact that you had taken more than you could well manage," Davies wrote him, and suggested that he go on the water wagon, ". . . or confine yourself absolutely and strictly to first what ale or claret you take *at the dinner table*. This is my rule and a good one."[1] These pious abjurations, "I beg you will believe in my friendship . . . ," were accompanied by an open threat that if matters did not improve the man would be sacked. This letter, like his letter to MacFarlane a few months earlier, set a pattern that was to be common in Davies' relationships with his subordinates. They must do precisely as he wished, or else there was no future for them in his business.

As a God-fearing and temperate man, Davies was seriously concerned about the evils of drink, which he saw all around him. His brother-in-law

Joseph Dredge was an alcoholic, who caused his sister untold pain and reduced his family to poverty. So when he warned associates against drink, Davies was acting from high moral principle and practicality; as far as he could see liquor brought little but trouble. He did continue to deal in liquor and beer, but the trade bothered him.[2]

The partnership with Janion each year became a lesser factor in Davies' business life. In February 1874, King Lunalilo died (his death speeded by whiskey, as Davies had grimly predicted) and David Kalakaua, another drinking man, succeeded to the throne. He came in like a lion, choosing for the symbol of his rule a burning torch: ". . . the increase of the people; the advancement of agriculture and commerce" were his aims. American Minister Henry Peirce was so distrustful of Kalakaua that he ordered up a succession of warships to show the Stars and Stripes in Honolulu, and prepared for a siege with a king who seemed to hate foreigners.[3] But Kalakaua's promise to further agriculture and trade was real and Davies was encouraged in a way, because he chose as foreign minister none other than William L. Green, the old Janion partner. To be sure, relations between Green and Davies had not survived the break-up of the partnership, but they still shared interests, particularly in trade and sugar. Green was never going to do any favors for Davies, but in his own interest he would help them all.

By this time the basic pattern of business power in Hawaii had taken shape. The trading firms were going heavily into sugar, as owners and agents.[4] Davies had his plantations and the Iron Works. Over on Maui he was backing Hind's machine shop, which was making sugar machinery for Alexander & Baldwin. His biggest customer for general merchandise was A.S. Cleghorn, English husband of Princess Miriam Likelike, who ran a general store in Honolulu, and who, in five years, had bought nearly $200,000 worth of merchandise from Davies-Janion. Similar business was being done by H. Hackfeld & Company, and F.A. Schaefer & Co., by the Chinese houses of Chulan & Co. and Afong & Achuck, and by C. Brewer, and Castle & Cooke, the Americans. All these major firms were deeply involved with sugar, and all were pressing the Hawaiian government to secure a reciprocity treaty with the United States that would eliminate or at least cut the prohibitory sugar tariff. In the summer of 1875 it was achieved, and "Sandwich Island Sugar," as it was called in America, was admitted free of duty. The provision was for unrefined sugar, which put an end to talk of building a big refinery in the Hawaiian Islands. The refining process would have to be carried out on American soil, but it was a small price to pay. There was still some outcry against the cession of land and independence to America (the treaty bound Hawaii firmly to America) but it was mild.[5] Davies was delighted. He foresaw prosperity for the Iron Works and had already lined up several sugar plantations to accept his agency. Kaalaea Plantation, about which he had despaired a few months earlier, was expected to begin paying dividends.

That fall of 1876, Davies had one shock. George MacFarlane, in whom he had placed so much hope, quit him altogether to go into business with William L. Green.[6] They bought a ship, the *Cowan,* and the Spencer plantation on the Big Island of Hawaii, and with Green's influence at court behind them, started a trading company. Davies felt that he had been knifed in the back; he had chosen MacFarlane at least partly because he was an American, and he felt an American was needed in the firm. More than that, he had made MacFarlane an executor of his will, and all this had to be changed. It never occurred to him that MacFarlane might have left him through simple ambition; he was not one to have any doubts about his own character or actions. In the letter by which he announced this change to Thomas Rain Walker, the junior clerk, who was on leave in England, Davies expressed the hope that Walker would "assume more authority in business" and then launched into a criticism of Walker's character. He was too shy and not sufficiently aggressive, said the critic of his employee. He had to develop more "cheek."[7]

On Walker's return he did become the senior clerk, but Davies' business was progressing so satisfactorily that he wanted yet another able man of business, and he turned to England to find him, having been once burned by an American. It would take a while. Meanwhile in Honolulu, business picked up remarkably almost the moment the reciprocity treaty

Charles Notley

Thomas Rain Walker

was signed. Henry Beecroft Jackson had been persuaded to invest in some properties Davies wanted to acquire. The Beecroft Plantation in the Kohala district of Hawaii island was one of them. After the treaty was signed Davies also persuaded Jackson to put money into a lease of land at Kaauhuhu. Many people in Honolulu wondered where Davies got his money. Much of it came from Jackson. Janion invested in some ventures, so did Mrs. Janion. Davies' father and his father-in-law also gave him small sums to invest. Davies also borrowed, loans arranged by Janion in England, and by his friend Henry Dimond in San Francisco. He needed a large flow of money, for he was backing several sugar ventures. He had started R. R. Hind on a sugar plantation in Kohala, after Hind sold out his interest in the sugar plantation he and H. P. Baldwin ran on Maui; Alexander and Baldwin took it over. Davies told Hind then that there were two really good sugar areas in the Hawaiian Islands, the Koloa district of Kauai and Kohala on the Big Island.[8] Hind had sold out for $23,000 and Davies persuaded him to start a mill in Kohala. The district was going to be a producer and might even amount to 10,000 tons a year, Davies said. He hoped to have the agency for most of it.

Hind went to Kohala in 1873 and erected a mill built by Honolulu Iron Works at Puehuehu. He bought that land and leased more (1,852 acres) and grew some cane. Davies became agent for the mill. To gain business he persuaded other men to come to the district and lease land and plant cane. He helped finance some of them, and he tried where possible to buy into the plantations. Davies' two sugar plantations in Kona apparently did not prosper. He did not mention them in correspondence that still exists, and he must have sold them around 1870. The Kona area was not very satisfactory for sugar cane propagation, but the Kona experience was useful. He met a number of other planters there. He persuaded one of them, another Englishman, Judge C. F. Hart (he had once been district magistrate of Kohala) to come over from Kona and plant on the Puehuehu area. Hart then bought a plantation at Niulii, which was financed by Theo H. Davies. Davies also wanted to become a partner in the plantation, but Hart refused. "No, no Davies," he said, "if I had you for a partner you would soon own it all."[9]

The other planters in the area were Daniel Vida, a relative of Janion's father-in-law, George F. Holmes of Kahua, and James Woods of Puuhue. The Hind Mill enterprise looked promising because the only sugar mill of any consequence was that of the Kohala Sugar Company, but Hind had barely put up the mill when it caught fire one night and burned to the ground. A few days before, Theo H. Davies had visited the mill and Hind had agreed to insure it with Northern Assurance Company, one of Davies' insurers. But no policy had been delivered and Hind was sure he was wiped out. He took the steamer to Honolulu to try to borrow money to rebuild. There he called on Theo H. Davies, who told him he would not need to borrow, the verbal commitment of insurance was enough; the policy application had been made for £3,000.[10] Northern Assurance paid off and Hind bought a new mill from Honolulu Iron Works. The new mill had a capacity of six tons of sugar per day (12 hours) and the first crop made it profitable. When the second crop was also profitable, Hind decided to expand and build a new mill at Hawi. He bought and leased lands for buildings and sugar cane, and as the third crop was coming in he was signing agreements with planters for the new mill. Then one night in 1875, another fire broke out at Puehuehu, and again the mill burned to the ground. Hind's commitments at Hawi were so heavy that he decided against rebuilding and sold out his entire Puehuehu holdings for $78,000. The buyers were Daniel Vida, two English brothers named Sneyd-Kynnersley (who introduced polo to Hawaii) and James Renton (an engineer at Honolulu Iron Works, also an Englishman and a friend of Theo H. Davies).[11] Each owned a quarter interest. Renton had capital, for he had made a fortune in the Australian gold fields. He moved from Honolulu to rebuild and then to manage the mill, and they changed the name of the company to Union Mill. When the mill was finished, the partners staged a grand ball to celebrate, and James Renton led the march, with Queen Kapiolani on his arm. It was a fine affair.[12]

Theo H. Davies was constantly expanding, and had excellent relationships with most of the planters and mill men in the Kohala district, most of them Englishmen. He retained a close connection with the Hinds because Beecroft Plantation, which belonged mostly to Davies and Henry Beecroft Jackson, sent its sugar to Hawi Mill for grinding. It was a short run, for the plantation was located only three miles from Hawi on the Mahukona side, although it could be a hard three miles. Planter Hart, for example, shipped his sugar cane by bullock cart to the Hawi Mill, at a cost of $20 a ton. The roads were so bad in those days that the bullock carts had to be half unloaded at the bottom of every steep gulch and two trips made to the top.[13] That tortuous method continued until the building of the Mahukona railway in 1880, but sugar was profitable enough to justify even such heroic measures. Sugar became *the* business of Hawaii, almost on the day the U.S.-Hawaii reciprocity treaty was signed. In 1856 the entire sugar crop of the islands amounted to 574 tons. Twenty years later the islands exported 18,000 tons, nearly all to the United States. [14]

One of Theo H. Davies' assets was his ability to perceive a trend, and then to act vigorously on his intuition. In 1876 he involved himself in a number of other sugar enterprises on the island of Hawaii as well. Around 1865, William Lidgate had acquired a large land holding at Laupahoehoe on the Hamakua coast of Hawaii and was interested in growing sugar cane. The problem was to mill the cane, and the land was too far from Hind's Hawi mill or the Hilo mill. Thomas Campbell wanted to participate by putting up a mill to grind Lidgate's cane, but as usual, money was the problem. That's where Theo H. Davies entered the picture; the Honolulu Iron Works could build the mill, and he would carry the debt for Campbell. His price included the agency for the sugar, which usually meant two per cent of the gross price obtained in California. In September, 1876, it was settled; Campbell would put up the mill on the flat down by the sea on a piece of land given him by Lidgate for the purpose. Lidgate agreed to plant enough cane in 1877 to produce 400 tons of sugar each year, and to plant an equal amount of land each year for ten years. Campbell would have a little stake, too: Lidgate rented him 50 acres of sugar land at two dollars an acre; Davies would sell the sugar, take his commission and split the proceeds between Lidgate and Campbell. That arrangement continued for three years; then, in 1879, Thomas Campbell transferred the mill, his lands, and the Lidgate contract to Davies for $20,000, and the discharge of all his debt to the merchant. Davies also held a mortgage on Lidgate's Laupahoehoe lands. The newspapers were full of talk about sugar, and they said of Laupahoehoe that it produced six tons of sugar per acre, "the best return heard of." The next year, 1880, it was common knowledge that Theo H. Davies was Lidgate's partner in the Laupahoehoe Plantation as well.[15]

In his travels to the island of Hawaii, Theo Davies met Charles Notley, yet another Englishman, and in looking over Notley's lands at Paauilo, he suggested that they were eminently suited for growing sugar cane. He made a contract with Notley that was nearly a replica of the Laupahoehoe arrangement; Notley would plant 150 acres a year for ten years in cane, Davies would put up a mill on 20 acres deeded him by Notley, and Notley would let him rent 50 acres to grow cane on his own account. Davies would pay two-thirds of the cost of constructing a landing at the shore and Notley would pay one-third. Notley would grow, and Davies would grind, and they would split the proceeds, although Davies would have the extra edge of the agency. All this took more capital than Davies could put up, so he arranged for the participation of Frederick J. Jackson, son of Henry Beecroft Jackson, in the plantation.

Soon Notley owned half the cane, Davies owned a quarter, and Frederick J. Jackson owned a quarter. Davies said he owned the mill himself. The plantation was called the Hamakua Plantation Company and the mill was the Hamakua Mill. To build it, Davies brought in Mrs. Domitila R. Janion, wife of his partner, and James Renton, who had all that capital from the Australian gold fields. The mill was put down in his books at $120,000.[16]

In 1878, Theo H. Davies became interested in the cane growing possibilities of the Hilo area. At first he persuaded several planters to put in cane, especially C. E. Richardson. He put up the most modern mill in the area at Waiakea (it was his last one). All this was done under the persuasion of Alexander Young, who was Davies' manager in the Honolulu Iron Works, and had been a blacksmith in Hilo years before. Davies put up all the money for the mill and brought C. C. Kennedy, an HIW foreman, over to erect it and then to stay on and run it. Alexander Young had some part of the mill under a partnership agreement with Davies. In the first few years, the mill did not do very well and was known locally as "Young's Folly." But they persevered. They put in the first steam locomotive on the mill railroad that ran through the Richardson property, and they delighted in coming over from Honolulu to ride the trains. One day in January 1880, they arranged a trip for a Sunday school picnic group on the train behind the puffing engine. In 1881, when the volcano erupted and threatened the area, for a time Young considered moving the machinery, and in July Kennedy and Richardson moved their furniture out of their houses as the flow drew near, and Kennedy built a wall along the ravine to stop the lava flow from going into his fish pond.

The reciprocity treaty came just in time for Davies and the rest. The whaling trade was dead, and the grave was dug in 1871 when 33 whaling ships were trapped in the ice of the Bering Sea and lost. The tomb sealed five years later when 13 more whaling vessels were crushed in the Arctic ice. In 1876 eight new plantations were started in the islands, and Claus Spreckels, a sugar refiner from California who had opposed the reciprocity treaty bitterly, saying it would flood California with cheap Hawaiian sugar, quietly went to Honolulu and contracted for the lion's share of the crop to be delivered to his refinery. From this real beginning, the sugar business was always intensely competitive. The struggle extended to the Honolulu businessmen—the old trading companies—which, having lost the whaling business, had to find new sources of revenue or perish. By 1879 Theo H. Davies had the agency for nine sugar plantations, but he was far from the most important agent: H. Hackfeld & Company had eighteen agencies. The other agents were W. G. Irwin Co. with ten plantations, C. Brewer with eight plantations, Castle & Cooke with five, C. Afong with two, F. A. Schaefer & Co. with three, J. T. Waterhouse with two, and G. W. MacFarlane & Co. with three.[17] For the next few years MacFarlane would be a thorn in Theo Davies' side, for the younger man bore a grudge against his old employer and seemed delighted to try to take business away from him. William L. Green retired from the firm in 1878, and MacFarlane blossomed forth in much the same way that Davies had done ten years earlier, selling general merchandise, machinery, insurance and fighting for plantation agencies. MacFarlane also went into business with Captain Makee to form the Makee Sugar Company of Kauai, and King Kalakaua took a quarter interest in the firm. Davies had been paying MacFarlane $2400 a year ("the highest I have ever paid") but the new MacFarlane was a different man, moving confidently in high circles. Davies was still piqued that the youth he had befriended would turn against him. He could not understand or forgive: MacFarlane, he wrote his agent in San Francisco, was "flying around doing nothing in particular . . . ," a claim that Davies knew was not true when he wrote it at the end of 1876.[18]

Not just the sugar entrepreneurs but the whole Hawaiian business community had become more competitive than ever; still sugar was the growth industry and the one most vigorously pursued.

One major difficulty was to secure planters who could succeed. Lidgate turned over some of his lands to his son Anthony, who agreed to plant 150 acres per year after 1882 and deliver those to the Laupahoehoe mill; that was one way to secure expansion. But outside the family relationships, the competition sometimes took ugly turns. Having established the Hawi mill, R. R. Hind also secured lands near Laupahoehoe at Waipunalei. The logical mill was Laupahoehoe's, so Hind made a deal: he needed a guaranteed water supply, and Lidgate had it; if Lidgate would give him the water, he would bring his cane to Laupahoehoe mill for grinding.[19] But when water was short, Lidgate did not deliver, and Hind sued him and won. Then Lidgate sued Hind for not delivering his cane, and he won. Theo H. Davies walked a straight and narrow path in this dispute, for he was agent for Hind's Hawi mill and Lidgate's partner. He was not immune to the irritability; he quarreled with Notley and Notley filed a suit, but they apparently adjusted their difficulties amicably. Theo H. Davies was inclined to do that where possible. They said that the Hind-Lidgate quarrel had made money only for the lawyers. That was not quite true; everything involving that operation was making money for Theo H. Davies.

Chapter Nine

MAN OF AFFAIRS

In *the middle 1870s*, a prospering Theo H. Davies took his position as an important member of the Hawaii business community. The year 1875 saw him elected to the presidency of the Honolulu Y.M.C.A. He marched in Kamehameha V's funeral procession, and King Kalakaua entertained him at breakfast. As vice-consul of Great Britain he was automatically a member of the diplomatic community. He was serious about his work, his government, and his place in society. He sued H. Hackfeld & Company for $25,000 in a dispute over wool marketing and collected a lesser amount. He quarreled with the Americans when they failed to honor Queen Victoria's birthday by flying the flag. He became a frequent, if not always accurate, commentator on affairs in letters to the editor of the newspapers. In 1873 he had opposed any cession of territory by the Hawaiian government to obtain a reciprocity treaty. He belittled the effects of the reciprocity treaty in a letter to the *Hawaiian Gazette*,[1] but four years later he declared that the treaty had been invaluable to business and that he had made more out of it than any other two men in Hawaii.[2] He was an active member of the Chamber of Commerce and was never shy about speaking up at meetings. He had strong views on the currency question (he favored a strict gold standard) and suggested that the under-financed government of Hawaii ought to establish an income tax. The vexing problem of securing adequate plantation labor troubled him as it did every planter; he wanted a Chamber of Commerce committee to deal with the problem, but instead the Hawaiian Immigration Association was established to bring in labor.

By 1877 he had just begun to bask a bit in his success. The ten years since he had come back to Hawaii to rescue Robert Janion had been good ones. The trading company had made profits totalling $192,000 in that period and the company owned half of Honolulu Iron Works, which Davies carried in Janion's interest as well as his own, although he assumed the $20,000 debt against the total 104 shares as his own liability. He wrote

The employees of Theo H. Davies & Co., Ltd. outside the firm's offices on Kaahumanu Street, around 1880. Theo H. Davies is the man in the bowler (derby hat) front, center, with his thumbs in his pockets.

Janion soon afterwards about their mutual investments and those of Henry Beecroft Jackson, but he did not write about his personal holdings, which were growing more important every year.

A week before Christmas, 1877, in the back of the Green-MacFarlane building, off Queen Street, a merchant named Adams was holding an evening sale. At nine o'clock, someone dropped a cigar butt into the straw and breeze fanned it into a blaze in a few moments. The northeast trade wind was blowing strong that night and soon the Adams sale dissolved in panic. Ladies fainted and strong men quailed as the fire spread.[3]

The firemen came in a hurry, but the trade wind had spread the blaze through the wooden buildings. Green-MacFarlane's roof began to go. Hopper's barrel factory caught next, and the rice mill was the third to burn. Robinson's wharf went up in flames, and the old James Robinson house went with it. Everyone came down to fight the fire; even King Kalakaua appeared and so did Governor John Dominis, husband of Princess Liliuokalani. George MacFarlane fought heroically, leading the bucket brigade. But it was no use. By morning the only structure standing in the block was the saddle and harness shop at the northwest corner of Fort and Queen Streets.

The newspapers estimated the destruction at $200,000. Green-MacFarlane had suffered $9,000 damage, and they carried $5,000 in insurance. H. Hackfeld & Company had lost $10,000, and they had $8,000 in insurance. Typically, the Hawaiian government, which owned several of the buildings, had no insurance at all to cover its $40,000 in damages. Also typically, Theo H. Davies, who had suffered $26,200 in damage, was insured for $26,200. Even bad fortune passed Theo H. Davies by, it seemed.

But what was to happen in the future was more debatable, for Hawaii was suffering severe pains. When Captain Cook had first come to the islands, he estimated the population at 400,000 Hawaiians. The white man's diseases and a strange malaise of the spirit accompanied the coming of the missionaries and the traders, and by 1823, the population had dropped to 142,000. Forty years later the official census put the population at 63,000 and in 1872, the total including *haoles* and *hapa-haoles* was only 52,380. The

Hawaiian race was dying. The foreign population just then was 4,500, with 900 Americans and 600 British, 400 Portuguese, 200 Germans, 90 Frenchmen, 1,900 Chinese, and 350 of other nationalities. The 900 Americans by 1872 dominated the government, society, and business, although the British were still powerful, particularly on the island of Hawaii, and similarly the Germans on the island of Kauai. Major Wodehouse and Theo H. Davies did their best to uphold British honor, and on the whole did well. On Queen Victoria's birthday in May 1878, Davies entertained his friends at the store. For once business was suspended for the afternoon, and a lunch (described by the *Gazette* as "sumptuous") was served "in a style of liberality and good taste such as Mr. Davies is famous for." Those were kind words, and welcome to a man who had come to the islands as a failure just over twenty years before. The next year business was so good that Theo Davies became more expansive, and gave a banquet for the Queen's birthday at the Royal Hawaiian Hotel. He opened the ceremonies with "remarks" and led the singing.

In the matter of business, the Davies leadership was growing. Friends suggested that he was on his way to becoming a millionaire. He was taking a definite lead in sugar matters; he wanted to bring in Indian laborers, but when his committee suggested it to the Chamber of Commerce, the opposition was fierce. The matter was tabled. Davies did have his opponents and his enemies, chief among them George MacFarlane, who annoyed him by trying to wrest away all his sugar agencies, and hurt him by importing sugar machinery in quantity from Scotland. Several sugar plantations opted to buy their machinery from MacFarlane rather than Honolulu Iron Works. It hurt, and all the more so because Davies was having trouble finding a replacement for MacFarlane. Janion suggested that he hire a young man named Francis M. Swanzy, but Swanzy wanted £400 to start, and Davies thought that was far too much for a man not yet thirty years old.[4] "Walker is 32 and has attained £400 after several years, and to start a younger man with the same salary and a prospective rise would upset all of my salary arrangements . . ." So Davies contented himself with a lesser man, named Housman, whom he paid £300 to start; "he could live *well* on

£250 a year," he said, forgetting that times had changed since he started out with Janion, Green & Co. without any real experience at £150. He was upset that Swanzy would not yield to his wishes. He had hired two clerks (one of them young Harry Luce, son of his old friend Captain Luce), but they were young fellows and would need some seasoning. He was desperately in need of a responsible associate. Housman left; Davies was so worried that he began offering $2,000 (the £400 Swanzy wanted) and seemed willing even to accept an American. But no American appeared who was satisfactory, and in the winter of 1878 Janion sent out another man on trial, Mr. Watson. But Watson, too, failed to meet the Davies specifications. He

Francis Mills Swanzy, circa 1905. By this time, he had become the central figure in management of the Davies enterprise in Hawaii.

hired a Mr. Tucker at $1,800 a year, with the usual high hopes. But by autumn, 1879, they, too, had vanished, and he was again writing Janion for help. The business had prospered so much that prosperity had become his burden. "We have a business that is second to *none* in Honolulu and in a few months more I hope to have carried the ship into smooth water, so that I can relax my hold a little."[5] But all was dependent on getting a good man; even Walker had disappointed him: "a first rate fellow but he has no vigor of character." In desperation he suggested that Janion's son Richard come out to Honolulu for three months trial; then Davies could place Richard and Walker in joint charge of the office at £500 a year, while he took Nellie and the six children who had been born in Honolulu back to visit England. His need bothered him constantly; he had a staff of eight, but still not the

Laupahoehoe Mill—1872

man he wanted. He had begun to speak lavishly of Harry Luce, "my right hand," but Luce was too young for grave responsibility, although Davies compared his activity to his own "ubiquitous" position at Janion, Green & Co. in the old days. Everything was going so splendidly and his assessment at the end of 1879 indicated it:[6]

Union Mill	THD and Janion owned a quarter, had built the $160,000 mill and paid off $90,000 of the debt; all but $10,000 of the capital was paid in, and Davies had the agency for the life of the partnership.
Hawi Mill	Davies had the agency.
Beecroft Plantation	Owned by THD and Henry Beecroft Jackson, with James Woods, manager, getting one-fifth of the net proceeds for his efforts.
Kaheai Plantation	Owned by THD and James Woods.
H.B. Montgomery & Co., C.J. Holmes, James Woods, Niulii Mill, Smith & Johnson	THD had the agency
Hamakua Plantation	Owned by Charles Notley and Fred J. Jackson, though THD had a secret interest and the agency.
Hamakua Mill	THD owned.
Laupahoehoe Plantation	THD had a half interest.
Waiakea Mill	THD owned with Alexander Young.
Waiakea Plantation	THD had the agency.
Kaalaea Plantation	THD owned one-eight; it was largely Jackson's property.

But, planning to sail for England, Davies still worried constantly about leaving the management to his associates. He had decided that Harry Luce should join what would be a triumvirate, with Walker as senior member and Richard Janion as the third member. Even so he was nervous about giving them such responsibility. He had hundreds of thousands of dollars at stake in sugar. The Honolulu Iron Works held its annual meeting on February 14, and the figures showed a capital stock of $100,000 and accumulated profits of $136,000.[7] The Iron Works was valued physically at $110,000 with merchandise and supplies on hand of $129,000, all paid for. Davies always believed in a strong cash position and not in doing as so many other companies: paying dividends from borrowed money. The result was that Honolulu Iron Works, although not paying much in dividends over these years, was highly profitable and totally unencumbered. Davies had high hopes for his "triumvirate" but he still worried; a wrong decision could be difficult and a series of them, made in his absence, might be fatal. His confidence was not increased when Richard Janion, even before arriving in Honolulu, began to complain about his salary. The result of this uncertainty and other difficulties Davies felt he must resolve before taking his pleasure, was to delay the home leave until late summer.

That summer of 1880 Davies had the great relief of finally unloading the Kaalaea Plantation to Sing Chong & Co. for $39,000.[8] It had, he said, caused him more worry and pain than any other aspect of his business. He had also negotiated large loans with Bishop & Company in Honolulu, putting up mortgages on Waiakea and Hamakua Mills and he was negotiating with San Francisco banks through his agents Williams, Dimond & Company (his friend Henry Dimond had done well) for $120,000 to carry the sugar interests until the crop came in. It was risky, but potentially very profitable. If only he could be assured of good management in the Honolulu office all would be well.

As summer drew on, in addition to all else, Theo Davies wrote out in his crabbed hand detailed instructions about all the problems of the mills, plantations, and every aspect of the business, to leave with his triumvirate. Richard Janion was to be in charge of remittances, Thomas Rain Walker was to have general charge of the office, and Harry Luce was to be his assistant, with special regard to the plantations, which he was to visit every three months. Walker and Janion were raised to $3,000 a year and Harry Luce to $2,000. In August, having made every possible move to guarantee a smooth running of the office and his complex affairs during a long absence, Theo Davies, Nellie, and the six children embarked for San Francisco and the long-delayed visit to his native England after twelve years away. He was supremely confident, and yet still worried; confident in his ability to meet any situation, but worried about leaving his affairs in the hands of others.[9]

Chapter Ten

THE END OF THE OLD FIRM

When *Theo H. Davies sailed* to the American mainland in the summer of 1880, he was supposedly taking a holiday from work. But the moment the train from San Francisco reached New York, he hustled wife, children, and the nurse off to the Fifth Avenue Hotel, and hurried down to the offices of Williams, Dimond & Company, his American agents.[1] What he discovered there sent him into a frenzy of activity. The price paid for sugar by Claus Spreckels in California was based on the price of "Manila Extra Superior," but an enterprising young man, J.C. Pfluger, Hackfeld's son-in-law, had discovered that the Hawaii producers were underpaid by the California refiners. Polarization—passing polarized light thru a sugar solution to measure the sugar content—was the key. Manila Extra actually polarized at 88° but the California refiners used a figure of 92°. The Hawaii sugar was being delivered at an average polarization of 92.5°, which by Pfluger's calculations should have meant four per cent or a half-cent-a-pound better price than they were getting. Spreckels was paying 7.415 cents a pound in San Francisco.[2] When Davies had first heard of the Pfluger claims, in Hawaii, he had dismissed them. Pfluger had not been discreet; he had erupted with a charge against the refiner. Davies had seen Spreckels in San Francisco and sympathized with the refiner, who said he was being victimized. Checking around New York, Davies discovered that

91

eastern refiners would pay 8.55 cents for 92° sugar and, deducting a half cent from this for the rail freight from California to New York, it still meant the Hawaii producers could get a price in the east more than half a cent a pound over that in the west.

Spreckels was so angry with Pfluger that he threatened to shut off from his refinery those who argued with him. Since he virtually controlled sugar refining in California, it was not an idle threat, but Davies was not intimidated. When he informed Henry Dimond of the situation, the San Francisco agent was so concerned that he wanted Davies to come back to San Francisco immediately to see Spreckels. Davies would not longer delay his vacation, but he promised to have new samples made by chemists as soon as he reached Liverpool. At the moment he was not even telling his office in Honolulu what he had discovered.[3] The matter was so sensitive that he wanted Spreckels to hear first, from Dimond. Davies was confident that then Spreckels "will appreciate my object and will see that my planters do not suffer by having placed confidence in him and me."[4] But if he was wrong in that confidence, he predicted that Hawaiian sugars would all flow to the east; certainly those controlled by Theo H. Davies would do so. Already he had a firm offer from an eastern refiner for a better price. Davies put all this in a letter and dispatched it to Dimond. He did not know it, but he was opening a quarrel that would last for many years and finally change the whole sugar industry of Hawaii.

Davies' voyage to England in 1880 was more than a trip home to see relatives and cast an eye on the old country. He had determined that he was going to return to England to live, and once there, he began looking for a suitable house to buy. Actually, his decision followed the pattern of the firm that was now in his name: Starkey had "made his pile" and gone home to England, to send Janion out. Janion had amassed enough money to return home, and dispatch Davies. This time, Richard Janion had taken his wife and family to Honolulu, and Davies expected the triumvirate of Janion, Walker and Luce to function for him in Hawaii. Eventually Davies expected to take over the Robert C. Janion position in the partnership and work from Liverpool. There was good reason for this plan; Janion had

The officers and staff of Theo H. Davies & Co., in January, 1890, keyed, as shown. Nos. 20, 26, 30 and 31 are unknown.

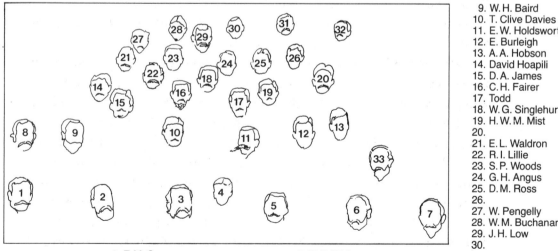

1. F. M. Swanzy
2. Alexander Young (Hon. Iron Wks)
3. Theo H. Davies
4. Harry Davies
5. T. R. Walker
6. C. H. Hedeman (Hon. Iron Wks)
7. J. A. Kennedy (Hon. Iron Wks)
8. J. C. Cook
9. W. H. Baird
10. T. Clive Davies
11. E. W. Holdsworth
12. E. Burleigh
13. A. A. Hobson
14. David Hoapili
15. D. A. James
16. C. H. Fairer
17. Todd
18. W. G. Singlehurst
19. H. W. M. Mist
20.
21. E. L. Waldron
22. R. I. Lillie
23. S. P. Woods
24. G. H. Angus
25. D. M. Ross
26.
27. W. Pengelly
28. W. M. Buchanan
29. J. H. Low
30.
31.
32. C. J. Day
33. T. R. Robinson

suffered a stroke in 1877 and had not fully recovered from it. When Richard had gone to Hawaii, Janion felt the loss sorely and complained about it. The coming of Davies to England could mean that Janion would retire.

Davies took a house at Alderley Edge in Cheshire, which he called Oak Bank,[5] and settled the family into English life. Clive was nearly ten, and it was time he began the proper English education, that would lead him to Uppingham public school, and then to university. In the manner of many a poor minister's son, Theo Davies had risen above his station, and now he and his family would live as English gentlefolk. The course was not quite clear, but he had no intention of returning to Hawaii to live. Nellie's health was precarious; six children born in nine years had not helped it, and he could think of several other reasons for turning Hawaii affairs over to subordinates. First however, he must make foolproof preparations for a secure business future. In that connection he looked up the expensive Mr. Swanzy, liked what he saw, and pondered. All that he had said about the deficiencies of Thomas Rain Walker remained in his mind. Further, Honolulu had not agreed with Richard Janion, and he had decided to return to England after only a few weeks there. The triumvirate had functioned so much less effectively in Davies' absence than he had expected that he knew a strong character was obviously needed at the head of the Honolulu office. Swanzy impressed him as just that person. In his earlier searches, Davies had hoped to find a man with sufficient strength to face down ebullient and sometimes arrogant Americans, someone about 30 years old, who would be responsive to Davies' superior experience and 46 years. Swanzy was an Englishman born in Ireland, of a landholding family there; he had an education superior to Davies' own, early years at the Portora Royal School in Enniskillen and later at Science College, Dublin.[6] At 16 he had gone to work for a Liverpool firm and had moved, always progressing, to others in Liverpool and Manchester. He was also a member of the Church of England, an important factor. They struck a bargain, Swanzy was to have his high salary ($2,500 for three years) and more later if the association was mutually satisfactory. Davies decided he would go back to Honolulu, taking Swanzy with him, although the Davies family had been home in England for scarcely three months. He would not take any members of the family, nor did he intend to stay much longer than to see Swanzy safely ensconced in the office.

On November 20, 1880, a frosty morning in Cheshire, he was up early. Clive was in bed with the sniffles, but Theo and Nellie and the other children had breakfast together, and knelt together to pray "commending each other to the care of the Shepherd of Israel who neither slumbers nor sleeps."[7]

The cab came leaving time for only a choking goodbye in the hall, and then Theo H. Davies was on his way to Liverpool and the steamer *Scythia*. Swanzy and his former Honolulu clerk, Charles Robertson, met him at the landing. He had sent Robertson back from Honolulu after Janion's illness to help with affairs in Liverpool, and Robertson accompanied them to Queenstown, Ireland so he could take back a last message from the loving husband and father to his family. They reached the harbor on Sunday morning, and all went to church together and for a walk, then lunched on chops, Irish potatoes, and draught ale. Then Davies and Swanzy boarded their steamer, waved to Charley Robertson and were off. They were seated at the Captain's table, as befitted Davies' position, but found no one of much importance or interest to them there. They passed the days talking and reading, and eating and waiting—and Davies' confidence in his new associate grew. Swanzy was pleased to accommodate his employer, and when they reached New York, he drove off to the Brevoort Hotel with the luggage, while Davies tended to business. They went to church three times on Sunday. They went to Tiffany's jewelry store, not to buy anything, even for Nellie, but just to look at $40,000 diamonds and $10,000 vases. Davies was delighted with the Brevoort because by sharing a room the cost was hardly more than that of a lesser hotel, and by ordering meals for only one person ("meals served for one are more than enough for two")[8] they may even have saved money. They travelled to Chicago, and by the Union Pacific line to the west. In San Francisco it was business all week and church on Sunday (twice) and then they sailed for Honolulu.

When they arrived in Honolulu they were met by all the triumvirate. Walker took care of Swanzy, while Harry Luce took Davies home to little Britain to stay with the family as he had done so many times before in his early years in Honolulu. Swanzy had been properly acquainted with his new job and by the end of the voyage certainly knew all that would be expected of him.

A few days after arrival at Honolulu, Davies went to the Big Island of Hawaii, taking Harry Luce with him, since Luce was in effect his manager of plantations. The ship took them down the Hamakua coast to Hilo, and from there they rode on horseback to Waiakea, to see the new mill put up by Honolulu Iron Works. Next day they took a ship back up the Hamakua coast to Laupahoehoe, where they negotiated the dangerous landing on the rocky beach. They stayed overnight with planter Tony Lidgate and then rode on to Hamakua plantation, about 11 miles from Laupahoehoe, where they stayed with the Charles Notleys. Theo Davies held a church service on Sunday for sixteen adults and a handful of children from mill and plantation, and then spent an hour with James Woods who had come down from Kohala Ranch to see him. The afternoon was spent inspecting Davies' Hamakua mill, and talking to Thomas Hughes, the old Honolulu Iron Works owner, who was now manager of the mill. Monday was spent worrying over the endless problem of transport of sugar. They made a decision to build a more effective "gravitation railroad" which would be powered by a stationary engine at the bottom of the grade, to bring cane from the plantation to the mill. Davies and Luce spent one night with Samuel Parker the cattle rancher, who was also in the sugar business in a small way at Paauhau. They visited several other plantations in the district, and then Beecroft Plantation in Kohala.[9] They saw Hart at Niulii and then met at Union Mill to look over that company, which Davies and three others had bought from R. R. Hind earlier. Everything on the trip seemed fine except one matter: "the wretched Kohala store," a retail enterprise Davies had begun a few years earlier which had never made profits and now seemed a more miserable and worse business proposition than ever. Davies decided then and there to shut down and go out of retail trade in

Kohala, but that was his only disappointment. On returning to Honolulu he was so satisfied with the condition of his investments on the Big Island, the prospects and profits of the Honolulu Iron Works, and the state of his offices on Queen Street, that Davies decided to return homeward via *The Australia* on February 14, a month earlier than he had expected to leave. The prospect improved his disposition remarkably, even to making it bearable to face the auction of the furniture at Craigside. He and Nellie had decided to sell all, since they did not intend again to live in Honolulu. He supervised the sale of everything, including the two horses Velpie and Gypsy, and the three carriages, and sent the two saddlehorses over to the Big Island. Then, free, without a care for business affairs, he boarded ship for San Francisco.

He gave his parting instructions to Walker but indicated that Swanzy would not only occupy the position young Janion was supposed to have taken but would "be prepared to aid in every branch of the business in which his judgement and ability may be useful."[10] He left a bank balance of $136,000 and a projected surplus for the next six months of $78,000. All in his world seemed serene.

In San Francisco, Davies stayed at the Palace Hotel, his usual place, and spent several days on business. He had a long quarrelsome meeting with Spreckels over the Pfluger report and Davies' subsequent proofs of the validity of the Pfluger premise through chemists' findings in England. They decided to test the argument: a new shipment of sugar had just come from Honolulu and two samples were sent to the refinery. Davies asked Henry Dimond to produce chemists to meet him there, and he and Spreckels drove down for the test. The Manila cane tested at 91° and, after seeing this, Spreckels agreed to pay on the basis of 91°, which meant $2.50 per ton more for Hawaiian sugar. They parted friends, for Davies had behaved with considerable restraint, unlike Pfluger who had charged Spreckels with cheating the sugar producers. Davies was pleased. By any standard he had accomplished a valuable piece of work.[11]

Davies then returned to Liverpool. He took the Union Pacific train to Chicago, transferred to the New York Central, boarded a transatlantic steamer, and was home in less than three weeks. He arrived in March 1881, to find that R.C. Janion was desperately ill and the doctors did not expect him to live through the summer. It was apparent that the partnership was coming to an end, and Davies' letters to Honolulu and Liverpool that spring and summer indicated his effort to wind up the affairs of the business so that it would be readily divisible. In May he made the decision to return to Honolulu again that fall but for only a few weeks, to be sure all was orderly for the transition. He rented a summer house at St. Leonard's-on-Sea in Sussex for the family and prepared for his journey. Ever since the day he left Honolulu he had kept up a barrage of correspondence, most of it with Walker, inquiring into every detail of the many business enterprises of Theo H. Davies & Co. By late spring, a note of irritation was beginning to creep into his letters to Walker over errors of detail, particularly in finance. But all this was forgotten on August 11, when Robert Janion died. The difficulties of ending the partnership meant that Davies had to establish a new company, and, if he wanted the business to continue as it had, he must secure for his own name the agencies of Lloyd's and Northern Assurance companies. It was important that Davies hasten to Honolulu to make sure all was done properly. There was another reason, too. After the discussions with Spreckels about polarization, the quality of sugars became a matter of new importance to all concerned. Each shipment was carefully tested by the refinery, and as a check, the agents for the plantations also tested. Williams, Dimond & Company made some grievous errors in tests and found a lower polarization point than the refinery. The refinery's tests were lower than those made in New York and London on the same samples, and soon planters, agents and refinery were distrusting one another.[12] By July Spreckels accused Davies of "giving me a stab in the back." By August, [13] Spreckels told Thomas Rain Walker that he would buy no more of Davies' sugars. Davies had said "so be it" and prepared to look for other markets; "I shall not beg him to buy my sugars." By October he was in Honolulu, arranging for the valuation of the assets of the partnership. He visited the Big Island to check on the plantations and mills, and was generally satisfied with what he found. In November he left

Honolulu again, not expecting to return for several years. He established the new firm, and registered with the government. There were some worrisome aspects of business, and they involved management. Hamakua plantation had a heavy crop and heavy debt to the Davies company which advanced money for supplies and labor. It was the same with Waiakea. As of the end of partnership with Janion, the firm held $240,000 in permanent sugar interests plus three planting interests which ran for three years more. The permanent interests were: one half of Waiakea Mill valued at $70,000; one half of Hamakua Mill, valued at $50,000; all of Kipahulu Mill, valued at $60,000; a fourth of Union Mill, valued at $10,000; and half of Laupahoehoe mill and plantation, valued at $50,000. In addition they held 52 per cent of the Iron Works, worth about $225,000. Davies' problem was to pay off the Janion heirs but retain control of these properties for himself. It was not going to be an easy problem to resolve, and within a few months he realized that if he was going to protect his interests, he might have to return to Hawaii again. With a reluctance that one can only imagine, given his previous plans, Theo H. Davies went home to England in November 1881, to think it over. He was no longer the young whirlwind of Hawaii business but a substantial businessman, faced with a major problem of success, how to secure what he had built.

Chapter Eleven

THE SPRECKELS AFFAIR

After *Claus Spreckels had exploded* and told Thomas Rain Walker that he would accept no more of Davies' sugar, Davies worried for a while but finally decided Spreckels was bluffing. He thought he knew his man. Spreckels had been in the sugar business for a long time, importing from Manila and the Far East before the Hawaii plantations were very important. With the signing of the reciprocity treaty, Spreckels had scurried over to Honolulu and, before competitors could act, had made contracts for more than half of the sugar to be taken off the land in the following twelve months. He had also gone into sugar growing himself with purchase of an interest in the Waihee plantation on Maui for his son John. Following that investment, Spreckels had returned in 1878, bought and leased more than 30,000 acres on Maui, cultivated King Kalakaua until he got a valuable water right on Mount Haleakala and permission to construct a water ditch, and established the Hawaiian Commercial & Sugar Company, which seemed to threaten to take over most of the economic activity in the kingdom. He also took ruthless advantage of poor Princess Ruth Keelikolani, a member of the royal family, who had no head for figures nor any concept of the value of land. For $10,000 he bought from her all her claim to the crown lands of Hawaii, and she claimed a half interest. (Eventually the Hawaii legislature paid him off with 24,000 acres of land, just to get rid of the claim.) By the time Theo Davies came back to

England, Spreckels had a fleet of steamers running to Hawaii, taking off the sugar. That same line, the Oceanic Steamship Company, was the principal American link with the whole Central and South Pacific. In accomplishing all this, Spreckels had made grand gestures and even more promises than he fulfilled, so although the industrialist was in no way "a paper tiger" there was a certain exuberance in his character that could be taken for bluff. No, said Theo Davies, Spreckels would not refuse his sugars; he might use the quarrel as a basis for reducing the price, but he would not cut Davies off.[1]

It was necessary for Davies to go to Honolulu to open the new books for the company and settle Janion's affairs, so he planned a trip in September 1881. He would stop off at San Francisco and see Dimond and Spreckels. He did stop, and saw Spreckels, but the argument was not resolved. He arranged for shipment of sugar from Manila to San Francisco so it could be tested against Hawaii sugars by Dimond's and Spreckels' chemists. Then, leaving the argument in abeyance, he went on to Honolulu to arrange for the settlement of Janion's affairs.

In Honolulu, Davies set about clearing the books. The whole Hamakua enterprise, plantation and mill, he valued at $150,000; Laupahoehoe, $200,000; Waiakea, $150,000. And there were Beecroft Plantation, the Kahei plantation of James Woods, Kipahulu Mill, various merchandise ventures involving shiploads of goods, Union Mill, and the Honolulu Iron Works, with a value of over $200,000. These investments were all encumbered with debt in one way or another, and the only sensible course was to wait for time and sugar crops to pay most of them off. Davies would devote most of his share of profit from all ventures to retiring such portions of the Janion investment as the heirs wished to relinquish in favor of cash, and he would make regular payments on the heirs' shares. It would mean some more belt-tightening, but in a few years it would all be worth the effort, as the Janion share was reduced and finally eliminated in most ventures.

The sugar refining negotiations with Spreckels were still unsatisfactory, so on his way home again in November, Davies stopped in San Francisco to resume the argument. He had discovered that although Extra

Superior Manila Sugar No. 10 had been laid down as the basis for payment on Hawaii sugars, Extra Superior Manila No. 10 was virtually never shipped from the Philippines. The sugar companies shipped Extra Superior Manila No. 9 which polarized at 87°, four degrees lower than Hawaii's sugar. But having once accepted that argument, Spreckels backed away and insisted on the No. 10 figure. New York sugar refiners regularly took the No. 9 so negotiations with Spreckels seemed to reach an impasse. The San Francisco *Chronicle* chose this time to make an attack on Spreckels and the Hawaii sugar planters, which did not improve the atmosphere. Davies wrote an indignant reply[2] and then went off to New York. The whole atmosphere on the West coast seemed to be growing so poisonous that perhaps the Hawaii planters would be better off shipping east. On his departure, Dimond said he was going the following Monday to negotiate with Spreckels and was sure it would turn out all right; the planters would have the higher price they deserved.

When Davies reached New York, no San Francisco agreement had yet been made for the next year. He secured an order from one refiner for 300 tons of sugar on an experimental basis, on which the price would be 6.5 cents after paying freight; not very satisfactory, but perhaps the best they could do. Then he sailed for England, promising the office in Honolulu that he was ready to return and make a deal in New York if Spreckels failed them.[3] The infuriating aspect was that Spreckels had them hanging on the line; he was buying their sugars, but he would not sign contracts. The alternatives were refineries in New York, St. Louis, and Chicago, none of them very attractive. But the other alternative was surrender, and by the end of January, 1882, Spreckels had indicated what would happen if they surrendered. He was talking about offering to ship sugars direct from plantation to refinery on the Oceanic Line *free*—but only if the planters eliminated their agents.

Hackfeld's son-in-law, Pfluger, happened to be in England, and Davies conferred with him. Together with F.A. Schaefer and Co. they represented the next most powerful factor to Spreckels himself in Hawaii sugar. They talked about establishing their own refinery in San Francisco. Meanwhile the St. Louis refinery was talking about taking up Hawaii sugars at a price that could be lived with. Hackfeld and Schaefer also dealt with Williams, Dimond & Co. in San Francisco. Together they represented 25,000 tons of sugar per year, and Williams, Dimond should be able to get a favorable freight rate, particularly since the owners of the Central Pacific and Union Pacific Railroads had started their own shipping line. Then New York made an offer, and the affair became so complicated that Davies decided to go once more from England to New York himself to confer with Dimond and others, who would meet him there.[4] He sailed on March 11, 1882, on the *Gallia*. He also expected to go to San Francisco but hoped he would be home in time for Easter—quite a presumption in those days before air travel. The San Francisco trip would be made to try one last time to reach an agreement with Spreckels before the latter sailed for Honolulu in April. Spreckels had heard of the negotiations of three important agencies with eastern refineries, and Davies inferred that he might be alarmed. Equally possible, however, was an assumption that Spreckels might try to bluff them. So when Davies reached New York, one of his first meetings was with H. O. Havemeyer, the investment banker, to talk over the construction of a new refinery in New York to handle the sugars of Davies, Hackfeld and Schaefer companies. Theo went on to San Francisco then, and discovered that the contracts Dimond had made for shipment of the rest of the year's sugars to St. Louis had indeed startled Spreckels. They went over the old argument, impasse threatened again, but then Davies took a gamble: he offered Spreckels a fixed price, 7 cents a pound, for sugar polarizing at 91°, no matter what the Manila price might be. Spreckels wanted to bargain, and held out for 6.90 cents, but Davies refused. Next morning, Spreckels must have read the newspapers, which were quoting a price of 7.28 cents a pound for Manila sugar and suggesting it might go higher, and Spreckels accepted the arrangement.

Davies insisted that the 7 cent price was a good one for the planters, because the average figures of Manila sugar over the past four years had been around 6.80 cents. Spreckels also wanted the freight for his Oceanic line, and Davies agreed that he should have 3,000 tons this coming year but would not go beyond that. Spreckels wanted to contract for 1883 and 1884, and asked Davies to come on to Honolulu with him and work out a

Nellie (Mrs. Theo H. Davies) at Southport
around 1900.

long-range contract. But Davies refused; it was better to let Spreckels stew,
he said. He wrote his planters[5] and then hurried back to England. He
sailed on April 19 and was home on April 29; he had promised himself a
"delightful May in England with the children" and the promise could be
kept. Just before he sailed he had a cable from Nellie. Her health had been
so poor that on their return to England there was a question as to whether
or not the doctors would let her ever go back to Hawaii. Davies knew that in
the fall he must return, and the thought of going without the family had
nagged him constantly. Jubilantly he wrote his friend James Woods in
Hawaii[6] that he had a cable saying, "Doctor says I may go in August;" Nellie
could go. He would be coming back in the fall to Hawaii "for good," he
said.[7]

Chapter Twelve

THE SUGAR BOOM

Boom *is precisely the* proper word to describe what was happening in Hawaii's sugar industry in the 1880s. What had been in the 1850s a cottage industry, and in the 1860s a dangerous speculation, suddenly blossomed under the Reciprocity Treaty of 1876, and five years later virtually everyone with a little capital was struggling to get into the most successful business Hawaii had ever known. Even King Kalakaua, who was not enthusiastic about foreigners and their works, declared that sugar would be the salvation of Hawaii.

On Theo H. Davies' visit to Honolulu in 1881 to settle Swanzy and reorganize the office after Richard Janion's departure, Davies had made some estimates as to the financial conditions of his various sugar enterprises. Waiakea, the newest of them, was also the most tenuous. There, Davies had engaged several men to plant cane and deliver it to his mill on a half-share basis; he supplied the land and advanced expense monies, and they provided the labor.

First of these men was C. E. Richardson, who had planted 100 acres of cane from which Davies expected a yield of 300 tons of sugar that year, plus 50 acres of rattoon cane, planted earlier to yield 75 tons. Davies' share would bring $25,000 that year. Second in importance was the land planted by a Hawaiian named Akana—100 acres plus 40 acres of rattoon, or second growth cane, but of better yield, to bring 80 tons of sugar. Davies estimated his share of this arrangement at $20,000. The mill, which he owned, would net him $45,000. The expenses, however, were going to be high. The cash required to finance the Waiakea operation in 1881 would be $155,000, while Waiakea would produce only $90,000 in revenue. Davies must find $65,000 to support Waiakea. At the end of the year he estimated that the mill would be bought and paid for and making profits and have a surplus of $30,000. The Davies theory was to finance improvements from profits.[1]

Laupahoehoe, which had been operating for five years, showed clearly what was happening. There Anthony Lidgate had planted 140 acres which should yield 560 tons of sugar, plus a late planting of 30 acres which should bring 90 tons and 30 acres of rattoons which should provide another 90 tons. The gross income for the 740 tons should be $88,000. Laupahoehoe, plantation and mill, had a total debt of $16,000, and running expenses for the year would be $54,000. Writing off all costs in one year, as was Davies' fashion, he came up with a net cash profit of $18,000 on Laupahoehoe. In 1882 he expected 880 tons of sugar there grossing $105,000, with a running expense of $60,000, for a surplus of $45,000. That, and what came after, barring expenses for improvements, would mean continuing high profit investment. Actually, in 1882 a severe storm and washout cost Laupahoehoe the loss of four boilers. Without complaint Davies made arrangements to replace them and changed the location of the mill to avoid a repetition; the profits and potential of Laupahoehoe seemed so immense with this first planting that what might have seemed a disaster to another could be taken in stride.

Hamakua was a different proposition. There Davies was in partnership with Charles Notley, the planter, and Frederick Jackson of England, Davies' brother-in-law. Hamakua was expected to yield 1100 tons of sugar, grossing $130,000. The mill at Paauilo still had a debt to Davies of $22,000, and running expenses were estimated at $24,000. For grinding, Davies had half the proceeds, or $65,000, which would give him a $19,000 surplus at the end of 1881. Hamakua Mill manager Thomas Hughes already had a debt of $60,000, and running expenses were estimated to be $65,000. Net profits at Hamakua would be subject to the closest scrutiny of Hughes' expenses, for Davies suspected him to be a careless operator.[2]

Davies also leased several hundred acres of land at Ookala from William L. Green and turned it over to Captain W. Toomey, who would have a third interest and $1,200 a year. This first year Toomey was to plant 80 acres. The plowing would be done by Notley with the new steam plow Davies had sent out from England in 1881. Davies and his partners were apparently the first to introduce steam plows into Hawaii. They used steam plows both at Hamakua and Laupahoehoe.

Davies was still in business with C. F. Hart in Kohala, and Hart was expected to bring in 1,020 tons from Niulii, to gross $122,000. Davies also was agent for Hind and Beecroft and a number of other plantations, and took 2½ per cent commission on the sales of all the sugar of these plantations, or about 5,500 tons of sugar, which at a price of seven cents a pound would bring commissions of $19,250 to the firm. It was no exaggeration to say that sugar was a burgeoning business. It was still also highly volatile, and dangerous in its way, subject to many threats, from those of competitors and refiners to those of nature. The Walker and Allen partnership of Honolulu, having restored their fortunes after the collapse of 1866, had gone heavily into sugar, and when the American market collapsed again in 1874, they had gone bankrupt. In 1881, with so much money at stake, and so many varied interests involved in his numerous enterprises, Theo H. Davies began to turn to the corporate structure as the best method of carrying on the sugar business.

The first Davies incorporation had been that of Honolulu Iron Works on December 22, 1876, with a capital stock of $100,000, divided into 200 shares worth $500 each. Davies held 52 shares, Janion held 52, Mrs. Janion held 26 shares, Mrs. Mary Green (William L. Green's mother) held 26 shares, and Alexander Young held 44 shares. The reason for incorporation of the iron works was obvious; it was the only one of Davies' enterprises in which an alien figure existed, Mrs. Green. Perhaps that is too harsh a judgement. Green's wife was a McKibben, daughter of Honolulu's English doctor whom Davies counted as one of his closest friends. But it would not be too much to say that the Greens had divided loyalties, and Green's interests were by 1877 often in conflict with Davies.[3]

The incorporation of the sugar plantations and mills came for the same reason, protection of a diversity of individual interests. First of these companies to be incorporated by Davies was Union Mill, in which Davies had a quarter interest along with Holmes, Woods and Renton. The partners applied for a corporation charter in 1881 from the Hawaii Privy Council. James Woods was to be president, G. F. Holmes vice-president, Davies' partner Thomas Rain Walker secretary-treasurer, and James Woods would also serve as auditor. James Renton would be manager of the mill and Davies would be agent. The capitalization of the company was $160,000. From the beginning Union mill had been profitable and it continued so; in the first year after incorporation the stock paid a dividend of 25 percent.[4]

The next incorporation was that of Laupahoehoe Sugar Company. In May, 1883, Hawaii Minister of Interior John E. Bush granted the company a 50-year charter and the right to issue $600,000 in capital stock. The first meeting was held at the Theo H. Davies office in Honolulu, where Lidgate took 2,500 shares and Davies took 2,500 shares. Davies became chairman, Lidgate president, and Swanzy was made treasurer. The value of the Davies and Lidgate holdings was $250,000 each.

By autumn, the affairs of Hamakua Mill Company had become so complicated that incorporation was necessary there, too. Apparently the ownership of Hamakua Mill had devolved to Davies, Mrs. Janion, and James Renton, with Davies handling Mrs. Janion's share as part of the investment account she held with him. In the incorporation, Hamakua Mill was set up with capital of $240,000. Davies controlled 2,100 shares of stock and Renton had 300. For the time being, Hamakua plantation was operated as a partnership;[5] eventually it would be amalgamated into Hamakua Mill Company.

It was small wonder then, that Theo H. Davies had come back from England to settle such complicated matters and disengage the assets of the old partnership in Theo H. Davies & Co., without losing them, as the obligations to the Janion estate were paid.

Chapter Thirteen

THE EVILS OF DRINK

Ohe day, not long after Theo H. Davies had re-
turned to Honolulu to live, he went to the funeral of a man he had known
for many years. The procession was moving along Beretania Street towards the cemetery up Nuuanu Valley. It passed the Commercial Hotel.
Suddenly a dozen drunken Hawaiians came charging across the street,
surrounded the hearse and chief mourner's carriage, laughing and shout-
ing, disrupted the whole funeral line and then ran into the hotel for
another drink.[1] As the procession turned on Nuuanu Street, several of the
Hawaiians rushed out again to laugh and shout at the foreigners. Davies
was badly shaken by the experience, and when he got home he began to
think about the evils of liquor, especially in Hawaii. Then, not long afterward, he was talking to a business acquaintance about a particularly brutal
murder which had occurred a few days earlier. The man should be
hanged, said Davies. But he was drunk at the time, said his friend; was that
not an extenuating circumstance? Not at all, said Davies, the murderer
should be punished to the full extent of the law. Drunkenness made no
difference; in itself it was, or should be, a crime. His friend looked at him
oddly.

"Davies," he said, "the man probably bought the liquor from your
company."

That remark made Theo H. Davies think even harder, until at the office he came to a sudden decision. Never again, he told the staff, would Theo H. Davies & Co. import another shilling's worth of liquor.[2] The orders from Ind Coope and the other distillers' agents were withdrawn and the business turned over to Schaefer & Co. although the economic sacrifice was considerable. Customs House figures showed that a quarter of British imports were in alcoholic spirits, and Theo H. Davies, as the most important British trading house, must have been doing at least that percentage of its business in the beer and liquor trade. Having taken so strong a stand, Davies also began examining closely his own habits and those of his associates. He had continued over the years to take beer and wine at the dinner table, although he did not often drink spirits; and although he had drawn the line twenty years earlier at taking a cargo of liquor to British Columbia for trade, he had never been known as a prohibitionist. Now, in 1882 he became one and might have been more strident about it had he not assessed the business liabilities of trying to force his views on strangers. But he became a teetotaler himself and encouraged his associates to do the same. Any indulgence he had ever before shown for alcohol and the men who drank was replaced by a stern disapproval of the practice and a sad compassion for alcohol's victims.

Theo Davies was also thoroughly disgusted with the Hawaiian royal court and its extravagances. As an old friend of Alexander Liholiho and Queen Emma, Davies was no stranger at court, and even in Kalakaua's reign, his official position as vice consul of Britain gave him entree to court functions. Still, his disapproval of Kalakaua's court was almost complete. One reason was the pattern of conspicuous waste the king had begun. Two years earlier, when Davies had been in England, King Kalakaua had undertaken a royal tour of the world, accompanied by W.W. Armstrong, his minister of state, and Charles H. Judd, and had visited London. Davies had done all he could to help with people in high places,[3] and even gone down to London to accompany the king. But he was snubbed by the royal party[4] and so when he returned to Honolulu he had little reason to be favorable to the royal person, even though Kalakaua had made a good impression on Queen Victoria, the Prince of Wales, Prime Minister Gladstone, and the British royal court. Hobnobbing with European royalty at the courts of Belgium, Germany, Austria, Spain, and Portugal had given Kalakaua a new perspective on royal behavior, and he decided to celebrate. He began construction of a new magnificent Iolani Palace. On the ninth anniversary of his election to the throne, he staged a coronation ceremony. He had ordered in Italy a grand statue of Kamehameha the Great. It was unveiled opposite the new palace on coronation day—or the replica was. The original had been lost when the ship bringing it to Honolulu was sunk; later it was recovered and erected before the post office on the Big Island at the birthplace in North Kohala of Kamehameha I. The story of the statue was symbolic; Kalakaua's attempt to create grandeur would have been laughable except that anyone who laughed was likely to have his Hawaii affairs come to a swift and unpleasant end. The coronation celebration went on for weeks. Feasting, drunkenness and the *hula* were much in evidence; Kalakaua defied the missionary party by staging a *hula* celebration that featured the most significant of the dances, one that lasted all one afternoon and far into the night, and the missionaries said it was disgusting. Even the *Gazette* complained that the "wantonness" and "phallic worship" had gone beyond all previous modern bounds. Theo Davies was piqued because he was snubbed by the court, he who had always been invited to the royal fêtes.* Equally important, his frugal soul was shocked at the sight of the king and his ministers "spending money like water."[5]

There was also the matter of business:[6] George MacFarlane and William L. Green stood very high with Kalakaua, and the MacFarlane company got all the government business. Theo H. Davies could do nothing about the royal intemperance, but there was everything he could do when he found the royal habits percolating into his own office. The first indications of trouble came in the late winter of 1883.[7] Allen Scrimgeon, the bookkeeper, had a tendency to drink, and occasionally he drank too much and was either unable to come to the office next day, or prone to error

---

*King Kalakaua did not like Theo H. Davies, perhaps because of the MacFarlane influence. This much is evident in the growing infrequency of Davies' unofficial contacts with the court after Kalakaua became king, and in the Kalakaua trip to Europe.

when he arrived. Characteristically, Davies had Scrimgeon up on the carpet, and the wretched man confessed all, and said he and his wife recognized the problem and wanted to get him far away from the fleshpots of Honolulu, for the sake of their two children. The confrontation came just at the time that Davies had received a letter from T.R. Keyworth, bookkeeper at Hamakua plantation, who wanted a job at the Davies office because he was eager to better his career.

The next shock was so great it made the Scrimgeon matter seem like a Sunday school transfer. Davies saw Harry Luce, whom Davies regarded almost as a son and in whom he had placed his total confidence, under the influence of drink at a royal ball, disgracing himself thoroughly, although probably no one else noticed; such were the royal balls of Kalakaua's day. Suddenly Theo H. Davies learned from the Luces that Harry had been drinking for several years, although until this time he had managed to conceal it from his employer. Characteristically, Davies put it all on paper,[8] he expressed shock and loss of confidence, and demanded that young Luce give him a written promise that he would abstain from ale, wine and spirits for one year. ". . . And the first time you break that promise . . . but I will not think so poorly of you as to think that you could break such a promise, if written . . ."

The threat was still only implied; the compassion was sincere:

"Dear Harry, my sorrow is greater than my anger. May God help you, for no one else can." No sooner had the chagrined Harry Luce signed the pledge and returned to his duties, than Davies had to face the problem of his own brother Fred's drunkenness, for even though Fred was far away in Australia, his wife called on Theo Davies as the steadiest (and most affluent) member of the family, for help. What help could he give? He was already paying Fred £2 10s. each quarter. He was willing to allow Fred's wife £40 a year if she should leave her husband. Could Fred not be placed in an "inebriate home?"[9] What he wanted was a man of the caliber of the Rev. J.T. Arundel, a friend who lived in Auckland, New Zealand, to take charge of his brother. But finding such a man in Australia was another matter.

Intemperance seemed to have seized control of Davies' life; what an irony for a man who had never once lost control of himself!

In the office, staff affairs went from bad to worse. Bookkeeper Scrimgeon never made it to the plantation; he had another bout with the bottle and Davies threatened to fire him. But the rub was that Scrimgeon was an excellent bookkeeper, and Davies had no other. Having taken the pledge, Harry Luce seemed to have gotten on the right path, but young Hay Wodehouse, son of the British commissioner, who had come to the office as junior clerk, soon gained so strong a reputation as a "hoodlum" that Davies felt impelled to take him to task. His drinking seemed to be controlled, but one night young Wodehouse and two companions were captured by the soldiers of the palace guard while riding at breakneck speed up King Street. This was too much for Theo H. Davies, who brought the young man in and lectured him, and delivered him another of those half threatening, half cajoling letters.[10] How could Hay do such a thing to his family? And his general behavior . . . his billiard playing in a saloon during working hours was reprehensible; his loafing in the salesroom; his *overdraft* on his salary! These were unacceptable acts and Wodehouse must either reform or leave.

Like Harry Luce, Hay Wodehouse promised to improve, but by November of that year he was back among his rowdy companions, roistering every night. Theo Davies gave him the sack, which infuriated Mrs. Wodehouse and annoyed Major Wodehouse, particularly since Davies took a high moral tone with the family in the proceeding. He had done it, he told them,[11] for three reasons:

(1) to shock Hay into a sense of the reputation he was making for himself. (2) To compel him to give you an opportunity to investigate any matters which he might otherwise have concealed and which you ought to know. (3) To vindicate the honor of my office which was so openly scandalized.

Wodehouse made it quite plain to Davies what he thought of the honor of the Davies office and the high-handed and pious proceedings[12] and Davies then complained that he was mistreated by the Wodehouses. Whatever the balance of truths, Davies had destroyed his relationship with the Wodehouses, and it never was the same again, although in the end they made sufficient obeisances to one another to preserve the forms. Hay Wodehouse came back to the firm for a time but did not prosper there. As for Harry Luce, he too fell from the straight and narrow path again, and to bring him around, Davies discharged him, then rehired him at a reduction in salary of $1,000 a year, thus as he put it, "combined justice with tenderness." But neither the justice nor the tenderness prevailed, for Harry Luce was caught drinking one more time at a party on the king's birthday and banished from the Davies world forever. Davies arranged for him to be sent off to Auckland, to live with his friend the Rev. Mr. Arundel.[13] He arranged with T.R. Walker, who was then on leave in England, to send out a new bookkeeper named W.T. Baird to replace Allen Scrimgeon[14] ("I am very glad you are sending a teetotaller"). The moment he arrived, Davies fired Scrimgeon, who reportedly said to him, "Luce and I are responsible for all the disorganization of the office, and if we had been dismissed as we ought to have been years ago, there would have been a different system now." Harry Luce did no better in Auckland and soon fell from grace there, too, and went then to Australia where Davies heard with a grim satisfaction that Harry was sinking into the depths. Davies was suitably distressed by it all, but somehow, his relations with the Luces were never quite the same again either. Still, there was not much time to contemplate the ingratitude of the Luces and the Wodehouses, or what might have happened to Scrimgeon had Davies yielded to his request for transfer, for business was bustling, and sugar seemed in a fair way to make Theo H. Davies a millionaire before the decade ended. Not even the impious and intemperate, who must have regarded Theo H. Davies as a dreadful old stick, could laugh at that.

Chapter Fourteen

BUSINESS AS USUAL

While the excitement and the challenge in Hawaii in the 1880s was in sugar, Theo H. Davies in no way neglected the merchandising side of his business. In 1883 there was enough business activity and responsibility for Walker and Swanzy that it seemed proper to expand. W.H. Holmes was brought in as merchandise manager of the firm. Holmes had been manager of a store in Honokaa on Hawaii Island and had done well enough to be called to Davies' attention. The merchandise department took over management of all goods from abroad except items brought for the Honolulu Iron Works and the plantations. Davies had already established a certain number of stores to serve his plantation workers and the people who labored in the mills. All this was made the Holmes responsibility and he was asked to make frequent trips to the rural areas to promote business. For this he received a salary of $200 a month and ten per cent of the profits of the merchandise department.[1] Walker became a partner in the firm in 1883, a reward for faithful service, but Davies still did not believe Walker was the man to leave in charge if he left Hawaii permanently. Whether or not he would quit Hawaii seemed debatable; his future was tied up in the islands, it was obvious, and on his return in 1882 he had settled in and involved himself in local affairs far more thoroughly than before. In the beginning this interest was indicated in sugar, which represented Davies' direct investment involvement, and the aspect which brought him to public attention was again labor. The Planters' Society was formed in 1864 to consider the mutual problems of the sugar growers. As the Hawaiian population continued to decline labor became the most important of these problems. The importation of Chinese contract laborers continued after the signing of the reciprocity treaty, but the social pressure exerted on the planters caused them to look for other sources of labor. In 1882 the planters organized the Planters' Labor and Supply Company to try to solve the perennial labor problem. Davies entered the discussion with his letter to the San Francisco *Chronicle* decrying the attacks on Spreckels and the planters for establishing "a system of cruelty and slavery." While he was in England in 1881 and 1882, newspapers in Berlin and Lisbon picked up the story. Davies wrote a letter to *The Times* attacking the attackers. He was particularly concerned about the effects of this propaganda on efforts then under way to secure plantation workers from Madeira.[2] The planters had tried people of various nationalities, even Norwegian, only to learn that most Europeans were unsuitable as plantation workers. Davies himself had employed 20 local whites as mill workers, on a year's contract. They had been happy for a month, but then began to complain of the isolation and food, and in six months he was glad to let them go. No more *haoles* for him.[3] He negotiated with Tatham & Company of London to send a shipload of plantation workers from Madeira if a thousand people could be persuaded to go. The arrangement never materialized, largely because of the stir created in the press and the anxieties of the Hawaiian government. Finally, through Foreign Minister William Green's intervention, George MacFarlane was sent to Europe[4] as a commissioner of immigration to arrange for Portuguese laborers. Davies so far forgot his quarrel with MacFarlane to write his friends at Tatham Company, recommending MacFarlane. Chinese were still coming to the islands, and they were quite satisfactory as laborers, but the United States in 1882 passed the Chinese Exclusion Act. The Reciprocity Treaty would end in 1884, and already considerable American agitation was registered against its renewal, largely on the grounds of the plantation employment of Chinese. Thus, in 1883, the Hawaiian government and the planters were looking hard for an alternative labor supply. Emissaries were sent to Egypt, to India, to Japan, and Japanese immigration soon began to replace Chinese immigration.

Davies was vitally interested in all aspects of life in Hawaii because almost any change affected his own affairs. One important aspect of his business life was banking. The sugar plantations and mills required a very large amount of cash for most of every year and were able to settle accounts only when the sugar cane was cut and milled, and the sugar sold.

In 1883 the Bishop Bank (now the First Hawaiian Bank) was still the only one in the islands. Janion, Green & Co. had been the bank's first borrower, and over the years Theo H. Davies had done hundreds of thousands of dollars worth of business with the bank. One day in the spring of 1883, an English ship with an unconsigned cargo appeared off Honolulu harbor, and learning of this opportunity, Davies sent a representative out by small boat, to board her outside and arrange to buy the cargo. The captain, however, had been instructed to deal through the Bishop Bank, and when he applied to Bishop, he was told to give the business to C. Brewer and Company, which he did. Theo Davies was furious[5] and expressed his surprise. Thereafter, he would do no more business with the Bishop Bank than was absolutely necessary. Davies was already leaning heavily on mainland sources for capital, money obtained through the guarantee of Williams, Dimond & Company in San Francisco. The system worked well enough, although it placed a large responsibility on Williams, Dimond. Davies contracted with Dimond to be agent for the purchase of the sugars of the plantations he represented. Williams, Dimond then borrowed from the banks, using notes from the agent which they discounted and guaranteed. By 1882 Davies had a line of credit of $150,000 with Williams, Dimond & Co. This was not enough money for him and there was still room for banking with Hawaii firms. In January, 1884, Claus Spreckels and several associates began a new Honolulu bank, which brought competition and an easing of Davies' difficulties with the Bishop bank.[6]

Spreckels had even bigger ideas. In 1882 Walter Murray Gibson, an

American who did not much like Americans, became premier of Kala-kaua's government. For the next few years, Gibson, the king, and Spreckels made most of the important financial decisions of the kingdom, much to Spreckels' profit. One of his schemes was to take over the coinage of Hawaii's money. He was to produce a million dollars worth of coinage, for which the Hawaiian government would give him a million dollars worth of six per cent gold bonds. Since the silver dollars would have an intrinsic silver value of 85 cents each, he stood to profit by about $150,000 in gold on the transaction. The scheme aroused the objections of businessmen. Theo H. Davies was chosen as a member of a Chamber of Commerce committee to consider the currency question, and he opposed the scheme publicly. In the end, Spreckels' control was broken and American gold coins became legal tender for debts above $10, but Spreckels went on from one scheme to another, mostly in America.

Of all the investments of Theo H. Davies, the one to produce the most outstanding and lasting effect on the islands' economy was the Honolulu Iron Works. In the summer of 1884, manager Alexander Young experimented with a new process of extracting sugar from cane.[7] In the beginning of the steam mill period, the mill consisted of a set of three rollers, one above the other two. The cane was fed into the rollers, which crushed the juice out. But at the end of the crushing, the pulp residue, or bagasse, still contained large amounts of sugar. More of this was recovered by adding a second set of rollers to the mill, and in some mills a third set of rollers. Even so, Young estimated that the mills were not getting more than 60 per cent of the sugar available in the cane. He set up an experiment which involved double crushing, but also the use of hot water, which recovered an extra 20 per cent of the juice. Soon the experiment was installed on a permanent basis at Waiakea Mill, and it was not long before other mills were turning to Honolulu Iron Works for installation of the new "maceration" process that had revolutionized the industry.

The Young development, however, did not help the planters a great deal in 1884. The United States was in one of the recessions that seemed to strike the economy about every eight years, and the price of

Alexander Young, circa 1910

sugar plummeted. Davies had expected to clear $250,000 from his planta-
tions in 1884, but by July he was talking about $75,000. Still, he was far
better off than many, especially his rival George W. MacFarlane, who had
overextended himself, gone into debt to Spreckels for nearly a million
dollars, and was being stripped by Spreckels of his sugar agencies and just
about all but his liquor business. Davies stayed clear of Spreckels after that.
For the next year, Davies required $200,000 from Williams, Dimond, he
said, and it must not be borrowed from the Anglo-Californian Bank, because Spreckels' partner in the Honolulu Bank, Frederick F. Low, was

head of Anglo-Californian.[8] He did not want Spreckels to know anything about the Davies business.

That summer, Davies and C. Brewer stood firm against Spreckels' demands for a lower price for their sugars. The old dispute had been resolved by Spreckels' acceptance of Manila No. 10, giving the Hawaii producers credit for the 91° polarization, and payment by the refinery 60 days after delivery. In view of the general depression, Spreckels had tried to better the prices for himself and had apparently convinced all but the two firms. "I've got 'em all in my hands, all except two firms—Davies & Co., and Brewer & Co.," he was reported to have said at a party.[9]

Spreckels then went back to San Francisco and tried to light fires that would burn Davies.[10] He was particularly annoyed with Davies because he had asked him to become a director of the Spreckels Honolulu Bank, and Davies had refused, having made his peace with Bishop. The first indication came when Anglo-Californian Bank made inquiries to Williams, Dimond about the financial status of Davies & Co., which the bankers indicated, seemed to be somewhat shaky. Someone said Bishop Bank had rejected a Davies check. Dimond passed the rumor on to Davies, who responded with a complete financial report. As of the end of 1883, Davies had owed the Bishop bank $300,000 on long-term loans and $88,000 on current account. Davies had just completed erection of a new sugar mill, Kukaiau Mill, which Bishop financed for him. His surplus in the Theo H. Davies Company as of June 30 was $80,000, and he had an inventory on hand, paid up, of $30,000. His sugar properties were by this time free of debt: $\frac{1}{2}$ Hamakua Mill, $\frac{1}{2}$ Kipahulu Mill, $\frac{1}{8}$ Beecroft Plantation, $\frac{1}{8}$ Union Mill, $\frac{5}{12}$ Waiakea Plantation, $\frac{1}{4}$ Honolulu Iron Works. (He was listing his *personal* assets, having deducted the Janion holdings which he intended to acquire as time went on.) He did not include in this Laupahoehoe Sugar Co. because it showed on the accounts as a debtor to the firm. As for prospects, even with the depressed price of sugar, he had received dividends on five of his seven properties, and the other two had paid off almost all their outstanding debt. In 1885, he expected "the whole seven will pay dividends two or three times..." And if there were any further doubts, he had one other little tale to tell.[11] A few weeks earlier, a Jewish money lender named Maguin (as well known in Honolulu financial circles as was the old miser-Robinson of the early days), had come to Davies to offer $12,000 at 8 per cent for two years, *without collateral.* He supposed, said Maguin, that Davies could use a bit of capital in his expansion. As everyone knew, Maguin had never run a risk in his life. That ought to be enough proof of the Davies financial position even for old man Spreckels.

The children of Theo H. Davies, circa 1892. George F. is at left in the sailor suit. T. Clive is the tall boy at the rear and at the right is Violet. Left front is Theo M. Alice, in the middle, holds baby Harry L. and Arthur W. is at right front.

Chapter Fifteen

HOME AGAIN, HOME AGAIN

T*heo H. Davies had settled in at Honolulu* and for two years had said nothing more about moving back to England. He had brought with him from Liverpool a complete household of furniture, including furniture for four bedrooms and servants' quarters and earthenware and china to serve 24 people. The house at Craigside had been rebuilt to meet the needs of the expanded family, and new horses, new traps and carriages had been sent out. In the summer of 1883 he had spent several weeks on the Big Island of Hawaii, most of the time at Volcano House. In part the trip was occasioned by his need to look carefully over his holdings, but more important had been the outing for the children, and the removal to the high, dry climate of Nellie, who was not very well. Yet Nellie was pregnant again in the spring of 1884, and in January the next year, Harry, their seventh child, was born. At first all seemed well, but Nellie developed a fever and then a serious infection. Perhaps it was puerperal fever; whatever the cause by March she was languishing, and Davies despaired for her life.[1] Frantically he brought an old retainer, "Nursie" Butcher, who had taken care of most of the children before retiring to Essex. Mrs. Lily Mackintosh, Mrs. Janion's cousin and Nellie's friend, who was the wife of Canon Mackintosh of St. Andrew's Cathedral, was with her day and night. Dr. Trousseau, her physician, came every day. She developed a swelling on her side, but it went down when Dr.

Trousseau treated it with iodine. All seemed well, but the swelling reappeared at the shoulder and the abscess broke, exuding infectious material. The doctor dosed her with quinine and brandy and she seemed to improve. But after the improvement she relapsed, and the pattern was repeated over and over from March until September 1885. She grew weak—one story reported that her life was saved by Canon Mackintosh, who held a prayer session after the doctors had given her up. Another tale said that she was saved by cocktails made of poi and milk, which Lily Mackintosh fed her.[2] Indisputably, Nellie was saved after a bout of illness that lasted until autumn. It was that long before she was out of danger.

The months of rigor, plus two business developments, persuaded Theo Davies anew that he should return to live in England. Richard Janion had taken over his father's business and acted as Davies' agent in Liverpool, although there was no further partnership connection between the firms. Richard had misused his inherited funds, and the business had failed, but out of the wreckage Davies saved his own good name. Davies commissioned Harold Janion to set up an office, which he intended to make into a separate partnership with young Janion, and he prepared to return to England and live in Liverpool.[3] The children were growing, and Clive at 14 was ready for public school. Before Davies left Honolulu, however, a number of matters claimed his attention. One of these was a long-standing quarrel with the Rt. Rev. Alfred Willis,[4] Church of England Bishop of Honolulu.* Davies had never gotten on well with the Church hierarchy; his Congregationalist background perhaps prevented his acceptance of theological discipline; certainly the churchmen resented Davies. It might be said that Davies suffered from the fault of innocence. He was innocent of any thought that he might be arrogant in his relations with others; it was obvious to him that all his associates, from erring clerks to partners, must be reminded of duty, and this attitude extended to his relations with the church. He had been a leader of the little band that

---

*Theo H. Davies said the Bishop was "well disposed but weak." He was surrounded by assistants who were neither. The result was that in Davies' eyes "the church was conducted in an arbitrary highhanded way."

brought the Church of England's Bishop Staley to the islands in the first place—and then he had quarreled with Bishop Staley. He had been a leader of the committee that had planned a magnificent cathedral, and of the finance committee that had decided to forge ahead with a very expensive building, despite discouragement from American-style Episcopalians, who seemed to have no proper appreciation of churchly grandeur. The result was St. Andrew's Cathedral in Honolulu, which was erected with much of the sweat and some of the money of Theo H. Davies.

He had in his way, made peace with Bishop Staley, but when Staley retired to England and a new bishop came out, almost from the beginning, Davies quarreled with Bishop Willis over any number of matters. In 1883 when Thomas Rain Walker was abroad, the matter swelled, and Davies wrote Walker that the bishop was becoming "impossible."[5] By 1885 the quarrel had spread; the large English faction of the congregation demanded a separate minister and separate services from the Hawaiian, American, and half-Hawaiian members. At first the bishop denied this request, although the dissidents pointed out that the cathedral was in use so little of the time that they ought to be allowed to have separate services without any disturbance whatsoever. They continued to press, and the bishop continued to argue that the request was divisive. King Kalakaua deprecated the action of the dissidents. Thomas Rain Walker, as warden of the congregation, entered the lists too, but Theo H. Davies, the real leader of the English faction, carried the battle with the bishop. It became virulent and personal, and at one point the bishop remarked that the Anglican minister who had admitted Davies to communion was a "traitor to his faith." Bishop Willis began publishing the acid correspondence with Davies, and in January 1886, Davies too turned to the press,[6] after proposing unsuccessfully that the quarrel be arbitrated. The quarrel had settled on Davies' activities as treasurer of the building committee, and the bishop accused him of misusing funds. The whole was bound up in church politics and personalities. The dissenters got their way: A.S. Cleghorn, Walker, Davies, T.H. Mist, W.H. Baird, W.C. Luce, and James Hay Wodehouse, all Davies associates or employees; a total of some 35 communicants. But the building fund fight went up to the Archbishop of Canterbury, who stunned Bishop Willis by saying he had blundered, and in effect, told the bishop to quiet down.

Davies made one far reaching business decision. Further carelessness by Thomas Rain Walker in his accounts had persuaded Davies that Swanzy must be made financial manager. Davies pushed Walker into making the suggestion himself, and as far as he knew, Swanzy was never the wiser, nor was Walker's apparent position as senior in the firm disturbed. Davies never gave any indication of understanding how Walker felt about the matter. So much for the business problem; by shrewd action he had weathered it with only the slightest of storms.

The saddest development of the year concerned the Wodehouses. Hay Wodehouse had sunk lower and lower into the depths of degradation

Interior of Craigside, the Davies residence in Nuuanu Valley.

and that year was discharged from his own father's employment for dishonesty that developed from drink. Mrs. Wodehouse maintained the friendliest of relations with Nellie Davies and with all the other members of the family and the firm. What Theo H. Davies could never understand was that she held him personally responsible for her son's downfall; in her mind that drive up Nuuanu years earlier had seen the settlement of a bargain, and in discharging Hay, Davies had violated the contract. Davies was first annoyed and finally puzzled. But he would go to his grave without understanding what had gone wrong. There was nothing in his makeup or his background to give him the slightest appreciation of a woman scorned.

In the spring of 1886, Theo H. Davies prepared to go home to establish the family in England forever. He devised a system of almost weekly

Craigside, No. 2. In the heights of Nuuanu Valley, overlooking Honolulu. The property remained in the hands of the Davies family until the 1950s, when it was sold, and it is now the site of a Japanese cemetery.

reports from the Honolulu office, followed by a constant stream of detail on every subject in the business. He would expect to return to Honolulu every two or three years to stabilize affairs, but he had every confidence that in Walker and Swanzy, at last he had the combination to secure his interests. As the time of departure neared, he made arrangements to abandon Craigside.[7] There would be another auction of furniture and belongings. The two Craigside houses would be put up for rent. The ponies and horses and carriages and wagons were sold, even the little girls' wagonette and Ashes, their pony. Late in May there was a grand reception at the Y.M.C.A. hall where Swanzy sang a song and Master Judd (son of the Chief Justice) gave the principal address, and Master Dillingham (son of the contractor) made the presentation of a going away sketch. Then it was time to go. After a brisk and refreshing sea voyage, they took a private rail car to New York and a ship to England. On July 7, 1886, the Davies party reached Liverpool, put up at the Albany Hotel, and Davies prepared for the new life. Nellie was taken up to Ludlow to her family's house. Davies soon took a house called The Elms at nearby Southport, and installed the family. Clive was entered in Uppingham and soon went off to board at school. He had been going steadily to day school in Honolulu but when he took Uppingham's placement examinations, his memory fled and he was dropped to the middle Third Form, which put him behind the boys of his own age. But he soon adjusted. All boys did. Davies announced to Honolulu that Harold Janion was doing very well, but that a little more gusto was wanted. He intended to supply that initiative and make the Liverpool office an important factor in the company. Obviously Theo H. Davies at fifty-five was just the man to do it.

Luau at Craigside. Edith (Mrs. Clive) Davies is presiding at the far end of the room (in front of palm tree). Note calabash collection on the table. Circa 1880.

Chapter Sixteen

THE TRIALS OF '86

Theo H. Davies' departure from Honolulu in 1886 was an indication of his self-confidence and the solid state of the Davies business. For in general the islands were suffering that year from the depressed price of sugar. The value of sugar plantations in the islands was estimated at $16 million, a meaningless figure in modern terms. Compare it with the value of the estate of Bernice Pauahi Bishop, the banker's wife and last of the Kamehameha line, who had died in 1884. Her immense land holdings, most of downtown Honolulu, Waikiki, and thousands of acres on Oahu and the outer islands were valued by the newspapers at $300,000 and by the government at $800,000.[1] So it was no exaggeration to say that sugar had become the economic foundation of the islands. Of that $16 million in sugar holdings, $10 million was in the hands of Americans, $3 million in the hands of the British, and the rest was owned by Germans and Chinese.[2] Since sugar prices were depressed, in turn, Theo H. Davies was depressed because his holdings that year were producing one of their finest crops.[3] Still, having reduced his debts so substantially, Davies was in a strong position; several sugar companies went out of business but Davies' most serious concern was the plight of the merchant A.S. Cleghorn, who that year failed and turned his assets over to Davies for liquidation. Davies managed to salvage enough from the wreckage to pay the debts and secure a little capital for Cleghorn and his daughter, the Princess Kaiulani.[4]

Just before Davies left Honolulu he managed a coup, when his competitor George MacFarlane got into trouble financially. MacFarlane held a mortgage of $65,000 against a sugar plantation owned by A.J. Horner at Honohina, near Laupahoehoe on the Big Island of Hawaii. Davies bought the mortgage from the Bishop bank for $20,000. Horner also owed $25,000 to adjoining Hakalau plantation on the other side but Davies expected to be able to settle the affair so that he would have the Honohina plantation and could add it to Laupahoehoe's holdings. Davies was pleased with himself when he announced this acquisition to planter William Lidgate.[5] Lidgate was astounded and delighted when he had the news.[6] He hurried over to Honolulu to confer with Walker and Swanzy, full of plans to take on the planting of Honohina, particularly the area called Lahaina, which he coveted. The best idea, he said, would be to move the Laupahoehoe mill toward Honohina, since that land ought to yield more cane than Laupahoehoe, perhaps even 2,000 tons a year. They had been talking about building a railroad to bring the cane from the far reaches of the Laupahoehoe plantation to the mill. It would be cheaper, Lidgate said, to move the mill. That summer they foreclosed on Honohina, but they did not reckon with Claus Spreckels, whose bank held the $25,000 Horner mortgage on Hakalau plantation.[7] Neither side would budge. Walker and Lidgate met with Horner and Spreckels, who claimed that Honohina was more valuable to his Hakalau plantation than to Laupahoehoe, and offered them instead a tract around Kawela which was held by the Spreckels bank and Samuel Parker, the rancher. Parker agreed to lease them 1500 acres for $5,000 a year, and sell 10 acres for a millsite at Kawela. Lidgate thought this idea excellent and proposed to undertake it, and move operations, including the mill, from Laupahoehoe to Kawela. As for Honohina, the best they could do, he said, was give Hakalau all the south portion, for $10,000 reserving the livestock, which was worth $5,000. That meant Davies would lose $5,000, instead of earning $20,000 in quick profit, but this could be recovered from the Lahaina land they would keep. Walker and Alexander Young both agreed that this was the best course. One reason for their approval was Lidgate's sudden statement that Laupahoehoe was not worth keeping. The lands were worked out, he said, and the prospect of profits was gloomy. He wanted either to sell Laupahoehoe or abandon it. He indicated the necessity of making high profits "so long as sugar holds out in the islands." Lidgate communicated this new idea to Davies in another letter.[8] Every time he went around the fields of Laupahoehoe, he said, he grew more dubious about the prospects. He had been badly shaken when Papaaloa, the field he considered his best, had failed to produce a satisfactory crop on second planting. The Ookala land adjoining was in even worse shape, he said, and the stockholders of that plantation stood to lose most of their money.

Theo Davies was nearly flabbergasted by the Lidgate letter, which raised all sorts of issues he had never before heard about. It would be impossible to sell just then, particularly on the basis of the gloomy reports from Lidgate, ". . . I never could recommend anyone else to buy what I did not want to keep." No, they must hang on.[9] The fact was, however, that Theo H. Davies was extremely jumpy about the future of sugar. For some months before his departure he had cautioned Swanzy and Walker against overextension of sugar enterprises, because he was not at all certain of the attitude of the Americans toward the reciprocity treaty, which was just then up for renewal. He had questioned the ability of the islands to produce and market as much as 80,000 tons of sugar a year. Nor was he alone in that belief: most planters shared the gloomy outlook.[10] The amounts of cash involved were high enough to give one pause: that year the Theo H. Davies sugar commission account with Williams, Dimond reached $602,000. Against future sugar deliveries Williams, Dimond had advanced $587,000 to Davies, who had disbursed it among the plantations and mills for expenses. Later Davies had shipped $615,000 worth of sugar to San Francisco for Williams, Dimond's disposal, and after all expenses were deducted Davies had a credit of $14,500 with Williams, Dimond. So, in such uncertain times, when the price of sugar was depressed, the investment seemed very large in terms of return. Walker sold off the Kipahulu mill and leases to H. Hackfeld & Company for $35,000, and credited the money to the account of the ailing Laupahoehoe Sugar Company.[11]

The long-standing quarrel between Claus Spreckels and the independent planters was eased that year, when Spreckels broke his close ties to King Kalakaua and the Hawaii government. The whole affair was deeply mixed in politics, and Theo H. Davies was affected personally and as a businessman. Davies had wanted appointment as the Hawaii representative in England, but that spring of 1885, the post was given to Abraham Hoffnung, who had been managing the immigration of Portuguese sugar workers for the Hawaiian government. Hoffnung had met Kalakaua during the 1881 trip to England, when Theo Davies had been snubbed; Hoffnung had been wined and dined at the old Iolani Palace;[12] Hoffnung in 1886 suggested to Kalakaua that what he needed was a fat loan from British bankers. Kalakaua could not have agreed more. He was talking about spending $10 million to establish an army and navy capable of integrating all the Pacific islands under Hawaiian control. Further, the government's budget for years had either come up to or exceeded the government's revenues as the king and his ministers lived their wasteful, dissipated lives. Earlier in the year Walker had informed Theo Davies of the visit to Honolulu and the Iolani Palace by Henry R. Armstrong, an ambitious promoter. Armstrong met that other promoter, George MacFarlane, who by this time was a member of the king's personal staff and of the House of Nobles, and they schemed to have the legislature pass a loan bill. When Spreckels heard of this, he rushed from San Francisco to Hawaii to be sure the loan, or part of it, got into the hands of his Honolulu bank. He was defeated, Walker reported, and bundled up all his Hawaiian medals and sent them off to Kalakaua. Banker Bishop dropped in at the Davies office to tell Walker for Theo Davies' ear that the loan was to be promoted in London. Bishop advised Davies to warn the bankers of London city with a simple statement of the financial affairs of the Hawaiian kingdom (which were terrible) but not to get involved in the politics of the loan.[13]

The advice was sound. In a few days George MacFarlane set off for England to negotiate the sale of $2 million in bonds. This activity created a new interest in Whitehall about the affairs of Hawaii, and Davies, who had never before been paid much attention by the Foreign Office, suddenly found his opinions in demand. Late in November, he went down to London and was closeted with several officials and even sent over to inform the Colonial Office of what was happening in the Pacific. The government was particularly interested in Davies' view that as soon as the trans-Canada railway and the Panama Canal threw open the North Pacific Ocean to international trade, the Hawaii dependence on the United States would cease.[14] The loan was "a dreadful mistake," Davies wrote Wodehouse and the Foreign Office.[15] In the end the loan raised £200,000 and the bankers exacted a cost from the Hawaii government of £40,000 for the privilege. Those bankers included Matheson & Company of London, and they paid George MacFarlane £2,000 for his part in the arrangement.[16] Davies and his associates were thoroughly disgusted, but business affairs so dominated their minds that they had little time to fret. Swanzy was of the opinion that they ought to be buying sugar lands, but Theo H. Davies totally disagreed. He told his junior partners (Swanzy was now getting an override of one percent of the profit of the company) that there was absolutely no sense in buying sugar lands if you could lease them.[17] The Davies' faith in sugar was considerably weaker than it had been before the quarrels with Spreckels and the difficulties about extension of the reciprocity treaty with the United States.

Swanzy was emerging as the strong figure that Davies had hoped he would be. He wrote from Honolulu that he was not overpleased with the office since Davies had gone away, "We are not yet up to Hackfeld's state of perfection. We have too many boys in Theo H. Davies Company who play at work." He was particularly disappointed in young Joseph Dredge, Davies' nephew, and son of his favorite sister, Margaret, who had come out to work in Honolulu. That being the case, Davies replied, Dredge was to have no raise in pay at the end of the year nor any ever until he had performed properly.[18]

The company became involved in one peculiarly Hawaiian farce that fall, an affair which showed Swanzy's strength and determination. Early in September word came to Honolulu that the ship *Dunnottar Castle* was wrecked on Ocean Island.[19] She belonged to Skinner & Company of Britain. Theo H. Davies was still vice-consul of Britain, although T.R. Walker performed the tasks in Davies' absence in England. But Walker was out of town when the word came. When Swanzy heard, immediately he made arrangements to charter the ship *Waialae* to go to the rescue of 22 men who were reported to have been left behind on the island while the first mate and a small boat crew sailed forth in an open boat to seek assistance. (The boat was picked up by a ship bound for Honolulu.) The cost of charter was $300 a day, which would eventually be borne by Her Majesty's government but it was no small matter to undertake such expense. Swanzy set about getting medical supplies from Dr. McKibben and ordered bookkeeper Baird, who needed a change, to go along on the voyage as representative of England and the firm. But before the *Waialae* could sail, she had to load coal. This operation took half a day. In the interim Major Wodehouse came to the Davies office to announce that the Hawaiian goverment had kindly offered to send its surgeon general on the voyage along with an assistant and all the needed medical stores, and that as an exercise in goodwill he had accepted the offer. It sounded good, too good. Swanzy smelled a rat. There was reason behind the Hawaiian gesture. The government also wanted to send along a carpenter and some lumber and put up a shed on Ocean Island, and raise the Hawaiian flag to signify possession of the island as a colony. Colony? Swanzy made some loud exclamatory noises. What sort of business was this—the government of Hawaii hitching a ride on a British charter to put up sheds and take possession of a desert island? He protested to Wodehouse, and he protested more loudly when he interviewed the carpenter who said it would take five men a day and a half to put up the shed. But the Hawaiian government was obdurate. Prime Minister Walter Murray Gibson also sent along an artist named Strong, who had recently been discharged from the local insane asylum. Strong was to chronicle the historic event on canvas, and Colonel James H. Boyd, the Queen's aide (known locally as 'Jimmy'), with a servant, was to raise the Hawaiian flag and take official possession.

On learning this last, Swanzy was truly furious. For two days he had turned the entire Davies office into a sort of Red Cross. It was all becoming ridiculous. Then the *Pacific Commercial Advertiser* came out with a story giving all credit for the proposition to the king, Prime Minister Gibson, and Colonel Boyd, and wishing godspeed to their brave expedition off into the wilds of the Pacific. By this time Swanzy was speechless. The *Waialae* sailed, but three days later when the ship reached Ocean Island, the crew found a note saying that the *Birnham Wood,* en route from Hong Kong to Valparaiso, had picked up the survivors of the wrecked ship on August 18. That in no way affected Colonel Boyd and the members of his Hawaiian expedition. In full dress uniform of red and blue and gold, with his huge Hawaiian medals on his chest, the Colonel came up onto the deck of the *Waialae* and made a speech, then went ashore with the Hawaiian flag in his pocket, affixed it to a stick, and annexed the island to the kingdom of Hawaii in the name of The Great Kalakaua. For the next 36 hours the *Waialae* stood off the island at $300 a day, as the ship's crew erected Prime Minister Gibson's shed on the barren rock. Then the expedition returned to Honolulu. The story of the event was given to the *Advertiser* along with a copy of Colonel Boyd's speech, and the newspaper editor ran it with a straight face, although nearly everyone else in Hawaii was convulsed with laughter. Swanzy wavered between hilarity and indignation, and finally the laughter won. He did have one small satisfaction: Commissioner Wodehouse let him bill the Hawaii government for the passage of Colonel Boyd, the servant, the carpenter, the artist, the shed, and for the services of the crew of the chartered vessel for 36 hours. Throughout, Prime Minister Gibson responded with such serious mien that it seems impossible to believe he had the slightest understanding of the comedy. Nor could the Europeans make too much fun of it all. Hawaii might have some of the attributes of a musical-comedy kingdom, but in sugar and trade there were too many millions of dollars involved for anyone to laugh very hard.

Chapter Seventeen

THE GROWING UNREST

In the summer of 1887 the Americans who lived in Hawaii were growing impatient. The reciprocity treaty was up for renewal and Washington wanted Pearl Harbor for a naval station as the price for signing. King Kalakaua was dead set against the cession and told Davies' superior in the diplomatic service, Commissioner Wodehouse, that he would never accept it.[1] But the cabinet and legislature were in the hands of the American missionary party, and they overrode the king under the constitutional powers wrung earlier from the monarch. Led by Lorrin Thurston and other self-righteous advocates of reform, the cabinet rode rough-shod over the Hawaiians, secured acceptance of the treaty, and various groups of Americans schemed to take power from the hands of the king.[2] In London, Theo Davies was a welcome guest at the Foreign Office and had several meetings with various highly placed officials to discuss events and trends in the North Pacific. Davies said that when the Canadian transcontinental railroad was completed and the Panama Canal opened, he hoped to see a greater ascendance of British influence in the islands. One of his own hopes[3] was for creation of a Canadian sugar refinery and establishment of a shipping line between British Columbia and Hawaii.

The yearnings of Theo H. Davies and other English businessmen in the Hawaiian islands were no secret to the Americans. The communications of the American ministers grew more urgent in tone, as they warned Washington about growing British influence. Minister George Merrill called attention to a long article on Hawaii in *The Times* and indicated that Britons were subverting the American influence. Private British capital was beginning to flow to Hawaii after a long hiatus. William Green, A.S. Cleghorn, and others were talking about making Hilo into a port comparable to Honolulu. The Big Island of Hawaii, as everyone knew, was the stronghold of the British and the Canadian Pacific Railroad, and the British cable plan to run west to the Asian colonies could be dangerous. Merrill warned darkly of "other influences" who were trying to change the sentiment of Hawaii toward Britain and away from the U.S., and he said there was no doubt that the most suspicious of these influences was Theo H. Davies, one of the richest men in the islands. Davies' presence in England made the Americans nervous. They did not know what he was doing and suspected the worst.[4]

Some of the Anglo-American rivalry was dissipated that year in a greater cause of common concern over native unrest. In the summer of 1887 the government dissolved into chaos. King Kalakaua called the foreign diplomatic representatives together [5] and tried to give them the country. Citizens' meetings were called to discuss the arming of native troops, and a confrontation was narrowly avoided when William L. Green was made premier of a new government. Swanzy attended these meetings, and so did Thomas Rain Walker; Walker was still the titular managing partner in Honolulu and was also acting British vice-consul. Eventually he would be vice-consul but not until Theo H. Davies was certain of his plans.[6] The Davies consular leave expired at the end of 1887, so he planned a trip to Hawaii to look over his affairs and decide whether or not to seek renewal. The uncertainty was still apparent: he had let the lease on The Elms expire and had taken another house, Sundown, in Hesketh Park nearby, but he had not bought it. As for the journey, there would have to be some changes. Swanzy had worked out well, and he had made the all important decision to settle down in Honolulu that year, when he married Julie Judd, daughter of Colonel C. H. Judd. Davies wrote him vaguely but promisingly, implying that a real partnership was in the offing but it would have to await the Davies trip to the islands.[7] Davies took the keenest interest in "the revolution" by which the foreign community combined to end Kalakaua's excesses. He was very pleased with the participation of Swanzy and Walker in the public affairs of Honolulu, and even more so with their restraint, which had brought the changes with "so much dignity, honour and success."[8] In London the interest in Hawaii grew; in midsummer Theo Davies called at the Foreign Office and the Colonial Office again, and was greeted with grave respect. Sir Robert Herbert, a senior official at the Colonial Office, asked him his views about the growing ascendancy of the United States in Hawaii.

"You can expect no British ascendancy, but you may maintain British equality, if you will."

"How could we do that?" Sir Robert asked.

"Don't always let the British representation be second to the American. Insist on equal footing."

Sir Robert said he agreed. Davies then went off to Westminster Palace for an appointment at the House of Commons. He was really becoming something of a political figure, it seemed. That impression was heightened in August when he spent an hour with Sir James Fergusson at the Foreign Office, and supplied him with a "brief" that was read by Lord Salisbury, the Foreign Secretary. By late summer Theo Davies' advice was openly sought by Whitehall. On September 9, he wrote a long letter to Salisbury, dealing with Pearl Harbor, the new constitution of Hawaii, and the Hawaiian loan, which was proving so unmanageable. He was also in frequent contact with Hawaii Premier William L. Green in Honolulu, and through the British Foreign Office he was put in touch with Canadian Commissioner Culmer, for a meeting that resulted in his change of itinerary to stop off in Ottawa on his way to Hawaii later in the year.[9] He did that; he met with Sir John MacDonald and other members of the government of Canada and with Rear Admiral Seymour at Victoria. He sent a long letter back to Lord Salisbury with reports and findings—more notable for their diligence than their prescience: Davies predicted that the United States insistence on cession of a base at Pearl Harbor was a meaningless token and not a serious effort to obtain a naval station.[10]

When Davies arrived in Honolulu in December 1887, he renewed his plan to achieve an official position for himself in England comparable to the vice-consulate in Hawaii. He arranged for another six months' leave of absence from the consular post, but advised Wodehouse confidentially that the Hawaiian government had decided to make him their new consul general in London. Consul General Hoffnung would have to be fired, but that was to be arranged after Davies left Hawaii.[11]

The trip to Hawaii had brought a series of shocks. Theo Dredge, son of Davies' sister Maggie, had to be fired and sent back to England for his own good, and Davies had to do it. By January 1888 these unpleasantnesses had become acceptable, if unsatisfactory, but what was not acceptable was the shock Davies found as he went carefully through the business ledgers. Thomas Rain Walker, his trusted partner, had let the financial affairs of Theo H. Davies & Co. deteriorate even more than Davies had feared. Of ten salary accounts, nine were overdrawn, and Walker was overdrawn most of all. "It is simply an education in embezzlement!" Davies exclaimed, "and it must cease immediately." Worst of all, in Walker's case, was that he was constantly overdrawing, over a five-year period, at the rate of $2,000 per year. Davies wrote Walker a stiff note, warning him that unless Walker showed total reform almost immediately, all financial affairs would be placed in Swanzy's hands "without right of appeal."[12] The departure was further clouded by the quarrel with Mrs. Wodehouse. Davies had served for more than 15 years as vice-consul in Hawaii. As he had prepared to leave the islands in 1886 and applied for the Hawaiian consular post, the Hawaiian Foreign Office took the matter under consideration. But at the same time, Davies asked Wodehouse for a leave of absence as vice-consul, with T.R. Walker to serve in his stead. Apparently this was to be insurance, to keep the consular post in the hands of the Davies company, and perhaps even to keep it open for Davies in case he had to come back to Hawaii. Major Wodehouse granted the leave of absence. Then, through his wife he learned of Davies' attempt to get the Hawaiian consulate, and she demanded that Davies resign his British post to avoid conflict of interest. Wodehouse was persuaded by her arguments, earnest ones, for she had never forgiven Davies' humiliation and demotion of their son Hay, and the embarrassment of the family by

Davies' communications directed to them. This matter had dragged on for weeks in the spring of 1886, and even as Davies prepared to sail for San Francisco in 1888, it was not settled that he would have the Hawaii consulate in England. Wodehouse flatly refused to extend his leave; instead he accepted Davies' resignation.[13] Davies was furious and frustrated, and threatened to complain to the Foreign Office for the "slight" he had received after long years of service. His reaction was typical of Davies. He finally demanded that his relationships be clarified in Whitehall. It was not a question of retaining the vice-consulate; by the spring of 1886 Davies had made the final decision to go home and stay. It was a matter of "honour" — a word Davies had come to use frequently.

Theo H. Davies was vitally conscious of his dignity and what he referred to as "chivalry." Five years earlier, in 1883 at the coronation of Kalakaua and Queen Kapiolani, Davies had been given place in the procession *below* several officers of a British man-of-war that happened to be in harbor. He protested to Wodehouse over the indignity: ". . . I felt keenly isolated to take rank below officers who had not done me the honour to return my call made fifteen days before, and not one of whom Mrs. Davies had ever met."

James Wodehouse-son of British Commissioner to Hawaii James Wodehouse. The younger Wodehouse married Nellie Ward, a grandaughter of "old miser" James Robinson.

He complained that he had no boat but was supposed to call on British naval ships in port. Could he not go with Wodehouse on his trips to the ships? Mrs. Wodehouse had suggested a ball for the following month at which she and Mrs. Davies would receive. But would that be proper, when the Davies were not even introduced to officers who had made the acquaintance of all the other English ladies in the community?[14] For a man singularly insensitive to the effects of his own harsh words on others, particularly subordinates, Davies was always quick to take offense and to bridle when offended.

Thomas Rain Walker was a partner, and Davies addressed him in the most friendly terms. But three years earlier, when Walker was in England, Davies was furious because the junior partner had not made it a point to see the Rev. Theophilus Davies and talk about Theo H. Shortly afterwards, old Theophilus died, and Theo H. chided Walker by letter. He was also angry because Walker had not seen the Davies' in-laws, the Cockings, and in his complaint he pointed out that Walker's habits were very unbecoming for a businessman, which on cold reading seems a very far-fetched complaint indeed.[15] His criticisms were broad and frequent and extended to everyone in his office. Swanzy was prone to error in the first few years of handling the finances of the company, and Davies never failed to point out the errors to Walker, as head of the office, and to express his disapproval. He did not like to have his people doing anything he did not do, or very much at all on their own initiative. Swanzy was addicted to amateur theatricals (as Davies had been in his youth). But the mature Davies complained to Walker "I hope he (Swanzy) is not giving too much thought to theatricals."[16] Swanzy, in 1883, had considered very seriously the idea of throwing up his job and returning to England.[17]

None of these affairs precipitated crisis, for one reason: the continued patience and loyalty of men of such ability as Walker and Swanzy, as much as the impatient desertion of George MacFarlane from the fold, were indications of the opportunity to be gained by association with Theo H. Davies.

As Davies prepared to take his leave in 1888, he settled up loose ends of business. He had sold Kohala ranch off in 1883, and Henry Beecroft

Jackson's interest in Beecroft Plantation to James Woods that same year for $110,000, thus reducing his financial dependence on the Jacksons. He did not need them any longer. The Bishop Bank and Williams, Dimond in San Francico met all his financial requests; that year his borrowings through Williams, Dimond came to $679,000.[18] His assets certainly justified such extensive borrowing, given the manner then of financing the sugar industry. Applying for credit at the North & South Wales Bank of Liverpool, Davies stated that the properties he owned outright were valued at $537,000. Besides this Theo H. Davies Company had a surplus of $115,000, and all of that but Partner Walker's one-eighth share belonged to Davies. He expected dividends from his sugar investments and Honolulu Iron Works of $160,000, and having just sent off $10,000 to Jackson's executors, his debt to the Jacksons was reduced to $50,000. He was also whittling away at the Janion debt and would soon have that cleared. His personal fortune was assured and growing.

The quarrel with Claus Spreckels had never really been resolved. By 1884 Spreckels had contracted for two-thirds of the Hawaiian sugar crop. There were by this time some 70 plantations producing around 60,000 tons of sugar. The principal hold-outs against Spreckels and his California Refinery were Davies and the Hackfeld Company. When a new venture appeared, the American Sugar Refinery Company, Davies and several of the others hurried to contract for their sugar with the new company, much to Spreckels' disgust. In the summer of 1886, the American refinery was very shaky; in the first four months of the year the profits had been about $1,500. By selling to American and to the St. Louis refinery, and delivering some sugar in New York, Davies was able to hold out quite satisfactorily against Spreckels. The plantations were paying excellent dividends in spite of sugar prices that were still not what they ought to be. Waiakea Plantation paid an $18,000 dividend for the first six months of 1886, and when the books were closed on the partnership in 1889 it would have paid $102,000. The other mills and plantations were paying handsomely: Laupahoehoe $113,000 and Hamakua $69,000 in 1888, for example.[19]

Changes were being made: Hamakua Plantation Company was acquiring the lands of the Aamano Plantation next door. Kukaiau Mill's

Garden Party at Craigside, Feb. 14, 1888.

manager wanted one of the new "maceration mills." These matters were of note, but certainly within the confines of normal business expectation. Decisions would have to be made, some of them in Honolulu, but the important ones by Davies in Liverpool.

The Davies departure from Honolulu in the winter of 1888 was preceded by a furious round of entertainments, the most sumptuous of them staged by Davies himself, "the host more than justifying his record of doing nothing by halves."[20] The Davies affair was a garden party given on the 20-acre estate in Nuuanu Valley. His Craigside house was scrubbed down and painted from roof peak to foundation, and the gardens were filled with tables, chairs and benches for people of all ages. Some 300 guests arrived, led by Queen Kapiolani. Princess Liliuokalani, the heir apparent to Kalakaua's throne, brought her husband John Dominis, commander of the armed forces and until recently governor of Oahu. Princess Ka'iulani came, notwithstanding the death the year before of her mother, Princess Miriam Likelike, but her father, A.S. Cleghorn, had made Davies Ka'iulani's godfather, and she was to be his ward. The other guests included all the officers from all the foreign warships in the harbor, the exalted figures of the worlds of government, church, the learned professions, and of commerce, with their wives and children. It was a family day—no drinking of course—and a very successful one. The Royal Hawaiian Band was there at two o'clock and played almost continuously until six, when the party ended. Two days later Queen Kapiolani entertained Theo Davies at breakfast in Iolani Palace, and again they were serenaded by the Royal Hawaiian Band. That evening it was as if the party had never ended; this time Theo Davies went to Princess Liliuokalani's mansion on Washington Place, for an even more brilliant reception where the band provided the music. A week later, Davies provided the music at a farewell party given him by the Young Men's Christian Association; he sang "Nothing Else to Do" in his pleasant tenor voice. It was his farewell performance, but anything but his swan song in Hawaiian affairs. For Davies in these last two years had become far more politically interested in Hawaii than before. He saw the threat of American domination; and in a new attitude in Whitehall,

The staff of Theo H. Davies Co. Ltd. before the company offices in 1895. Swanzy is the man standing before the open door in the heroic posture, wearing a bowler hat and a lei.

sparked by the westward movement in Canada, he thought he saw a way of containing the American influence at least enough to maintain a powerful British economic presence in the islands. Although King Kalakaua had not been very friendly to Davies, neither had he warmed recently to many foreigners, and Kalakaua's star was obviously on the wane after the constitutional revolution of 1887 wherein he had been forced to yield to reform. There was talk in Honolulu in 1888 about the abdication of Kalakaua in favor of his sister Princess Liliuokalani. Such a course would only please Theo H. Davies, who stood high with the princess. She did not much care for Americans, having been educated with rod and birch at Amos Starr Cooke's Chiefs' Childrens' School, and then seen her mentor desert the ways of God for those of mammon to become a merchant. Davies' feelings for the preservation of the Hawaiian monarchy were well known and strongly expressed over the years, and the royal family appreciated them. Thus, in 1888, when the bereaved A.S. Cleghorn wondered what to do about the education of his daughter, the Princess Ka'iulani, it was arranged that she should come to England to become an English lady. It was already understood that Kaʻiulani was the favorite of Liliuokalani, and in the absence of any direct heir (Liliuokalani was well into middle age) Kaʻiulani would succeed to the throne. To be prepared there was no better training ground than an English girl's finishing school. Thomas Rain Walker was planning to send his daughter, Beatrice, to England in the spring of 1889, accompanied by Mrs. Walker. It was arranged that Kaʻiulani should have as her headquarters the Davies house in Southport, and that Davies would look after her financial affairs.[21]

Theo H. Davies left Honolulu then, in a flurry of activity, having in the past two or three years achieved an entirely new position as a political figure.

Chapter Eighteen

THE COMING OF KAʻIULANI

A s *Theo H. Davies settled down* to the life of an English gentleman in 1888, the business in Honolulu was secure. The Janion estate would be finally settled that year,[1] and so would that of Henry Beecroft Jackson, in which Davies had been involved through Jackson's investments in Hawaii. The future of sugar was as well assured as it could be with the extension of the Reciprocity Treaty by the United States, and although Theo Davies and some others hoped to retain a certain British influence, even *The Times*[2] suggested that the island kingdom was moving inexorably toward the American umbrella. As an Englishman, this motion made Theo Davies uncomfortable; as a businessman he could not but welcome the stability it promised, and these conflicting sentiments, more than in the past, bothered him in the late 1880s and 1890s.

Theo H. Davies & Co.'s merchandising department was expanding satisfactorily. A number of Davies stores had been opened in communities around Oahu and the neighbor islands, and business was so satisfactory that Theo H. Davies & Co. ran full-page advertisements in the newspapers to announce the arrival of ships with new consignments. Walker and Swanzy had undertaken the building of a new retail store at the corner of Queen and Kaahumanu Streets. There was certainly movement in the business: the Kealia store on Kauai did not prove satisfactorily profitable, so Walker lopped it off and sold it to the MaKee Sugar Company. All this activity made the partnership profitable too. Davies drew about $30,000 a year for running expenses. Walker's small share netted him about $5,000 in addition to his fees as manager. The firm employed half a dozen other Englishmen, and a number of local porters and salesmen in the stores. In the fall of 1889, Davies decided it was time to take Swanzy into partnership and did, with Walker to have 20 percent, Swanzy 13 per cent and Davies 67 per cent profit since he supplied the capital.[3] Theo H. Davies & Co. at that time had assets of $650,000.[4] The new partnership, he could hope, would be even more satisfactory with the management team he had finally assembled. Davies took one extra precaution: if the profits exceeded $50,000 a year, he was to have 75 per cent of the rest.

Theo H. Davies & Co. represented certainly not more than half of Davies' Hawaii assets just then. He had bought out the estates of his former partners (with a few exceptions: Mrs. Janion continued to hold Honolulu Iron Works and other stocks). His sugar holdings were constantly increasing. In 1886 Laupahoehoe paid dividends of $100,000[5] and Davies' interest in Laupahoehoe became greater when he threw Anthony Lidgate's sugar plantation debt of $152,000 into the Laupahoehoe pot, added those lands to the plantation, and brought Anthony Lidgate in to follow his father (who had died) as manager. In Davies' situation as capitalist and sugar agent, it was easy for him to pick up lands without even trying. For example, next door to Hamakua mill, on the Hilo side, was the Aamano plantation, which used the mill's facilities. By 1885, Aamano owed Hamakua mill $19,000, and it seemed unlikely that the cash would be forthcoming. So Davies took over the lands, leases and equipment, and added them to Hamakua plantation, which he owned with Charles Notley. Three years later Aamano was completely swallowed into the Hamakua complex. Its addition made a difference: in 1886 Hamakua mill paid dividends of $19,600; by 1887, the year prior to amalgamation, it paid $73,000, and the next year jumped to $183,000.[6] Such jumps worried the conservative Theo Davies. He was making a fortune in sugar but still had no faith in the industry's long range future. In the summer of 1888,[7] Alexander Young, his associate in Honolulu Iron Works and Waiakea mill, sought Davies' advice about buying into a plantation on Hawaii Island owned by the Afong family. Davies advised Young against it, citing "the precarious state of the U.S. tariff" (on foreign sugars) which he feared might be eliminated at any moment. No, he said, sugar was a bad investment with a murky, worrisome future, and was not the sort of investment a man should undertake in the 1880s. He was offered sugar lands and refused to buy; sugar was all right in its way, but he could not see a future encumbered with virtually useless Hawaiian lands when, as certainly must happen some day, the sugar market dried up. Alexander Young weighed his friend's advice, but in the end he bought into the Afong property anyhow, and prospered.

In May 1889, the fourteen year old Ka'iulani and her half-sister Annie Cleghorn left the beautiful sunny estate Ainahau, in Waikiki, and sailed for stormy England. The decision to send the princess to England for education was greeted with dark suspicion by the American community, which had begun to be extremely wary of Theo Davies as he emerged into the political sphere. For years Davies had spoken out when he felt it necessary, but usually in matters of commercial interest, wherein he was joined by other merchants and businessmen. But, his fortune assured, Davies now felt impelled to exert his energies in new ways.[8] In Southport he became active in Conservative Party politics. He transferred his Hawaii allegiance to the Y.M.C.A. to the Southport branch, and was an active churchman. He began to travel widely. In the spring of 1889 as the Walkers were bringing Ka'iulani to England, Davies took Clive out of Uppingham for a trip to Germany.[9] Later he and Clive travelled around the world,[10] by way of India and Australia, and Clive had his first look at Honolulu since his days at Iolani School. Theo H. Davies also made a momentous decision about Clive's future that indicated his dichotomy of mind on the political and economic problems of Hawaii. The norm for country squires who had made their fortunes abroad and come home to England to enjoy them was to enter their sons at Cambridge or Oxford universities. Theo Davies' second son, George F., would go to Cambridge, but his first son, Clive, who was designated as his father's business heir, would go to the Massachusetts Institute of Technology, to take courses that would fit him for the complex industrial world in which he was growing up. Times were changing and Theo H. Davies was going to change right along with them.

On February 8, 1890, Theo and Clive were in Honolulu.[11] It was a Saturday, and Walker had closed down the office to meet them and take

Theo H. Davies and Princess Kaʻiulani on their historic voyage to America to plead with President Cleveland for intercession to restore the Hawaiian monarchy. This photograph was made in Boston, Massachusetts. Circa 1890s.

them to his house. On Sunday they visited St. Andrew's and Davies made a little speech to the Sunday school. On Monday they went to the office, and Davies was astonished at the number of new members of the staff. They were needed, he soon learned, for the business flourished in the growth of the community, and Walker and Swanzy had divided it into three parts, drygoods, groceries, and hardware. Every effort seemed to show the most exhilarating profits. Father and son visited the Honolulu Iron Works, and Davies was pleased with what he saw there. After two weeks of business and pleasure, they sailed to the Big Island, to make the rounds of the Davies properties. They travelled in a style befitting the richest man in the islands — in the "President's cabin" abroad the inter-island steamer *Kinau*.[12]

In the old days Davies had ridden by horseback everywhere, and if he wanted to send a message, a horseman or a runner carried it. But almost on arrival he was able to telephone the manager of Union mill and tell him he was coming to visit. Soon they were at Waiakea, where manager Kennedy met them and drove them to the mill. They had brought Alexander Young along on this journey, so Davies could consult with him about improvements and expansion of the mills. They visited Hakalau plantation and Laupahoehoe. It was raining hard, but that did not deter Davies from making a thorough inspection. He marvelled at the extensive water transport system of flumes and the perpendicular railroad that had been installed to harvest the difficult lands of Laupahoehoe. They seemed to answer William Lidgate's complaints of the past.

After William Lidgate had died, the settlement of his affairs had been awaiting just this meeting. Davies and Clive went to the Lidgate house, where they were met by Mrs. Lidgate and Anthony. That night the adults talked long. They agreed that all the Lidgate shares in Laupahoehoe would be transferred to Davies, and he would cancel the plantation's debt to the Honolulu company and give them a bonus of $15,000. He was pleased with the arrangement, as were the Lidgates, so with many expressions of goodwill, next day the Davies, father and son, went on to Kukaiau to visit the Horners.

They met George Renton at Kukaiau mill and rode in the rain, wear-

Anthony Lidgate

ing yellow foul-weather gear, to Hamakua mill. They stayed the night with manager James Renton. At Honokaa they planned to take the steamer to Kohala, but it was the weekend. The *Iwalani* would take them over on Sunday—but the strait-laced Davies would not travel on Sunday. The *Pele* would take him on Saturday and then work its crew Sunday loading cane. That would not do either. Finally, the captain of the *Iwalani* said he would take Mr. Davies on Saturday if that is what he wanted, and it was. They went down to the Honokaa landing, a hundred feet above the sea, and were swung off in a box by a crane and lowered a hundred feet into a boat that appeared below.

"The sensation was most odd . . ." said Theo H. Davies—in what Clive must have thought was the understatement of the month.[13] The steamer took them along the Hamakua coast, past the deep Waipio valley and steep cliffs that graced the shoreline between Hamakua and Kohala. It was a fine day and they could stand at the rail and enjoy the sight of the land's wonders slipping by.

Soon they were at the Henry Rentons—at Union mill—old friends of Davies, where they stayed four days. They went to Beecroft plantation and visited various families in the area. After five days they started back to Oahu, first travelling by train to Mahukona, where the brig *Ella* was loading sugar for San Francisco. They boarded the *Kinau*, and learned that the glass was falling—bad weather in the offing—although it was as sunny as anyone could wish just then. Through the Hawaii channel the weather held, but beyond they went into the gale, and since the *Kinau* was travelling without cargo, she tossed like an empty bottle in the sea. (Later they learned that the *Ella* went up on the rocks that day and was a total loss.)

They were nine hours late reaching Honolulu and then could not cross the bar in the furious sea, so joined the steamers *Australia* and *Alameda* outside, to wait. The rest of Davies visit was, as he put it, "occupied pretty well with church and state."[14] He wrote a letter of advice to the legislature to the editor of the *Commercial Advertiser*, and although the editor cordially detested Davies, the Englishman was too important a figure to ignore. It was printed and he was "gratified" to learn that Wodehouse had sent a copy to No. 10 Downing Street. "It also resulted in the withdrawal by the Hawaiian cabinet of a treaty clause with the U.S. on which I had reflected." Yes, by 1890, Theo H. Davies was very much a factor with which the United States must reckon in the political affairs of the Hawaiian Islands.

Portable cane flumes in the field on the edge of Waipio Valley.

Mahukona Landing on the island of Hawaii. The sugar was brought down in bags, hoisted into the boat and carried out to the ship waiting in the safe water beyond the reef.

Sugar operations at the Paapaloa factory on the Hamakua coast. This mill is typical of the sugar operations from the beginning of sugar planting until bulk shipment took over. The cane fields are in the background (top) and the plantation operations, living quarters and mill work down the hillside to the very edge of the steep cliff that drops down into the Pacific. Along the edge of the cliff is the railroad that went nearly around the island, serving most of the sugar growers and processors. Thus raw material, manufacturing and shipping processes were highly centralized.

Early steam locomotive on the Hamakua Plantation. Anthony Lidgate, the manager of the plantation, is the man in the dark suit. Theo H. Davies is in the light suit.

Steers ready for shipment at Kukaiau.

The Kohala Railroad, which ran to Mahukona Point, crossed many gullies like this one and served the plantations well for years.

A Caterpillar tractor in use on Hamakua plantation in the 1930s. The Davies "marriage" with the Caterpillar company was successful and lasting. Pacific Machinery Company, a Davies subsidiary, is still the Caterpillar dealer in Hawaii.

Chapter Nineteen

THE HAWAIIAN REVOLUTION

M*rs. Walker installed* Princess Ka'iulani and her half-sister Annie Cleghorn in the English boarding school for girls conducted by Mrs. Caroline Sharp at Great Harrowden Hall, near Wellingborough.[1] At holiday time they came to Sundown where they settled into the large Davies family without a ripple. It had been anticipated that the girls would go home at the end of a year of "finishing," but King Kalakaua died in San Francisco in January, 1890. He was succeeded by Liliuokalani on the throne. Suddenly Ka'iulani was, in fact, heir to the kingdom. Annie went home that year to marry Hay Wodehouse (which must have galled Theo H. Davies more than a little) but Cleghorn, Liliuokalani, and Davies decided that Ka'iulani must have more education to fit her to be queen, so she stayed on beneath the cloudy skies of England, while her sister went back to the sunshine.

The death of King Kalakaua raised a whole new series of spectres in the minds of the American jingoists, whose leading figure was U.S. Minister to Hawaii, John S. Stevens.[2] Almost as soon as Stevens presented his credentials at Iolani Palace he began writing Washington about the British danger. His letters nearly screamed in frustration and anger against the British: their commercial interests were growing too powerful (primarily that meant Theo H. Davies); if Ka'iulani ever came to the throne, the British would control. Whether or not Stevens started the rumor, which seems likely, given his unremitting proclivity for mischief, the story got about that Theo H. Davies was plotting to marry Ka'iulani off to his eldest son Clive. Stevens was a ferocious gossip, and much of his conversation made its way into his official reports. It might be, the American minister said hopefully, that although Cleghorn was reputed to be Ka'iulani's father, that she was really the child of Princess Miriam Likelike and an officer of the U.S. warship *Maine*. That information, apparently, was supposed to indicate to Washington that even if Ka'iulani came to the throne all was not lost. But the tenor of all reports belied such optimism; Stevens' insistence that Hawaii must be annexed by the U.S. grew more shrill every month.

Theo Davies did nothing to lower Stevens' blood pressure with his new habit of visiting Hawaii every year. The reason was obviously more political than business; Theo H. Davies & Co. was stable and profitable, and the other investments caused no worry. Davies was back in Honolulu, however, in April 1891, in his new found role as unofficial representative of Canada and London. His friend Cleghorn arranged an interview with Queen Liliuokalani, at which Davies displayed a map of the world with the British Empire colored in red. He drew her particular attention to the British possessions in the Pacific, Australia, New Zealand, a cluster of islands in the south and central Pacific, and the vast expanse of Canada, on which he enlarged verbally. Oh, yes, Canada, said the Queen. She knew that her brother had often spoken of wanting more trade with Canada, to balance the American influence. For both had known that it was unhealthy for any one nation to predominate in Hawaii. But what was to be done, the queen asked ruefully? The Hawaiian race was undoubtedly diminishing, and the foreigners were becoming more powerful every year. If only the great powers could come to an understanding among themselves to guarantee Hawaiian independence, perpetually . . . Davies was totally sympathetic. The queen was saying precisely what he had been telling them at the Foreign Office. He felt sure that British sentiment favored the guarantee of Hawaiian independence. With that the queen smiled and they passed on to talk of Ka'iulani and other matters, but later Cleghorn reported to Davies that the queen had the definite feeling that Britain really did not care much about what happened to Hawaii.[3] Davies could hardly but agree, given the lacklustre performance of the Foreign Office, but he could, and did, report to London that the queen was disappointed.

Davies, and for that matter, the queen, could only suspect the depth of the determination in high American circles to have Hawaii as an American possession. Secretary of State Blaine was an outright advocate of annexation; so was President Benjamin Harrison; they were admittedly only looking for an excuse to seize the islands.[4] Stevens was their willing servant, the eager advocate of action *now*. And so the clouds closed in around the islands. In the fall of 1891 the *U.S.S. Pensacola* was sent to Honolulu on more or less permanent station, in spite of the queen's disapproval, to guard American interests. Guard them against what?—the nefarious British, of course, and among those British the shadow of Theo H. Davies loomed so large that it dwarfed all others. Davies' business interests were becoming increasingly involved in the political struggle. The McKinley Tariff of 1890 had raised the U.S. import tax on goods to almost 50 per cent of their value, which destroyed most of the value of the Reciprocity Treaty (except for raw sugar) and brought a depression to the islands. Davies was in favor of expanding Hawaii trade with British colonies in the Pacific, but he got little support from London. Still, he wrote letters to the editors of newspapers and engaged in correspondence that kept interest high in the islands. In October 1892, he returned once more to Hawaii, and Minister Stevens reported to Washington with some excitement that Davies' coming had "intensified the ultra-English feeling" centered around Iolani Palace. This man, said Stevens, was the agent for the Canadian Pacific Railway, and for Canadian and British steamer lines, he was a Tory, and he was not to be trusted. The other English houses in Hawaii were "thoroughly Americanized" but the house of Theo H. Davies stood alone—dangerous to the American interests.[5] It was true: Davies had secured various new agencies in his trips west and east, which these days almost always took him through Victoria and Ottawa. On the strength of the commitment, particularly for a new Canadian-Australian steamer line, Theo H. Davies & Co. opened a new steamship department in 1892, and it immediately prospered, in the increased commerce between British colonial ports and Hawaii.[6]

Davies' 1892 visit aroused Minister Stevens to absolute frenzy. "This man," said the minister in warning to Washington, "is a resolute and persistent opponent of United States predominance . . . the death of Liliuokalani would virtually place an English princess on the Hawaiian throne . . ."[7] In a way, Stevens' agitation was symptomatic of the time, for Hawaii was rent with factionalism, some parties advocating a new constitution, some retention of the old, some a republic, some wanting annexation to the U.S. In 1892 one faction, led by Colonel V. V. Ashford, tried to stage a rebellion; it was suppressed and a degree of tranquility seemed to be returned to the islands. But beneath, the atmosphere was anything but tranquil. Lorrin Thurston and his annexation committee were at work and had encouragement from no less personage than President Harrison.[8] London attempted to indicate a greater interest by raising Commissioner Wodehouse's status to that of minister resident—but the wheels of change were already grinding too quickly for any such indications to be effective.

In these hectic months, Theo H. Davies was heavily occupied with the political situation. In October 1892, he was in Hawaii and was startled to hear from friends that the queen expected troops of the *U.S.S. Boston* to be landed to seize her government. The next month the American presidential election of 1892 shocked the annexationists, because it brought back to power in America, Grover Cleveland, who was unalterably opposed to foreign excursions. The air seemed to lighten, but the effect was illusory; Davies involved himself in a newspaper argument about the disadvantages of the Pearl Harbor naval base to Hawaii, and then went home again, en route aboard the *Gallia* to write a long public letter to the Rev. Sereno E. Bishop, chiding him for coming out publicly in favor of American annexation of the islands.[9] Perhaps it was unfortunate that Davies was in Honolulu during this period and not in London. Minister Wodehouse was keeping the Foreign Office completely informed and suggested the need for British warships to prevent an American takeover. But the Earl of Rosebery, the Foreign Minister, had no intention of extending the lion's paw into the Hawaiian situation. Davies had hoped, and had been encouraged to hope, it would seem, that Britain wanted an independent Hawaii. But under Rosebery, Britain wanted an independent Hawaii only as long as Hawaii could manage on her own; there would be no British interference with the Americans. Just as Theo Davies was leaving Honolulu, Rosebery was writing Wodehouse the fateful words: warning his commissioner in Honolulu to be ". . . careful not to say anything which would lead Her Majesty to rely on Her Majesty's (Britain's) government for support in the event of pressure being put upon her by the United States."[10] What Davies might have done had he been in London is uncertain; he might have had no influence at all, but anyhow, he was in the wrong place at the wrong time, if anything he might have said would have made a difference.

While Davies was going home to Sundown, the queen (Hawaii's) was pondering ways to strengthen her rule. She hit upon the idea of promulgating a new constitution, whose effect would be to weaken the missionary party that had taken control of the government. This attempt triggered a rebellion led by Hawaiian subjects who were mostly American-born. Lorrin Thurston was their leader, and he made the proposal that they seize power. They might suffer a queen who wished to reign, but not one who insisted upon ruling. Hardly had the Christmas decorations been cleared away at Sundown, and Ka'iulani gone back to Great Harrowden Hall for the new term, when Hawaiian affairs were in an uproar. Theo H. Davies was privy to the innermost secrets of the palace, for Queen Liliuokalani, having lost her husband a few months earlier, had turned to Cleghorn, her brother-in-law, and her niece Ka'iulani, as the only people in the world still dear to her. Cleghorn was collector of customs and Governor of Oahu, but far more, he had the queen's ear and he reported faithfully by letter to Ka'iulani on the events of the palace.[11]

But Davies would soon enough have known, anyhow, for his position was such that he could not be ignored. Sanford Ballard Dole, the president of the provisional government, had been Davies' attorney for many years before he became Hawaii's Chief Justice. Dole was not at all certain of the propriety of what the Annexation Party had done, and he favored the removal of the headstrong Liliuokalani in favor of the hopefully pliant Ka'iulani, who was expected to be content to reign, not rule. He suggested they seek Davies' advice. But there were others who remained adamant, and so the scene shifted to Washington, for as all concerned knew, the revolution could not have been staged without the assent of American Minister Stevens, and thus implied, that of the U.S. government. Since Washington was in a period of transition (the Cleveland Administration would not come to power until March, but the Harrison administration could take no binding action) there was time for maneuvering. From Honolulu came assurances that Ka'iulani would be granted a large pension by the provisional government; Davies did not believe these statements. He could take Ka'iulani to the United States, to appeal to the new administration, and above all to American public opinion, in which he was ostensibly pleading the cause of the monarchy, but with an implied promise that Ka'iulani, not Liliuokalani, would be the queen. This attitude was really engendered in Honolulu by Cleghorn and others, who knew that the headstrong Liliuokalani would create trouble again if she were restored. For his part, Davies decided to take Ka'iulani to America to see the incoming President and to make her case. They sailed in February, and went to Washington. On the voyage across, Davies carefully wrote statements and speeches for Ka'iulani, and when she arrived in America she delivered them.[12] The reception was generally good, although some believed that in the way he made his case, Davies created difficulty by setting Ka'iulani up against her aunt, instead of pleading only for restoration of the monarchy.[13] They also visited Boston, where they saw Clive Davies, busy with his studies at Massachusetts Institute of Technology, and Davies gave interviews to the press at which Ka'iulani said her orchestrated piece. The Boston newspapers were much taken by the princess. One mentioned the "romance" between Ka'iulani and Clive Davies, and praised the Davies family because although the princess no longer had a kingdom, there was not the slightest backing away from "the engagement" by the Davies family. Forever after, Theo Davies denied there was any romantic attachment here, but Clive Davies kept that particular clipping in his papers, and it was found among them when he died.[14]

All the Davies family were immensely fond of Kaʻiulani, perhaps more so because they saw this delicate flower of Polynesia transformed over the years into a cultivated Englishwoman. With the uncertainties of the revolution, no one considered sending Kaʻiulani back to Hawaii. She remained in England, at the school and visiting the Davies and other friends during holidays. But Kaʻiulani, with all her grace and beauty, was a sore trial to Theo H. Davies. She could not keep her checkbook balanced and was forever running out of money and applying to Nellie. This shook the Davies applecart, because the master of the house was strict with everyone, including his wife, in the matter of money. No one ever had any excuses for extravagance as far as he was concerned. But if Kaʻiulani was one part spoiled schoolgirl and one part English gentlewoman, she was still one part Hawaiian princess, with the sort of temper that the *aliʻi* could show. Theo H. Davies, with his limited imagination in such things, somehow really believed he might persuade Kaʻiulani to stop spending what she wished when she wished; had she been one of his young men she would have been discharged or set back for her monetary intemperance; as it was, Davies spent countless hours abjuring her by voice and letter to mend her ways—but she never did.[15]

That famous royal Hawaiian temper, as exhibited by Kaʻiulani's aunt, Queen Liliuokalani, put the end to any hope that the house of Kalakaua might be reestablished in the islands. Up until December 1893, there had been hope. Some of the revolutionaries were not very comfortable in their position and would have welcomed a reasonable constitutional monarchy, particularly since Grover Cleveland made it quite plain that in his term of office, the U.S. would never annex Hawaii. He sent James H. Blount, former chairman of the House of Representatives committee on foreign affairs, to ascertain the facts about the revolution. Blount approached his task openly,[16] if anything, sympathetic to the royal claims for restitution. Blount's report was favorable to the queen, for he found that the native people of Hawaii overwhelmingly wanted her return. He did not concern himself much with the attitudes of the "missionary party" which were obvious, or with that large number of footloose half-castes, whites and various others who did not care who won as long as the islands had tranquility. Blount went home, and in spite of Lorrin Thurston's masterly propaganda for the revolution, American opinion had swung against the rebels. Then Albert S. Willis came to Honolulu as American minister, with the inherent task of arranging for the orderly transfer of power back to the queen, as Cleveland desired. The one important provision was that she grant full amnesty to those who had moved against her (men misguided by Minister Stevens, they believed in Washington) and assume the obligations of the provisional government as legal debts of Hawaii. But Queen Liliuokalani could not refrain from exhibiting the royal fury at the revolutionaries. In an interview with Willis she said that if she were restored, she would behead the revolutionaries and confiscate their property. Willis was taken aback and tried to make her understand that she was destroying herself, but she would not or could not comprehend what was demanded of her as the price of restitution of the monarchy. She stuck to her position, and thus pulled the teeth of her friends. Davies, back in Honolulu, wrote Princess Ka'iulani hopelessly that "The Queen has committed a great blunder . . . the future looks very gloomy in Hawaii . . ."[17] The provisional government had the ammunition it needed to protect itself, and if Cleveland had once considered using American force to undo American wrongs, public opinion turned against him so that there was no chance of it.

As for Ka'iulani, she became a princess in exile. Her schooling finished, she began a round of European travel, for "broadening." She travelled to Germany where she entertained, but finally rejected a proposal of marriage from a German nobleman. Davies, who was feeling more than a little frantic under the financial responsibility for her, suggested that with her income, she ought to settle down as an impoverished English gentlewoman would: find "some nice, refined family in England and live there on whatever your income is . . ."[18] He knew then, although he could not even admit it to himself, that all Ka'iulani's dreams and all his own hopes for Hawaii's future had been dashed by the wilful, stubborn queen.

Chapter Twenty

THE CORPORATION

For the next several years, although Theo H. Davies really had virtually no hope of success, he continued to function as the prime polemicist of the royal party. The newspaper editors of the *Gazette,* the *Commercial Advertiser,* the *Star* and *The Bulletin* detested him, attacked his statements and reviled him, but they could not fail to print his many letters. Theo H. Davies & Co. was too important a factor in Hawaii for its senior officer to be ignored. He spent much time in Hawaii, and everything he did there was subject to the closest public scrutiny. When he discharged one of his employees during a visit to Hawaii the *Advertiser* printed a rumor that the man was fired because he expressed opinions in favor of the provisional government. By 1894, some worrisome suggestions began to emerge in Honolulu. The *Star*[1] suggested that Davies was on the verge of becoming "dangerous" and indicated obliquely that it might not be long before he was jailed, deported, and banned from returning. Such talk would give any businessman pause, and Davies was no exception. When the *Advertiser* began wondering in its editorial columns if Davies was guilty of sedition, it was worrisome.[2] When Lorrin Thurston, the Hawaii Republic's Minister in Washington, denounced Davies as a "professional mischief maker" it was more worrisome, and this concern was not lessened by a report in the San Francisco *Chronicle* that Davies was "hatching a conspiracy"[3] against the provisional government of Hawaii. As a matter of self preservation, Theo Davies began to consider the idea of incorporating his holdings in Hawaii under the new government's laws. That would certainly lessen, if not completely eliminate the danger of expropriation of his property. In the spring of 1894, Davies went to Boston to see Clive get his degree from Massachusetts Institute of Technology, and then to travel to Honolulu. They stopped off in Ottawa to attend that year's important Intercolonial Conference, as representatives of the Honolulu Chamber of Commerce, and then went to Honolulu, where Davies, Walker, and Swanzy worked out the details of incorporation.[4] The capital stock was set up at $700,000 in 7,000 shares of $100 par value. Under Hawaii law it took five persons to incorporate, three of whom must be residents of the islands. The resident directors were Walker with 560 shares, Swanzy with 280 shares and W.H. Baird the bookkeeper, with five shares. The other two incorporators were Theo H. Davies with 6,055 shares and Clive with 100 shares. Theo Davies was managing director; Walker and Swanzy were "resident directors." In effect, the company would run as before, but with a greater protection for all of the directors against loss.

In spite of the uncertainties about the future of sugar in the islands, the Davies' enterprises continued to prosper beyond any dreams young Theo H. Davies could have nurtured when he first came to the Hawaiian islands. That year, 1894, the new corporation showed profits of $113,370.[5] True to the Davies tradition, half that profit was kept in reserve, and $56,000 paid out in dividends. Theo Davies believed in financing capital improvements on the spot from profits, and in borrowing no money unless it was absolutely necessary, and then against such tangibles as the coming sugar crop. To be sure, there was risk in borrowing against futures, but that was a risk the planters and sugar factors had long accepted as essential in a country where capital was always in short supply.

The Theo H. Davies company earnings hardly represented the income of the Davies family. The Honolulu Iron Works continued to be a key to Davies' success, although the company had ups and downs in the uncertainties of the early 1890s. In '91, for example, the company did a business of $468,000 but showed a net profit of only $18,000. The reason was low prices charged, purposely, to keep the works going in difficult times. The next year the company showed a business volume of only $172,000 and paid no dividends. But Davies and the other board members were confident of the future: they bought the stock and assets of George Mac-Farlane's competitive Pacific Iron Works for $54,000. In 1893 sales were back up to $249,000 at a profit of $5,500. These modest profits, however, did not indicate the value of the company, which in 1894 was listed at $345,000.[6] The capital stock, valued at $200,000, was split into 200 shares. Davies owned 52, the estate of R.C. Janion owned 52, Janion's widow owned 26; thus Davies had effective control. Twenty shares still belonged to the estate of Mrs. Anna Green, William Green's mother, and 6 shares to Mrs. Mary Green, his wife. Alexander Young had wanted to assure HIW business from the other important sugar factors, particularly when George MacFarlane had begun undercutting Honolulu Iron Works with sugar machinery imported from Scotland. So Young had sold some of his shares to Castle & Cooke and H. Hackfeld & Company. As shareholders, these plantation and mill owners naturally brought their business to Honolulu Iron Works. But by far the greatest benefits were derived by Theo H. Davies & Co., which was purchasing and sales agent for Honolulu Iron Works. Davies was quite content to let the HIW bills run, and in 1894 the company owed Theo H. Davies & Co. $118,000. Because he controlled the HIW board, he could do as he pleased: in 1894, as had happened several times in the past, the Iron Works passed its dividend because of the large amount owing to Theo H. Davies & Co. Further, as the years went on, Davies acquired the stock of the Janions, and after Alexander Young retired as manager in 1896, the Davies company owned 130 of the 200 shares.[7]

The Davies sugar properties were like gold mines. By 1888 Waiakea Mill was capitalized at $600,000. Over the years, Davies had been taking capital stock against the mill's debts to him. In 1881 he took $120,000 in stock for debt; in 1882 he took $60,000. Eight years later Waiakea was incorporated; Davies and Young each held 1250 shares and Mrs. Janion held 375 shares. The manager, C.C. Kennedy, had 125 shares. By this time, Waiakea was the most efficient mill in the islands, thanks to Alexander Young's perfection of the maceration process of cane grinding, which added 20 per cent to production in 1885 alone. By '89, Waiakea produced 3,100 tons of sugar, with a new record of a ton of sugar for each seven tons of cane. These were astounding figures for the day and kept the reputation of Alexander Young and Theo H. Davies as high as the profits. In the next ten years Waiakea would pay dividends of $1,177,000, out of profits of $3,600,000, and finance all improvements from income![8]

One of Davies' oldest, but least important sugar investments from the standpoint of capital, was in Union Mill in the Kohala district. In the early '90s, he held 20 shares of the total 160 shares, and Clive had another 5 shares. But the major owners were the Renton family with 90 shares, valued at $1,000 each. Union Mill paid fair but not spectacular dividends: in 1893 the dividend was $100 per share. Davies continued for years to retain a small but comfortable interest, partly because of friendship for the Rentons, partly because the interest guaranteed his retention of the agency contract and virtual assurance that machinery would be bought from Honolulu Iron Works.

Far more spectacular and complex were the dealings of Theo Davies in Laupahoehoe Sugar Company, which began as a partnership with William Lidgate. At one time (1884) Lidgate was carried on the Theo H. Davies Company books as owing $347,000. It was not much wonder that all those years, whenever Davies was away from Honolulu, he pored over the letters from Walker and Swanzy and reacted immediately to changes in Laupahoehoe's situation. Late in the 1880s, Davies acquired all the capital stock in the company. In the uncertainty of the sugar market, Laupahoehoe's income jumped up and down like a boy on a pogo stick. One year the company would earn $100,000, the next it would pass its dividend. From 1892 to 1898, no dividends were paid, and Davies would cheerfully have unloaded the company if he could have found a buyer.[9] Part of the trouble was indeed the apparent non-productivity of the land; part was the general condition of the sugar industry. In 1892 Davies had made arrangements with Western Sugar Refining Company to take about a third of his crop, but that volume soon increased.[10] The troubles with Spreckels were over; he had never managed to secure the stranglehold he sought on Hawaii sugar, but the whole industry was dislocated by the McKinley Tariff of 1891, which paid American sugar producers a bounty of two cents a pound and admitted raw sugar from all foreign countries free of duty. This law wiped out the price advantage the Hawaii sugar producers had enjoyed in the years when the Reciprocity Treaty meant something. The industry would be years in recovering, and yet some of Davies' sugar interests paid handsome profits even in the worst of times.

The best sugar investment in the Davies portfolio in the 1890s was at Hamakua,[11] where Davies had gone into business with Charles Notley. The mill at Paauilo was profitable, and so was the plantation. James, one of the Renton boys, had become manager of Hamakua Mill Company in 1883 and did a fine job. Hamakua was expensive in its way; the landing at Koholalele demanded the building of bridges and roads and a railroad leading from the mill. These costs were easily met from income, and the dividends were still paid out. In 1885 the Kukaiau mill was built. In 1889 Aamano plantation was incorporated into Hamakua. In 1896, the complicated affairs of Hamakua plantation and mill were resolved by bringing all under the Hamakua Mill Company, Ltd., with 7,600 shares. Davies, the Davies Company, and Mrs. Janion owned 4,150 shares, which meant that in case of difficulty there was no question about who controlled Hamakua, although Charles Notley was actually the largest shareholder, with 3,000 shares. Theo Davies had a way of coming up with such divisions. There was little dissention among the stockholders, however, because the dividends were most satisfactory: between 1887 and 1898 Hamakua paid out $958,000 to stockholders while retaining a strong reserve and financing improvements out of income.[12]

In the middle of the 1890s, Davies might lament the course of political events that had so changed the Hawaii he knew, and so unfairly deprived the Hawaiians of control of their native land, but his economic interests were advanced by the movement beneath the American umbrella, and he knew that very well. The anomaly of his personal predilections and the

Above left and lower right: The sugar loading operations of the 20th century improved over the old method, but the principle was the same: the ships stood off the Hamakua coast and the sugar in bags was run across the water on long lines. Only after the 1946 tidal wave wiped out the railroad on the Big Island did sugar loading move quickly to a bulk operation, carried in trucks to the port at Kawaihae and there handled much as grain is handled in the American middle west.

Above right: Aerial view of Haina Mill at Honokaa, October 1951.

Lower left: Paaua Mill around 1920, showing camp of homes of workers.

course of fortune was a burden he bore with more equanimity than most men might have managed, and after it became certain that there was no turning back, Davies reduced his royalist polemics to the point where even the *Commercial Advertiser's* attacks lessened. Thus, while Theo H. Davies & Co., Ltd. was "British to the core," as had been any of the preceding partnerships, the Davies company was accepted as a part of the new Hawaiian scene. In 1895 a branch was opened in the growing town of Hilo. The Canadian Pacific Railway brought agencies for the Cunard Steamship Company, Anchor-Donaldson, and the White Star Line.[13] The days of challenge and adventure seemed to have ended and what remained was a solid mercantile venture, one of a handful of survivors from the early days. The entrenched sugar companies, Waiakea, Hamakua, Laupahoehoe, and Union Mill, which, like the successful ventures of Castle & Cooke, Alexander & Baldwin, and H. Hackfeld & Company, continued to swallow the small plantations around them. In the middle of the 1890s, Theo H. Davies could indeed contemplate retirement and the life of a country squire.

When Davies bought the house called Sundown, after several years of leasing it, he had expected to live there for the rest of his life. But Nellie never did recover completely from the dreadful long bout with infection in Hawaii, and the climate of Merseyside began to bother her. This concern distressed Davies, because much of his personal life was bound up in Southport. He was active in the Church Missionary Society, the British and Foreign Bible Society, and the Church Pastoral Aid Society. He was a busy supporter of Lord Curzon and the Conservative Party and, in the 1890s, of the Unionist government. He had helped build Emmanuel Church in Southport and was a bastion in the Y.M.C.A. there as he had been in Honolulu, serving for three years as president. He was also president of the Southport Working Lads Club and a hearty supporter of the Church of England Temperance Society.[14] Nellie had been equally involved in good works. The drawing room at Southport, when not full of giggling schoolgirls from Ka'iulani's boarding school, was likely to be the scene of a meeting of the church auxiliary or the ladies' sewing circle. The children, too, were involved in community affairs. Clive was an active member of the Working Lads Club and a member of the committee that found premises for the clubhouse in Eastbank Street. The other children grew, learned manners and the ways of the new found gentility in this house. Alice Marion grew up and went to boarding school; so did the second girl, Violet Mary. George F. went to university, and later so did Arthur W. Harry Llanover, the youngest, was a baby when the family came back to England, and his entire childhood was spent in this house at Sundown. He never really knew Hawaii. The child who did know the islands, and in terms of time had spent more years there than in England, was T. Clive. Soon, at Sundown, the future of Clive was settled: he was educated for the sugar business, primarily to understand the mechanics of building sugar mills and the intricacies of engineering. Of the other brothers, neither Arthur W., Theophilus M., nor Harry L. Davies showed any inclination for the business, and they would be encouraged to seek their own ways of life. Only George F. Davies decided that he, too, would take a hand in Hawaii, and he prepared himself at Cambridge to spend several years in Honolulu.[15]

By 1896, when Theo H. Davies was looking about for a new home for Nellie and the family, Clive was ready for his venture into the business, and George was not far behind him. There would be fewer and fewer of the family brood at home from this time on, but it was still necessary to have a proper gentleman's house. Davies chose a mansion called Ravensdale in Tunbridge Wells, Kent, about 35 miles from London, and in 1897 he moved the household to Ravensdale. He was still making an annual trek to Hawaii and at 63 looked forward to a continued vigorous career as merchant, capitalist, philanthropist, and churchman.[16] His life had been extremely satisfying until this point and there was no reason that it should not continue to be. His one great regret involved Ka'iulani, so harshly deprived of her birthright by circumstance; but certainly no one could chide him for inattention or lack of zeal in promoting his ward's welfare. The rumor still circulated that the Machiavellian Davies schemed to marry his son Clive to Ka'iulani as a part of his master scheme to take over Hawaii.

But even this tale lost credibility in the spring of 1896, when Clive became engaged to Edith Fox, daughter of a famous British civil engineer. From the Davies point of view the world of 1896 was a pleasant place; the children were marrying well and the business in Hawaii prospered. What more could a man want of life?

Chapter Twenty-One
CLIVE

I*n January 1896,* Theo Davies was abubble with plans for the future. He would take Clive out to Honolulu that month and introduce him properly to the business. First, however, Clive must be officially engaged to Miss Edith Fox who, from the Davies point of view, was a "catch". Her father was a civil engineer of international reputation and the family, was, if not as wealthy as the Davies family, superior in the social world. There was a certain amount of tension between the two young people after Edith learned that Clive would be expected to remain in Honolulu at least two years before coming home to get married.[1] Clive travelled nervously down to the Fox estate at Wimbledon on January 20, to pick up Edith and bring her home to "meet the family." Edith knew the Davieses already; she and Clive had met through his sister Violet Mary, who was at school with Edith; but this January visit was a formal meeting of the engaged couple with the fiance's parents. Leaving Edith with his mother, Clive journeyed to London to buy the engagement ring, returned with it, and that afternoon he gave her the ring. A photographer came to take pictures and the seal of finality was fixed to the engagement.[2]

On the foggy afternoon of January 25, Clive and his father boarded the steamer *Umbria* in Liverpool harbor, and she sailed at midnight when the weather lifted. It was a typical Davies voyage: they were placed at the captain's table and Davies took over as lay minister on Sunday; he read the service and Clive read the lessons. In the evening they assembled the first-class passengers and Clive played hymns on the piano in the saloon. In a week the ship docked in Boston and they travelled across country to San Francisco, where Clive was introduced to Claus Spreckels and Henry Dimond of Williams, Dimond & Co. Then they were off on the *Australia* to Honolulu, and to Craigside, which would have to be refurnished for Clive.[3]

The first few days were occupied by social functions —the introduction of the Davies heir apparent to the Honolulu *haole* community. There were receptions at the houses of Davies' friends and a party at the Britannia Tennis Club. Clive was entered in the British Club. He joined the Honolulu symphony orchestra as a clarinetist. But on February 25, the festivity ended and business began; Theo Davies would be going back to England in a few weeks and there was much that he must show Clive about their domain. On the 25th and immediately thereafter were the annual meetings of Theo H. Davies Company, Honolulu Iron Works, Hamakua, Laupahoehoe, Union Mill, and Waiakea sugar companies. The books of all these firms were kept in the Honolulu offices of Davies company and the Big Island board members came over for the meetings. Clive displayed his engineer's education in discussing the values of a turbine-driven water wheel for one of the mills, and he pleased his father by copying over a business letter for him. Then, in the first week of March, they were off to the Big Island to see the sugar mills and plantations. Harry Llanover Davies had come over separately with Thomas Rain Walker, who had just ended a leave in England. Harry accompanied Davies and Clive to the sugar lands. They landed at Hilo and spent the rest of the month of March touring the island. At Pepeekeo they watched the awesome process of loading sugar by hoist. The sugar was brought from the mill warehouses to the landing on the cliff, 80 feet above the blue sea. Outside the reef line stood a ship at anchor, and a boat came from the ship to bring a light line that carried the cable to the ship. The cable was raised onto a boom, and then the slings of sugar bags were sent high above the water from shore to ship, as the waves danced below and surf crashed on the coral reef. In a good wind the ship tossed out there like a cork, the cable swayed and dipped ominously, and the spindrift from the wave tops damped the outsides of the slings. This was the way they loaded sugar along the Hamakua coast![4]

They travelled down to Laupahoehoe, and Clive and Harry were instructed in the growing of cane by Manager McLennan. Clive spent some time studying the mechanics of the mills and the question of more rollers, which McLennan had raised. That would be taken up with Honolulu Iron Works back in Oahu. McLennan took them to Hamakua on horseback through a blinding rain, and then they began the rounds that would introduce the boys to Davies' old associates, the Lidgates, Notleys, and Rentons. Clive divided his time between learning about sugar production and studying waterpower problems with his engineer's eye. He went about the mills with little notebook in hand, pipe in his teeth, taking notes on everything in a tiny hand.[5]

On April 1 they all returned to Honolulu, for Theo H. and Harry must soon sail for England, and Clive must get down to work in the office. His routine began the next day, April 2, when he arose at seven-thirty, had breakfast at Craigside, rode down Nuuanu valley to the Davies Company offices in downtown Honolulu and was at his new desk at nine o'clock learning to calculate interest under the eye of bookkeeper W. H. Baird. From that day on, all day long, all week, a full day on Saturday, and evenings when necessary, Clive sat at a desk learning to be a clerk. There was time for amusements and he joined the Y.M.C.A. and regularly attended symphony practice. He was accepted by his family's friends, and he made new friends, most of them in the British community, most of them within the congregation of St. Andrew's Cathedral. Clive Davies was taller and more of a "gentleman" than his father, having never known any life but that of wealth, but he was every bit as much an Englishman, and an aloof, diffident Englishman at that. He was also a respectful son, honoring his father's wishes and following parental authority. He had come to Hawaii to learn the business and make his place in it, and this he set out to do with total concentration. The opportunity was created for him: he was to be cashier, but he found himself much like the boy thrown off the end of the dock with a rope tied around his waist and told to sink or swim—the going was not easy. His career as cashier began on the morning of June 1, at eight-thirty.[6] Almost immediately he was in trouble. That first morning he took in a sum of cash from a customer, and forgot to enter the man's name. He mixed up his figures and had difficulty in balancing the cash. On the third day his accounts were off by $100—he had cheated someone, some-how, because he had that extra $100. Finally it was tracked down, and the mistake rectified; which would have put him right with his father, had Davies known. But that first week, Clive very nearly made the sort of mistake that Theo H. Davies would not forgive. Clive's friend Baird tried to cheer him out of his depressed assessment of his potential as a cashier by taking him in the evenings to call on the Mackintoshes and other old friends. James Renton and Manager McLennan showed up in town from the Big Island and Clive went to call on them at their hotel in the after-noon.[7] They got to talking and so involved that he very nearly missed getting the cash to the bank that day. Such an error, involving activity outside the office, had brought Hay Wodehouse and other young clerks down in the past. But Clive managed to squeak through the doors of Bishop & Company just before closing, and even had he not, neither Swanzy (who was just then in England on leave) nor Walker (who had just returned) was the martinet type. But it was as well that Clive's father did not know.

Walker and Swanzy had been advised to give Clive every exposure as rapidly as possible. He made his first solo appearance at a board meeting on June 3 and was so impressed with his own temerity at managing to speak up that he noted it in his diary. For the first weeks he had a dreadful time with the cash; it was his responsibility to balance up all the cash records at night. All day long the clerks in the hardware, dry goods, and grocery departments were selling and taking in money, and each day before Clive could leave he had to make sure the books were in order. Some nights he burned the lights until late; one night he finally gave up and went home with 41 cents still missing somewhere. That did not seem a large sum, when he was dealing with perhaps $20,000 a day, but debits and credits must cancel out, and that night he had been at it until eight-forty-five. Next morning which was Sunday, he was back to find the error. He was assiduous, and he was also lucky. One day he made out a check to a payee for $5,000 instead of $500, but the man returned it. By midsummer he was much more adept and confident, and in August, when the Honolulu Iron Works cashier turned up sick on payday, Clive volunteered to take over, went over to the Iron Works, paid the men, went back to Theo H. Davies & Co., Ltd., balanced his cash books for the day, and was home at Craigside by five-thirty.

His social life continued busy, if restricted. For a time, when Walker went to visit a neighboring island, Clive took his Sunday school class at St. Andrew's. He dined out with family friends two or three times a week. He went to the British Club for luncheon, and to orchestra rehearsals one evening a week. The Y.M.C.A. took a certain amount of his time. Writing letters to Edith took another segment—and more as the months rolled on, and Edith let it be known that (1) she was growing restless about their continued separation and (2) there were other fish in her sea. From the other side, anxious letters began to arrive from Theo H. Davies to Swanzy, worrying letters in which the father wondered why the son was not getting on faster. "Neither his letters nor yours give me the idea that he is getting at all familiar with the inside of the business—that is, with the confidential parts . . ."[8] Why was Clive not spending more time on the Big Island? He had not been over since May. Swanzy must draw him out, and he was not doing it. Walker wanted to take a long furlough in 1897; could Clive not be brought along to be Swanzy's "alter ego" at that time? Swanzy must redouble the training efforts; let him begin by giving Clive all the correspondence between Theo Davies and Honolulu to read.[9] So poor Clive was caught between a rock and a hard place, and by 1897 he must have been sustained against opposite tuggings of his father's and his fiancee's impatience by the stolidity of his character. He did learn as his father said he must. Davies warned Swanzy not to let Clive become "groovy" (it was his favorite phrase to describe a plodding clerk) and he pressed Clive for ever more exhibition of knowledge and more decisive attitudes towards business affairs. Clive responded. He read everything dutifully. He began to learn to write the company's letters. He researched into the past, even studying Theo Davies' quarrel with Bishop Willis. The Bishop's behavior was "shocking," he said. He did ask for more exposure, but Swanzy, who in all but name had now become the senior in Honolulu as Walker's thoughts moved more and more toward England, obviously disagreed with Theo Davies that haste was essential and that Clive should be sped along. One day in the summer of 1897 Clive came to dinner at the Swanzys and they had a long talk. Clive, as goaded by his father, said he thought he should be getting more experience.[10]

"Oh, I think you're getting on fine," Swanzy said.

So the education of Clive Davies continued at Swanzy's pace, with Theo Davies clucking in the background. Times were changing in the business world; among other things office machines and the typewriter made their appearance, and the Davies correspondence began to appear in typed letters. The copies, however, were still made by the old process of heat transfer in the letter copy books, and it would be several years after the turn of the century before the Davies company discovered carbon paper.[11] Not only methods, but personnel were changing. E. H. Wodehouse, another of James Wodehouse's children, joined the firm and applied himself vigorously. He did not share his brother's social proclivities, or if he did, there was no Theo H. Davies in the Honolulu office to watch over every leisure and business activity of the young men. These were modern times, and Swanzy, in particular, was a modern man, a good deal more sympathetic to human foible than Theo H. Davies.[12]

Back in Liverpool, Davies had reason to be pleased with himself and the firm. He had finally secured the Hawaiian consulate and his stationery now bore the proud legend: Theo H. Davies & Co. Liverpool and Honolulu, T.H.; Hawaiian Consulate; and the Hawaii seal and crown in a circle, with the legend *Kanikele Hawaii Ma* around it. By 1897 he announced his move to Ravensdale, with its 100 acres of land, and wrote Swanzy that he was thinking seriously of opening a London office because he hated the thought of Hoffnung & Co., who were still the Hawaiian agents in London, having the final say with the government on Hawaiian affairs.[13] Davies also spent a considerable amount of time recruiting Britons for the enterprises in Hawaii, whose personnel needs were growing. He wanted his to remain a thoroughly British firm, and he wanted his plantations staffed with British *haoles,* not Americans or the flotsam that turned up on the Hawaiian beaches. But Davies' real preoccupation was with the future of his two eldest sons in the business. George would receive his Cambridge degree in German and French literature in June and would then be sent for three months to a London accounting firm. At the end of October, 1897, he would accompany Theo Davies to Honolulu and for three months would be put to work as a clerk under W.H. Baird. Early in 1898, Theo H. Davies would bring both sons home. He and George would open an office in London and George would move to London to man the office, while Theo H. continued in charge of the Liverpool office, although he would live in Kent. But it was his intention to remove himself gradually from day-to-day concern about the business in favor of his sons. Clive would get married on his return home, spend six months on a honeymoon leave, and then return to Honolulu. In a few years the sons would probably change places, although it was Theo's intention that George make a special study of finance. Davies regarded finance as the most important aspect of such a business as theirs "and one in which I am singularly deficient."[14] Actually, in 1897, Theo Davies was ready to retire altogether from the business, he said, and would, except that he wished to see his sons and his old partners and their associates so well-established that nothing could dislodge them. He sensed Walker's growing disinterest in the business and it irked him mildly, but he could hardly be annoyed; Walker had been with the firm nearly as long as he had, and had worked for the Jacksons in Manchester before coming out.[15] He did not command now so much as counsel. Swanzy had been making a study of the coffee business, which seemed to offer possibilities, but Davies warned him that until he had better top-level assistance (of the type that Davies hoped Clive would provide) any such expansion would mean nothing but greater burdens on Swanzy's shoulders. These would not have been the words of Theo H. Davies in the 1870s, but a quarter of a century had passed and the founder of the firm was slowing down. His idea of a fine investment was the Hilo Hotel, which was soon coming up for sale with an upset price of $60,000. He advised Swanzy to watch that sale, and if he could get the hotel for $75,000 to take it. The Davies' taste in investment had changed.[16]

Davies did follow the program he had outlined for his boys. He did go to Honolulu in the fall of 1897 with George, and the three did return to England in the winter of 1898. Theo Davies caught cold on the voyage home across the Atlantic and his resistance was so low that he seemed to be unable to shake it in the damp English winter. April came and he was still confined to his room. He hated being sick, and being seen to be sick, so he stayed in his room. He wrote letters almost every day, but did not appear even for meals unless he felt that he could dress and carry on properly. By May, George was at loose ends. On their way home, he and his father had consulted with bankers in Montreal, who had suggested that George could best learn finance by starting with a year in the firm of a chartered accountant. Then he could spend six months with a merchant banking firm in New York, and another six months in Canada, learning the intricacies of finance. But all was in suspension because his father was ill. George wrote all this to Swanzy on May 4,[17] fully expecting that his father would be up and around well before the June wedding of Clive to Edith Fox. But two weeks later Theo H. Davies developed complications; his "cold" became a severe gastrointestinal attack. Apparently there was something in the food or water, for three of the household servants also fell ill. The doctor was called and prescribed for them, but Theo Davies grew worse, and then quite suddenly, on May 25, 1898, Theo H. Davies died.[18] So swift and so serious was the fatal illness that the family could hardly believe the facts. An autopsy showed nothing more than severe intestinal disorder; but since other members of the household were ill, too, the family suspected typhoid fever or cholera. They engaged experts to assess the Tun-bridge wells water supply, but it was given a clean bill of health, and Davies' death went down as one of those mysterious occurrences that baffle medical science. The shock was profound on both sides of the world. Even the Honolulu newspapers managed to work up a bit of sympathy for this strong figure they had fought for so long. There was an immediate panic about the coming wedding, but Nellie and Clive and George counselled together with the Foxes and decided to carry on. Literally a few days after the death of Theo H. Davies, Clive and Edith Fox were wed and, after a brief honeymoon, left for Hawaii. George agreed to settle the estate and undertake his father's program, and so the Davies dream was not forgotten or abandoned. He had planned well, and everything was proceeding according to plan.

Edith (Mrs. Clive) Davies taken around 1900, probably at Craigside.

Clive Davies

Chapter Twenty-Two

THE EMERGENCE OF SWANZY

A*s befitted a man of many affairs,* the will of Theo H. Davies was long and complicated. Essentially, after providing bequests ranging from £1,000 down to £50 for relatives and servants, the will set up an annuity fund for Nellie and a trust for the children, since all but Clive and George were under 25 years of age. As recognition of Clive's adherence to the business in Honolulu, Davies left him his personal stock in Honolulu Iron Works. He left George outright title to real estate and buildings in Winnipeg, Canada. The executors were to be Swanzy, Walker, Clive and George, and for their effort each was given 100 shares of stock in Theo H. Davies & Co., Ltd. The houses in Honolulu and England were sequestered for the use of Nellie and the children, but all else was thrown into the general trust. In that trust, Arthur, Theo, Harry, Alice Marion and Violet Mary each was given a £10,000 share, but the disposition of the assets remained in the hands of the executors, who would pass the estate along to the trustees in time. After Nellie died, and after the children were grown, the trust would be broken up into equal shares for all the children.[1] For the purposes of probate, the estate was valued at £97,158 19s. 1d., or about half a million dollars. The actual value of the holdings was perhaps ten times that amount. When the executors came to examine the estate they were astounded at the diversity of Theo H. Davies' investments. They included mortgages in Waikiki, Vancouver (Canada), and San Francisco, and stocks in British railroads, American railroads, utilities, and banks. Almost all the investments were substantial and gilt-edged, except for a £12,000 loan to Davies' brother-in-law, Frederick James Jackson, which was unsecured—an example, along with the dozens of legacies for nieces and nephews, of Theo H. Davies' strong sense of family bond.

With considerable acumen Davies attempted to exercise protective power over his fortune from beyond the grave. He designated Swanzy as managing director of the Honolulu company, which could have come as no surprise to Walker by this time. He also specified that two-thirds of the net income from the sugar properties must be returned to the residuary estate as capital; that was protection for the future against possibly rapacious heirs who might grow restive in waiting for the whole estate to be shared out.[2] Those sugar investments, even more than Theo H. Davies stock, were the key to the future. At the time of Davies' death his personal holdings consisted of 6,060 shares of Theo H. Davies & Co., Ltd. stock, which represented $606,000 of the $900,000 capitalization of the company. He also held $30,000 worth of the company's five per cent debentures. He had 20 shares of Union Mill stock, 1,250 of Waiakea Mill, 1,200 shares of Hamakua Mill, 450 shares of Kahuku Plantation Company, a half interest in the Kukaiau Mill, and all the stock of Laupahoehoe Sugar Company. That year the real value of Theo H. Davies & Co., Ltd. was probably about two million dollars.[3] The company's profit was $245,000 of which $140,000 was paid out in dividends. Honolulu Iron Works that year earned $120,000; Waiakea Mill earned $540,000. Laupahoehoe was earning money, but paying no dividends because the earnings were paid into Theo H. Davies company each year to reduce the indebtedness that had caused Davies to take over the company from the Lidgates. For much the same reason, Hamakua Mill showed only a small profit and paid $25,000 in dividends that year, and the other sugar investments were about equally productive. But during that first year after Theo Davies' death, the estate paid Nellie her £2,000 a year, which was quite a high income for those days—and each of the Davies children received $26,000 as his or her share of the earnings of the estate, which converted to over £5,000, a princely income.

Clive Davies, after a briefer honeymoon than he would have liked, took his bride to Honolulu to pursue the program laid down by his father, while George commuted from Kent to London to do his share and conduct the British affairs of the estate. Clive was immediately thrown into the deep water of responsibility that Theo Davies had wanted, and worked in the most intricate and confidential levels of the business. Thomas Rain Walker's role diminished month by month. In 1899 he was in England; his father died that year there, and he had that estate to settle. The real truth, however, was that Walker had lost all taste for the business and Hawaii, and looked forward only to his retirement to England, although he was only in his mid-fifties. In 1899, he announced his decision to quit, and the next year he resigned his directorships in Theo H. Davies & Co., Ltd. and the various other holdings, and left Hawaii to settle on the Isle of Wight in a house in Bonchurch.[4]

As the century turned, most of the old Hawaii that Theo H. Davies had known was drifting away. The Spanish-American war and its jingoism had brought a sense of "manifest destiny" to Americans, who now seemed to wonder why it had taken them so long to join the colonial game. Resistance in America to the annexation of Hawaii collapsed in 1898 after the victory of Admiral Dewey at Manila Bay, and Hawaii was made an American territory that summer. With Theo H. Davies dead, the issue resolved, the old hatreds began to dissolve.

Annexation—the running down of the Hawaiian national flag on the pole outside Iolani Palace—put the finishing touches on the despair of the Hawaiian people. Their proud nation of 300,000 people had been reduced in a century and a quarter to a handful of dispirited survivors. The happy, vigorous past was only a dream; Queen Liliuokalani, now citizen Dominis, retired to the gardens of her house at Washington Place.

Poor Ka'iulani, the brightest star of the Hawaii constellation! After the establishment of the Republic had become indisputable, Theo H. Davies had advised the princess to settle down, and, hopefully, to make a good marriage in England and live out her life as an English lady. But Ka'iulani was drawn to Hawaii, where she felt her duty lay as the last representative of the rulers of her people, and she went home. For several years she had led a desultory existence, visiting friends on the outer islands and listening to Hawaiian plaints about the tragedy of the kingdom. In the spring of 1899 she fell ill with a cold. It persisted into the summer and suddenly she was desperately ill. She died within a few days. Swanzy, Clive Davies and James Wodehouse were all pallbearers at the funeral, and then it was over and business called. Almost the last Davies connection with that past was ended.

The Honolulu Iron Works was so successful that Swanzy and Davies became worried about its monopoly control of sugar mill equipment in the islands. This ended when the Riston Iron Works became a competitor. That created a new worry after they lost an important contract to Riston. If enough of the other planters grew restless they might start more competitive works. In the spring of 1899, profits were so great that it seemed wise to broaden the base of stock. A 25 per cent stock dividend was declared and 1,150 treasury shares were allocated for sale to new investors. The idea was to bring into participation customers and potential customers. C. Brewer was offered 250 shares; the trading and sugar firm of W.G. Irwin, 150; Ben Dillingham, the construction man, was offered 100 shares; others were to go to the Schaefers, Waterhouses, Wilders, and other important persons of the business community.[5] The idea was sound, rumblings in the community stopped, and the Honolulu Iron Works settled down. Sales for 1899 were around half a million dollars; in 1900 they went over $1,250,000. The Iron Works leased land from the Bishop Estate in Kakaako (the site at Punchbowl and Ala Moana) and built a new factory there.

The business was almost unbelievable: they employed 525 men in the shops, 50 of them boilermakers. They had a contract for a new mill at Kihei, one at Spreckelsville, at Wailuku, and one for McBride Sugar Company. The manager, Charles Hedemann, was fishing for a contract to operate shops for a drydock for the U.S. Navy.[6] It seemed nothing for a sugar company to order ten miles of 60-inch irrigation pipe.

It was like that all over the islands, business had never been better than it was in the first days after annexation, and the Davies Company business was better than most. Merchandising sales leaped in 1899 from $84,000 the previous year to $188,000. The next year they went to $194,000. That was an enormous year for Davies: the company earned profits of $410,000 and paid dividends of $140,000. From that point until the depression year 1932, the profits never fell below $150,000, and generally the curve was upward.[7] Sales were computed in the millions of dollars.

In spite of Theo Davies' warnings, Swanzy did take the company into the coffee business, with a mill at Kailua, Kona, and Clive approved completely of the move.[8] Clive and Swanzy got on probably better than Clive might have managed with his own father; their personalities were complementary. Clive was studious and diffident; Swanzy was outgoing and decisive, and the younger man admired the elder.[9] The fact that the growing prosperity of the company and the other investments was unclouded by reverses in these early years of their association meant that there were no questions in the relationship at this crucial period. The combination of Managing Director Swanzy and Junior Director Clive Davies seemed as effective as had Theo H. Davies' personal management of earlier years.

With the virtual retirement and then death of Theo H. Davies, Swanzy emerged as a major figure on the Honolulu business scene. He was an active and respected senior member of the Chamber of Commerce, and several times president of the Hawaiian Sugar Planters Association. In this connection he spent considerable time around the turn of the century on the labor problem that dogged the planters and had troubled them since the American exclusion of Chinese laborers from the mainland had put pressure on Hawaii to stop the import of Chinese labor, too. In the years after the revolution, many Chinese came in, but the pressure was always there, and with the annexation, the U.S. Chinese Exclusion Act became Hawaii's law. Seeing the handwriting on the wall, the sugar planters in 1896 had begun heavy importation of Japanese field laborers. They also considered other races, and around 1900 the Portuguese began arriving again to join those who had come in from Madeira years earlier.[10] When Swanzy visited England and Ireland, which he tried to do every two or three years, he explored the possibilities of bringing in more workers—it was the planters' greatest headache, for sugar cultivation was a slogging, labor-intensive industry, from the plowing of the fields to the cutting and delivery of the cane at the mill. On behalf of the planters, Swanzy explored many avenues. He talked about Koreans, and Italians, and even North Europeans. The Japanese had been growing nervous as they watched and listened along the U.S. west coast and found the signs of agitation for an exclusion act against their nationals as well as Chinese. So the Japanese government, shortly after the turn of the century, frowned on emigration to Hawaii, which further complicated the planters' labor problems. In all this Swanzy spoke for the company and the family. He was in every way, the head of the Davies interests in Hawaii.

Chapter Twenty-Three
SUBTLE CHANGE

A *subtle change had settled* into the relationships between Swanzy and Clive Davies. When Theo H. Davies had been on his deathbed, Clive had asked him what course he should follow in life. Did his father want him to give up Hawaii and remain in England to care for his mother? Or did his father want him to go on as planned? The months of weakening illness, and a failing heart had left Theo Davies virtually exhausted in the face of this new illness, and he could not bring his mind to deal with the subject. He gave no reply. In 1896, Theo H. had read his will to Clive while they were both in Honolulu. "If I should die," the father had then said, "of course you would go back to England." But puzzled at the actuality of death, Clive had asked Swanzy what to do and Swanzy had advised him to come to Honolulu as planned. By 1905 Clive Davies had spent most of nine adult years in Hawaii, and one thing he knew: he did not intend to spend the rest of his years there. Early in life, Clive kept a diary, and at about this time the diary entries indicated how much more he enjoyed the frequent and long holidays he began to take in England. Shooting, fishing in Scotland, cycling on the country lanes, and a beloved automobile (which broke down constantly) dominated his English stays.[1] All the children still made Ravensdale their headquarters and would as long as their mother lived. Ravensdale and all it meant were the parts of life dearest to Clive Davies. Honolulu meant drudgery in a foreign clime, among people he really did not like for the most part: Americans, whose points of view were foreign to his own, in spite of his youth in Honolulu and his four years in the Boston area. That is not to say that Clive shirked; when Clive was in Hawaii, he worked dutifully, addressing himself to the complex problems of the sugar industry in particular.

Laupahoehoe Sugar Company continued to be a perplexing problem for the Davies' interests. Clive appeared in its councils for the first time in December, 1898, when he came to represent the estate of his father. That year Swanzy was elected president of the company, and Clive vice-president. Clive listened as Swanzy explained how the sugar companies worked together. Lorrin Thurston had just returned from Washington, where he had promoted the Hawaiian sugar interests with the new home government. He had spent $60,000, and now Laupahoehoe, along with all the other members of the HSPA had to put up its share of the cost of the mission: 30 cents per ton on the 1898 crop. Clive also began to refresh himself on the intricacies of the refining contracts. Laupahoehoe, like all the other Davies' interests, sent its sugar to the Western Sugar Refining Company in California, but was going to split its crop between that firm and American Sugar Refining Company, for reasons of safety.

The planters were really not very pleased with their refinery relationships and had not been since the quarrel with Spreckels. In spite of the uncertainties of sugar, and the questions about refining, Laupahoehoe was going ahead. In 1901 they harvested 900 acres of new (plant) cane. For 1902 they harvested 1,375 new acres.[2] Throughout they were bedevilled by the labor problem. The HSPA collected contributions from all the plantations to try to bring in new labor. A brief strike of plantation workers at the height of the harvesting season in 1901 emphasized the seriousness of the situation. Next year Laupahoehoe intended to cut cane on 2,395 acres, but the planting system had to change in view of the coming of U.S. laws and the labor difficulties. The Davies' interests began to convert to contracts with individual planters, most of them Japanese, who had leased land from the company or from the Hawaii government. Laupahoehoe, for example, lent money to the planters against the crop, provided fertil-

The C&H Refinery established at Crockett, California, in 1906. The California and
Hawaiian Sugar Company was set up as a cooperative owned by the Hawaiian sugar
industry to refine and market Hawaiian sugar production.

izer, and through its supervisors managed the cultivation and the harvest. The 1901 crop was not a good one; the water supply failed in mid-season and the extensive flume system developed at Laupahoehoe had to be abandoned for the year. Two hundred perfectly good acres of cane could not be harvested at all and had to stand over. Labor was scarce, half the Japanese planters left the area, totally discouraged by their inability to make a living. Then in November came rains, which brought down 40 inches of water in 36 hours, and floods. All the high trestles but five were washed out. It was a completely local storm, affecting no other plantation, but it cost Laupahoehoe 4000 tons of sugar that year.

The next year, the plantation leaned even more heavily on individual planters; its expenditures for labor in 1902 were $99,000 and advances to planters were $65,000. Even though the company was not paying dividends it was making profits: in 1902 the earnings were $195,000, on a gross income of $495,000. The shipments of sugar were split among three refineries: 29 per cent went to New York, 21 per cent to San Francisco and 49 per cent to Philadelphia. Laupahoehoe, they were finding, could be extremely profitable, if the right cane were used. They had discovered that one of William Lidgate's problems had been in his cane. They were experimenting constantly, sometimes successfully, sometimes not. The Lahaina cane that did so well elsewhere was no good at all for the North Hilo lands. But they were finding and developing their own varieties, and the results were increasingly successful.[3]

In 1905, Hawaii's sugar companies decided to get together and work in common to end the refining difficulties that had dogged them since the quarrel with Spreckels. In all, 37 Hawaii sugar companies agreed to set up Sugar Factors, to deal as a whole with the Hawaii crop. In the year just passed Laupahoehoe had shipped 6000 bags of sugar for sale in San Francisco, 34,500 bags to San Francisco that went by rail east for sale, 12,000 bags east by sailing ship around Cape Horn, and 39,000 by steamer around Cape Horn. The price secured in San Francisco was 6.8 cents per pound, in the east 6.1 cents, and for that sugar shipped by sailing ship 5.1 cents. It was hardly a satisfactory state of affairs. A sugar mill had been established long before at Crockett, California, but it had been expensive and in the long run unsuccessful. The HSPA planned to reorganize the Crockett operation and try again as a cooperative. So the California and Hawaiian Sugar Refining Co. was organized in San Francisco and Crockett.[4] On his way back to Honolulu from home leave, Clive stopped off in San Francisco to confer with President George M. Rolph. Clive was anxious lest this effort prove as unsatisfactory as the earlier one. He made a number of suggestions about management, all of which Rolph apparently accepted. So, they prepared to butt heads with Western refinery, and the various sugar companies (33 of them finally) subscribed to the stock, on the basis of the tonnage they shipped. The issue was $2,000,000 in shares, Laupahoehoe holding 310 shares at $100 par value; in all the company represented 80 per cent of Hawaii sugar production.[5]

The Davies' interests continued to be broad. Clive became a director of Theo H. Davies, Liverpool, which opened a Vancouver office, and started an iron works, called the Vancouver Engineering Works. George was involved in this company as well, more perhaps in spirit than he was in Theo H. Davies, Hawaii. For while George came out to Hawaii dutifully to take on his responsibilities as director of the trading company and various other holdings, he did not leave much impact on the Hawaii scene. The Davies company under heirs was an entirely different company from the company when the founder was alive.

Swanzy bore the major responsibility, which had to be managed in a new way, since he was not the major factor in the company. He did it very well; there was never a whisper of complaint about Swanzy's management. The work was telling, and so hard on his health that in the spring of 1906, on a business trip to the United States, he collapsed in Chicago and had to be hospitalized. It became apparent then that considerably more help in management was needed than Swanzy was getting. For several years he had been struggling with ghosts. When it became apparent that the boys did not share their father's passion for hard work, Swanzy wanted to bring more directors into the company. It was not good having only five directors, with two of them absentee, which seemed to happen more and more.

Clive argued for the ways of the past, but in the end the number of directors had to be increased, although Swanzy was unable to persuade Clive that the number should be left indefinite, which would have made it possible to appoint new directors with a quorum.[6] Swanzy did win a struggle to have E. H. Wodehouse, younger son of James Wodehouse, made a director, and Wodehouse then joined the inner circle of management.[7] All this activity was essential because Theo H. Davies Company under Swanzy was expanding. They had bought the Pearl City Fruit Company, a pineapple cannery, west of Honolulu. Pearl City was to pineapple what the original Davies sugar mills were to sugar; it produced no pineapples and did not own any land. The agent for marketing was T.H. Dole Company.

When George and Clive Davies were in Hawaii, they attended board meetings, but they seemed to be in Hawaii less and less. Having finished a long vacation in England in the fall of 1905, Clive and Edith came out to Hawaii. Clive and George were filled with good intentions; Clive had bought a lot on Tantalus mountain, overlooking Honolulu, and proposed building a country house up there, to indicate his commitment to Hawaii. He did build and stayed his two years (George went home). In 1906 Arthur L. and Theo H. came out and were elected to the boards of various Davies corporations. But the exposure did not take. Arthur quickly decided that his vocation lay in the ministry and he studied for ordination in the Church of England. Theo had no head or inclination for business, and needed none; his father had provided so well in the will that none of the children need bestir themselves in trade. Harry was still a schoolboy.

So in 1906 it was apparent that of all the Davies children only Clive was willing to apply himself to the business fully, and George much less so. It was also clear that Clive was not totally engrossed in business the way his father had been. He was much more enthusiastic about his current motor car, or his tennis game and the heavy social schedule of *haole* Honolulu, than about the prospects of the next shipload of merchandise. It was odd, in a way, because he did have a head for business, and a phenomenal memory (aided by meticulous note-taking) and in emergency, such as Swanzy's illness in Chicago, he functioned very efficiently as manager of the company. He and Wodehouse brought off a contract to build a million-dollar Hamakua Ditch[8] which ran 16 miles through the rugged mountains, to bring a steady supply of water from Honokaa to Hamakua and other plantations on the Hamakua coast, which would also add guarantees to their own sugar lands against droughts such as those that plagued Hamakua Mill from time to time. But England called loudly, and after Nellie Davies died at Ravensdale in 1907, somehow the yearning to establish home base in the mother country seemed to grow rather than diminish for all of them. Clive and George were in Hawaii at the time, George managing the financial end as planned, and Clive taking charge of sugar and detail in Swanzy's absence.[9] In 1908, Clive went home again to England. The pattern was now established: one year in England, two in Hawaii, with overlap between himself and George. That year it also became apparent that none of the other heirs had any but a financial interest in the earnings of the Hawaii enterprises.

Harry Llanover Davies, the youngest son, came of age that year, and his attitude was plain. Swanzy wanted to buy the outstanding stock in the Ookala plantation on Hawaii island, and asked Clive what position the family would take if asked to invest in it along with Theo H. Davies & Company. Clive thought the boys would be interested, but probably not the girls, since their sugar dividends remained in trust under Theo H. Davies' will. But how far the other brothers would be willing to invest remained an unknown factor.[10] Everything about the family and the business was changing. Clive had already made up his mind that in a very few years he would leave Hawaii and the real responsibility he bore for a far less demanding role with the company. Swanzy had seen this change coming for years. In the spring of 1909 he told George Davies, who was in Honolulu, that Clive's plans must be made clear; the staff had sensed Clive's growing lack of interest, and the whole process was corrosive to morale. So George wrote Clive and asked for a decision. Clive squirmed. He had not wanted to be so blunt, but it was true, he admitted, that he had been thinking for half a dozen years about the date that he would "follow Father's course of establishing myself on this side". He had been thinking about 1913, he said. He wanted to withdraw then, but continue as a director, and hold himself ready to come out to Honolulu to meet any emergency, and to spend every alternate winter in Hawaii. But Swanzy said this really would not do in terms of the company. If he was going to withdraw from active participation, that had to be made clear to everyone. Wodehouse was Swanzy's candidate to take over Clive's areas of responsibility, but Wodehouse had to be given the responsibility if the plan was to work. Could not Clive come out in the next month or so, and settle it?[11] No, Clive could not. There was an "important" function involving his wife's family that must be attended to in June. So he could not come until the 12th of June, and then he wanted to be back in England for Christmas. Swanzy saw that was no good, and he realized that the problems, such as they were, would have to be resolved without consultation with Clive until after the fact. So the hurried trip was abandoned, and Clive spent the summer touring about England. After his mother's death, and the sale of Ravensdale as provided in the will of his father, Clive had taken a house in Tunbridge Wells, but he had no intention of settling there. The area was too close to London, and was becoming commuting territory for men who spent their weeks in business in town. Clive wanted to be further away, and secluded. He found just such a spot in the middle of Hampshire, a high hill, almost like the site of a medieval castle, surrounded by rills and valleys, as secluded as one could wish. Here he would build his house, and after two more years in Honolulu he would come back to England just as his father had done, to take up life as a country gentleman, with three farms, 325 acres, and all the gardens and appurtenances of a fine estate.

Chapter Twenty-Four
CLIVE DAVIES GOES HOME

A*fter the turn of the twentieth century* and annexation, the Honolulu Iron Works suddenly began to expand with explosive speed. No move could have been wiser than to bring new capital and participation from the Honolulu community, as had been done. By 1907 the company was doing business all over the world. Eventually it would build factories in China and Cuba, Formosa, the Philippines, and half a dozen other countries. Swanzy was president of the company; J.H. Robertson of C. Brewer & Co., Ltd. was vice-president. Davies' control of the directorate was maintained by the presence of Clive Davies as treasurer and E.H. Wodehouse as secretary of the company. But here again, control was no problem because under manager Charles Hedemann the Iron Works could scarcely handle the business generated. There was no quarrel about the direction of the company.

Sugar planters in Cuba expanded their operations as soon as American forces drove the Spanish from the land, and it became an American economic appendage if not a political possession. Theo Davies' long cultivation of Henry Havemeyer paid off for the Iron Works, for Havemeyer, the merchant banker, was interested in Cuban sugar. More and more planters looked to Honolulu for their machinery, the Cuban-American Sugar Company, Colonial Sugar Co., the Aguirre Co., among them. Honolulu Iron Works had kept a New York office at 11 Broadway, advertising its services as "Consulting and Contracting Engineers, Sugar Factories, and Equipment." Williams, Dimond, which had also opened a New York office, was instrumental in helping the Iron Works. For example, in 1907 Williams, Dimond arranged to charter a ship to deliver an entire sugar factory to the Taiwan port of Takao. Not all the components were built in Hawaii; HIW bought centrifugals and dryer machinery in Boston, and some machinery in Germany, assembled the lot with its own Honolulu machinery and parts, and shipped it off to the Japanese owners. Hedemann, who went to Cuba that year, wanted Swanzy to go with him, but in the uncertain state of the management of the Honolulu business, Swanzy did not feel that he could be away for so long.[1]

For many reasons, Swanzy kept pressing Clive Davies for a definite decision and timetable for his future with the company. For reasons of his own, Clive Davies kept delaying. Perhaps it was conscience; his father had remained active in the Honolulu business until he was 55, and Clive was talking about "retiring" twenty years earlier than that. Swanzy's insistence reflected his assessment of the many tasks that could be accomplished only by a dedicated senior management. The labor situation was growing increasingly murky. In 1907 the Japanese government restricted the various Japanese firms handling emigration to Hawaii to about three dozen emigrants each, per month, with half of these to be women. (This was a result of the "Gentlemen's Agreement" of 1907 between the U.S. and Japanese governments.) Hawaii planters were seeking plantation labor all over the world, from Madeira, Puerto Rico, and the Philippines in particular. The California and Hawaii sugar cooperative demanded attention from the planter-owners. The banking arrangements in San Francisco no longer met the needs of the Davies enterprises, and Swanzy hoped that money could be found in London, since the Davies business was British business. The whole merchandising operation needed a good overhaul to bring it up to modern standards. But to undertake these tasks, Swanzy needed first-class, dedicated assistants; he felt he was not getting the full attention of either Clive or George and that a crisis was approaching because of it.[2] And then came the first strike of sugar workers.

One can only say that the sugar planters brought the trouble on themselves through short-sighted labor policy. Japanese had been coming in by the thousands for seven years. By 1907 there were 100,000 Japanese in the islands and they were the majority of the population. But Japanese laborers were paid less than Portuguese and Puerto Ricans, one theory being that since they were orientals their standard of life had no relationship to that of occidentals. The occidentals received $21 a month for work in the fields, and the Japanese sugar workers got $18 for the same work. So in the spring of 1909 about 5,000 Japanese sugar workers went on strike. The strike came at a time when Swanzy was away, and Clive Davies was taking one of his long holidays in England. George was alone to face the crisis. It was a worse situation than even Swanzy's absence indicated: H. Hackfeld, H.P. Baldwin and J.P. Cooke were also away from the island when the strike broke. The planters' association lawyers immediately brought pressure on the territorial government, and charges of riot and conspiracy were levelled against the strike leaders. In Honolulu the strike went to court, but in the fields, the machetes were idle until the planters could bring in strikebreakers. The Puerto Ricans and Portuguese began to arrive, with some Filipinos, and they were hired at $1.50 a day to cut cane—twice what the Japanese were being paid.[3] The Davies were no more enlightened than the rest; from England Clive wrote congratulating the HSPA for refusing to make any concessions to the strikers. "It is a fight on the question of control of the labour force,"[4] he wrote Swanzy from his comfortable perch in England. Perhaps it was, but Clive Davies did not seem to realize that he was parroting the ancient cry of the capitalist, that he must have all but life-or-death control over his working force. This was a question, Clive said, of breaking the "Makino gang" and the planters must show "no quarter." For in the final analysis, as Clive understood very well, "it is a question of dollars and cents." "It is a pity," he said also, "that wages were not raised a little before the agitation came to a head." And once the planters had won, and the workers had gone back to work, then certainly they must go into the wage matter and make some raises. So Clive Davies, the capitalist, showed himself to be a man of good will and probity; he simply shared the attitude of his contemporary capitalists. For some reason he never equated the demands of the sugar workers for a living wage with his own family's situation.

Laupahoehoe's revenue for 1908 had been $803,000 with a net profit of $196,00 or nearly 25 per cent on sales.[5] To Clive's satisfaction, the sugar planters won the strike within a few weeks. The Japanese workers had virtually no resources to sustain them, they were ejected from company housing, and the editor of the Japanese newspaper *Nippu Jiji* was arrested along with the strike leaders and brought to trial for conspiracy. So the strike failed, the Japanese went back to work, and the plantations raised wages a little. The major result for the Davies family, was the realization that it could happen again, and some guarantees must be secured against a repetition. The best guarantee was to find new labor sources. Swanzy, on behalf of his own interests and those of the Hawaiian Sugar Planters Association, was encouraged to make a world trip to survey the market and try to solve the labor problem. But before he could do this, he absolutely must have a commitment from Clive Davies so he could put the management house in order. One did not make a long trip around the world and leave loose ends.

Clive was still reluctant to commit himself to any change. Swanzy wanted him to abandon the vice-consulate, which Clive had inherited from Walker, and George seconded the matter because he could not get on with British Consul Forster. If necessary Clive would resign the post. And as for his plans, he finally committed himself: he would go out to Honolulu in 1910 for two years, and then resign as a managing director. He would come back every other winter, alternating with George. So finally the die was cast, and Swanzy knew what he faced. Wodehouse would have to be brought along, and they should have another director. But there was no one in the organization with the experience or capability at the moment. For the time being, they would just have to make do.

Clive did do one major service for the company during that 1909 holiday. He was well acquainted with R. L. Barclay, of Barclay and Company, the bankers, and he went to see Barclay to try to secure loans for Honolulu. Why could not Barclay expand into the Pacific? R. L. Barclay explained that they could, indeed, and as Clive said, they could secure much higher rates of interest than they were getting in England. But to have their money so far away, no matter how effective their agents, would make the Barclays nervous. It was just not worth the effort, said Banker Barclay, and Clive soon found that other banks agreed. He went to the London & Westminster Bank, which did a large business in India and in the Straits Settlements of Malaya, but all the firms in Asia to which they lent money had London houses, and the loans were made to the London firms. If the Davies company wanted to borrow in England, then the whole business would have to be reorganized with headquarters in London. Otherwise there was no way money could be borrowed except on bills of lading for sugar, and then the bankers would demand such swift repayment that the whole purpose would be lost. If Swanzy was concerned about the ability of Williams, Dimond & Co. to find the capital to meet their expanding business needs, he must look to America for the money.[6]

Another growing burden to the harried Swanzy was the burgeoning of the merchandising department. Hilo, in particular, was growing rapidly. Adam Lindsay was the manager in Hilo, and he was doing a good job; but he needed more support than just the one assistant he had, T. Guard. James Wakefield of the Honolulu office was sent over and came back with a recommendation that Lindsay and Guard be given a percentage of the profits, on a two to one basis, and that the grocery, dry goods and hardware departments all be expanded, a lumber division added, and a new, large warehouse be built at Hilo.[7] All these changes were made, and Hilo continued to grow in importance to the company.

Before Swanzy could go off around the world, as he intended to do on his labor quest, he had to help resolve the problems of the Hawaii sugar factors with their Crockett refinery. Since California and Hawaii had managed to line up most of the planters, Western Sugar Refining Company was reduced to buying sugar for its customers from C & H. At the moment Western was buying on a year-to-year basis, but the Hawaii producers wanted a more substantial agreement—a five-year contract. Western was not willing to sign such a contract, largely because, as both parties knew, a sugar surge had begun in the Philippines, and Western Refining hoped in a few years to have enough 96° Philippines sugar available to forget about the Hawaii market. President Rolph began negotiating with Western as Swanzy prepared to set out on his long trip.[8] When Swanzy left, he went to Europe and then to various places in the far east, including India, Hong Kong, Japan, and the Philippines. It was the Philippines which commanded most attention, for Swanzy and the other planters saw that in the islands they could solve their labor problems if they could make the necessary arrangements. The advantage, of course, was that the Philippines, as an American protectorate since 1898, were not subject to the strictures that covered orientals in general in a racist American society. The Hawaii planters were already talking to various businessmen in the Philippines about growing sugar there, and Honolulu Iron Works wanted Swanzy to look into the possibilities of selling machinery. A man named Carman came to Honolulu to try to raise capital to build a sugar plantation and mill on Mindoro Island, and suggested that Honolulu Iron Works build the mill, taking half its pay in stock. This suggestion was greeted coolly by Clive Davies, who was involved in the negotiations, and Mr. Carman went off to the mainland to try.[9] Davies asked Swanzy to look into the matter, and particularly the feasibility of a sugar installation near Iloilo. By this time the HSPA had opened an office in Manila to encourage immigration, and various businessmen there were seeking Hawaii capital to help them start their own sugar business. Just then the idea did not get very far with the Honolulu businessmen.

After Swanzy's return from Asia, Clive prepared to leave Hawaii and settle in England, as he had so long threatened to do. Since there was no changing that plan, Swanzy and the others fell in with it, although Swanzy felt strongly that the business would suffer because of the determination of the second generation of Davies' to be absentee owners. It was quite different from Theo H. Davies' departure, for the firm's founder had made sure two of his sons were involved in the business before he finally opted to remain in England. What Clive and George planned was entirely different, but there was no stopping them; they had their minds made up, and neither yet had a son. Clive went home and began building his dream house in Hampshire, a 38-room mansion he called Hawkley Hurst, which demanded ten inside servants and a force of six gardeners. The Hurst had three tennis courts (two grass and one macadam) and extensive gardens on the hill overlooking the Hampshire countryside. It was a magnificent house, fit for a very rich squire, and that, of course, was precisely what Theophilus Clive Davies now set out to be.

Chapter Twenty-Five

MANAGEMENT TROUBLES

Management,—*that was the problem* created by the insistence of Clive and George Davies that they should spend minimal periods in Hawaii. Swanzy carried almost all the responsibility for management, assisted by Ernest Wodehouse as junior director and by Baird, who now functioned as a director and officer of most of the companies. The Davies brothers opened an office in the City of London and dutifully manned it, dealing by correspondence with the problems that arose in Hawaii. But if this was management, it was able to succeed only because of the sharp attention to detail by the hard-working Swanzy. Many a time he must have wished that Walker had not quit at the turn of the century. But Walker had been unable to stand more strain; he was a big, ruddy-faced, hypertensive type, and the tensions of working under the beady eye and sharp pen of Theo Davies had exhausted him. In 1908, when Swanzy was visiting London, Walker came up from Bonchurch for a reunion and discussion of business affairs. For even from afar, Walker had continued to function in the business, helping out where he could. Walker put up at the Wilton Hotel, his usual place, and Swanzy met him there on September 21. They had a pleasant evening and, at the end of it, they parted at the foot of the marble staircase, and Walker began to go up. On the staircase he suffered a stroke and fell backwards, striking his head on the edge of a marble stair. Swanzy rushed to his side, and the hotel staff summoned an ambulance. Walker was hurried to the hospital, but he lingered only a few hours.[1]

By 1913, Clive Davies was as well ensconced in Hawkley Hurst and English country life as if he had never left home. He had two motor cars now, a Packard and Renault. Usually one of them was in the shop for repairs, and the other busy motoring various members of the family about the Hampshire countryside.[2] Motoring was always an adventure; usually a drive of 75 miles involved at least one flat or blowout; on one occasion Clive was caught by the local police in a speed trap, but got off when the officers could not prove that he was travelling at the outrageous speed of 35 miles an hour because their clocks were inaccurate.[3] He was the real gentleman; as a staunch Unionist he worked for the party, and went to the Marchioness of Londonderry's receptions when he was in town. He went to Parliament, and the Horse Show. In the country he was the squire, a member of the vestry of the Hawkley Church, and a gentleman farmer. He helped organize the local cricket club. He hired keepers and established a shoot. He hired a landscape gardener to build a formal garden at Hawkley Hurst. His secretary, Mr. Bird, attended to the details in town, so that Clive could go up on Tuesdays and return on Fridays, except during the summer and in holiday times, when often he did not go to London at all. In the fall of 1913, he journeyed to New York to meet with Swanzy and settle certain business affairs.[4] This pattern repeated itself, and Clive never did actually resign his directorships or leave all in other hands. Swanzy seemed content to work with Clive as a non-resident chairman of the board, with Swanzy functioning as chief executive officer. Of course, those terms were not in use, but the concept was the same.

By 1913, the Davies family pattern was clear, too. The others had come of age and were marrying. Alice married Wolcott Warner (they had no children). Violet Mary married Major F. H. Young. George married Lady Mary Ellen Birney and had five children, three boys and two girls. Arthur, who became the Rev. Arthur Whitcliffe Davies, married Lilian Mabel Birney, and they had two boys and a girl. Theo M., in the throes of a broken engagement in 1913, would go off to Canada to forget and, having done so, almost immediately would return to marry Dorothy Mitford and have five children, four girls and a boy. Harry Llanover would marry Barbara Childeroy and they would have one son. Finally, Clive and Edith would have six children, four daughters and two sons. And already in this last year before the Davies world was turned upside down, it was apparent that five of Theo H. Davies' children were interested in the Hawaii business only as a source of dividends. No problem had yet developed, but that was because the dividends were eminently satisfactory. In 1910, dividends from the company were $154,000. In 1911 they came to $175,000. In 1912 they totalled $238,000. True to the conservative philosophy Swanzy had learned from Theo H. Davies, dividends represented about half of income: the company was investing the surplus. It owned 500 shares of Hamakua Plantation stock, worth $50,000; 5,000 shares of MacBride Sugar Company, valued at $100,000. It also owned 797 shares of Honolulu Iron Works, greatly undervalued at $79,700, and $50,000 in stock in

Clive Davies' famous Packard motor car in 1913. He had two autos then. One was usually in the shop and the other, on the road, almost always had some sort of breakdown on any journey over a mile or two. Here the chauffeur changes a tyre. (No, not a tire. This was Hawkley Hurst.)

American Hawaiian Steamship Company; and shares in Pacific Chemical and Fertilizer Company and the Pearl City Fruit Company, Swanzy's venture in the pineapple business.[5]

That $50,000 in American Hawaiian Steamship Company stock represented one of Swanzy's brave ventures. Captain Matson had done so well in the early years of the Hawaii sugar trade that he decided to attempt to monopolize the whole trade. In this he was backed by Hackfeld, Castle & Cooke, C. Brewer, and Alexander & Baldwin, but the Davies Company balked at the rates and at the monopoly and threw its business to the fledgling American Hawaiian Steamship Company. To be sure, this decision angered Matson, and certainly did not endear Davies to the other Big Four. But that was the sort of vigorous management that Swanzy maintained as he took almost single-handed command of the business.

The change in management was apparent in the office. Swanzy occupied the first and largest office on the ground floor of the building on Queen Street. Wodehouse had an office of almost that size next to Swanzy's. Clive's office was next to Wodehouse's, and next to that was an office of similar size, occupied by George and J. N. S. Williams. Out in back at desks in a bullpen were Baird and Tim Healy, another clerk. Upstairs, a large office without partitions was used by the rest of the staff, nineteen members, from clerks to office boys and a telephone operator.[6] From here Swanzy managed the Davies businesses; from the moribund Kailua Coffee Company (which had lost $50,000 in 1901 and was finally closed out in 1906) to the struggling Pearl City Fruit Company and the immensely successful Honolulu Iron Works and sugar investments. As for sugar, Laupahoehoe had begun paying dividends in 1908 and paid them (small but steady) until 1913, when a bad year brought a loss of $50,000. But Hamakua was more typical of the Davies sugar investments; it paid dividends of $300,000 in 1908.

Even there a new element had entered the Davies picture. In 1909 Hamakua Mill had a profit of only $162,000, but paid dividends of $165,000. It was true that the company had an earned surplus on hand of $722,000, but Theo H. Davies would never have countenanced payout of such a sum, given the profits of the year. And in 1913, although Hamakua too suffered from the drought of that year and actually lost $1,600, the company paid out $40,000 in dividends.[7]

The change in approach represented the change in the attitude of the owners of the companies. Alexander Young, Theo Davies' old manager of Honolulu Iron Works, had used his income from the investment in Waiakea Mill to go into the building business. In 1910 and 1911, when Waiakea paid *only* 30 per cent on investment and the Youngs were not very happy because they wanted more money, Swanzy, Wodehouse and Baird tried to make them understand a few of the financial facts of life: for one, in seven years Waiakea's lease on its sugar lands would end, and the company should be building large reserves. No one knew what attitude the government would take in seven years. It might declare all those lands up for homesteading by settlers. It might hold them for release to assure the survival of Waiakea Mill. But the company had to be prepared for any of several developments, and that meant saving money.[8] So, although the Davies interests had kept on expanding the sugar holdings (they also owned Kaiwiki Sugar Company now), investors began to have a different attitude. Nor were all those investors outsiders.

In 1905 Theo M. Davies and Arthur had become stockholders in Hamakua, for example. In 1910, Harry Llanover Davies became a stockholder. These three stockholders represented absentee ownership in every sense of the word. None of them had more than a nostalgic interest in Hawaii, and Harry hardly had that, since he left the islands when he was about a year old. Swanzy, Clive, and George represented conservative management, although Clive's level of expenditure had risen when he built Hawkley Hurst, but they were subject to outside pressures from the rest of the family. All of them were basically living on dividends and raising a large number of Theo H. Davies' grandchildren, twenty-four in all, who in time would claim their own shares of the inheritance.[9]

Of the new ventures, the one that seemed to have the most potential in the first years of the 20th century was Pearl City Fruit Company. Swanzy had made a careful study of pineapple before buying the cannery. He established an office in San Francisco to handle this and other business, and by 1909 was much encouraged about the prospects. The competition was stiff, particularly from Dole, but Swanzy had Alexander & Baldwin as agents in Tacoma and Seattle, and he was confident that eventually Pearl City Fruit Company would be very profitable. Dole found the marketing of canned pineapple equally difficult, and he began selling "filtered juice" on the market. Clive Davies thought that a futile operation. Someone told him that Dole was not getting any repeat orders for his juice, and that it cost more to manufacture than he could get for it.[10] So much for Clive's prescience in the matter of pineapples: Dole pineapple juice created a fortune for his company. But who was to worry? Everything was going up, up, up. Laupahoehoe's capitalization was increased in 1911 to $500,000, but its assets were $1.1 million. To be sure, some additions and changes were needed—but the company still financed these out of earnings and surplus as it always had and paid handsome dividends even when they were not called for. The new method of control was for Clive or George, or whoever was in Hawaii, to serve on various boards, and then to resign from the boards as he left the territory, in compliance with the law that stipulated that the majority of directors must be residents. Under Swanzy all was going extremely well. Like Theo Davies before him, he managed to bring all sorts of new bits and pieces of capital to the firm. They took over the agency for the Kauai Fruit and Land Company with $5,000 in stock. They had interests in schooners and steamers and, as the steamers took over, they sold off the schooners, usually at a profit. In 1913, they started Kukaiau Ranch at the top of the lands of Kukaiau sugar company, next to Hamakua. The object was to grow mules for the plantations and mills, and cattle for the grocery departments of the Davies company in Honolulu and Hilo. They made contracts with the slaughter houses in both places. Together with Humuula Sheep Station Co., Kaneohe Ranch Co., and Haleakala Ranch, they owned the Hawaii Meat Company. It was a big operation for greenhorns to take over, $80,000 worth of cattle, $16,000 worth of horses, $2,400 worth of mules and an assortment of sheep, pigs and other livestock. But from the first it was profitable and paid a two per cent quarterly dividend on the stock, all of which was owned by Theo H. Davies & Co. except the shares necessary for directors to qualify*.[11] Clive Davies was in England when Kukaiau was acquired, that winter of 1913–14; it was George's turn to spend it in Hawaii. In the spring, after a holiday in Switzerland, Clive went out to Honolulu. He spent the month of May largely on Hawaii Island, going over the plantations and mills, and then returned to Honolulu. Because the Davies company was a shipping agent, they had some advance warning of the worrisome state of political affairs in Europe that July. The British Embassy in Washington cabled Davies, asking them for information about German warships in the Pacific. The light cruiser *Nurnberg* of the German East Asia Cruiser Squadron sailed on July 27 from Honolulu, after putting in for coal and supplies, and Clive reported this fact to the Embassy. The Foreign Office had carefully established lines of communication with its offices around the world. Consul Gordon of Honolulu had a copy of the secret Foreign Office code, and messages began coming in, asking for information. Gordon had gone on home leave, and Clive Davies was in charge of consular affairs. But Gordon had taken the code book with him, and Clive could not understand a word of the messages. He sent all the information he thought the Foreign Office might want, in the clear, but it was not a very satisfactory arrangement. And then came August, and war. The lives and the affairs of the Davies family would never be quite the same again.

---

*Later some Kukaiau stock was sold, and Wodehouse, for example, secured about 20 percent of the total.

Chapter Twenty-Six

WAR FOR THE DAVIES

The beginning of the war with Germany appalled the Davies family as it did so much of the world, and they sought participation in England's effort. Clive was 43 years old, with four children, and not regarded as combatant material. George tried to enlist in the volunteer army and was turned down because of his age. In those early days anyone over forty was "over the hill." But George persevered and managed to secure a commission in the Territorials. He was not only patriotic, he was lucky: his headquarters turned out to be only 18 miles from a house he had recently bought in Gloucester. He commuted, and as soon as the fighting began, his wife took in refugees. So did the Clive Davies family.

The tragedy of the war was brought home to the Davieses almost in the first drive. Harry Llanover Davies, the baby of the family, held the King's commission and was one of the first to go across the Channel with General Sir John French's British Expeditionary Force. Harry was an artillery officer, and his battery soon moved into the Artois sector of Belgium to stop the German drive toward the sea. The British moved up, but were pushed back as the Germans rolled through Ghent and Ostend. On the night of October 23, the battalion was again moved back and ordered to dig in at a new position. They reached the position around midnight and then began placing the guns. The Germans were on the move and threatened to overrun them. Lt. Harry Davies was supervising the section, when he was hit in the abdomen by a rifle bullet. They moved him into the aid station, which was a farm house, and put him down in a bed of fresh hay. Captain R. G. Finlayson, his commanding officer, wrote a cheery note to Barbara Davies, saying that although Harry had been badly wounded, he should recover. That was October 25. Two days later, the battle raging within three hundred yards of the farmhouse, Harry Davies died of his wounds and was buried in the farmyard next to one of his soldiers.[1] Harry and Barbara had been married four years, and all the family marvelled that their union seemed to have been touched by some superior force of happiness. Barbara had learned to hunt, so she could participate in Harry's favorite activity. He had comforted her when she was depressed, and she him, and they spent almost all their time together, oblivious of the rest of the world. They had one child, a boy, now not quite four years old. A distraught Barbara took the boy to live, at least for the next few months, with Harry's older sister Alice, who, childless and married to an invalid, welcomed them as a mother. Somehow the tragedy brought all the family closer than they had been in recent years.[2]

The war in Hawaii was an entirely different matter: if the Davies in England suffered, their interests in Hawaii prospered almost indecently. The price of sugar leaped as the British began buying every bag in sight. Laupahoehoe Sugar Company, which had shown a loss of $40,000 in 1913, earned a profit of $140,000 in 1914, and two and a half times that much the following year.[3] The United States was neutral in the war in these early years, and so there were only indirect reverberations of the struggle in Europe and on the sea. The German cruiser *Nurnberg* returned to Honolulu for provisions and coal on September 1, taking care to observe the neutrality laws of the United States. But after leaving Honolulu she headed straight for Fanning Island, where the British had finally located their Pacific cable station. The German crew went ashore and blew up the British cable buildings, cut the cable, and looted the office safe of $3,000 in gold. When the Germans left, the survivors wirelessed the British consulate in Honolulu for help. The Davies company (a British company) dispatched a ship with provisions and dispatches, and her captain (British) took pictures which he brought back to show the world how much unnecessary damage the Germans had done.[4]

In October, 1914, the German gunboat *Geier* arrived from Tsingtao. She had been sent away by the Admiral Graf von Spee when he began his dash around South America, heading for home with the German East Asia Cruiser Squadron. The *Geier* was too old and her guns too small to be of much use. In fact, her guns had been transferred to steamers to create auxiliary cruisers. She steamed into Honolulu harbor and made a great show of planning to steam out again. Two Japanese cruisers rushed up to cover the waters offshore and sink the *Geier* if she dared go out. But had the Japanese captains spoken to the men of Honolulu Iron Works they would not have wasted their time for three weeks, hanging about Honolulu harbor, waiting. For as the HIW men discovered when the *Geier* sent a few pieces of machinery ashore, the German gunboat was incapable of going anywhere. At the battle of Coronel, Admiral Von Spee destroyed a British squadron and the *Geier* had accomplished her purpose — tying up the Japanese and preventing their joining up with British Admiral Cradock's force in time to save it. So the *Geier* was interned. The Japanese did offer the Americans of Waikiki a thrill or two. One night they captured a German motor schooner that tried to thread its way around Diamond Head but did not come in close to shore. Her crew was captured and she was burned in front of the beach. A few nights later, a sister schooner sneaked in around Koko Head and Diamond Head, braving the reef rather than the three mile limit, and she made it into port.[5]

The Davies company occupied an odd position during these months. Nine German freighters were in Honolulu harbor and some of their cargo was consigned to British customers, including Theo H. Davies & Co., Ltd. For years, Davies had probably been closer to the Hackfeld company than any other in Honolulu; Theo H. Davies and H. Hackfeld were friends, and the relationship had lingered. But now Hackfeld's manager was the German consul. The addition of the crew of *Geier* and those of the merchant ships to the German population made that group quite formidable. Hackfeld published the official news daily in German in the local newspapers and spread rumours about German successes and British defeats. The atmosphere grew strained. At the Chamber of Commerce it was hard for Swanzy to sit down at the table with the Hackfeld people. But what could not be changed must be endured, if alone. All the Davies family had gone back to England, leaving Swanzy in complete control for the first time and, of course, with more worries than ever. But the difficulties were at least palliated by the large profits the war brought the trading house.

Clive Davies had little thought to give the Honolulu business, for his life was bound up in England's war. His patriotism had asserted itself the moment he headed home in August ("A blessing to be once more on British territory," he wrote in his diary as he boarded RMS *Laconia* in New York Harbor). At home ("43 years old, not one grey hair, and I weigh 154 pounds soaking wet") he registered for special constabulary duty and then tried to organize the home guards at Liss, a nearby market town in Hampshire. He was appointed to "the committee." He was eager to "do something for England" but England did not seem to want him very badly. At least he was made commandant of his unit of the Home Guard, got into his drab uniform two or three times a week, and drilled with the troops. They also practiced firing on a rifle range a few times. By the end of 1915 drills were down to once a week and suspended during such holidays as Christmas week. But they took it seriously. Colonel Otter-Barry, a neighbor who was a retired army officer, lectured them on outpost duty just before New Year's day, and then came to tea at Clive's home. The next day there was supposed to be a standfast shoot on the Davies hunting preserve, but it was a wet day and the shoot was postponed until Saturday. So instead, Davies and Otter-Barry "reconnoitered" on the East hill (in deadly seriousness). Davies valued his farm stock for the end of the year, and went to church at noon. Then on Saturday, January 1, they held the shoot.[6] As was Clive's fashion on the first day of the New Year, he assessed the old year in terms of expenses and income. He was still building on Hawkley Hurst and had spent $25,000 on the place that year. But his income for 1914 was $164,000, and when one deducted all expenses, Hawkley Hurst construction, living expenses, charities and subscriptions, (which were

$19,000) and all taxes, which came to $12,000, Clive Davies had a surplus that year in his personal account of $102,000.[7] It was not, all considered, a bad life for the grandson of an impecunious Congregational minister from Ludlow.

The war dragged on. George F. Davies went to France with his unit, the 5th Gloucestershires. Clive took a course in musketry and went to camp where he was a platoon leader. Colonel Otter-Barry was his commander, and it was embarrassing to have Mrs. Otter-Barry insisting that Davies take all his meals with them; Mrs. O-B did not forget that back at Hawkley Clive was *the squire*.[8] But Clive's attention was dragged to Hawaii in September, 1916, by word from Honolulu that Swanzy was seriously ill. Poor Swanzy had literally wrecked his health in carrying the business load of the Davies. He had suffered a heart attack and was in bed at home. The news was disquieting, for it meant something drastic must be done about Honolulu. Swanzy was not alone, of course. Wodehouse was there, and a new man, J. N. S. Williams, who had joined the firm just before the outbreak of the war. Williams was married to one of William Green's daughters; he was an engineer, and a sugar man. He had taken the sugar problems off Swanzy's shoulders, but the overall responsibility remained and the war made it harder than ever. They had bought E. O. Hall hardware company, which added new lines to their old ones. New developments in agriculture must be examined, and they had recently gone into use of the new Caterpillar tractors, which were proving admirable for plowing the steep lands of the Hamakua coast. The Davies company was again (as Theo H. Davies had been in the beginning) in the forefront of the Hawaiian sugar industry. Their Caterpillar operation was the most advanced method in the fields. They continued to innovate and lead in the mechanization of the sugar industry. Swanzy had taken all this in stride, but now he had reached his limit, and was flat on his back.[9]

Clive Davies had been talking about joining the Garrison Artillery, which might possibly have been a way to get to France, but the news about Swanzy continued to grow worse. George was in France, and the only other Davies males of his generation, Arthur and Theo M., knew nothing of the

Hawaii business. Arthur was busy with his church work. Theo could be left to manage family affairs; he had been declared unfit for military service of any sort and would stay put in England. So Clive decided he must brave the dangers of the submarines and make a trip to Hawaii. When he arrived he was appalled; Swanzy was in worse shape than he expected, and it was apparent that he would never recover sufficiently to resume management of the company. The annual meeting of Theo H. Davies & Co., Ltd. was held at Swanzy's house in February, 1917. They fixed the value of the shares at $225. The capitalization of the company was $1,460,000, and it showed profits for 1916 of $789,000. They declared dividends of $467,000.

So if the Davies family were suffering the ravages of war in Europe, they were at least not suffering the pangs of want.[10] In years past Swanzy had always made it a point to have all ready for the annual meeting, and it had gone without a hitch. But this year he had been unable to prepare, and they found that several strings had been left undone. Most important, the new articles, necessary for recapitalization, had not been digested, and so the meeting had to adjourn till the following day so the paperwork could be completed. Swanzy was growing weaker every day, and Clive took over. He went to the governor's office on February 9 for a meeting of all the Big Five with the governor and a committee of military men. The purpose was to ascertain Hawaii's ability to survive without regular shipments from the mainland, in case the U.S. went to war against Germany. The military asked all purveyors for a confidential estimate of their stocks on hand and asked them to make sure that they had at least a three-month supply of necessities.[11] Changes had to be made; a new director added. W. H. Baird was made a director, along with George H. Angus, James Wakefield and J. N. S. Williams. Clive had to take over the problems of staff; clerk Tim Healy, for example, came to see him to complain that he was loaded with too much detail work.

On February 21, Clive had the worst of news, confirming all that he suspected; the doctor said that Swanzy's heart was weakening rapidly and that there was no prospect of recovery. Indeed he might die at any moment, and the slightest bit of worry could bring on his death. So Swanzy had to be kept from any worry, which meant no further consultations with him on business affairs. Clive had the total responsibility. All through March he carried the load, trying to bring Wodehouse and Williams into more active roles. The American declaration of war on Germany in April brought new shipping problems, particularly in the insurance division. The purchase of the Kukaiau lands, which were owned by the Lidgate family, was agreed at a price of $450,000 in the Davies company stock. It was the first major land purchase made by the Davies interests in many years.[12]

Having made the best arrangements he could, Clive left the business basically in the hands of Wodehouse, Baird and Williams, and sailed for Vancouver. At New York he took the *RMS Carmania* for England. Clive Davies was no Theo H. Davies, and when he was seated at the purser's table instead of the captain's, he made no objection. The voyage was uneventful if a little frightening; Edith had cabled her worries— perhaps he ought to stay on the American side until the war ended, she suggested—but the submarine menace had largely been conquered, he assured her, and there was no incident on the voyage.[13] In a few days he was back at Hawkley Hurst, preparing to drill his Home Guard troops once more.

Chapter Twenty-Seven

THE MAZES OF FINANCE

With Swanzy's passing, some of the heart went out of the Davies enterprise. Swanzy was, after all, one of the original partners, the last who had actually seen the business and its offshoots emerge from the pack of trading companies to become one of the "Big Five" of Hawaii, as the major firms had come to be known. The other directors, Clive Davies, George Davies, assistant general manager Ernest Wodehouse — were of a second generation. Under the new articles they would form a triumvirate to operate the business, all three carrying the "Managing Director" title, but it would not be the same as the old triumvirate of Davies, Walker and Swanzy. None of the second generation had the same stakes, and Wodehouse represented something new in the company. With his appointment as resident managing director, for the first time the company was in the hands of a non-Briton.

Minister James Wodehouse had lived for years in Hawaii, and Ernest Wodehouse was Hawaii bred. He married a Hawaiian, and his entire horizon was bounded by the Pacific Ocean. In another way, Wodehouse represented a change; he was the first to come into the company from outside. When he joined the firm, he already had a successful law business in Honolulu, representing various trading firms and the estate of Queen Emma. Clive and Swanzy had debated how much of this he would have to give up; more important, Clive had to insist that Wodehouse buy stock in Theo H. Davies & Co., Ltd. if he was to join them as a director, and Wodehouse acceded only reluctantly. So here, in charge, was a man with ideas that had little relationship to the past, but of course all Hawaii was changing. The most notable change came with the end of H. Hackfeld & Co. the most powerful of the Big Five. When the United States declared war against Germany, Hackfeld's assets were seized by the U.S. government, and eventually after the war, they would be sold and go into the possession of an American firm called American Factors, or Amfac.

At the moment, in 1918, the change did not seem drastic, or important. The vital matter was to get the war won, and that occupied the full attention of the Davies family in England. George was in France, still. Theo finally managed a commission as a captain with the Garrison Artillery and went to France. Clive secured a post in the Ministry of Munitions, the agency in charge of war production and procurement for the armed forces. It was an important job although not a glamorous one. He spent the work week in London, staying at a flat he had taken near Whitehall. He would go to London on the seven-thirty train from Liss, Hampshire, every Monday morning and go back to Hampshire on Friday afternoon, or Saturday morning if work detained him.[1]

In Hawaii business seemed to be going very well, making allowances for the war, which put major changes in abeyance. The company had bought a piece of land at Alakea and Merchant Streets, the whole block bounded by Merchant, Queen, Bishop and Alakea, and they proposed in 1915 to build a new four-story building. But shortage and confusion caused delays, and then when the U.S. entered the war in 1917, the whole project was put off. All through the war the company was making enormous profits on its capital of $1,500,000; in 1917 the profit was $868,000; in 1918 $751,000; in 1919 $748,000. In those three years Theo H. Davies Co., Ltd. *alone* paid $1,200,000 in dividends to its stock holders.[2] That did not include the sugar dividends. So who could complain about management?

Actually the management was a serious problem to Clive Davies, who had not expected to have to take an active role in company affairs. With Swanzy's death, Clive became president of various corporations. Wodehouse was managing director, but he did not function as Swanzy had. And there was much concern in England over the lower echelon of the company, which had been split up into departments. J.N.S. Williams was in charge of the plantations and doing very well. Long ago the merchandise department had been split into grocery, drygoods, and hardware. But with the vast expansion of the company (total merchandise was doing a business of $4,000,000 with a profit of ten percent) it seemed logical to regroup them all under a merchandise department. The obstacle was James Wakefield, manager of the drygoods department and senior man, who was very unpopular with the rest of the staff. But the likely candidate to run merchandising was George Angus, who was in fact, regarded as potential managing director material. They went 'round and 'round in the meetings of the board and in letters.[3] But after Swanzy's incapacity and death there was no satisfactory resolution; Clive and George Davies had suggested that Wakefield's contract be allowed to expire and not be renewed, but in the end he became a director of the company and remained until 1922. Another of the troubles of absentee ownership involved Laupahoehoe Sugar Company. Clive and George Davies had inherited their father's deep suspicion of sugar, and of Laupahoehoe in particular. The reverses of 1913 had convinced them that either their manager, Colin McLennan, was incompetent, or that Laupahoehoe was destined to fail. Sugar was selling at $45 a ton that year, and Laupahoehoe's cost of production was $63. The brothers were buttressed in their belief by much better production records at Honokaa, Ookala and other plantations. Clive had gone to Manager McLennan and in a not particularly subtle manner had suggested that unless cane could be grown much more cheaply they must close down Laupahoehoe — and was McLennan's health equal to the Herculean task of rescuing the plantation? McLennan had gotten the hint without trouble and promptly resigned, although Laupahoehoe had, until recently, been earning huge profits. Clive and George were distraught; they took seriously their responsibilities as lords of industry, and McLennan had been their faithful servant for a quarter of a century. Clive wanted to make McLennan a director of Laupahoehoe, but Swanzy, even in his last months, balked. If McLennan was incompetent as a manager, why put him on the board? In the end, Clive and George together bought McLennan 50 shares of Laupahoehoe stock as a token of their appreciation, and thus salved their guilty consciences.[1]

This sort of dealing at long distance created many problems, and after Swanzy was gone, only the war economy saved the company from the consequences of its management mistakes. There was embezzlement at the Hana store; Pearl City Fruit Company was involved in labor disputes and troubles which ended with the stabbing of a foreman by a worker,[5] and thorough deterioration of morale. The Davies company had troubles with their sugar-refinery contracts, and the California and Hawaii Sugar Refinery had management problems that bothered all the sugar factors.

Swanzy's independence in the matter of Captain Matson's virtual freight monopoly drive now cost the Davies company dearly. The operators of American Hawaiian Steamship Company decided the Atlantic Ocean offered more opportunity and took off, leaving the Davies company apparently in the clutches of Matson. The other four of the Big Five had very cozy deals with Matson. In the 1920s, 1930s and 1940s they would ostensibly act as Matson's agents for shipment of their own sugar and collect a commission on the revenues charged by Matson, which meant they had a rebate on shipping charges.

The offending Davies company had to pay full freight on anything it shipped from Hawaii to the mainland of the United States. In the short and medium ranges, the effect was seriously troublesome, but it caused the Davies company to seek competing lines, and they brought in the Waterman Steamship Co., States Marine and States Lines in the 1950s and 1960s. Eventually the Davies company in the 1970s became the largest surviving shipping agent in Hawaii, and when States Lines went bankrupt in the late 1970s, Davies found a successor.

In the immediate postwar years, however, the shipping situation was just another of Davies' management woes, of which there were aplenty. The amateur ranchers—for that is what they were—made serious mistakes regarding the management of Kukaiau ranch. In 1915 Kukaiau paid dividends of six and a half percent. In the heavy rains of 1916 they lost some stock, including a pair of imported Hereford breeding bulls worth $500 each. At the end of the year manager Donald S. McAlister said they needed ten new bulls, a new stallion to keep the horse herd up to quality, and a new road. Clive was president of the ranch company after Swanzy's death, but he was absent in England. Wodehouse and the others did not want to spend the money so they did not. That winter of 1917 the company paid six percent dividends — and the road washed out. Donald McAlister said they needed water storage tanks to handle half a million gallons — and he wanted a raise. The directors scoffed at the need for water storage, and turned down his raise. For the next two years, the area suffered drought so severe that Manager McAlister had to send scrawny beef to market — at a loss — just to keep the herd down.[6] But with the high prices of virtually everything, who was to complain?

Replacing Swanzy in the councils of the Sugar Factors was hard but the demands were not too great just then. Even refinery difficulties did not seem great when every bag of sugar sold without question. The HSPA's major difficulty had continued to be in assuring the labor supply, and the Philippines had apparently been the answer to troubles with Japan as a labor source. But with the war, the Philippines became restless. The island of Negros supplied most of the labor for Hawaii. In 1915 the Philippine government announced that it intended to erect two sugar factories, and to man them and the cane fields, and discourage emigration abroad. The Hawaii sugar planters became alarmed and decided they must make an important gesture to the Philippines to smooth over the differences. In 1919 they organized the Hawaiian Philippine Company, with a capital stock of $2,000,000, seven-eighths of it held by the Hawaii plantations, and they engaged Honolulu Iron Works to build a sugar mill, or *central,* for shipment to Negros. All eight major sugar planters subscribed to the stock, in sums relative to their sugar tonnage.[7] Amfac was the biggest subscriber, with its ten plantations and 159,000 tons of sugar shipped each year. C. Brewer was second with thirteen plantations and 151,000 tons. Davies was fifth with six plantations and 48,000 tons shipped. So the *central* was built

Sugar being loaded into barges at Bogo-Medellin Milling Co., Inc., Bogo, Cebu. (December, 1961)

Sugar workers in cane fields at San Carlos Milling Co., Inc., San Carlos City, Negros Occidental. (Photo taken in 1961)

near Silay City in Negros Occidentale, and landowners began planting cane. This *central* was the direct cause of the first Davies investment in the Philippines, for when Manager Hedemann of Honolulu Iron Works went to Manila to look over the ground, he discovered there a machine shop and boiler factory on Manila Bay called Earnshaw's Docks. He came back to Honolulu to suggest that Honolulu Iron Works buy Earnshaw's Docks.[8]

Don Manuel Earnshaw was interested enough in the idea of bringing more capital into his business that he made a trip to Honolulu, and arrived shortly after Clive and George Davies made their first postwar visit to the islands. Clive took the Earnshaws on a tour of Oahu and saw that they were well entertained on their visit. On November 19, 1919, Clive, George, and Earnshaw agreed on terms for the Davies interests to buy into Earnshaw's Docks.[9] Shortly after that meeting, George sailed for England, but

A locomotive hauling cane at Hawaiian-Philippine Company, Silay City, Negros Occidental.

Clive stayed on. There were matters of importance that a member of the family must settle. Most serious of these was a suggestion by E.D. Tenney that Castle & Cooke and Davies amalgamate, in order to present a larger competitive figure against Amfac. Tenney and Clive were old friends, and Tenney served on the board of Honolulu Iron Works. Clive was noncommittal; there was no need to make an issue of it anyhow, for Tenney just then was recovering from an illness at Queen's Hospital. But that same day, Frank Atherton of Castle & Cooke brought up the amalgamation idea with a sniff of distaste. Wouldn't the Davies family rather sell out and take their capital back home to England? That idea, said Clive Davies, had never even been considered by the family. But as of that moment, it did come under consideration and for years it was to lie in the corner of Clive Davies' mind.[10] Not that he was thinking only of selling — he was considering buying. He tried to buy the F. A. Schaefer firm of merchants and sugar agents, since old man Schaefer had virtually retired. But the family did not want to sell as long as the founder was alive, and Clive had to be content with a first refusal.

In January, Clive and Earnshaw made a trip to Manila to make the final arrangements for their business venture. Earnshaw wanted to continue to manage the shipbuilding activities of Earnshaw's Docks, and give Honolulu Iron Works charge of all the shops. In Manila they thrashed out more details, and Clive went to meetings of the Hawaiian Philippine Company. Earnshaw balked at selling at one point, and had to be shown his agreement of sale to bring him around. Clive now began to exhibit the financial management that would be his hallmark in the Davies businesses. He went to the Philippine National Bank and secured a $\frac{1}{4}$ percent premium on the rate of exchange on the $630,000 he had to change to pesos to pay over to Earnshaw and cement the deal. On Saturday, February 21, 1920, they signed the papers and exchanged cheques and certificates of shares, and the Davies family had a foothold in the Philippines.[11]

When Clive Davies returned to Honolulu in March, he faced an accumulation of difficulties that had grown up during the war years. Wakefield had continued to prove unmanageable and, although a member of the board of directors of Theo H. Davies & Co., Ltd. he contributed little but bad temper and negative argument. Clive wanted to offer stock to the employees and put a motion through the board to that effect. Wakefield complained, and when the complaint was overruled, in a fit of anger he resigned from the board, thus accomplishing in one brief meeting what Clive and George had wanted to do for five years.[12] For "face" purposes Wakefield was to remain with the company until after the new building was opened, but as of the end of 1920, he was finished.

The new building on Merchant and Queen Streets was creating worry and trouble for the company, coming as it did with the heavy capital outlay for the interest in Earnshaw's Docks. Clive Davies was particularly concerned about the method of their financing; the Davies companies operated entirely on short-term loans, backed by inventories and sugar futures. Much of this financing was still handled in the old way, with Williams, Dimond & Co. of San Francisco and New York guaranteeing the loans. Ernest Wodehouse had wanted to force the matter of a new $500,000 stock issue for Honolulu Iron Works that year, but Clive Davies had persuaded him to drop the matter for the moment.[13] Still, Wodehouse's concern was for working capital, and even with the enormous profits of the war years, the dividends had been so high that the working capital was not what Clive wanted it to be. The new building, largest in Hawaii, with four stories and a magnificent arcade and total fireproof construction, was costing many thousands of dollars more than anyone had expected four years before.

So in San Francisco and New York, Clive Davies called on bankers. He worked at this harder in New York, not wanting to upset Williams, Dimond & Co. He called The Corn Exchange Bank, which offered the Davies company a line of credit of $500,000. National City Bank gave Honolulu Iron Works a line of $500,000. In New York, Clive Davies met John E. Russell, who had gone to work there for Williams, Dimond & Co., and they made some of the bank rounds together. It became obvious that Williams, Dimond could no longer meet Davies' financial needs, so he proposed that their firm continue as sugar agents, but that Davies move out independently to manage its own financing. Davies would pay two-thirds of John E. Russell's salary in the interim, if Williams, Dimond would assign him primarily to the Davies account.[14] This change and the gossip that spread around Honolulu after the Tenney and Atherton conversations, started a widespread rumor that the Davies family had sold out to Castle & Cooke, and that the American firm would take over the Davies building when it was completed. The rumor was given credence by the extreme friendliness between Clive Davies and E. D. Tenney and the election of Tenney to the board of directors of Theo H. Davies & Co., Ltd., a move taken by Clive to strengthen the board and, perhaps half in the back of his head, to keep the possibility of a sale open.

Clive, obviously was spending a good deal of his time in this period dealing with Hawaii affairs; too many problems hanging on from the war had to be solved. The sugar refinery was certainly not the least of them. During the war the United States government had controlled sugar prices at 7.28 cents a pound, which was profitable for the producers, particularly when every sack was sold without question. In 1919 the controls were removed and the price of sugar jumped to 23.5 cents a pound. That was in May. But in December, as various governments released or announced their intention of getting rid of enormous sugar stocks, the price dropped to 4.6 cents a pound. The C & H refinery had been paying for sugar on delivery, which meant that by December it had enormous stocks of sugar on hand for which it had paid the planters 20 cents a pound and more. But suddenly the world price was less than a quarter of that amount. Had C & H been a private business it would certainly have gone bankrupt. All its surplus was wiped out, and then all its capital. The refinery was dead broke. The planters had no recourse but to bail out the refinery (they had been the recipients of the 23.5 cents a pound), and they set about doing so. They provided $10,000,000 in new capital, through bonds subscribed by the various sugar companies. Davies had to take their share. The Crockett refinery was operating so unsatisfactorily that in the fall of 1920 the HSPA appointed a committee to go to California to try to straighten out the mess. Chairman of the Committee was E. D. Tenney of Castle & Cooke.

There were four other members, including Clive Davies. They sailed on December 1 for San Francisco. At San Francisco Davies divided his time between sugar problems and financial problems of his own companies.

J.E. Russell came over from New York and they discussed the requirements. Clive called on the British-American Bank and asked for a line of credit of $500,000, but before action could be taken word came from New York that banking arrangements had been made there as specified, and that they met the Davies company's immediate needs. True to his nature, Clive Davies "spread the wireless before God, and thanking Him, took courage." He had been more worried over the cash flow than he had admitted even to his diary.[15] As the year ended, he could sigh with relief. The Crockett meetings were successful; the surplus in the Davies Company and the line of credit resolved immediately the problems of the building and sugar advances. But "this regular annual worry about finances will not do," he wrote in his diary. "We must make better plans in the future." Had old Theo H. Davies been alive, he would have taken a look at the two million dollars or so paid out to the family shareholders in the last three years and said that they could solve the problem very nicely: declare a moratorium on dividends until the cash reserves were built up adequately. But this was 1920, not 1890, and some fifty people, plus all their servants and employees depended on those dividends from Hawaii. Even old Theo might have been stumped at that.

Chapter Twenty-Eight

THE BREAK IN THE DIKE

The difficulties of 1920 spilled over into 1921, and it became obvious that the Davies company was going to have to take financial action to better its position. A new issue of 15,000 shares of Theo H. Davies & Co., Ltd. stock was authorized, to raise $1,500,000. Of this, a million dollars was in common shares and half a million in six per cent convertible preferred stock. By 1922 the capitalization had been raised from $1,500,000 (1917) to $2,300,000. The Davies family bought some of this, but not all, and the dilution of the Davies family control began. Immediately the situation would be made better by a $2,500,000 bond issue, floated at seven per cent to meet the sugar company losses and the enormous expenses of the new building. But that bond issue, along with the stock dilution, changed the nature of the company, and over the years, the Davies family's attitude toward the investment. Each such change removed a bit more family responsibility and control.

In the early months of 1921, Clive Davies had a sad task to perform. The money market and the affairs of the Davies company and its subsidiaries had so changed over the years that the relationship with Williams, Dimond & Co. was a burden. The Davies company marketed most of their sugar through C & H, so Williams, Dimond had little to sell. The Davies company had opened its own offices in San Francisco and New York, and so it did not need Williams, Dimond to buy for the company.* The Davies empire had become so large that Clive was talking in terms of line of credit of $2.5 million and Williams, Dimond could not handle so large an account. In February, in San Francisco, Clive Davies gave notice to end a relationship that had served his father's company well in the early days.[1] They would have to deal directly with banks and other institutions from this time on.

Davies thought he had made a firm arrangement with John E. Russell the year before to take over the Davies office in New York. But after Clive gave notice to Williams, Dimond and returned to Honolulu, there came a telegram from Russell, who had gotten cold feet and decided to remain with Williams, Dimond.[2] Nothing was to be done about it at the moment, so Davies did nothing. In June he went to San Francisco to assure the Honolulu Iron Works line of credit of $500,000 with the Bank of California, and then on to New York to talk about more credit. National City Bank offered a line of $750,000 to Honolulu Iron Works. Clive took his balance sheets to Corn Exchange Bank and those bankers said he could have a line of $1,000,000 for the Davies company. Clive saw John E. Russell and expressed polite disappointment that Russell had reneged on his arrangement, but no more than that. Then Clive Davies, who would never have had to make the trip east just then if Russell had lived up to his word, said goodbye and went back to Honolulu. He wanted to divest himself of responsibility, but Wodehouse spoke to Tenney, and Tenney, whose opinion Clive respected, said it was imperative that Clive remain as president of the various companies to assure stability. That would mean far more time in Honolulu than Clive wanted to spend, but there was no avoiding it just at the moment.

In the summer of 1921, Clive took Edith and daughter Muriel, who had just turned 21, on a pleasure trip to Japan, Korea and North China. They went to Shanghai, then Canton, and finally to Manila, where Clive had business with Don Manuel Earnshaw. Clive wanted to buy him out, and

---

*The Davies company had opened these offices to fortify the merchandising department's expansion in Honolulu by more careful purchase of goods, but those offices were also capable of dealing with banks and other financial institutions, and this became a major part of their job.

did. He increased the capitalization of Earnshaw's Docks to ₱12,000,000 ($1.8 million), and Don Manuel agreed that he would retire on October 31 from the company with his capital. His son, Don Tomas, would remain as manager of shipbuilding. Clive had anticipated some difficulties in buying out Don Manuel, but none of them seemed to materialize, and he was able to spend part of his time in the Philippines looking over the sugar operations. He took a ship to Iloilo, and then went to Bacalod, where the Murcia Milling Company had a factory. They drove to Talisay, then to Silay and stayed at Hawaiian Philippine Company's *central*. There Clive Davies went thoroughly into the finances of Hawaiian Philippine on behalf of the Hawaii planters and found them sound, if peculiar to Philippine ways. There were 105 planters in the district, 60 of whom needed loans against future crops from the mill in order to survive. In Manila Clive conferred with Mr. George Fairchild, the organizer of the Philippine sugar industry, and approved of Fairchild's plan of borrowing heavily from the Philippine National Bank to finance planters. It was, after all, not so very different from the old system under which Theo H. Davies had borrowed in San Francisco against sugar futures in Hawaii. Clive approved, but he did send a cable to Honolulu, reminding his fellow directors of HSPA that Hawaiian Philippine Company was committed to pay off the bank on June 30, whatever happened to the price of sugar. The loan guarantee was the price the Hawaii planters had to pay for a labor supply.[4]

At the very end, just as the final papers were to be signed that would transfer control of Earnshaw's Docks from Don Manuel to the Honolulu Iron Works, a snag developed. It was the Davies' first encounter with *amor propio,* the highly developed sense of Spanish pride mingled with Oriental "face" which lay behind the geniality of the Filipino. The issue developed over titles of officers of the company. In the beginning, Clive Davies would be President and Don Manuel first vice-president, which was no problem, since Clive represented a powerful family with immense holdings. But almost immediately Don Manuel would retire, and Clive would give up the presidency in favor of someone from Honolulu Iron Works, probably Charles Hedemann. The Davies faction proposed to bring in M. Simpson of

HIW as general manager, but here Don Manuel balked. It would be unseemly, he said, for an *extranjero* with no Philippine experience to be placed in charge of the company (and over Don Tomas Earnshaw) in the beginning, and would reflect badly on the Earnshaws and on Don Manuel's management in the past. It would never do. So they wrangled over details. Finally the matter was settled by giving Simpson the title of business manager with the duties of general manager, and the crisis was ended.[5] Before Clive Davies left the Philippines, he was satisfied that the investment was sound and prospects bright. There was plenty of work for the new Honolulu Iron Works operation, with its factories already in operation at La Carlota, Maao, Bacolod-Murcia, and Talisay. All these would need parts and repairs, and there were more factories to be built in the future, to say nothing of the new opportunities offered by the proximity of Earnshaw Docks to Indonesia and the rest of Asia.

November 21, 1921 was a banner day for Theo H. Davies & Co., Ltd. in Honolulu. That was the day of the formal opening of the new Davies building that fronted on the corner of Merchant and Bishop Streets. A special section of the *Star-Bulletin* that day commemorated the event and told Hawaii residents of the glories of the new edifice.[6] It would still be standing in a thousand years, boasted L. C. Mullgardt, the architect, unless, he corrected, it might be torn down. In any event, Honolulu needed a lot more buildings of this "unique" style. Persons familiar with the arcades along the waterfront of Singapore and the old South China Building in Hong Kong might not think the architecture so unusual, but at least it was an impressive change for Honolulu, and it was fireproof, with the interior divided into firewalled sections, and with internal fire hydrants. The building had two passenger elevators on the Merchant Street side, and four freight elevators on the Queen Street side, plus special circular chutes, and dumb waiters to bring merchandise down from the top warehouse to the street level. The theory in those days of low ground rent was to store the goods as close to the point of sale as possible. Cost of handling did not seem to be an important factor. The Davies company employed 200 persons, about half of them involved in warehousing and delivery.

The special newspaper section contained glowing articles about the company, its history and its officers. No mention was made of dissention in the ranks; Wakefield was still treasurer for the record, and Clive was still chief executive officer; but the treasurer was packing his bags, and the chief executive was on a ship somewhere between Rangoon and Calcutta, winding up his Asian tour. He was more than a little troubled about the monkey wrench thrown into his personal plans with the death of Swanzy and the need for reorganization of the company in Honolulu. He knew that the solution they had reached was not very satisfactory—Wodehouse was far too quixotic to be a good executive—but he could not at the moment offer a better one. Still pondering the problems of Hawaii, Clive and Edith and Muriel arrived in style at Hawkley Hurst two days before Christmas. The gardeners had put up two lines of flags along the road to greet them, and the other five children, Gwendolen, Lorna, Harold, Geoffrey, and Elizabeth were all there.[7] Christmas was a happy feast, with proper observance of the rites: Clive went to church three times that day. Boxing Day came, with its exchange of gifts, and then Clive prepared for a major family conference to discuss the affairs of Honolulu.[8] It was held at Hawkley Hurst four days after Christmas and was attended by the four remaining brothers, George, Arthur, Theo and Clive. Arthur wanted out, which meant the sale of his share of their father's residual estate as well as his own holdings. It seemed wise at the same time to get the estate of Harry Llanover Davies out of the picture, since it could be nothing but a burden to management, and Barbara could use the money in other ways. The problem, particularly for Arthur, was that he did not want to unload just at the moment, and with good reason. The end of the war had brought a glut of sugar stored in the warehouses of the western powers. The same factors that caused the inflation and then the worldwide recession of 1921 had hurt the Davies company and its subsidiaries. Their profits, for example, had dropped from $906,000 in 1920 to $429,000 in 1921. Laupahoehoe Sugar Company, with profits of $760,000 in 1920, showed a *loss* of $24,000 in 1921. Hamakua Mill had lost over $500,000 that year! At least the lesson of 1921 had taught the Davies to stop denigrating Laupahoehoe and look to solutions for its sugar problems, rather than abandonment. Of course, with its immense loss, Hamakua paid no dividends in 1921 (nor did most sugar companies) but because of the demands of the heirs, Laupahoehoe was milked of $120,000 for dividends, all of it coming out of surplus.

What the meeting meant, in essence, was that Arthur had panicked in the face of adversity. Theo M. did not want to sell out, but all had to agree to the dispersion of Theo H. Davies' estate before it could be done. So they did agree that day, with Clive and George telling the others they would buy up any shares that came for sale, unless they saw a chance to dispose of some to strengthen management in Honolulu. Three of the brothers had no intention of deserting their father's business, but with Arthur's defection the first hole had been bored in the dike of family control of the Davies enterprises. They met again the next month.[9] George and Clive amended their earlier statements to make sure all understood that they had no intention of continuing as active directors in Honolulu or even of being there very often. Arthur said he would like to retain a few shares of the Davies company, obviously for sentimental reasons. At that meeting the four brothers prepared a statement for all the other heirs, which would be added as an exhibit to the minutes of the most recent meeting of the company. Conditions in Hawaii had so changed, they said, that the way was now open for all the family who wished to realize their investments in Hawaii, and the two estates would be liquidated as soon as reasonably possible. From this point on no member of the family could be said to have any further responsibility to the rest.

Chapter Twenty-Nine

EXPANSION IN MANILA

O*ne reason for the economic* troubles of the sugar industry was the strike of sugar workers in 1920. It began with the Japanese again. They were joined by the Filipinos, who by this time were a major force in the sugar fields. But the Filipino strike effort collapsed in factional bickering, and the sugar planters, who had no intention of yielding an inch, turned their full attention to the Japanese, once again ejecting them from plantation housing and the plantations themselves. Strike breakers were brought in to work the fields, and there were enough to do the job and stop the strike.[1] But as always, even a strike which the planters won necessarily cost them dearly in terms of future planting and the next year's crop. Racism just then reached a sort of pinnacle in Hawaii, with the Japanese as its major victims. But not a word of that is to be found in diaries or papers of Clive Davies. Even the strike of 1920 was of relatively little moment when assessed against the greater problems he saw ahead.

Finance was the key to all of it. Clive had been disappointed to learn that John E. Russell had backed away from the job of company representative in New York. But apparently Russell had second thoughts when he learned of the Earnshaw's Docks purchase, for he changed his mind once more, and the Davies company honored its commitment. Russell became their New York representative, and they sold him 100 shares of stock, taking his note.[2] But Russell's joining did not solve the problems; the fact was that in 1922 the Davies company was overdrawn on its various credit lines. Clive told one of his bankers that he did not intend to continue an active role in the company, and the bankers erupted.[3] It was only because of Clive's participation that the Bank of California had granted them a credit line, and that was certainly true of the National City in New York and the Corn Exchange. Until those overdrafts were paid, the bankers would hold Clive personally responsible. So Clive backed down and wearily agreed to get into harness again. He resented it terribly; on September 28 he marked his 51st birthday with a lament, "There is not much of life left for all the things I wanted to do and have not done . . ."[4] He must go back to Hawaii much sooner than he had hoped. At least the contentious Arthur left that year; he went off to become a missionary in India, a path that would lead him to eminence in the educational field and advancement in the Church of England.* His removal brought sighs of relief from Clive. George was as busy as Clive setting up as a country gentleman. He had bought an estate for £42,000 but by the time he refurbished it and put in a new water supply it cost him £67,000. And George had the political bee in his bonnet; he wanted to stand for the House of Commons.

Clive refused to go out to Honolulu in 1922; after all, he had just gotten back and it was George's turn, if anything. But George was taking a new interest in politics. He would stand for Parliament and be elected. His interest in Hawaii had changed to that of an investor only. So Clive puttered at Hawkley Hurst, doing a good bit of shooting, and spent four days a week in London, trying to run his business affairs from long distance and not succeeding very well. It became apparent that he must go back to Hawaii, so in February, 1923, he sailed.[5] The pressure was really on, he found. He called at the First National Bank of Chicago, where they had one credit line. The officer who handled their account said that in view of the reduced financial showing of 1921 and 1922, the bank intended to reduce their credit line at the end of the season. In San Francisco the Bank

---

*Arthur became Dean of Worcester Cathedral.

of California was a bit more pleasant, and Vice-President McIntosh congratulated Davies on holding distribution of the company's 1922 profits to fifty percent. (He did not know about the sugar dividends.)

In March Clive Davies was in Honolulu, attending annual meetings of the companies. For the first time pressure was brought on him by one of his outside directors; Tenney did not want Honolulu Iron Works to pay dividends, given its shaky profits. And of course, that attitude came into direct conflict with the known views of the English heirs. Clive managed to weather the meetings without any real incidents, and then went off on a tour of the sugar plantations to bring himself up to date. Back in Honolulu, he began talking with Tenney about the family holdings that the others wanted to sell. The problem, as Clive had seen from the beginning, was the retention of these stocks in friendly hands. He had tried to persuade several intimate friends in England to buy into the companies, but Hawaii was just too far removed from London, as his earlier experiences with Barclays' Bank had shown. His best chance, he knew, lay in Honolulu. Before Clive left Hawaii that spring, he had arranged with Tenney to buy a few shares. But there was a sticking point on the value the Davies family set, $200 a share. Frank Atherton balked at paying so much· and told Clive he might as well buy them up himself at that price; no one else would.

One of Clive Davies' most serious matters of concern was the Davies building and what it had done to the finances of the company. Costs had proved so high that the company had been forced to issue $750,000 in bonds to cover, and the amortization program called for the bonds to be fully redeemed by 1940. Further, the company had written off $900,000 from the profit-and-loss account to pay for the building, and this was one of the major cash problems.[6] As an exercise in accounting it was all wrong, because the company, as user of the building, was paying only $41,250 a year, which did not meet the upkeep, charges, and redemption costs. For the first time since Clive could remember, the Davies company was in so precarious a position, because of this luxurious building, that he wondered (in his diary) if he had not gone too far in setting up his expensive gentleman's estate at Hawkley Hurst.[7] He returned to Hawkley Hurst, however, and pursued the life of the squire: four days a week in the city working on his business affairs and lunching almost daily with George, and three days of heavenly escape in Hampshire.[8]

In the beginning of 1924, Ernest Wodehouse in his blunt way laid out the problem: Theo H. Davies & Co., Ltd. had gotten itself into a position, with the large payments of dividends, the new building, the Pearl City Fruit Company (which demanded advances to pineapple planters) and poor business conditions, that it needed a million dollars in new capital, either through another bond issue or an issue of preferred stock. What Wodehouse had suggested earlier was the issuance of 7,500 shares of common stock, but the Davies heirs could not agree to take that up among themselves, and Clive and George were not anxious to broaden the stock ownership base by taking in outsiders. Still, the cash problem was serious: at the end of February, 1924, the Davies company owed banks $1,385,000 on short-term notes, and although the amount due from the plantations alone was $2,000,000, they did not have the cash.[9]

In 1924, John E. Russell came to Honolulu to serve as Wodehouse's treasurer. W.B. Craig was the manager in New York then, and his assistant was a young man named Harold Weidig, for whom Wodehouse had great hopes.[10] The Russell addition was a direct result of the refusal of the two Davies brothers to remain active in Honolulu affairs. In fact, conditions were changing so rapidly in Hawaii in 1923 and 1924 that Clive Davies' absence put him out of touch with much that went on. The sugar plantations, in particular, were undergoing change. The Territorial Government had begun active encouragement of homesteading government lands and discouragement of long-term leasing to sugar companies. The Filipinos and Japanese were on strike again all over the territory, and Waiakea Mill, for example, had now become surrounded by homesteaders. So in February 1925, Clive and Edith went to Hawaii so that he might give a hand in unravelling some of the more serious problems. They stopped off in San Francisco, where Clive called on the Crocker Bank and the Bank of California and opened some discussions about turning Laupahoehoe Sugar Company into a commercial timber preserve. During

John E. Russell. Circa 1924

six months in the islands, he spent nearly a month on the Big Island of Hawaii and the remainder of the time in Honolulu. Subtly, the Clive Davies relationship with the company had changed. He was now functioning as chairman of the board, but as a non-operating chairman. Various employees felt no fear of coming to him with their complaints about treatment within the company or with their problems. Leslie Wishard, manager at Union Mill, told Clive he was thinking about getting out of the plantation business because of the educational problems of life in such lightly populated areas. John E. Russell came to complain that Managing Director Wodehouse did not give Russell proper recognition for his financial dealings.[11]

Theo H. Davies & Co., Ltd. and its various subsidiaries had decided under Russell's urgings to refinance its debt with long-term securities. Waiakea Mill, Niulii, and Union Mill all issued bonds (Union Mill's for example, totalled $200,000). Waiakea issued $250,000 in six percent bonds, which were sold to the Pacific Trust Co. at 98 cents on the dollar, a two percent discount. By this method Wodehouse and Russell managed to clear off the Davies company's overdrafts at the various banks, and by the middle of 1925 only Pearl City Fruit Company was drawing heavily on the cash of the Davies company. Pearl City Fruit was a continuing problem; the pineapple market had not materialized as Swanzy had hoped it would. There were no apparent buyers for Pearl City Fruit Company, and the debt was so great it would have been a shock to close down and write it off. So the firm kept going, hoping for the best.[12]

For the first time, during the 1925 meetings in Honolulu, the question of "Americanization" of the Davies company was raised openly by Wodehouse and Russell.[13] Wodehouse wanted to approach Castle & Cooke to buy more shares of Davies stock and thus show the broader base of the company. The stock was available, about a thousand shares, representing the sell-out of some of the English heirs. Clive had insisted that the tight control of Davies shares be maintained, so they had been bought up by the treasuries of Kukaiau Ranch and other affiliated companies, but Wodehouse wanted them sold. In fact, under Governor Farrington and his land commissioner Andrew Adams, the whole future of the sugar industry seemed shaky, because the government was pressing hard against the holders of big land leases to relinquish the land for homesteading. This development caused the sugar lands to be cut up into tiny portions and increased the administrative expense of the plantations in dealing with a number of small growers. The Waiakea Mill came under a special investigation ordered by the legislature after charges were made that the Davies interests were trying to strangle the homesteaders.

The new financing method brought its own shadow, which would have upset Theo H. Davies more than a little had he still been alive. The profits of the Davies company in 1925 were $500,000, an increase of about $60,000 over the previous year. But all the new financing brought its penalties: dividends on preferred stock came to $56,000; $100,000 had to go into a sinking fund for the company bond issue. The company had paid out dividends of $235,000 on common stock in 1925. Then there were taxes, and money for pensions. At the end, there was a surplus of $70,000 which was comforting, but not adequate for any sort of capital improvement. So what the new financing meant was that the days of pay-as-you-go had ended forever for the Davies company, and the owners and managers had to learn to live with debt and a much higher interest cost than in the past.[14] Added to that difficulty was the spottiness of the Davies company business:

Profitable	
Theo H. Davies & Co., Ltd.	$498,000
Honolulu Iron Works	425,000
Laupahoehoe Sugar Co.	206,000
Hamakua Mill Co.	45,000
Waianae Lime Co.	11,000
Kukaiau Ranch Co.	30,000
Unprofitable	
Waiakea Mill Co.	$132,000
Halawa Plantation Co.	18,000
Kaiwiki Sugar Co.	71,000
Niulii Mill & Plantation Co.	22,000
Union Mill Co.	66,000
Pearl City Fruit Co.	268,000

The sugar plantations and mills could be expected to show that sort of fluctuation; it was apparently inherent in the sugar business, depending on sugar variety and weather, as much as on management. But Pearl City Fruit was an enormous drag. They tried everything. In 1926 Wodehouse tried to make arrangements with Armour & Company to market the pineapple instead of trying to do it themselves through the San Francisco office. But that did not solve the problem. It dragged on, and on the horizon some other difficulties loomed. The sale of Honolulu Iron Works stock by the Janion and Davies families had for the first time cost the Davies family actual control of Honolulu Iron Works. After 1926 they depended on their relations with Castle & Cooke to retain control. In the fall of that year, one of the Janions offered some Theo H. Davies & Co., Ltd. stock for sale. Since it was not a listed stock, the Hawaiian Trust Co., which held the shares, offered them to Wodehouse, but he declined to accept them for the company and suggested that Clive and George might buy them. Thus was posed a major problem: how much defensive buying could Clive and George Davies undertake, and to what end?[15]

One aspect of the Davies affairs to which Clive addressed himself earnestly was the development of the Philippines operations. In January, 1927, he sailed for Manila, by way of the Suez Canal and the Indian Ocean. He stopped off at Agra to visit his brother Arthur, who was developing the university there into a prominent institution. Then it was on to Manila, for meetings of the Earnshaw directors and a trip south to inspect the Hawaiian-Philippine operations for the Hawaiian sugar planters. Back in Manila all seemed satisfactory with Earnshaw's, which was doing a good business in sugar-factory construction and maintenance in connection with Honolulu Iron Works in Hawaii. But this year Simpson, the manager, became ambitious and decided to open a merchandise department in Manila proper, and expand. He did it without consulting the board of directors, and Clive was furious.[16] But Simpson was right in a way; the opportunity for expansion did exist in the Philippines, and Clive saw it for himself. He wanted to send Guard from Hilo to take over the business in Manila, but Wodehouse would not let him go. They would begin with an agency to handle plantations, insurance and other business, Clive suggested. Finally W. G. Hall of Honolulu Iron Works went to Manila to open an office for Theo H. Davies & Co., Ltd. The expansion in the Philippines was about to begin.[17]

Chapter Thirty

THE BIG CHANGE OF 1929

By the beginning of 1927, Clive Davies was certain that a major change had to be made in Honolulu if he was going to be able to carry out his plan of moving back into a comfortable English retirement. Ernest Wodehouse was dynamic and very positive but not an easy man for others to serve, because he was didactic and stubborn. In particular, John E. Russell found Wodehouse blocking him although, largely because of Russell's financial efforts, the over extension of the Davies company's debts had been converted into long-term loans and possible financial disaster averted. It was all very easy to say that the company directors should never have allowed conditions to get out of hand, but the major factor was really the skyrocketing cost of the new building in Honolulu, and that could be attributed to the inflation of the postwar period. In the winter months of 1927, after several conversations with Russell, Wodehouse, Tenney and others, Clive and George were undecided about the future of themselves and of Wodehouse. What they did not wish to do was in any way disturb the public relationships of the company.[1]

Business affairs seemed stagnant in the middle 1920s. The sugar business went along, with its usual ups and downs; the most important development was the purchase of a third interest by the sugar agencies in Western Sugar Refining Company, with Davies' share costing about $300,000. The really difficult problem was Pearl City Fruit Company. In

1927, Theo H. Davies & Co., Ltd. wrote off $600,000, which represented the value on the books, cancelled all the leases, and prepared to sell off the machinery. The labor troubles in the sugar plantations continued to flare and subside — with no real solution, no matter the nationality of the workers. At the beginning of 1928, T. Guard was brought up from Hilo to take over the merchandising department and become a vice-president and director. Russell was a director, so was A. G. Budge of Castle & Cooke, and Tenney; and of course, Clive and George Davies. It was not a very strong or cohesive board, particularly since Clive and George Davies came less and less frequently to Honolulu. Frank Atherton wanted to increase the power of Castle & Cooke in the Davies directorate to offset the influence of Wodehouse, whose powerful personality seemed to cow the Davies directors. There was no way Clive could do much but make pleasantries.[2]

The Philippines investment seemed to be progressing well enough, but the problem of managing the dual operation of Earnshaw's Docks and the Davies company fledgling offices had not really been resolved. What was needed was a strong character to emerge from the Philippines or for Clive to find one. That need was much on his mind, even as he turned his attention to his affairs in England, the children and the company. The three girls, Muriel, Gwendolen, and Lorna, would of course have no direct connection. Geoffrey, the youngest son, had more or less been earmarked for the Navy almost at birth. He was eleven in 1927, almost ripe for a midshipman's post if the naval career was to become a reality. Harold, the oldest boy, was tentatively slated for the company; he was entered at Uppingham and would go to Cambridge to read engineering. Clive had found no particular advantage in his father's depriving him of an English university education in favor of American. As for the girls, they had beaux and romances. One of these was a subject of some concern in 1927. Lorna had met a young man named Gerald Wilkinson, son of an impoverished but excellent family, who was at school at Winchester.

The attraction between Gerald and Lorna had blossomed, and in the summer of 1927 everywhere Clive turned he seemed to trip over the Wilkinson boy. Lorna had him over for a weekend to Hawkley Hurst in

July. The next month the family took a house named St. Hilda's on the Isle of Wight, and Gerald showed up there too, by invitation. Wilkinson embarrassed him by asking for a talk, and then proposing that he and Lorna become engaged. It took all Clive's tact to fend him off; he did so with platitudes about "conducting themselves as good friends" until such time as Gerald was out in the world, securing a career for himself in which he could support a wife. At that moment, 1927, the prospects seemed far off. Clive attempted to still the obvious disappointment by approving heartily of the young people's declaration of love for each other, but there were the cold facts.[3] Still, Clive could not but be impressed by the bearing and openness of the Wilkinson boy.

One of Clive Davies' new ways of avoiding long stays in Honolulu was to make brief trips to New York to confer with various executives when they came to the eastern shore of the U.S. mainland. In October 1927, he and George went to New York, where they held a series of meetings with Wodehouse and Tenney about the company. Tenney was not happy with Wodehouse's management. He was joined in this view by Director Budge, and of course, Russell. Clive also met with W. G. Hall, head of the Philippine operation, and discussed personnel, always the problem. The result of these meetings was to "clear the air," whatever that meant; the session did not resolve outstanding problems but did reassure underlings that Clive and George Davies were sympathetic to their difficulties though Wodehouse was not.[4]

By the summer of 1928, business life had become even more tense in Honolulu. Clive went to New York again to meet John E. Russell, who told him of his woes. Clive had expected the misery of fending off demands that he come back to Honolulu and take charge, which he was prepared to resist. But apparently all concerned had given up hoping that Clive Davies would come to the rescue of the company; no questions were raised. There was one unpleasant task to perform; the bloom was off the sugar-factory market and the New York office of Honolulu Iron Works was to be cut down. The older employees were to be retired and some of the younger ones released. But that accomplished, Clive Davies could return to England with a lighter heart. Obviously, he bore the weight of his own decision to eschew Honolulu heavily on his conscience, but he was determined on this course and did not falter.[5]

In the 1920s, a new business problem began to face the Davies heirs—the income tax. For the first time care was being given to the details of trusts and income in view of taxation. Clive spent a considerable amount of time on the subject, on his own behalf and that of his sisters and other relatives. He was also thinking ahead, about the children. Harold was preparing in 1929 to enter Cambridge University; it would not be long before he would be going out to Honolulu.

Clive went to the islands himself in the spring of 1929, to put the stamp of affirmation on a decision he and George F. had made over the winter, based largely on the advice of Tenney and Budge. Wodehouse was to be superseded by Russell as managing director of the company. Officially it would not occur until December 31. Actually the change was already in effect. It was expected that Wodehouse would retire, with a pension of $10,000 a year for five years and then $5,000 a year for five years. The retirement posed one nagging problem: Wodehouse held 800 shares of Theo H. Davies & Co., Ltd. stock, which he intended to sell. He offered it to Clive and George, but they had by this time accepted the theory (long advocated by the banker J. Pierpont Morgan) that control of a business could be maintained without majority stockholding. They declined the offer.[6]

In 1928, Davies Company and the Honolulu Iron Works had bought $150,000 in shares in Bogo-Medellin Sugar Company, which they sold around the Hawaii community (S.G. Wilder took $5,000, Robert McCorriston took $2,500, J.E. Midkiff took $2,500). The idea was to establish the financing of Philippine sugar mills with guarantees by Honolulu Iron Works and the Davies company and then to retrieve the capital by such sales for another venture.[7] The proxies would be turned over to Hall to vote, so the control would remain in the hands of the Davies company. This arrangement represented the Davies concern over their investments in the Philippines: the problem was cash; together the Davies company Manila branch and Earnshaw's Docks had deferred payments of about $2,000,000 financed by Theo H. Davies & Co., Ltd. Honolulu, and Honolulu Iron Works. W.G. Hall was ambitious and wanted to expand, but the Filipinos were strapped for cash, and expansion meant financing with American dollars. Hall wanted to make crop loans to Filipino planters; Honolulu was dismayed, but did authorize ₱300,000 for the purpose.[8] To handle the increased business, Hall hired an assistant, G.C. Hunter. The Manila office had picked up several insurance company agencies, including the London & Scottish Assurance Corporation, which came to them in 1928. W.G. Hall, who had been working very hard for the Davies companies, wanted to make a trip to Europe in 1929. Begrudgingly, Wodehouse approved the idea (although he told Clive Davies he thought it was cheeky of Hall to make such a trip) but Wodehouse made a point of denying Hall any expenses, even if he did business in Europe for the companies.[9] On December 20, the bombshell came: Hall resigned. Wodehouse was almost stricken with panic: for just then the Davies interests were negotiating through the H.S.P.A. to secure the agency for Hawaiian-Philippine Sugar Company for Davies in Honolulu, and their presentation depended on assurances that a man of Hall's experience would be in charge. But Hall seemed adamant: no amount of backstroking at this point would change his mind.[10] Wodehouse sent Russell out early in 1929 to arrange for a transition. When Russell arrived, he did manage to smooth Hall's ruffled feathers. Wodehouse had not known, and not made any attempt to discover, that Hall's problems involved the education of his daughter and his wife's determination that it be accomplished elsewhere than the Philippines. The compromise was made "in the family"; Mrs. Hall would take the girl to Honolulu and Hall would spend several months of each year in Hawaii.[11] With the expansion of the Davies interests in the Philippines, Mr. Robinson, the chief accountant of Honolulu Iron Works, went to Manila to manage the books of Earnshaw's Docks, Honolulu Iron Works, and Theo H. Davies & Co., Ltd. G.C. Hunter would manage Theo H. Davies, and Hall was to take responsibility for all three companies, and have the title of General Manager of the Honolulu Iron Works. Clive Davies, who had come to

Honolulu in March, 1929, for the annual meetings of his companies, wrote a placating letter, indicating that Hall could go to Europe when he wished, and the company would foot the bill.[12] Hunter was made executive director of the Theo H. Davies Co. Philippines, on the recommendation of John E. Russell. Clive asked Hall to spend a certain amount of time each year in Manila, overseeing the joint affairs of the three companies.

At the spring company meetings, Clive also supervised a major change in the management of Theo H. Davies & Co., Ltd., foreshadowing the emergence of Russell as the key figure. Russell was elected a managing director, to replace George F. Davies, who remained only as a director. Although Castle & Cooke did not like it, the triumvirate system was retained, for the moment at least, but the way was paved for Russell's emergence. In their conversations that spring, Russell warned that Frank Atherton was preparing to make an offer to buy the Davies out, lock, stock and barrel, as he put it.[13] Five days later Atherton did just that.[14] He wanted George and Clive Davies to sell all their interests in the Davies company to Castle & Cooke, plus control of Waiakea Mill Company and Laupahoehoe Sugar Company, for cash and stock, and a seat on the board of Castle & Cooke. The sugar agencies would all be transferrd to Castle & Cooke. Theo H. Davies & Co., Ltd. would remain only as a merchandising business. As for the personnel of the Davies Company, the only person Castle & Cooke wanted was possibly John E. Russell.

Clive Davies gave Atherton an equivocal answer. Next day he discussed the offer with John E. Russell, who advised against taking it. There was nothing wrong with Davies' ownership now that the management problem seemed to be solved, said Russell. So Clive equivocated more.

In discussions with Castle & Cooke's Atherton and Tenney, Clive asked how they valued the Theo H. Davies shares.

"Oh, about $150 a share," said Atherton.

Davies sat, unmoved.

"Or maybe a little bit more," Atherton corrected himself.[15]

After the meeting, Russell told Davies that Atherton's holdings had recently been valued in settlement of Charles Atherton's estate, and the value placed by the government appraisers had been $180 a share for the Davies Company stock.

By May 21, the discussions continuing, Atherton and Tenney were beginning to talk more sensibly about appraisals of the stocks of the Davies family, based on yield against capital. Atherton had hoped to purchase only control but now realized they would have to buy up all the Davies heirs at the same time. They talked about $200 per share, so the offer became more tempting, until Clive asked Atherton what Castle & Cooke would do about the many pensioners of Davies and the other companies who were carried from year-to-year. And what would they do about the staffs of various subsidiaries and the Davies company?

Castle & Cooke would have no use for the pensioners—they would be lopped off. So would the staffs.[16]

Atherton could not have realized that in that casual remark he cost himself the control of the Davies companies. Clive was tempted. The Castle & Cooke men did not thoroughly appreciate the restlessness of the other heirs, and the degree to which Clive leaned toward the sale. But Atherton and Tenney did not understand, either, the extreme "Englishness" of Clive Davies, and the *noblesse oblige* which guided him. He would not think of abandoning the people who had served his companies for so many years.

On May 21, the whole idea of sale to Castle & Cooke was squelched in Clive Davies' mind, and his only remaining purpose was to try to disengage from the discussions without angering the Castle & Cooke men. Over the years, moving slowly in, Castle & Cooke had brought an estimated $15,000 a month in new business to the merchandising department, and their management assistance had helped quell local arguments about absentee ownership. Clive asked openly if a refusal would anger Castle & Cooke, and Tenney replied that it would not, but Atherton said it would certainly end Castle & Cooke's interest in acquiring any further shares.

So the Castle & Cooke attempt to take over the Davies' interests came to a sudden end in the spring of 1929. There were a few repercussions; the rumor had gotten out and Clive Davies had to reassure his principal executives that the Davies family were not selling out. That accomplished, the air was really cleared, and in the mid-summer he sailed for England. Theo H. Davies & Co., Ltd. had earned a profit of half a million dollars in 1928: the sugar companies had again shown an overall profit (controlled by local circumstances at each mill or plantation); the old Halawa plantation of Dr. Hart had been taken over by C & C and the question of what was to be done with Niulii was just then under consideration. The plantations' managers were moving to a new degree of mechanization with growing importance attached to the railroad lines; and the Philippines investments seemed to hold a great promise for the future, now that the management had been secured in Manila. All in all, Clive Davies' heart could be lighter as he contemplated the family business than it had been since Swanzy's death.

Chapter Thirty-One

CRASH IN AMERICA

By 1929 the irritating Rev. Arthur W. Davies had troubled his brothers so much they approached him about selling out all his interests to them. Arthur had a tendency to complain about the size of the dividends and the management of the companies, without the slightest bit of knowledge about the activity in Hawaii.[1] The matter came up at this time because, although Clive Davies felt the Castle & Cooke offer was ridiculous, when he returned to England he felt honor-bound to mention it to the other heirs. George and Theo M. agreed that there was no validity to the Castle & Cooke proposition, but Arthur was of a different mind. George and Clive met privately and agreed that it would be desirable to buy Arthur out before he created serious problems.[2]

Fall and winter of the year 1929 were troublesome times for Clive Davies. The American stock market suffered a severe collapse in October 1929. Of course the American market was forever collapsing; it seemed endemic in the system that seven or eight good years would be followed by a panic; the last had come in the grain markets of 1921. The disaster of 1929 at first seemed to be more industrial than agricultural, but when the market did not recover, and to this were added personal problems, the last months of the year were not very happy ones. Edith was found to have a breast cancer and had to go to the hospital for a mastectomy. In spite of Clive's cautions and precautions, Gerald Wilkinson had persisted in his attentions to Lorna. He owned a motorcycle which he kept just outside Winchester school's wall, and once or twice a week he would come over to see Lorna (who was studying privately with tutors at home, having not adjusted well to schools). On January 31, 1930, Gerald's 21st birthday, so much pressure was brought to bear on Clive Davies that he consented to their engagement. But he continued to warn that he would never consent to the marriage until Gerald was self-supporting.[3]

Scarcely a week after the engagement party, it became apparent that the American disaster was worse than had been expected. Clive and George had the profit-and-loss figures of 1929, and they agreed that they were "not exhilarating." Theo Davies Company's profit was down from $519,000 in 1928 to $446,000.[4] Laupahoehoe's profit was down from $220,000 to $160,000. Hamakua had dropped from $137,000 to $59,000. Waiakea Mill showed a loss of $13,000.[5] The figures were distressing; actually distress was not the word; discomfort was more the reaction.[6]

The Rev. Arthur Davies was in England on leave from his post; George and Clive lunched with him on February 4. They found Arthur almost as difficult as ever. He had been so eager to get out of the inherited investments that George and Clive had made him an offer, considerably less than the last sale price of the securities, in view of the market. Arthur was willing to sell his investments in Honolulu Iron Works, Union Mill, and certainly Waiakea at the figures mentioned. But when it came to Theo H. Davies & Company, Ltd., he balked. He could see no reason to take one penny less than $200 for the stock. That was the figure carelessly mentioned earlier by Clive in rejecting the Castle & Cooke nebulous offer of something over $150. No, said Arthur, he did not see why he should sacrifice any bit of advantage in selling out of Theo H. Davies & Co., Ltd. "for the sake of regard towards the purchasers."[7] Thus, in the conditions that prevailed in the market, Arthur's "sell-off" was delayed.

Clive Davies spent a leisurely winter at Hawkley Hurst, in the south of France, and Egypt[8] but by May, Russell said it was imperative that he and George go to New York, at least, to confer with Russell and set a course for the Davies companies during the continuing American crisis. The banking situation was serious because the Corn Exchange Bank and the National City bank had attempted a merger and failed. Davies began negotiations to move the company accounts to the Banker's Trust Company, and spent a long morning with the chairman, president and other officials.[9] Another reason for the trip was to meet with the heirs to the estate of C. F. Hart to discuss the Niulii plantation, which had a large debt because of several bad sugar years. Clive and the others agreed to try to buy Niulii and put the wheels in motion.[10] But the most important matter of all was brought up by Russell: the need for new capital to help weather the current crisis. Clive and George went home to confer with others of the family. At a meeting in London on July 29, the seriousness of the situation and the danger of ignoring their deep involvement was brought home to Theo, Alice and her husband, Violet and her husband, and Arthur. Muriel was not there — she had just been married by Uncle Arthur in a ceremomy at Hawkley Hurst to Lt. Col. Percy Montgomery Medill of the Royal Artillery and after the honeymoon would settle down with him in Norwich.[11] Even Arthur saw that this was no time to sell, and all agreed to take new shares. So the capitalization of the company was increased (it now reached $2,800,000).

As Clive was making plans to go to Honolulu for several months in February 1931, Gerald Wilkinson and Lorna were trying to make plans to get married, and Clive was the stumbling block. Gerald, fresh out of Winchester, first decided he wanted to become a chartered accountant (CPA) but quickly changed his mind and took a job with the Northern Assurance Company selling insurance;[12] but his annual income was only £250. Gerald's family intervened in behalf of the marriage, before the elder Davies' left for Honolulu, but Clive would not be pinned down. He would write, he said.[13] Privately, the next time Clive had opportunity, he looked up Gerald's superior and asked some questions. The answers were strongly affirmative: the Northern liked Gerald Wilkinson very well and wanted to keep him and advance him rapidly.[14] In fact, they wanted to send him to South Africa for experience.

Gerald Wilkinson continued to press; he and Lorna wanted to get married right away so she could go to South Africa with him, if that change materialized in Clive's absence. Bedevilled, Clive and Edith finally agreed to a date for the wedding: the fall of 1931. Edith told Lorna, who told Gerald. In his impetuosity, Gerald Wilkinson bridled, sat down and wrote a letter to Clive Davies telling him that the young couple would do as they pleased, unless they were allowed to get married in January, before her parents left England.[15] When that letter reached Hawkley Hurst, it caused an eruption in the Davies library, and within hours Mr. Gerald Wilkinson was ordered to appear. He came on August 29. After lunch he was taken up to the *sanctum sanctorum* and asked to explain the impertinent letter that lay on the desk before the master of Hawkley Hurst. For the first time, Gerald Wilkinson took a good look at his future father-in-law, and saw beneath the mildness of the round face a jaw remarkably like that of Theophilus Harris Davies. Having delivered an ultimatum by post, he began backing water in the interview. No, he had not realized that Mr. and Mrs. Davies had some reason for giving the fall date of 1931. He did not realize that Clive had any convictions on the subject and that is why he had never spoken to Clive about it. He did not really mean to have delivered an impertinent ultimatum. He had not meant to nag, or threaten his future parents-in-law with defiance. In the end, Clive accepted all the apologies and peace was restored to the household. The wedding, however, would be held in September 1931, as planned.[16] If Gerald were sent to South Africa in the meantime, he would have to go alone.

The remainder of the year in England was calm enough. Young Geoffrey had his tonsils out. Harold went up to Cambridge where his tutor found him "of average intelligence" and "probably" capable of achieving a degree. He took his honors entrance examinations to Magdalene college and squeaked through with a little help from friends in the proper places.[17] Then Harold came down with appendicitis and had to have an operation.

But by the first of the year serenity had returned to Hawkley Hurst, the farms seemed to be in good shape, and Clive and Edith Davies went off as scheduled on their duty trip to Hawaii, by way of Bermuda and Havana. Honolulu Iron Works had acquired an interest in MacFarlane's foundry in Sagua la Grande, Cuba; the investment had soared to $135,000, and Clive wanted to find out where the money was going.[18] Some serious decisions had to be made about expenditures, expansion, and investment. The Davies family still regarded their Hawaii investments as a family enterprise, and the family, generally speaking, still retained majority control of them. (The exception was Honolulu Iron Works.) John E. Russell was very eager for Davies to arrive. He was thinking about pulling the Davies company completely out of their investments in Kohala, on the Big Island, in order to recover capital. The Davies family had settled on a rise in capitalization by a 20-percent issue of preferred stock of Theo H. Davies & Co., Ltd., and that was their limit at the moment.[19] But Russell was not sure the $750,000 this would raise would be enough. Russell was a very conservative man; he felt nervous unless his cash position was just right. Already this nervousness was affecting some operations. In the Philippines, G.C. Hunter wanted to expand the merchandising activity of the branch, but Russell warned him that "we do not wish to go blindly into something that may involve large amounts of money." The Russell concern was not for solidity, or return, but to keep the company neck well within the company collar.[20] That is not to say he opposed what he saw as progress: he was enthusiastic about Manila's plan to take over the sugar agency for all the Hawaiian-owned or Hawaiian-controlled sugar properties. By 1930, Hawaii influence had spread wide, and Russell was talking about Bogo-Medellin, Cebu Sugar Company, San Carlos Milling Company, and Hawaiian Philippine Company.[21]* Affairs in the Philippines were going much better than those in Hawaii, largely because the competitive situation was far less serious. Honolulu Iron Works got a big new contract for a wallboard factory, which meant profits for the year from Manila. Hunter reported a rise in the price

---

*John E. Russell's selection of sugar properties with a future indicated considerable foresight about the management and futures, since he chose what turned out to be among the best properties of all.

of sugar, and good prospects, particularly for Bogo-Medellin company, in which the Davies company had the agency.[22]

In a way, the Hawaii sugar problem was illustrated by the Niulii Plantation situation, which was directly related to the Hawaiian homestead pattern. Between 1917 and 1921 leases on 200,000 acres of government land expired, including 26,000 acres of sugar lands. In 1920 Congress had passed the Hawaiian Homes Commission Act, and since that time, the sugar companies had been dealing with far more small planters than before. The Davies people referred to "homesteaders" and "friendly homesteaders"—the latter being the ones they could control. The economic pinch brought a new struggle between sugar mills of competing companies, where their territories overlapped, as in the Hilo district, and Kohala, on the north side of Hawaii island. Castle & Cooke had acquired control of most of Kohala district. Union Mill, in which Davies Company owned slightly more than 50 percent interest at this time, was literally fighting for its existence.[23] Niulii plantation was an important asset in this struggle. In his meetings with the Niulii heirs in New York, Clive Davies had offered $50,000 in cash and $55,000 in Theo H. Davies stock for the plantation. At that time the heirs had thought the offer generous, but back in Honolulu the lawyers who were in charge of the trusts thought they might get a better deal. So most of 1930 was spent in jockeying. The Davies people knew their offer was a fair one, so they encouraged the lawyers to talk to Castle & Cooke, which they did. Castle & Cooke was not interested in Niulii at the price, for the debts of the plantation were immense. So it came back to Davies. Russell proposed to merge Niulii with Union Mill, giving the Hart estate $50,000 extra in common stock and raising the capitalization of the new concern to $1,300,000. Of that, bonds would account for $380,000 and the control would remain the same, in the hands of the Davies company and the Davies family.[24] The dickering continued, and at one point Davies suggested that the heirs offer Niulii to Castle & Cooke for $620,000 (which would include the debt to the Davies company as agents). Castle & Cooke were not interested at that figure, and so by December it seemed certain Davies would buy and amalgamate Niulii with Union Mill.

The lawyers were sitting down to sign the papers on December 8, 1930 when a telephone call came from another lawyer, saying he had been asked by one of the heirs to the Hart Estate to secure an accounting. Suspecting a "double cross," John Russell broke off negotiations right there. By the middle of the month four firms of lawyers were involved, representing heirs who were making sure their individual interests were guarded, and the negotiations were at a standstill. The situation grew more complex as the heirs quarreled about the division of the estate. In the interim, the Davies company, as agents, and Clive Davies, as a trustee of the Hart estate, had to continue to operate as though Niulii was going to become a part of the Union Mill complex. The trend was toward bigger operations—the combined Niulii-Union Mill sugar business would produce 10,000 tons of sugar a year. Of course, this would mean new, expensive equipment, and more financial worries about building it. Sugar, one might say, was in a holding period.[25]

In February, 1931 Clive Davies took Harold out for a look at Hawaii, stopping in Cuba en route. The annual meetings of the various companies were mostly concerned with finance, in the growing depression of the American economy. The Davies company's profits were down again in 1931, to $275,000, but the demands for dividends were inexorable, and the past dividend was reduced only slightly; $211,000 was paid out. In part, this high dividend with falling profit was a fault of the Davies dividend system. Dividends were calculated quarterly and semi-annually in the Davies scheme, and then paid, and always had been. Thus a good first half year would produce a fat dividend, when a bad second half would make the total dividend disproportionate to profits. That system reflected an earlier period, when the company operated on a cash basis with heavy reserves. Times had changed, and Davies would be caught by them. For 1932 would be a disastrous year in Hawaii, and the Davies company profits would drop to $55,000. Yet dividends paid in that year would be $68,000, most of it paid before the management fully understood what was happening to the economy.[26]

In the spring of 1931, signs of this difficulty were already showing—if

Clive Davies had been willing to see them.[27] The Castle & Cooke management asked for a meeting with Davies and John E. Russell, his general manager. The meeting was held on April 14, with Frank Atherton, E.D. Tenney and A.G. Budge, the two Castle & Cooke directors of the Davies company. Tenney opened by saying he was thoroughly disgusted with his investment in the Davies company, and that in his opinion the company was on the way to disaster. Budge complained that he was never consulted by Russell before decisions were made and action taken. Atherton said Russell was carrying too heavy a load—an implied charge that Clive Davies was carrying too light a one. Clive Davies ignored that innuendo. The stock issue was approved by the Castle & Cooke men as essential, but they parted grumbling about management, and Clive Davies was shaken.[28] He began to understand the difficulties more in a day or two as he went about the community seeking "safe" homes for the new stock issue. He went to Swanzy's widow, confident of acceptance, only to learn that she had no cash margin for further stock investment and all she could give him was her blessing. Just then, the Theo H. Davies & Co., Ltd. stock consisted of 25,000 shares, 12,487 of them safely in family hands, 9,116 shares unissued, which assured family control, 3,397 shares in other hands. Actually at that moment both Arthur and Theo Davies owned more Theo H. Davies & Co., Ltd. stock then Clive did, and it would not take many sales to change the entire balance.[29].

On May 13,[30] Clive had precisely the same sort of discussion with his internal directors, John E. Russell, Angus, and Guard. Russell said that Clive and George Davies should spend far more time in Honolulu, particularly in view of the difficult times through which they were passing. He wanted Clive to come back forever. Since the refusal to sell out to Castle & Cooke, Tenney and Budge had been of no use as advisors, Russell said. Worse, he suspected them of complicity—at least of inaction—in the rumors that flourished in Hawaii that the Davies family was selling out. Those rumors had nearly destroyed the morale of the company; they were dissipated only when Clive was in Honolulu.

Ted Guard, the merchandising manager, spoke up, saying that the business had always revolved around the Davies family. He pleaded with

Clive to come back and live in Hawaii. He would like to see Clive "home" again, and Castle & Cooke out of their business. Angus said he was worried about sugar. They needed Clive in Hawaii in the winter, when some serious decisions must be made.

Clive Davies was very uncomfortable. Asking him to reverse a plan of 30 years standing, he said, was asking an enormous personal sacrifice. And they must not forget, there were other lives involved (his family's). There was no point in talking about George; as long as George was in Parliament, he could never involve himself in Honolulu. As for himself, they were already demanding more than he wanted to give. He had stipulated every second year a visit to Hawaii, and the last year he had also been forced to make a trip to New York on company business. He then turned the discussion to the third generation. Russell wanted Harold, and Harold was coming out to work—the only member of the third generation who showed any interest in the company.[31]

Russell and the others saw they were getting nowhere in pressing Clive to take an active role in the business, and they concentrated on a plea for another visit the following January and February. Times were going to grow worse, Russell said. Clive could not ignore that threat, and reluctantly he agreed to one extra trip, but that was all. It was not a very satisfactory meeting from the management's point of view. Clive Davies ended up talking about "fuller exploitation of the possibilities of consultation by correspondence," and on that note the company directors gave up the struggle. They were loyal men, every one of them certain that the answer was for Clive Davies to reverse himself and heed all that others had been telling him over the years. But Hawkley Hurst called, and that call was not to be denied. In September there came Lorna's wedding to Gerald Wilkinson, a happy time, but in October the clouds from Honolulu drifted even over Hawkley Hurst. Clive Davies gave notice to one of his farm workers, the first servant to go as a result of the economy.[32] In December came more depressing news: the company dividend was reduced to $1\frac{1}{4}$ per cent (and probably should not have been paid at all). The year went out with Clive Davies worried once more. The words of Atherton and Tenney, and of John E. Russell must have been ringing in his ears.

Chapter Thirty-Two

THE CONSCIENCE OF
CLIVE DAVIES

When 1932 began Clive Davies, as promised, went
out to Honolulu again. E.D. Tenney had been talking about resigning
from the board of Theo H. Davies & Co., Ltd. but on Clive's appearance he
agreed to remain for another year. He said he was doing so on a completely
personal basis. "There aren't many damn people I have any affection for,
but you're one of them."[1] So there was obviously good reason behind
Russell's demand that Davies come. There was more: Clive found the Davies
company's merchandising business was so dismal that spring that on
Good Friday General Manager Russell refused to close the firm. They
could not afford the loss of business when their competitors were staying
open, he said.[2] The financial difficulties were emphasized two weeks later
when the executive committee voted to cut company salaries to save perhaps $100,000. (With 500 employees, this was not impossible.) A few more
weeks' stay, and then Clive Davies sailed back for England, leaving Russell
and the professional management to face the problems of an uncertain
world. His excuse was that the Davies' interests, actually, were in better
condition than many. The company was not losing money, although some
divisions were showing losses. Honolulu Iron Works was making profits
through its continued sale of machinery and sugar factories around the

world. (Tabacalera gave them a ₱500,000 order that spring.) The Philippines operation had become important enough that Clive Davies and John E. Russell agreed to amalgamate the Davies company office in Manila with Earnshaw's Docks. Laupahoehoe Sugar Company had a surplus of $1,300,000 and would make a profit of $85,000 that year. But that just went to show how volatile and local sugar was — Hamakua Mill, which lost $160,000 in 1930, and made a profit of $9,000 in 1931, was expected to lose again (it did).[3] Union Mill was finally to be amalgamated with Niulii, and they had high hopes for the future. Waiakea Mill's situation indicated the difficulty that many plantations were having just then: Waiakea would make 16,500 tons of sugar, but the more it made the more it would lose — because too much of the cane was bought from homesteaders at prices established by contract when sugar was selling at a much higher price. The lawyers said the contracts could not be breached without running into lawsuits. Only in 1933 would the new contracts, stipulating lower prices, begin to come in, and those for a third of the crop.

In August, Russell cut the employees' pay again, on a formula that gave each department a minimum monthly revenue to attain. If the grocery department revenue fell below $250,000 in a month the grocery clerks could lose up to 20 percent of their pay for the month. Russell told Clive Davies this was as far as he could go; only von Hamm-Young Company had made similar cuts, and the other big companies—Amfac, Castle & Cooke, Alexander & Baldwin—had made no cuts.[4]

To the English stockholders, the first blow came in September, when Russell notified Clive Davies that the company was passing its quarterly dividend.[5]

The dismal state of affairs in Hawaii demanded constant consideration and decision, mostly on the conservation of pennies and the screwing down of all avenues of expenditure. The hope, it seemed, lay in the greater picture: in Honolulu Iron Works' commissions from abroad, which brought work to the Kakaako shops, in the growth of the Philippine Sugar Industry, and in new avenues. The Philippines was less affected by the world depression than most areas because the country was so poor to begin with. The improvement of sugar resources was undertaken largely by very wealthy families, and they were not threatened by such temporary conditions. Thus in the fall of 1932, Charles J. Henderson, the assistant treasurer of the Davies company and a man on whose judgement Russell and Clive Davies had come to rely on considerably, was sent to the Philippines to make a survey of the business potential.[6] Henderson visited the southern islands, spent time in the sugar *centrals,* and then went back to Manila. After several weeks of talking with various people, he returned to Honolulu with a number of recommendations. First, was that Don Tomas Earnshaw be retired to cut the overhead of Earnshaw's Docks (and stabilize management). Second, that they encourage development of Cebu Sugar and Bogo-Medellin. They had just taken over the agency for Cebu, a coup in itself. Then he recommended that more attention be given to merchandising by the Davies company, which was spending 95 percent of its Philippine funds on Bogo-Medellin. The company was agent for London and Scotish Assurance Corporation for fire and earthquake, and for Century Insurance Company Ltd. for the same sort of coverage. It represented St. Paul Fire and Marine Insurance Company for fire, and marine insurance. It had the agency for Solignum & Norusto paints. It maintained a small warehouse at the rear of the Perez Samanillo building and it was doing about the same business as it had been for several years. Another function of the office in Manila was to buy hardwoods for the building department of the Davies company, Honolulu. But building was off in Hawaii, and with that business was too.

The biggest problem of the Manila office was the need for an assistant for G. C. Hunter. He could not take a vacation, or afford to be sick, because he was the only responsible person in the office. As for Hunter, Henderson had the highest praise, and recommended that his views be given complete credibility in Hawaii.[7]

Henderson's report was read carefully in Honolulu. Clive was asked to write a letter retiring Don Tomas (who was mayor of Manila, so it was a ticklish matter). Clive had already mentioned his son-in-law, Gerald Wilkinson, to John E. Russell, and when Russell read that a young man was needed to understudy Hunter, he suggested Wilkinson could fill the bill. Another man was under consideration, but these were hard times and the other was experienced and expensive. Gerald Wilkinson was young and would not cost the company dearly. The other had been all but accepted, his recommendations checked out, and Clive was ready to hire him when Russell made his suggestion. Hunter had been elected to the board of Earnshaw's Docks and Honolulu Iron Works, and he obviously needed help, depression or not.[8]

Russell's recommendation regarding young Wilkinson was prompted by his feeling that the Davies family must be involved in this company if it was to survive under their ownership. Clive knew precisely how they felt in Honolulu. He had been more shaken by the meetings of the previous year with Tenney, Atherton, and the internal directors than he had indicated. Indeed, Clive seldom revealed himself even on paper, but he devoted a full page in his business notebook to an explanation of his actions:

> Two events have recently released Clive and George Davies from any charge that they owed the company more personal services—(1) George has responded to the suggestion that he relinquish his former fee and Clive has specified a visit every two years as that which is covered by his fee; (2) the Davies family has responded to a request for a fresh set of Articles of Association. Thereby a break with the past occurred and the responsibility attaching to the office of Managing Director was relinquished by any member of the Davies family. The company cannot have it both ways. They can not ask the Davies family for concession (e.g. the sale of shares to Castle & Cooke, new articles, etc.) and at the same time hold that the family (with its reduced stake in the business) responsible for its outcome . . . [9].

The fact remained, however, that Clive Davies had a guilty conscience about his own behavior in the pattern of events that had led to all these changes. The reduced stake of the Davies family in the business was only in a minor way occasioned by the entry of Castle & Cooke at Russell's behest. (Russell felt then, and forever after, that Theo H. Davies & Co., Ltd. should be a local company, owned by local people, preferably Americans.) As Clive knew very well, the diminution of family influence would continue as heirs with no emotional stake in the business sold shares for capital to build chalets in Switzerland or houses for their children. One sop to that conscience would be Harold's eventual coming to Hawaii. Another could be the dispatch of Gerald Wilkinson and Lorna to Manila. In January, in his careful way, Clive set out to ascertain Gerald's fitness. Gerald had been assigned the territory of Exeter by Northern Assurance, with a stenographer and an assistant salesman. Clive visited Gerald's regional supervisor and asked how he was getting along, and whether the supervisor, Mr. Leach, would recommend him for a post as assistant manager in Manila. Mr. Leach was almost rhapsodic in singing Gerald's praises. He had never had such a business-getter, he said. There was no one else in his division with such outstanding ability at making contacts. He was tactful, too. If there was a fault it was only his youth; there had been that one occasion on which Gerald had pressed and pressed and gotten a nice piece of business for his branch, from a national company, but cost London the whole of the company's business, when it was discovered that one branch had insured locally. But that was youthful zest; only an older man would have thought to check on such a matter. As far as Gerald was concerned, there was no post to which he could not rise. If he stayed with Northern Assurance, he could look forward to becoming a branch manager with a salary of £1,000 a year and a pension on retirement. (Mr. Leach did not realize he was talking to a man whose income from Hawaii alone was thirty times as much.)

The Davies' association with Northern Assurance was more than half a century old, so it was no problem for Clive to secure a talk with K. K. Peters in the home office. Peters was as enthusiastic about Gerald as Leach had been, but he did warn that Gerald had no inside experience; his was a sales job. To remedy that, if Clive took him away, Peters would bring him up to the home office for a few weeks to send him out with the inspectors. That way he could learn about big risks. As for the change, Peters would be sorry to lose him — he had never seen a man of Gerald's class (upper middle) who could get on with his social inferiors so well in a business way. As for going to Davies, then Northern would not feel it was losing a man at all.[10] Within a few weeks it was all settled: Gerald would get a little more seasoning with Northern Assurance and take advantage of Peters' offer, and then go out to Honolulu in 1934 for a short stay. He would then be assigned to Manila as Hunter's assistant.

In the spring, Clive Davies was back in Honolulu. Almost on his return, he had a call from Frank Atherton and E.D. Tenney to discuss Russell's administration of the company.[11] His notes on the meeting indicate that the Castle & Cooke men had not given up hope of acquiring the company; they were subtly trying to undermine Davies's faith in Russell and the local management. This time they brought up Russell's health. He had once been threatened by tuberculosis, they told Clive, and now he had a cough. He was nervous and he was carrying so much weight. Atherton then began enumerating on his fingers. There was one loss occasioned by the failure of a customer. Russell should have known more about the customer's finances. The sugar plantations and mills were spotty. Union Mill was losing money, while Castle & Cooke's Kohala was making money. (Atherton did not go into details, which would have shown very little similarity between the problems of the two operations.) The sugar companies suffered from inept management. Russell had gone into an enterprise called Cane Products, which was to make use of byproducts. But he had done so without good management and it had been experimental all the way. The Castle & Cooke directors had fought the move but had been outvoted. And, Atherton continued, what if something happened to Russell? Who would take his place? Henderson, the assistant treasurer, was a man with great promise, but he was too young and had no experience. He was not even on the board of directors yet.[12]

Since frankness seemed to be in the air, Clive Davies unburdened himself with some of the Davies complaints about the Castle & Cooke directors. The behavior of the Castle & Cooke directors on the executive committee led the Davies company men to suspect their motives—they were serving Castle & Cooke at the expense of the Davies company.

Atherton and Tenney erupted in angry protest. What did he mean? Who said they were against the Davies interest? Let him cite some specific instances. Davies could not or would not; these were the impressions he had from discussions with the internal directors of the Davies company. The Castle & Cooke men were extremely disappointed in their investment in Theo H. Davies & Co., Atherton said. Tenney broke in to say that he had been responsible for Matson Navigation Company investing in Davies, and he was chagrined by the poor performance. Davies replied that he had been persuaded over his best judgment to let Castle & Cooke buy into Davies because Russell wanted their counsel and association, and the Davies family was disappointed, too.[13]

They parted with expressions of goodwill, but much better mutual understanding of the limitations of cooperation, particularly when a group of directors, brought in and hoping to take over a company, has failed to do so.

The Castle & Cooke position seemed very strong, and Clive Davies must have had some hard thoughts about his own business, for while Davies was making $55,000 in 1932, Castle & Cooke had earned ten times as much, and its agricultural companies had done remarkably well: Ewa, $760,000; Waialua, $556,000; and Kohala Sugar Co., $137,000. The same old question stood out: was Clive going to be willing to sacrifice himself and come to Hawaii to bring the business up to where it should be?

The answer was the same. Clive revelled in his position as an English squire. At Christmastime he had written Russell about the difficulties of being a squire, and the grave responsibilities, such as the right to select a parson for the church (which he was doing) and all it entailed.[14] It seems doubtful if Russell could really appreciate Clive's problems, so enwrapt was he in those of Honolulu. For a long time Russell had warned that the refusal of the Davies to participate in management was creating rumors. One such reached Clive that summer in the form of an inquiry from a London law firm about the control of Davies company, and whether the owners wished to sell. Clive was not averse to selling, at the right price. He said he could not answer the question. The stock was controlled by a group of the family and he was the spokesman, but they would have to be consulted. What was the price? Also did the purchaser contemplate buying only the merchandising firm, or did they want the sugar plantation companies and Honolulu Iron Works "which form the constellation in which THD & Co is the sun?"[15] The lawyers went away and did not come back, but others would come again. Clive knew that, and with the unpleasantness of his recent visits to Honolulu, he was in 1933 far more ready to talk sale than he had been a few years earlier. The problem was that prices were so depressed and the performances of the companies so spotty, that the family would lose heavily by a sale. The estimated net profit for the first half of the year was $61,000 — not good, but better than 1932. And from Honolulu came word that the other companies, which had been forced to make salary cuts too, were restoring them. HSPA put back its bonus, and all the other major Honolulu houses restored all cuts. Davies and Russell agreed that the company should restore five percent to the salary level. That would mean a $17,000 extra expense, which in view of the minimal profits was a new burden. They must hang on.

Chapter Thirty-Three
DISSENSION IN THE RANKS

I*n the early weeks of 1934,* Clive conducted his own program of educating Gerald Wilkinson. Gerald had finished up with Northern Assurance and was getting ready to go to Hawaii. Clive took him around London to meet bankers with whom the firm would be dealing in the Philippines, those of The Chartered Bank, in particular, which had extended a line of credit to the Davies company in the Philippines.[1] On January 12, the young couple (plus one baby) sailed, amid expressions of goodwill and hope for a successful future.[2] But success in the American business scene meant expansion, and in the spring of 1934, for the first time, Clive Davies quarreled openly with the management of his Honolulu interests. The quarrel, as might be expected, was over money.

When Clive and George Davies had divested themselves of their "managing director" roles, they had placed the power of decision in the hands of General Manager Russell and the boards of directors of the companies. Since they chose not to attend most directors' meetings, the power of the Davies' family over business affairs could be exerted only by their ultimate stock control. One could not operate a business at the annual stockholders' meeting. There managements could be made and unmade, but for day-to-day affairs, even important ones such as the payment of dividends, the board of directors and the management would control. In the spring of 1934 Clive Davies was furious when he learned that the board proposed to pass the 1933 dividends, and retain the slender earnings as surplus, to be used for capital improvement.[3] Clive and the other members of the Davies family were living very well, and they wanted to continue. George could not possibly manage on his pay as a Member of Parliament; it scarcely covered his secretarial services. The Davies family in England had adopted a way of life that demanded large amounts of income, and so Clive Davies, as spokesman for the family, took a position about the Hawaii investments that would have shocked his father. Clive had many ideas different from those of Theo; his father had dreamed for years of living as a country gentleman, and had managed to attain that position only for the last year of his life; Clive was not going to follow that course. And if Clive was concerned about dividends more than the company, then one can imagine the views of Arthur, Theo, and the sisters and their children, most of whom would never set foot in Hawaii. The angry letter Clive wrote to Russell produced its results: it was followed by a cable from Russell announcing the payment of the dividends on May 15.[4] The quarrel was inevitable once the Davies brothers gave up their management roles, and the schism would grow year after year, until privately Russell would begin to refer to Clive Davies as "the cross I have to bear."[5]

In Honolulu, Gerald Wilkinson went through every department of the company under Russell's supervision. He was amiable and created a good impression. He very nearly brought off a coup when an American life insurance company suggested it might want to open a Philippine office and he had the inside track for the agency—but it did not materialize and that was probably just as well for his entrance onto the Philippine scene.[6] While Wilkinson was still in Honolulu, a subtle change appeared in the relationships of G. C. Hunter and the Honolulu management. Following Henderson's glowing report, Hunter had been on top of the world. Russell liked him and felt he was doing an excellent job. Clive had some reservations about Hunter's intellectual capacity and leadership but no quarrel with his performance over the years. But this spring Hunter quarreled with Simpson at Honolulu Iron Works and with others at Earnshaw's Docks. Actually the fault seemed to lie with the manager of Earnshaw's

Docks, and that fact was duly appreciated, but Hunter's lack of tact had shaken confidence in his abilities. None of this was resolved by the time Gerald Wilkinson left Honolulu for Manila that summer, but he was aware that there were straws in the wind. His ebullient character had already created waves in the company.

George, Theo, and Arthur Davies were all talking about selling some of their Davies company stock. They could hardly do it in 1934, the probable price of the stock was around $50 a share instead of the $150 or more they expected to receive, but the future course was clear. Also, Mrs. Swanzy was very old and expected to die soon; her stock probably would be sold to pay estate taxes.[7] So stock would be available, but would junior members of the firm be allowed to buy? Nothing, certainly, could be done immediately, but Russell had made Clive Davies extremely conscious of the problems of future management and control.

Wilkinson's duties were to make himself familiar with purchasing for Honolulu, insurance, and the administration of Bogo-Medellin sugar company and Cebu sugar company, whose agencies the Davies company held. It was expected that he would be elevated to a directorship of Bogo and Cebu. He was also to spend at least a quarter of his time at Earnshaw's Docks, learning the finances, operations and control from office manager Robinson and to travel around Negros, Panay and Luzon with manager Simpson. Honolulu Iron Works had just signed contracts to put up some sugar mills in China, and it was expected that Wilkinson would take over the relationship there, too.[8]

In mid-September the Wilkinsons were aboard the *Empress of Japan* which stopped at Hong Kong. Gerald left Lorna there and went to Canton and the new factories. He met Yui Ming, counsellor of the central government's Ministry of Foreign Affairs, and they talked over the Honolulu Iron Works plans. The Nanking government of China was watching jealously over the sugar mill experiment because it was generated under the auspices of the provincial government of Kwangtung. In general the Nanking government did not much care for private government monopolies; the great problem in China was the continued existence of independent governors and warlords. John J. Erhardt was the Honolulu Iron Works representative in Canton, and he was setting up the Sun Tso factory just then. Theoretically, the governor wanted sugar factories, but actually, as Wilkinson learned, his people were engaged in a very lucrative smuggling trade. They brought sugar up from Java, smuggled it past the central government authorities by Kwangtung provincial gunboat to the Honolulu Iron Works Canton Mill, rebagged it, and sold it without paying the central government duty of 150 per cent. This meant a profit of a million Canton dollars a month[9] ($US 200,000).

On September 20 Gerald Wilkinson was in Manila, after a voyage that indicated what a remarkable man he was. Aboard the *Empress of Japan* he had been invited to join the captain's table. (Clive usually made it no higher than the purser's.) It was there he had met Yui Ming, who promised to visit him in Manila. He had also met the Norwegian Ambassador to Japan, who gave him a briefing on the Far East, and Mr. Drummond, the oriental manager for Canadian Pacific Railway, who began talking about an agency in Manila. In Hong Kong Gerald had gone out of his way to see Mr. Costello, the general passenger agent of C.P.R. on the same mission. They both promised to come to Manila and consider the idea.[10]

Once in Manila, Gerald Wilkinson lost no time in plunging into business affairs. Within a month he was negotiating for a Best Foods mayonnaise agency and talking about Kona coffee and relishes. In Honolulu his enthusiasm caught the interest of Ted Guard, the merchandising manager, who endorsed his suggestion for Best Foods.[11]

Wilkinson made a fine impression on Hunter, and they were almost immediately on a first name basis. Hunter embarrassed him by instantly recommending an increase in his pay. Gerald so wrote John E. Russell.[12] At least that was the purported purpose of the long, handwritten letter. Actually the letter was a masterpiece of subtlety.[13] Duncan, another assistant, had just been transferred to Earnshaw's Docks through Gerald's efforts. "... It took me the devil of a lot of argument with Charles H. ..." He found Duncan an engaging fellow "and more popular than Charlie ..." He confided that DeWitt, head of Earnshaw's, had suggested that Wilkinson take over if DeWitt went on vacation, but "we must not put me over Charlie's head in Earnshaw's unless it is essential. . . ." There were five more pages of this report, and in every page was some putdown of Hunter. ". . . a board meeting fixed for the following day and not one item on the agenda had been discussed between Hunter, Simpson, or DeWitt. Charles had not mentioned my future status . . . ." He spoke highly of the Earnshaw's crowd and praised their willingness particularly since "Charlie's attitude to them had been absolutely damnable." But then he was saying how good Charlie was in the office, how he spoke Spanish like a Spaniard and was a go-getter for business and following that with a note that Charlie showed "the most egoistic, cocksure, uncompromisingly offensive attitude" that he had ever seen.

There were eight pages in this masterpiece, written two weeks after arrival. Wilkinson indicated that the whole business was about to collapse because of Hunter — until Wilkinson had come to smooth things over. But everything was all right now, he said, and the last page of the letter was a paean of thanks to Russell. Never had a subordinate more swiftly skewered his superior and planted the seeds of distrust in the home office minds than Wilkinson had in this wide-eyed innocent letter to Russell. All he said was news, shocking to the core, and it was said in such a manner that Honolulu could not ignore it, or fail to investigate. What was remarkable, aside from the hatcheting of his superior, was Wilkinson's swift grasp of the essentials of the business, and his ability to attract confidences from men who were almost strangers.

One day in November, Wilkinson bearded Hunter and the twenty-three-year-old assistant dressed down the fifty-year-old manager mercilessly. Wilkinson gave details of Hunter's faults, most of them sins of personality. He told him black stories of his atrocious treatment of other Davies' employees. He completely cowed Hunter.[14] And, strangely, instead of throwing the upstart out of the office, Hunter listened. Or was it so strange? The young man was, after all, the son-in-law of the chairman of the company. It seemed incomprehensible that he could so speak without the authority of Honolulu. In fact, Gerald did have some backing for his behavior. In August, Clive had written him about the "slush fund" in the Manila office, to which four Davies company officials charged "incidental expenses" and asked Wilkinson to look into it, since the whole idea was repugnant to him.[15] So Clive had given the young man an indication of his special position; no more was needed. On December 10, Gerald Wilkinson wrote Russell, demanding that Hunter be fired. His candidate (he said) was G. G. Gordon, the head of the Philippine Milling Company's agency. Gordon was about 45, competent, and experienced in the Philippines, Wilkinson reported. But he also damned Gordon with faint praise, and indicated such complications in employing him that Gordon appeared less than desirable to head the Manila operations of Theo H. Davies & Co., Ltd. There was another candidate, indicated in the letter by implication: Gerald H. Wilkinson. "... I am quite familiar with the delicate buying problem caused by our dual relationship to Cebu stockholders and Earnshaw's Docks." And he lulled criticism with an obvious truth: "In justice to Hunter, however, I would ask you to remember my youth and inexperience and the fact that youth's opinions are frequently impulsive and superficial, and that in this case, with all the desire for true honesty, it has not been easy wholly to disassociate from this matter the element of my personal ambitions."[16]

It had already been established that Clive and Edith Davies were coming out to Manila just after the turn of the year 1935.

Clive's conscience, plus Edith's desire to see Lorna and Gerald, took Lorna's parents to Manila in January, 1935. Clive did not know Hunter and he wanted to see the man for himself. When he arrived, he plunged into work with the vigor that made Russell and others wonder why he had ever deserted the business. He spent the first afternoon with Hunter, dined with Gerald and Lorna, and the next morning he was at Earnshaw's Docks for an inspection. Then he went on to the oil refinery they had taken over. He lunched at Gerald's and then made half a dozen calls in the afternoon to learn about the general Philippines business situation.[17] He called on the Tabacalera people (they were the most important merchants in Manila) and on several other firms. He went to Cebu, came back, and for a week carried on a furious social life interspersed with business calls. But there was more than sight-seeing and social life in this period. He met daily with Gerald Wilkinson and went over all Gerald's letters, and his reports, and heard his tales about Hunter's ways. He also talked the matter over with C. A. DeWitt, the head of Earnshaw's Docks. DeWitt recommended Wilkinson in the highest terms. He had indeed, said DeWitt, done all that he had told Russell; since Wilkinson's arrival, many difficulties among the three Davies factions had been resolved.[18] After that conversation, Clive was convinced and wrote in his notes that "G. Wilkinson has shown himself able to handle successfully and quickly the most difficult personal situations. He has had himself known and liked all over Manila. He is fully able to handle the position of manager of THD Co., Manila. . . ."

From these meetings, Clive had also gained some of Gerald Wilkinson's enthusiasm for the prospects of merchandising expansion of Theo H. Davies & Co., Ltd. His original thought had been to settle the problem of a financial manager, but he quickly expanded that view.[19]

On February 4, Clive undertook the unpleasant task of firing G. C. Hunter.[20] At 2 o'clock Hunter came to him at the Manila Hotel, and Clive handed over a letter John E. Russell had sent him for possible use, giving details of separation. It meant six months pay "and the sincere hope that you [Hunter] will in the meantime be able to make some other satisfactory association . . ." There was little chance of the latter. Hunter was around 50, and there were few jobs for foreigners in Manila. He asked for any job. He would work for Gerald Wilkinson gladly. He would take a reduction in salary. But Clive was firm. The answer was no. The period was extended, Hunter would be paid through December 31, but that was all. So the deed was done, and that evening Hunter came back to the hotel, along with Gerald Wilkinson. On February 17 Hunter delivered his resignation, dated June 30, but it was understood that he would take a "long vacation" before that time. On February 20, Clive and Edith Davies sailed for Honolulu, leaving Gerald H. Wilkinson as the new head of Theo H. Davies & Co., Ltd. in the Philippines.

Chapter Thirty-Four

NEW DAVIES BLOOD

After Harold Davies left Cambridge, he spent a year at Massachusetts Institute of Technology to improve his engineering skills and learn more about dealing with Americans. He had done only fairly well at Cambridge—he had failed his honors examinations—but had taken a first in the ordinary bachelor's degree, which was as much as Clive Davies thought he could expect.[1] After his year at MIT, Harold spent some time in the Vancouver office of the Davies business, concerned especially with the Vancouver Iron Works, a small copy of Honolulu Iron Works. This phase of the Davies business was operated as it had been in Janion's day, as a separate entity from Honolulu, and never assumed a major importance in the Davies family scheme. Soon, Harold would move to the larger arena of Honolulu, for Clive continued to be conscious of the peculiar relationship of his company and the community to which the family no longer belonged.

In considering the future of the company, history, custom, and circumstance made Clive think still in terms of a triumvirate, although one quite differently placed from those of old. He hoped that in the next generation the company would be in the hands of Harold Davies, Gerald Wilkinson, and C. J. Henderson, the bright young American who had now served a number of years as assistant treasurer, but more important, as chief assistant to John E. Russell. Henderson had Russell's confidence and that of virtually everyone else in the organization. He had but one real problem: his health. Several years earlier Henderson discovered that he suffered from diabetes, and although he took insulin to maintain a normal life, he was not quite sure that his health was up to the demands of senior office in the company. In 1933, when Henderson had been in a hospital in Boston, his brother Wellington Henderson, a Philadelphia businessman, had offered him a place in his company that promised to be less demanding. At the same time, Clive had written Henderson with promises for the future if Henderson wished to remain with the Davies company. Henderson had remained, but he had never responded to the question. In the spring of 1935, Henderson had a long interview with Clive Davies to settle the future.[2]

He had decided to stay with Davies if there was opportunity for him there. He wondered how many young Davies would be coming into the business.

Clive responded that there seemed to be no likelihood of any Davies coming in except Harold and Gerald. The latter, he said, had come because Russell wanted him (this was a defensive position Clive adopted and maintained).

Clive's second son, Geoffrey, was a complete disappointment. He had gone to Uppingham, in the family tradition, but had not proved to be a scholar and had announced that he would not go on to university. He would rather be a farmer, he said. What does a squire do with a son like that? Clive went to see Farmer Edgar of the Old Place Farm, and Edgar agreed to take Geoffrey as a farm student at a fee of £75 a year. There seemed small hope that Geoffrey would ever join the firm in Honolulu.[3]

Clive indicated that he regarded Henderson as a sort of American son, and valued him for "his capacity, his ideals and his breeding" and welcomed him as one of the trio. He went further: in the future none but American citizens could become general manager of Theo H. Davies Co., Ltd. in Honolulu.[4]

Henderson asked about buying some stock. He could buy some on the outside, but he wondered if he could not take over some stock held by

Kukaiau ranch at treasury cost. Better than that, Davies said, he could look forward to buying much more stock, for Clive's three brothers all wanted to begin disposing of theirs. But when Henderson examined the market, he discovered that just then he could buy stock from outsiders at $75, rather than $150, and it was agreed that he should buy some shares from the estate of F. H. Young, the husband of Clive's sister.[5]

At the end of his Honolulu stay in 1935, Clive Davies felt better about the company than he had in several years. That September, Harold sailed for Honolulu to begin his apprenticeship. A few days later Clive celebrated his 64th birthday sobered by the recollection that his father had been but four months older when he died.[6] Yet he was thankful for the change in his affairs, with "relief in the business's improved stability."[7]

It was true that the business had stabilized in 1935. The coming of the Roosevelt administration had been greeted with distress by the Honolulu business community, and for several months in 1933, the Davies company had postponed all major policy decisions, pending examination of the Roosevelt revolution. But the reds had not come marching in, and the country had not collapsed in spite of the 1933 Bank Holiday. Soon adjustments began to come which were thankfully welcomed by the sugar community, particularly in 1934 the inclusion of sugar in the Agricultural Amendment Act (later to become the Sugar Act) which that year provided the Davies company nearly half a million dollars in federal aid for its sugar plantations.[8] Still, the Honolulu and Hawaii businesses were no more than slowly recovering lost ground. With the exception of a flurry in 1936 which brought the Davies company an income of $450,000, it would take a new war to bring the company profits up to the level of the 1920s, and even then the ratio of profit to capitalization would not achieve the old levels.[9] The future had to lie in other directions, and in the case of the Davies company that meant sugar, Honolulu Iron Works, and the new Philippine venture. Sugar remained spotty, with Waiakea Mill falling into more trouble, Hamakua's performance no better than fair, and Laupahoehoe emerging as the queen of the Davies sugar investments.[10] By 1934 Honolulu Iron Works had grown to be a large business, with assets of six and a half million dollars and liabilities of only $1,370,000. Through dividends and new issues, the common stock totalled 30,000 shares, and 15,000 shares of preferred had been authorized, although not all was issued. So Honolulu Iron Works was quite prosperous, due largely to business generated from Manila.[11]

There, the 23-year-old Wilkinson suddenly thrown into command of this industrial kingdom was eager to make a showing, and of course the way to do it was to increase the *profit* in that profit and loss statement at the end of the year. One avenue could be China and the Far East. General Manager W. G. Hall of Honolulu Iron Works wanted to retire, and Gerald thought perhaps he could be replaced by Erhardt—that's how important the Canton operation was considered as a potential, in spite of the unsettled conditions of China.[12] Honolulu Iron Works was building mills in Kweihsen and Waichow and hoped for large profits from them. Hall had made a trip to Thailand and was hopeful about new contracts in that area. But there were conquests to be made in the Philippines, and Wilkinson was determined to make them. He hired G. G. Gordon as his second man, a situation he had prepared in that original letter that ostensibly touted Gordon as manager potential but actually cut him down to number two size, and was applauded for the action in Honolulu. But his first real challenge came just after the beginning of the year 1935. The Davies Company was offered the agency for Crown Life Assurance Company if Gerald would take personal charge of the business. On February 8, Wilkinson cabled Honolulu for instructions. Clive Davies was in Hawaii, but on the Big Island and could not be reached. With Davies in the area, Russell was not willing to make a commitment. He assented to the arrangement but subject to approval of Davies. When Wilkinson had that message, he tried to reach Davies independently, and failing, signed the agreement, then wrote Russell blithely ". . . it was unfortunately impossible for us to comply with the first condition of your cable . . ."[13]

By the spring of 1935, Gerald Wilkinson was moving at full speed. Davies expanded its sales of mining machinery; J.F. Taddiken, who had begun in the New York office of Honolulu Iron Works, was sent to Canton to expand the company's China trade. He dispatched a commission sales-man to Southeast Asia to sell Philippine exports (a novel idea). As Russell and Davies knew from the first,[14] with Wilkinson it was not a question of jacking up the effort, but of holding it down. Wilkinson was reminded that his office was a branch and that he was not to commit Theo H. Davies & Co., Ltd. to new expenditures without Honolulu approval. But by September Russell was chiding Wilkinson for falling victim to "the old, but serious malady which causes Branch office and subsidiary concerns . . . . to forget they are but part of the whole and that they must accept the decisions of the Head Office.[15] His complaints about Wilkinson to Clive Davies became so strident that finally Clive advised Russell to make a trip to Manila the next spring.[16]

In the fall of 1935, Harold Davies went to Hawaii to begin his appren-ticeship in the business. Russell sent him to the Big Island to learn about the plantations, with the idea of moving up through the plantation depart-ment. He started at a salary of $150 a month, half again as much as his father had received from Swanzy in 1896.[17]

The late summer of 1935 was disturbed by the dismissal of several key executives of the Manila operation, at Earnshaw's Docks, Honolulu Iron Works, and T. H. Davies & Co. Wilkinson had spoken about these people to Russell, and his views were backed by Taddiken, who had come in as Far Eastern Manager of Honolulu Iron Works. The change was distressing and expensive, involving more payoffs, but at the end of it Clive Davies and Russell hoped that the mistakes of the past had been corrected.[18]

Near the end of the year, Harold Davies returned to Honolulu from the Big Island, steeped in sugar lore, tanned and healthy, and eager to get into the plantation department's affairs. Russell told Clive he had high hopes for Harold's rapid rise in that branch of the company. The problems in the sugar plantations continued to be the same: climate, labor, and management. In the past few years the Davies company had suffered badly in the latter division, through quarrels and incompetence and the necessity of buying out small landholders and old contracts. The combined Union Mill and Niulii operation was improving, in spite of management problems, although the milling cost was still high. Hamakua, after some bad years, was turning around; there, in 1933 the plant harvested 11,000 tons of cane from 3,600 acres. Two years later they took more than 15,000 tons from 3,300 acres. Everywhere, of course, they were moving to increased mechanization, using cane trucks, mechanical weeders and every possible device to cut the cost of labor. Crop controls by the federal government created some difficulties, but Russell indicated that these could be managed.[19] Kaiwiki Sugar Company, which Davies had acquired in Swanzy's day, was beginning to show profits after a bad year in 1934. Laupahoehoe's only problem was to hold down production to stay within the new Agricultural Adjustment Act quota, and Waiakea Mill was showing profits.[20]

Honolulu Iron Works was profitable, and so was Theo H. Davies & Co. Ltd. Clive wanted to increase the dividend since the net profit was up more than a hundred percent ($272,000) over 1934. Castle & Cooke's director, Budge, objected. Davies had valued its three million dollars in investments at book, and many of those investments were not worth their book value in 1935. So, said Budge, the Davies balance sheet was inflated. Clive and Henderson launched into a long series of justifications; but the result was about a 50 percent increase in the dividend to $85,000 that year. Clive Davies might not be running the company any more, but when he spoke, those who ran it listened. The Davies company and its subsidiaries were still very much Davies operations.

Chapter Thirty-Five

THE UNION MENACE

T*he Davies properties were long on assets* and short on performance, and this was a troubling note all during the 1930s. In 1935, Kaiwiki Sugar Company, for example (one of the newer acquisitions), had assets of $1,333,000 and made a profit of $143,000, which was respectable enough. But the parent company, with assets of $9.5 million and a capital of $3.5 million, was earning less than seven percent on the investment, which was hardly better than putting the money out to loan.[1] Even though Clive refused to spend much time in Honolulu, he spent most of his work week on the company business in London. In February 1936, Russell came to London for a round of conferences and they went over the company finances. There was good news and bad news. The bad news was that the United States Supreme Court had just outlawed the Agricultural Adjustment Act of the Roosevelt administration, under which sugar producers were paid various benefits. Unless Roosevelt could think of something new, that change would mean a sharp reduction in the revenues of the sugar companies.[2] Russell had been planning a trip to Manila to impress young Wilkinson with his responsibilities to Honolulu, but instead he had to go to London. The cash positions of four of the five sugar companies were excellent (Union Mill still had its troubles). Kukaiau Ranch and Waianae Lime Company were both making small profits, and Davies profit was up. Most comforting was the comparison in financial position between that of the end of 1935 and five years earlier. The company's bonds, building bonds, and short term debt amounted to $1,600,000 as compared to $4,780,000 at the end of 1930.[3] So while there was much complaint within the company about Draconian measures, it could be seen at Hawkley Hurst that only those measures had saved the company. How Davies had gotten into such a pickle in the first place was not a matter for discussion with Clive; Ernest Wodehouse was virtually retired, and had Clive been bearded about his own responsibility he would have been surprised.

While Clive and Russell were talking about affairs, including those of Manila and its headstrong young manager, Gerald Wilkinson sent a cable announcing that he had done it again: this time he had a firm offer to take the agency in the Philippines for the Lincoln National Life Insurance Company of Indiana, and proposed to go to Fort Wayne in a few weeks. Honolulu Iron Works' Taddiken, in whose judgment Clive and Russell had great confidence, agreed.[4] How much criticism could one heap on a man who kept bringing home the bacon, when most of the other divisions seemed content to just keep feeding the hogs?*

When Russell returned to Hawaii in the winter of 1936, he found that the simmering labor unrest of the last few years had begun to come to a head. At the end of 1935, representatives of the International Longshoremen's and Warehousemen's Union (ILWU) began appearing at the docks in Honolulu and Hilo to organize the stevedores. "Union in Honolulu is only partial and, we believe, and hope, it is fairly well blocked," Henderson reported to Clive.[5] But in Hilo, the ILWU managed to sign up almost all the dockworkers, and in January the union had called a strike in Hilo and Honuapo. The seamen also walked off, tying up half a dozen Matson Line ships, but the Mariners' Union in San Francisco sent its members back to work. The company was warned and was doing all it could to stop unionization from creeping into the sugar ranks. "Bad situations or low pay will

---

*To be absolutely fair to the Honolulu office, it must be noted that Honolulu's Theo H. Davies & Co., Ltd. already represented Lincoln National Life Insurance Co. in Hawaii, and that Louis Baron, then manager of the insurance department, was helpful in securing the agency for Manila.

be corrected (if found) as soon as possible."[6] So although the ILWU men did not know it, their activities in the islands were already improving the lot of the workers. The Big Five were getting a long overdue push. They did not welcome the change. Assistant Treasurer Henderson referred to the "destructive agitation" of the "radical leaders," and the sugar factors responded by establishing an Industrial Association of Hawaii to monitor and counter union activity. Soon the association had branches in Hilo and on Kauai.[7] Henderson was the committee member for Theo H. Davies & Co., Ltd. The association began publishing a bulletin; one issue was an analysis of communism, "a world revolutionary organization" with allegiance to Moscow, complete with seven footnotes to give verisimilitude and importance to the material. There was not one word about local labor. But most issues were more pointed; they gave industrial statistics (selected) and reports on labor activity. They also presented propaganda to keep up employer morale. "No union man is loyal to any company.—Statement made by a local union representative." Under the heading "More Facts," the editor charged that the unions which had invaded the islands had no interest in Hawaii. "What are some of their motives?" the editor asked.

> First, to enlist support of their mainland campaign. Second, to create positions of power and personal gain for some loyal henchmen whom they desire to reward. Third, to obtain money from workers by splitting up the work to include hundreds who have never worked on the waterfront, in order to get a larger monthly income for themselves. Fourth, to get wages high enough so that their surplus labor, from whom they have collected dues for years but who are hardly earning enough to keep alive, can again be in a position to pay up regularly.[8]

There was, of course, a certain truth in this diatribe. The ILWU and the Sailors Union of the Pacific were locked in a mortal battle with the waterfront employers of the mainland. Before it was finished it would destroy the port of Portland, very nearly destroy that of Seattle, and bring San Francisco business to the starvation point. And it was certainly true that Harry Bridges, the leader of the ILWU, was radical and primarily concerned with the West Coast waterfronts. It was essential to his plans that he tie up shipping, particularly Matson Navigation Company's, at both ends of the line. But that did not mean that the union men he sent in to organize the workers of Hawaii were not doing something for those workers. Many of those union men were communists, as history proved. They had hidden loyalties; but for the moment their aim was to enlist the dockworkers, lumber workers, sugar workers and pineapple workers of Hawaii, and bring higher wages and better working conditions. The practical deficiency of the propaganda the Big Five fed themselves through the Industrial Association was that it was self-deluding and prevented some of the key executives from understanding the real issue as far as they were concerned: which was to make wages more clearly reflect the contribution of the workers to the high profits of the sugar industry.

Yet Henderson was anything but blind. He sent L. M. Judd over to Hilo to discover what had brought about the success of the strike there that had failed in Honolulu. Judd gave him an informative bill of particulars. In the first place, the conditions at all the little ports on the Big Island were different and that meant working conditions, wages, and employers. The unions could go from one port to the next and cite the better conditions of X over Y. The second reason for dissatisfaction was the behavior of the Matson Navigation Company in Hilo. Matson kept a hiring list of enough stevedores in Hilo to work three ships. But often there was only one ship in the harbor, or none. Matson's system of splitting the work meant that many of the stevedores were earning $16 a month, on which they obviously could not support themselves. Worse, favoritism was in control. The Matson manager, Frank Harlocker, played politics and used jobs as rewards for political adherence. Thus, the port captain was an incompetent who did not have the respect of the men he employed. The timekeeper on the wharf was another political henchman of Harlocker's. As to conditions, sometimes the stevedores were worked from early morning until 8 o'clock at night without any food or rest. The employers ought to have corrected those conditions, said agent Judd.[9] The solution: higher pay and better working conditions. But the immediate action: "Get Mr. Bodie [the union organizer] out of Hilo and if possible out of the territory of Hawaii. The other local leaders who are at present in Hilo do not have sufficient ability and knowledge of the method of organizing and carrying out a strike to make it effective. If Bodie could be eliminated and no other leaders, as Moll and Luning, be permitted to come to Hilo, the situation could be cleared up."[10]

Had the employers attacked the source of difficulty they might have avoided the fierce labor conflicts that were to come in the next twenty years, but it was expecting a great deal of human nature to ask those employers to give up their old ways and voluntarily reduce profits. The Davies men were no more enlightened than the rest; they had been quick enough to cut wages when the pinch came, and slower than some others to restore them when conditions bettered. In recent years, since Clive had abandoned his managing directorate, he had adopted a protective ploy in his relationship with all employees. He was always inquisitive on his visits to Hawaii, sympathetic and understanding of men's troubles. But if a person wanted something, he was inevitably referred to his supervisor; when old employees were fired by a new manager of a sugar company, as happened frequently in the 1930s, Clive always deafened himself to their complaints, and said he could not go above their superior's heads. It was not true, of course. Whenever Clive wanted to go above the superiors' heads he did so. In 1935, in a bloodletting in Manila, Gerald Wilkinson forced the retirement of Secretary Simpson, who had served the company for many years. Simpson complained to Clive[11] that this was shabby treatment for one who had given his life in service to the company, and Clive forced Russell to make the settlement more generous. Leslie Wishard, the manager of Union Mill, was very unpopular with Russell and the plantations department of Davies, and for three years Russell talked about firing him. Clive interceded time and again. But generally speaking, by 1935 Davies had adopted the habits of "the soulless corporation"[12] and thus was a prime target for labor organization. In response to threat, instead of bettering conditions, remarkably Davies joined the other employers in espionage, propaganda, and strike breaking. Secret agents were employed to infiltrate the ranks of the workers, and report on activity.[13] The union responded by increasing its activity. For example, on January 28 in Hilo, Filipinos flocked into the ILWU hall to join the union. Who were they? Employees of the Davies company lumber division, brought in by Harry Kealoha, the union agent. How had he "enticed" them (as the secret agent put it)? He had told them that as soon as the union was well organized they would be working for $1.00 an hour instead of twenty-five cents an hour. Harry Kealoha infected them with a vision: some day, he told them, the Big Five would recognize the Longshoremen's Union because all the steve-adores and laborers from the sugar plantations and different big companies would one day be hired from the Longshoremen's Union. Already, by January 30, he had signed up 1250 men in Hilo.[14]

By March 1936 the HSPA was expecting a strike which was supposed to come as soon as the Honolulu chapter of the ILWU received its charter.[15] By June 14 the demands of the union were known: recognition of the union as bargaining agent, Pacific coast working conditions, and Pacific coast wage scales. The HSPA tried at the eleventh hour to mend its ways; on August 15 its members agreed to adopt the eight-hour day.* But this new sign of concern for the workers came too late. The dock strike was voted on October 31. It was the first of Hawaii's major labor disruptions.

---

*Technically, the HSPA was not involved with stevedoring in Hawaii. However, four of the Big Five, as agents for Matson, were so involved, and that is part of the reason for the ILWU's success in organizing the sugar workers (as opposed to the AFL unions that were also active at the time).

Chapter Thirty-Six

WILKINSON VS RUSSELL: ROUND I

The dock strike of 1936-37 did not hurt the Davies company seriously. Kukaiau ranch, selling meat to Hilo and to Honolulu made better profits than ever. The company's indebtedness was reduced because new inventories could not be brought in, and the inventories were depleted quite satisfactorily by a product-hungry public, partly at least cut off from the usual sources of supply on the mainland. Profits of the trading company for the year turned out to be almost twice as high as they had been in 1935.[1]

Minor changes continued in Hawaii. The company had bought E. O. Hall Company, a retail hardware firm. It had acquired the Piggly Wiggly store franchise from Western States Grocery Company, and all these were satisfactory businesses. There was talk of selling Union Mill to Castle & Cooke's Kohala sugar company, and Clive was eager to get rid of a sugar operation that seemed to have gone sour for the Davies over the past few years.[2] A purchase of F. A. Schaefer and Company nearly materialized but collapsed, much to Clive Davies' disappointment; he had long wanted to acquire Honokaa Sugar Company, which the Schaefers owned. Honokaa was a prime property. Once he had it, Davies would then control most of a forty-mile section of the Hamakua coast, from North Hilo to the edge of Kohala. But generally speaking, Hawaii matters did not change a great deal; the new arena was westward, in the Philippines and China. Manager Erhardt in Canton and Taddiken in Manila had negotiated with Chinese in the far western province of Szechuan for mills, and it seemed likely that business would also open in North China. The Japanese had occupied Manchuria, and their designs on China were apparent, but Chiang Kai-shek had managed to wrest control of Kwangtung from the warlord in control, who also owned the sugar monopoly. This threatened to put a crimp in the Canton business, but China seemed no more in upheaval than it had been for twenty years.

In Manila Gerald Wilkinson was making friends for himself and the company and increasing, at least slightly, the profitability of the Theo H. Davies enterprises. It was decided in 1936 to legally merge Earnshaw's Docks with Honolulu Iron Works, recognizing the physical reality. Don Manuel Earnshaw had committed suicide, Don Tomas had been eased out of the company, and it was a Davies creature anyhow. Without apparently moving, Gerald had his hand in the retirement of DeWitt and Simpson, the older executives of the group in Manila, and emerged with Taddiken as one of the powers of the company in the Far East.

Many of Gerald Wilkinson's actions were considered to be precipitate and ill-advised in Honolulu and, had Gerald not been the son-in-law of the chairman, he probably would have been accused of insubordination. As it was he aroused Russell's annoyance, which was not very well concealed, even to Clive.[3] What upset Russell was that Wilkinson seemed to do as he pleased and get away with it. He had been in Manila for only two years, and everyone knew that the time-honored stint for an expatriate was three years, followed by six months' home leave. Yet when Gerald announced the Lincoln Life Insurance coup, in the same cable he said he was going on to England, to take the vacation he had planned to take in 1937. Russell fumed at that, but Clive pretended not to notice. After all, his daughter Lorna was coming to see her mother, and bringing their daughter, Mary June, who had been born in England before the Wilkinsons left. A second child, Rupert, was born in England[4] in 1936.

While Wilkinson was in England, he approached Clive with the request that he be allowed to buy stock in the company. Clive had no objection. George, Theo M. and Arthur all wanted to unload shares, and Henderson had bought shares from Mrs. Swanzy and others. Twenty years earlier, Clive would not have considered explaining such a sale to anyone. But conditions had changed. Once Theo H. Davies & Co., Ltd. had been a family company. In 1936 the company was still controlled by the Davies family, and its stock was still privately held in that it was not traded on any exchange, but many outsiders had been brought into the company. Castle & Cooke owned 2500 shares and, through them, Matson and Company owned 2600 shares. Alexander & Baldwin had 360 shares. Walter Dillingham owned 600 shares. Other outside holdings brought the total outside ownership to about a quarter of the 26,976 issued common shares.[5]

Clive felt no demand to consult with any of these people, but he did feel the need to inform them. When the matter was taken up with Russell, and he learned that Clive proposed to sell Gerald Wilkinson 633 shares in the company, Russell was upset. Further, for months, Wilkinson had been touting Philippine gold mines as an investment for Theo H. Davies & Co. and Russell had been holding back, wanting only to handle Philippine gold on an agency basis. In 1937, when the stock purchase was being discussed, Wilkinson admitted to Clive that he could not pay for the stock because he had borrowed £30,000 on a note signed by his father to buy Philippine gold stocks, and they had subsequently dropped in market value. If he sold them, he would lose thousands.[5] This bit of information troubled Clive Davies, but it annoyed Russell, who expected his subordinates to inform him of their outside dealings.

By the winter of 1936-37 the growing animosity between Russell and Wilkinson upset Clive Davies. He went to New York in February, and when he met one of his associates who spoke very highly of Gerald, his concern spilled over and in a most untypical manner, Clive unburdened his soul to the other on the subject of Russell's unbelievable rancor toward the young man.[7] Clive did not seem to understand that he was suddenly giving Gerald a chance to buy, *on credit,* nearly as many shares in the company as Russell owned. The older man was jealous.

Clive Davies went on to San Francisco, where he saw C. V. Bennett, the San Francisco manager, in whom he had great confidence. They discussed the quarrel between Russell and Wilkinson, and the discussion moved to the future ownership and control of the Davies interests. Clive told Bennett what he had said earlier, that he hoped Harold Davies, Wilkinson, and Henderson would run the company when he was gone.[8]

Wilkinson had a fine sense of timing, and over the past few months he had obviously sensed how much his relations with Russell had deteriorated. Just before Clive Davies left San Francisco, Wilkinson cabled Russell asking if Russell wanted him to come to Honolulu for that delayed meeting. Wilkinson knew very well that Clive Davies was on his way to Hawaii, and there could be no safer time for him to appear. Russell indicated his feelings by cabling Clive in San Francisco, asking if he "wanted Gerald to be allowed to come to Honolulu on April 2." Clive showed that message to Bennett, and the San Francisco manager helped him work out a careful message of reply to indicate that Russell might want Gerald to come to Honolulu to discuss difficulties.

In March Clive Davies was in Honolulu. He spent his first evening with Harold and heard some of his woes. The second evening he spent with Russell, to thrash out Russell's attitudes toward Harold and toward Gerald. The latter demanded most attention, for in this conversation for the first time, Clive Davies learned that Russell believed Wilkinson was disloyal.[9]

Life continued then, on an even enough keel, for several weeks. Russell had shown his superiority by delaying Wilkinson's trip to Hawaii until May 14. In the interim, Clive was like a man waiting for the other shoe to drop. He took Harold over to the Big Island on one of his inspection tours and was delighted to see how well everyone there liked his son. The affection was spontaneous and real, and several people went out of their way to comment to Clive about the boy's marvelous personality.[10]

On May 14, Gerald and Lorna Wilkinson arrived in Honolulu aboard the *President Hoover*. The tugs warped the big liner into the Aloha Tower dock, the boats went out, filled with divers and laughing Hawaiians covered with leis. More leis were stacked around the necks of the incoming guests and the band played *Aloha Oe,* and it was hard for anyone to resist a tear of greeting. Clive and Harold were there, bearing leis and smiles, and so were

Russell and his wife Olive. Then they all went up to Craigside, where Clive gave them lunch in quiet splendor. After lunch, Clive, Russell, and Wilkinson went to the Davies building downtown, where Clive left the other two closed in Russell's private office. They remained there until after five o'clock.

In the next two days, Clive spoke with both principals in the quarrel.[11] Russell had opened the conversation with a frank accusation that Wilkinson was disloyal. He had heard remarks, he said, that indicated Wilkinson did not have much use for John E. Russell. Wilkinson denied it, and said that he had learned from a mutual friend (and named him) that Russell did not like his work or his personality. Russell denied that (but later told Clive Davies that he had been "let down" by the friend, who had repeated remarks about Wilkinson to the younger man).

Wilkinson had obviously converted his defense to attack, and he went on to assure Russell that he was prepared to work "as a loyal member of a team of executives of which Russell was general manager." After that, somehow Wilkinson managed to come out of the encounter as victor. Russell, who had been sour about the Wilkinson stock purchase, begged Clive Davies to put it through immediately, and Clive did. Not one word was said about Clive Davies putting up the $60,000 for Wilkinson's shares.[12]

In the next few days, Clive Davies congratulated himself that the waters of truth and mutual confidence had washed the past clear. Russell agreed that it had been right to bring Wilkinson to Honolulu just then (although he had resisted it with every fiber) and that the interview had gone well. He agreed that his contacts with the branch managers at Manila, San Francisco, New York, and in Cuba were not frequent enough, and promised to arrange for meetings every six months. Having reduced the disagreement to a corporate level, Clive Davies was content.[13] But on May 27, the night before Clive was to sail on the *Empress of Canada* for Vancouver, Russell came to him, distraught. He had awakened the night before and at two o'clock had finally gotten up and written out a "paper of complaints" which he now showed Clive. The paper was passed, Clive Davies read it, and "the floodgates now opened and with them, his heart." Russell said he wanted Clive to deal only through him. No other person was to report to him. At this juncture, Henderson sent financial reports to Clive, Guard sent merchandising reports, the San Francisco office sent monthly reports, as did New York, and Manila. Ah, Manila, there was the rub! All these reports, all these people in direct contact with Clive Davies. Russell was losing prestige in the eyes of all, he said.[14]

Clive Davies soothed Russell. To do as Russell asked, he said, would be to upset tradition. Always the head of Honolulu Iron Works had reported to its president. Always the managers of the plantations must report to their president. And Clive was president of each of the sugar companies and of Honolulu Iron Works. Russell realized that, and in the discussion, the question of Clive's contacts with his son-in-law was conveniently forgotten.

There was one other incident. Gerald came to Clive, not to Russell, to report that Taddiken, the HIW man, was interfering with Wilkinson in his exercise of the financial duties of the company in Manila. There really was no way of telling Clive Davies that Wilkinson should have brought that information to Russell.

But when Russell left Craigside that evening, he seemed happier than when he had come, and next day the Russells, Lorna and Gerald Wilkinson, and Harold Davies all came down to the Aloha Tower to see Clive off. It was a happy crowd, the band played Hawaiian music, Clive went aboard laden with leis and all the crowd were smiling. At the end the band played *Aloha Oe* again, and the *Empress of Canada* sent forth a great blast on her whistle and moved out toward the sea, as a few leis were thrown into the water, and the waving of the visitors on the dock continued until faces could no longer be seen.

The Wilkinsons and the Russells parted company then and went their separate ways. That was nothing new, Gerald and Russell had been doing it for two years.

Chapter Thirty-Seven

A SEA CHANGE

I*n 1936,* when Clive Davies and John E. Russell were exchanging anguished letters about Gerald Wilkinson, Clive stated his current thinking about the Davies firm. Clive's aim, he told Russell, was to create an "inner circle" which had four purposes: (1) to maintain the tradition of the family name of Davies; (2) to provide a business enterprise in an American community for British interests; (3) to provide careers for members of the Davies family and other associated with the business; and (4) to control the sugar and other investments of the family.[1] Thus Clive wanted stock in the hands of Wilkinson, Harold, and Henderson. Russell wanted that circle broadened to include Ted Guard and Bennett, the San Francisco manager. And, of course, Russell did not at all like the prospect of seeing Wilkinson or Harold with more stock than he had,[2] although he made little of this in the discussion. What really annoyed Russell was that Wilkinson had spoken privately to Henderson and Harold about the future. Also, the pressure under which Russell had been placed to resolve the difficulties with Wilkinson had left scars. Davies had behaved with heavy propriety throughout; he had told Russell that if Russell did not approve, Wilkinson's stock deal would not go through. Russell could sense that if Clive refused Wilkinson (which Russell would have preferred over all else), and Wilkinson left the company, that it would not be long before Clive Davies would be getting rid of John E. Russell. So, in this exchange, the relationship between Russell and Clive Davies was the real sufferer.

Clive had been willing to sell out in the 1920s when there seemed no prospect of any young Davies taking over, but there was no more talk of that. George was knighted by King George V in 1936, and that, too, somehow made a change. Sir George had a son, George T. Davies, and although his bent seemed to be toward literature, one never could tell. Even Geoffrey Davies, Clive's second son, who was having so hard a time finding his way, had begun to settle down. The farming experiment had come to an end.[3] After the farm, Geoffrey decided he would become a policeman, and his father duly helped him get located. But by the autumn of 1936 Geoffrey was willing to try Cambridge, and with much relief Clive saw him off to university. After a year it became apparent that Geoffrey was not cut out for an honors course. His tutor, Mr. Sinker, suggested that the reason was that he had not applied himself sufficiently at Uppingham and did not have the reading behind him to do honors. Nor was Geoffrey really concerned about applying himself at Cambridge. He told Clive he was switching to Railroad Management. While Harold had gone to Cambridge with a pledge of sobriety and only after two years had applied for the right to drink wine and an occasional glass of port, Geoffrey became one of Cambridge's more social blades, and beer was very much a part of his Cambridge career. (He ended up taking a "gentleman's degree."[4]) What attitude would he now take to the business? By 1938 it seemed quite unsure. Geoffrey enjoyed Cambridge, and stayed there. His tutors suggested that the army would take him at the drop of a hat—he was just the sort of person they wanted to give a commission. But Geoffrey was not pointed toward an army career. He did not have any idea of what he might do, he was living from day to day. Geoffrey was a very different sort from his brother Harold. He was shyer, and their appearances were so different it might be hard to tell they were brothers. Harold was by far the most handsome of the Davies men, but one could still recognize the jaw and nose of Theo H. Davies and Clive in him. But Geoffrey's face must have been modeled on the Fox line, for he looked little like his grandfather, his father, or his brother. He was tall, six feet, and rangy. Like his father he smoked a pipe, but he had none of his father's calm about him. In that sense he was very much like Gerald Wilkinson, whom at one stage John E. Russell had seen as possessing "strong evidence of ambitious independence amounting at times to rebellion."[5] Russell might have been talking of Geoffrey Davies.

Poor Clive! It seemed that no matter how he tried he could not get the management team set. For even as Gerald Wilkinson was being stuffed down John E. Russell's throat, Charlie Henderson quit the Davies company. Perhaps he saw handwriting on the wall with Wilkinson and Harold in the running for the chief executive's job. Perhaps it was just youthful impatience, but in the spring of 1937, Henderson was offered a job as No. 2 man in the Hawaiian Pineapple Company, and he took it.[6] Russell was truly anguished because he lost his understudy. There was no other in the organization. Shortly after Clive returned to England that spring of 1937, Russell began writing that he hoped to bring Harold along rapidly enough to take over Henderson's chores in a few months.[7]

Russell understood what Clive Davies wanted and, in spite of his own misgivings, as a conscientious and loyal employee he did his very best to carry out Clive's wishes. As promised, he went to Manila to see Gerald Wilkinson within six months. While there he behaved with such generosity and courtesy no outsider could have known of Russell's deep suspicions of Wilkinson's ambition. Russell suggested the expenditure of $20,000 to build a suitable house for the No. 1 man in the Philippines, and $12,500 for the building of two vacation cottages in Baguio, to be used by staff members. The justification, he told Clive, was that this move put a stamp of permanence on the Davies presence in the Philippines.[8] Clive could not have been more delighted with the turn of events. He endorsed the addition of Harold to the board at an early date and applauded Russell's forbearance toward Wilkinson.[9] He was furious with Henderson for "deserting" them, but there was nothing to be done about it.

Russell was spending most of his time on sugar affairs in the late 1930s. He was always very shrewd about sugar. Kohala was sold. After much soul searching, Union Mill was sold to C&C, and the company disincorporated; the assets were not sufficient to pay all the liabilities and the stockholders' investment was worthless.[10] But the other companies prospered, with Laupahoehoe making about a quarter of a million dollars in 1937. Russell's heavy attention to sugar affairs was caused by several events. He was elected president of the Hawaiian Sugar Planters Association in 1937, and also of Sugar Factors. These were responsibilities, and the agricultural policies of the Roosevelt administration demanded a considerable amount of lobbying in Washington, Russell's position meant he served on the committees that traveled to the national capitol once or twice each year. The labor situation was serious, apart from the shipping strike. Sugar workers on a number of plantations on Maui walked out, and production there was stopped. The Davies plantations managed to avoid stoppages, but the future was clear: unless the labor situation was remedied eventually the plantations would all be hit.[11]

The sugar planters were taking action just as strong as they dared, to strengthen their positions. They formed company unions to try to keep the CIO unions out. Russell worked constantly to modernize the plants, cut the labor force, and thus the cost, looking forward with acuity to days when labor costs would rise sharply. In the 1930s Russell was talking about mechanization far beyond the plantations' ability (then) to operate. He wanted trucking to replace the railroads and flumes. He wanted labor-saving harvesting devices. Hamakua Mill company experimented with a bulldozer cutter, which eliminated hand cutting of cane but created a mess of rock and trash that was hard to eliminate. Hamakua was a good example of the state of the Davies sugar interests in 1937; "good" in the sense that Laupahoehoe and Kaiwiki were superior. Much "progress" had been made in seven years. In 1931, Hamakua produced 38 tons of cane per acre. In 1937 the plantation produced 64 tons. But the quality of the cane was the problem. Climate and fertilization of the wrong sort had taken a toll. In 1931 it took 9 tons of cane to secure a ton of sugar; in 1937 Hamakua was grinding 12.5 tons to get a ton of sugar. In seven years half a million dollars had been spent on modernization; the result was that the payroll had dropped sharply, from $450,000 in 1931 to $363,000 in 1932 and only in 1937 was coming back to $450,000, largely because of wage raises given to try to offset union organizing. Actually the number of men on the payroll was down from 854 to 737.[12] Russell had nearly panicked, along with the other planters when Atherton Richards, president of Hawaiian Pineapple Company, jammed through his board a move to pay pineapple workers a $2-a-day base! Worse, the company would pay time and a half for overtime. The sugar planters went to Richards in force and persuaded him to hold up on the move. They said it would destroy them.[13] The real labor troubles in the sugar fields that year were confined to Maui, where the ILWU organizers had concentrated their effort and closed down most of the plantations. The labor strife had not spread formally yet to the Big Island, but the effects of the difficulty and the shipping strike were already making the Davies interests suffer. The shipping strike, Russell said, would cost them $10 a ton that year. The HSPA had also voted to share out the losses of any plantation through strikes, so Davies would have to pay a portion of the Maui strike costs.

What Russell really dreaded was the inevitable wage increases. It took 13.75 man days to make a ton of sugar, and if Davies had to pay $2.20 per man per day it woud add $5.50 to the cost of each ton. The solution: mechanization and stalling as long as possible in the face of labor agitation. Russell never deluded himself about the outcome. They would have unions. The question was: when?

So bemused with sugar problems was John E. Russell that he did not have the time to spend with Harold Davies that Clive wanted him to devote to the education of the young man. By the end of 1937 this default had created new tensions within the company. Several times Clive reminded Russell by letter that he expected Harold to be elected to the Board of Directors of Theo H. Davies & Co., Ltd. at the annual meeting in the spring of 1938—and he was. Clive did not suggest that Gerald Wilkinson also be chosen—that would have been too much for Russell to swallow, and Clive knew it. Besides, Wilkinson had gotten himself into financial difficulties. Manila in 1936 had gone gold crazy. Ore strikes in the hills had started an investment fever in the Philippine capital that raged all summer. In the summer, Wilkinson, for example, had offered to take $1000 of C.J. Henderson's money, and had run it up to a "value" of $1750 in about a month in gold speculation. But in the winter the bottom dropped out of the gold market, and Wilkinson and hundreds of others were left with serious stock market losses and heavy debts. When Russell went to Manila in the summer of 1937, he was dismayed to discover that the three major officials of Theo H. Davies & Co. in Manila were all in debt. Wilkinson owed $61,000 and his collateral was worth only $23,000. G.G. Gordon, Wilkinson's assistant, had plunged even more recklessly: he owed $113,000 and his collateral was worth only $69,000. Even the third man, I.M. Duncan, owed $8,000, with a collateral of $5,000.[14] Russell, as part of his *volte-face* on Manila, suggested that Clive and the company fund the debts of these executives, to relieve them of the embarassment of facing local creditors. This plan was given serious consideration. Some of the difficulty was relieved in 1938 by a partial recovery of the gold market, but Clive Davies took on a guarantee of some of Wilkinson's debt. Russell would have had grim satisfaction in airing the problem had he been vindictive, but he could not be, for as he put it "virtually all Caucasians in Manila were taking in each other's washing" in the gold fever of the day, trading back and forth ever higher until the bottom dropped out.

Sometime in the late 1930s John E. Russell came to one conclusion that was to direct the rest of his corporate life: Theo H. Davies & Co. Ltd. must be Americanized if it were to catch up to the others of the Big Five. Castle & Cooke's Tenney and Atherton had said the Davies company was falling behind. In 1930 Castle & Cooke's net profit had been $840,000 and the Davies company's profit only $319,000.[15] At the outbreak of World War I the Big Five companies had been nearly equal, but that situation was changing. In 1938 Castle & Cooke's Tenney was dead, and Atherton was retired, and Budge, the Castle & Cooke director in Davies company, had nothing like the same interest the others had shown, so Russell did not have the goad of past years. Still one of Russell's major concerns was always the quality of his executives. By the end of 1937 he had decided that Harold Davies was not the material for leadership, although Davies had performed well enough in acting as *charge d'affaires* during the months that Russell was away in the Far East. Russell's discontent was emphasized by some other events. Sir George Davies had begun transferring stock in Theo H. Davies & Co., Ltd. to relatives, which underlined the change in ownership. Now in the late 1930s, each time stock was moved, Russell wrote Clive Davies the exact position of the management, and the number and location of proxies needed for control. This was all new ground and gave rise to new ways of thinking. Russell allowed himself to grow unhappy with Clive's constant demands for information and Clive's continued correspondence with executives on all levels, often without sending copies to Russell. So while Clive Davies wrote Russell in his annual Christmas letter in 1937[16] how pleased he was at the turn events had taken, how much he appreciated Russell's efforts to get on with Wilkinson and bring Harold along in the business, all was not as it seemed. Clive said he was delighted to see that he and Russell shared "a common outlook on the more fundamental things of life." If he meant membership in Honolulu's St. Andrew's Cathedral congregation, perhaps he was right, but if he meant business, he was not as right as he had been the year before. In August Russell had indicated a new discontent with the ownership, in letters to Bennett in San Francisco and Ted Guard, who was on vacation in England.[17] A change had come over Russell, and the relationships between Chairman Davies and President Russell would change several times from this time forward. In 1938 Russell tended to go his own way more than before. In 1939 his independence became so noticeable that it created a crisis in the company.[18]

Clive Davies came to Honolulu in the spring of 1939 on his bi-annual trip. The first evidence of difficulty came from A.G. Budge, the Castle & Cooke president, who called on Clive one day. Speaking as a Theo H. Davies & Co., Ltd. director, Budge indicated that Russell thought he ought to have more money than the $25,000-plus-bonus he was getting as president of the company. Clive believed this discontent must have been registered by Russell. Budge also brought up the need for a good No. 2 man. Clive thought Russell had settled all that in the letters of 1937, in which Russell had indicated he was bringing Harold along. But on the visit to Honolulu,

Clive had learned it was not so; Harold was *not* being groomed for leadership. The Budge interview underscored his concerns.[19] Clive Davies really became upset when he took Harold on a trip to the Big Island to visit the sugar plantations and discovered that Harold was seriously considering quitting the company. On May 9, then, Clive braced himself and called Russell for another of those "frank talks." He began with Harold's plight. The boy had been pushed into a corner and was not being brought into the inner councils of the business. Clive said he was "very distressed." He could not expect Harold to make Honolulu his career if he were unhappy. Only a keen interest in his work would "atone for a residence in exile."[20]

If in 1937 Clive had upset Russell by insisting, if ever so gently, that Russell accept Gerald Wilkinson as a member of the business inner family, in 1939, Clive did not mince words. He was, after all, 68 years old, and he did not know how much time was left to him to make sure the business was protected. Budge's parting remark had been that he considered the present management situation "dangerous."[21] Harold *must* be brought into the inner councils of the family holdings. Since the Davies family owned or controlled nearly all the firm's clients, it meant Harold *must be* in general management. If Russell did not want to use Harold as a Theo H. Davies & Co., Ltd. executive, it made no difference. Harold *would be* made privy to *all* doings, just as if he were Clive Davies. Otherwise Clive would have to bring in someone else; he mentioned Gerald Wilkinson. Or, if Russell refused to accept that course, then Clive would move to dispose of the Davies family interests in all the companies.

Russell was taken aback. Anger was a facet of the Clive Davies character he had not before seen. Russell offered to resign, an offer to which Clive did not reply. On this uneasy note the meeting ended.

Back at Craigside, Clive Davies confided concerns to his notebook.[22] How could Russell be jealous of Harold? It seemed impossible. Russell did not seem to believe Harold was competent. But all the outside reports indicated that Harold was most competent, and the best-liked man in the company. Well, he had said his piece. Unless Russell came around, he would have to think carefully of the course of action. He had observed in the past two years a deterioration; more and more Russell and the resident board of directors took actions without consulting him. Nor was he being kept properly informed. In 1938 Harold had made a trip to Manila, and submitted a complete report. The report went into Russell's office and was never mentioned again, nor did Clive ever hear of the report or have a copy of it.

The next day Russell came back and responded to some of the questions Davies had raised. If the Davies family were to continue in Hawaii, a member of the firm must be in residence. Russell had always said that in the past. He definitely did not want Wilkinson; Harold was his choice. He had been bringing Harold along to manage finances and accounts, but recently he had noticed a change for the worse in Harold's frankness and hopefulness of outlook. He promised to have a talk with Harold. On this assurance Clive gratefully abandoned the unpleasant subject.[23] It was nearly sailing day, and his thoughts were turned toward England. He would be in touch with Harold, and with Russell, and the future course would show itself soon enough.

Chapter Thirty-Eight

AND THEN CAME DECEMBER. . . .

W*hen Clive Davies returned to England* in the spring of 1939 he plunged into the life of the country squire with a new vigor, remarkable in a man his age. In recent years he had become more personally involved with the Church of England than before. He was chosen as delegate to various church conferences, and he dined occasionally at Lambeth Palace with the Archbishop of Canterbury and lesser lights. This year he had become churchwarden to the Hawkley village church.[1] He also occupied himself with the business of his estates and of the village. There were cottages on his farms to be refurbished, and the local water system needed some work. He attended meetings of the local fire brigade, and went to Lloyd's Bank in Liss to straighten out the church's accounts.[2]

For more than a year the threat of a European war had hung in the air. War in China had already disrupted the Davies company's business in the Far East, but war in China and war in Europe were two entirely different matters. Spurred by the war atmosphere, Geoffrey, who had come down from Cambridge, decided he wanted to make a career of the Royal Navy and went up to take his Admiralty Board examinations.

From Hawaii came a disturbing letter from A.G. Budge, who did not like the way the Davies company management was performing.[3] Clive talked it over with George F., who told him the time had come to cut loose. The Honolulu situation had so deteriorated, from what Clive said, that the family ought to sell out lock, stock, and barrel. Of course, George admitted that he had felt that way since 1920 when he had urged the sale of that initial block of stock to Castle & Cooke, ostensibly to secure their management advice on the board of directors. How did Clive feel about a sale now? It would depend on what position a purchaser would take about retaining the active staff of the various companies, said Clive. As in the 1920s, he insisted that the Davies obligation to those who had given their lives to the company must be observed. Anyhow, let George in all his Parliamentary splendor regard the international situation. This was no time to be talking about sale. When somebody came up with a good offer, they could talk more.[4]

August came to England, and with it the bad news that Geoffrey had not managed to make the Admiralty list for naval appointments. What to do? He was a member of the naval reserve and had been since November 1938. On August 9, Clive Davies called on H.E.O. Wheeler of the Southern Railway, and subsequently Geoffrey was engaged to begin work there in January 1940, in railroad administration.[5] But as he waited, the news grew so much more threatening. By the end of the month women and children were being evacuated from London and Hawkley was taking its share of them. On September 3, war was declared with Germany, and four weeks later Geoffrey had his naval commission, as a sublieutenant in the Royal Naval Volunteer Reserve, and was off for the fleet anchorage at Scapa Flow. It was a "hostilities only" appointment, not the career post he had sought, but in August 1939, that was no longer a question. With England threatened, career became just another word.

The Wilkinsons happened to be in England just then on home leave, but that was cut short and Gerald and Lorna and the children hurried back to Manila. In Honolulu, Harold began talking about a commission; after all, he was a trained engineer, and once during a summer had sailed across the Atlantic as a trainee engineering officer aboard the *Aquitania*. Just then the Armed Forces were chockablock with applications at home, and those from overseas were not getting much attention. Harold was told to settle down and wait.[6] John E. Russell sympathized with Harold's posi-

Harold Davies, the heir apparent to the company fortunes in the mid-twentieth century in his naval officer's uniform shortly before his death on active duty with the Royal Navy, in November, 1941.

Harold Davies on the eve of his departure to join the British Navy. Left to right, Harold Weidig (New York Manager), H.W. Taddiken (Manager of Honolulu Iron Works), Harold Davies and Ted Guard (Mdse. Director).

tion. Indeed, after that last talk with Clive in 1939, Russell had gone out of his way to bring Harold into the "inner circle," and they were getting on much better. Russell even made the sublime gesture: if Harold went into service, Russell would welcome Gerald's coming to Honolulu for the duration of the war![7] But Gerald was in no position to come, although he could not say as much in a letter to Russell. With the outbreak of war he had written the Home Office in London, asking what he could do, and had been promptly enlisted in MI-6, the secret political intelligence service, as chief officer in Manila.

Spurred by Geoffrey's success in joining the Navy, Harold asked his father to make some discreet enquiries in London, and Clive replied that with his engineering background, Harold would have no trouble securing a naval commission if he returned home. So in the spring of 1940, Harold Davies packed up his bags and sailed for England. He found his homeland in a state of siege. The Battle of Britain was about to commence, and soon even the Hampshire countryside was alerted. Clive was doing air-raid warden duty, often manning the telephone in the center all night long. Geoffrey had become the executive officer of a converted trawler on coastal convoy duty and some patrol work along the eastern coast, assigned to the area of Suffolk county around the River Stour and the port of Harwich.

By July 1940, Harold was assigned to a corvette as a deck officer and sent to the West Coast on convoy escort duty. There he met Miss (Jane) Hester Patience Bullough, a pretty young woman, intelligent and of good family. She was at the time an officer in the Women's Royal Naval Service (WRENS) and the Davies family approved of the match, if perhaps not of the timing. They were married February 1, 1941, and managed a few brief days of leave for a honeymoon.

The war grew worse. In May, Clive Davies' London office was bombed out. Fortunately it happened at night, and neither Clive nor his secretary, Cecil Bird, was there. A friend offered him a desk, a typewriter, and the use of a telephone, and he took it gratefully. That was no small offer for 1941.[9] The local records, of course, were destroyed, but Honolulu could supply copies.

There were problems in Honolulu, financial for the most part, but Russell had to deal with almost all of them himself. He wrote and cabled Clive, but letters were slow and often the cables were delayed in delivery, and it had become virtually impossible to make a long distance telephone call from London to Honolulu. Clive tried for several days in June and then gave up.

But there was little time for concern with such matters as dividends and bond-retirement programs just then in the Davies lives. Harold and Jane came to Hawkley Hurst as often as they could, and so did Geoffrey, but most likely over a holiday they would be duty bound, and the two young men might be on the sea anywhere within a thousand mile range of England. Seldom did many of the family manage to meet. On May 23, for example, Geoffrey left Hawkley Hurst to go back to his ship, and next day Harold and Jane arrived at lunch time.[10]

The news was often grim. Friends were killed, and many old haunts in London disappeared into bomb craters. On June 26 came the sad message that John Davies, son of Harry Llanover Davies, had been killed in North Africa. Father and son had both been victims of the Germans, a quarter of a century apart.

Lieut. Ronald, youngest son of Sir George, was killed in the evacuation of Greece. H.W. Davies, eldest son of Rev. Arthur Davies, was serving as a lieutenant in HMS *Electra,* a destroyer that was engaged in the Battle of the Java Sea. His ship attacked the enemy through the smoke of battle and was never seen again.

Harold Davies' ship, HMS *Candytuft,* was assigned to Iceland that summer to try to take off some of the pressure of the German U-boats and their wolfpacks. On September 9, the ship was at sea on convoy, and Sub. Lt. Davies was in the wardroom, off duty, when one of the boilers burst, sending a cloud of live steam through the engine room and the wardroom, which was immediately forward. Several officers including Sub Lt. Davies, were killed. Eighteen men were in the engine room and none of them survived. They were buried at sea, and the Admiralty sent one of its terse, lugubrious messages to Hawkley Hurst.[11]

Early in 1941 it became apparent in Washington that Britain did not have the cash to continue the war against Germany. The British government soon ran out of dollar credits and even loans and guarantees from Canada were not sufficient to carry the enormous volume of war supplies that was being shipped. In the U.S. Congress the pressure grew for payment of British debts, and was directed against British holdings in the United States. "Why don't the Goddam limeys pay their debts" was the general tenor of the questions asked.

In Honolulu a suggestion appeared in the *Advertiser* that British securities be auctioned off.[12] C.H. Hemenway of the Hawaiian Trust Co. was so upset he hastened to write John E. Russell, who was in Washington. The pressure reached the White House, where President Roosevelt was extremely sensitive because he was engaged in a secret and possibly illegal alliance with Winston Churchill to support Britain's efforts with every means short of war. Roosevelt would have gone to war, except that too was illegal, the warmaking power being delegated to Congress, and that authority never then having been breached. Roosevelt called in Secretary of the Treasury Henry Morgenthau, Jr., and they discussed the possibilities. One was to force the sale of all British assets in the United States to support the loans. All the competitors of the British companies would have liked that very much, particularly if they could have bought the assets and taken over the businesses. Immediately when Clive Davies heard the threat he began looking for alternate programs that would not cost the Davies family their business in America. John E. Russell conferred with bankers and financial authorities in San Francisco and Washington. In New York, Harold Weidig, the company's eastern representative, was in touch with Sir Edward Peacock, the head of the British purchasing commisssion, who obviously had a vital interest in seeing that the flow of goods to Britain did not slack off.[13]

In the summer of 1941, much of the effort of John E. Russell in Honolulu and Clive in England was devoted to preparing a scheme by which the Hawaiian securities of the Davies family could be used to secure loans for the British government in its time of need. An elaborate plan was drawn, which would have yielded loans of $2,000,000. An alternative scheme called for sale of the Davies properties at more than $4,000,000, but this was rejected. Finally, the American Reconstruction Finance Corporation and the British Treasury came to a much larger agreement, in which assets of British companies and British citizens in the United States were to be pledged against the American loans needed so that Britain could buy the essential weapons of war and the food to keep her going in the struggle against Hitler.[14]* All this rigamarole seemed necessary be-

---

*The Davies loans were repaid by the dividends that otherwise would have been received by the British stockholders, who were compensated in the United Kingdom, with War Loans.

cause the United States was still technically neutral in the war against Germany, although in fact, American warships were escorting British convoys in the Atlantic and American destroyers were engaged in deadly battles with German U-boats. But in Congress and in the Middle West, in particular, anti-British feeling still had a strong base, and even stronger was anti-involvement feeling. Many Americans, even in 1941, truly believed the U.S. could hide behind its oceans and stay out of the wars that raged on both sides.

As in the first world war, the struggle of Britain brought greater profits to Theo H. Davies & Co., Ltd. and its subsidiary corporations. In 1940 Theo H. Davies & Co., Ltd. earned $448,000 after paying taxes of $160,000. When $58,000 was transferred to surplus and $90,000 was written off to amortize losses on Union Mill stock, the profit was still $298,000. Honolulu Iron Works that year earned $320,000, Laupahoehoe earned $58,000, Waiakea Mill earned $93,000, and Hamakua earned $42,000. The next year these figures leaped, but so did taxes, which suddenly jumped even higher than profits in comparison. In 1941, Theo H. Davies & Co., Ltd. earned $1,377,000 before taxes, which came to $635,000 that year, representing the enormous increase in American expenditure for defense.[15]

There was one other change, an extraordinary expense that represented a complete change in the uneasy position of the Davies family, citizens of a belligerent nation, whose profits were going to support a war that some Americans even in Hawaii did not like. Theo H. Davies & Co., Ltd. wrote off $250,000 for 1941. That figure represented the cash, accounts receivable, the inventories, and the other assets of the Manila branch. For on December 7, 1941, or December 8 as it was in Manila, the position of Theo H. Davies & Co., and the Davies family changed completely. All that enormous stack of documentation for the British securities loan suddenly became no more than a huge pile of paper.* Americans, who had been

---

*As Geoffrey Davies pointed out, there was still a loan to be paid off before the Davies company shareholders had control of their shares and could receive dividends themselves.

bystanders for three years in the war against Hitler, were suddenly catapulted into war themselves by the Japanese attack.

Gerald Wilkinson in British officer's uniform at the entrance to Hawkley Hurst during World War II.

Chapter Thirty-Nine

WAR IN THE PACIFIC

By 1941 the Manila office of Theo H. Davies & Co., Ltd. was doing better financially than it had been in the 1930s, a time when profits were slender or non-existent. The Manila branch had been brought into existence to handle sugar companies' sales and purchases, and to act as fiscal agent for the Honolulu Iron Works-Earnshaw's Docks business. Gerald Wilkinson had set out to acquire more business for the Davies company, and Davies had purchased E. J. Nell Company, a small but profitable engineering firm, and added marine insurance under Tito Luling, a local man who had joined the firm. In December 1940, the branch had made a profit of ₱10,000, which was very satisfactory. Wilkinson also persuaded Honolulu to let him invest in the Hume Pipe Company, and the Philippines Asbestos Products Company. All this was a part of Wilkinson's policy of "growing up with the country." By the mid-1940s the Philippines would have total independence from the United States, and Wilkinson believed that those foreign companies which truly served Philippine interests would be the ones to survive. He proposed to invest in "small factories with a skilled process." The Philippines had lagged behind other oriental countries in the matter of industrialization. When the independent government came to power, Wilkinson expected that those companies making Philippine products would be less likely to be discriminated against than others.[1] Earlier a bill had been presented in the legislature that would have outlawed foreigners from participating in the retail business. It was aimed at the Chinese, but its blunderbuss approach augured badly for all foreigners; although the bill failed, it would have been unconstitutional under the U.S. law anyhow.

So by midsummer 1941, Wilkinson had: a life insurance business under an American named Slane that was progressing and beginning to make profits; a successful, if small, marine insurance business under Tito Luling; a nitrate department under John D'Authreau, an Englishman; and a merchandise department under a Swiss named Gustav Laurent. Soon they would take on the Sherwin-Williams Paint agency. That year the company suffered an embezzlement by a Filipino employee in a trusted position. Russell worried over this and suggested that Wilkinson was putting too many local people into positions of authority.[2] Wilkinson replied to his charge with some heat, indicating he felt strongly that men of ability should be brought along, regardless of race.[3]

All that summer of 1941, the knowledgeable businessmen of the Philippines had been half-ready for war. But one could not batten down the hatches and stop doing business under the circumstances, so business went on, more or less as usual. Toward the end of November, Wilkinson knew the Japanese were going to attack. That was part of his responsibility as a "spook" working for MI-6. He sent a coded message of warning to the British agent in Honolulu, asking him to tell Admiral Kimmel and General Short that a Japanese attack on Hawaii was imminent. He also had that word transmitted to Russell. But when the British agent transmitted the warning to the military and naval authorities, it was simply put in the file with other reports. He tried to send Lorna and the children out on a ship scheduled to sail from Manila to Honolulu early in December. He had kept Lorna and the children with him during the past year very queasily. She had wanted to stay, and John E. Russell had seconded her decision; he did not believe there would be an attack on the Philippines, and if there was one, that Caucasians would not in any way be mistreated.[4] The sailing of Lorna's ship was cancelled, and the morning of December 8 arrived in Manila with the Wilkinsons all still there, and that same morning, December 7 in Honolulu, the American battleships were lined up in nice neat rows next to Ford Island at Pearl Harbor.

The Japanese did attack in the Philippines but that first week the action seemed far-off and inconclusive. The first attack was an air strike by 22 Japanese carrier planes on the U.S. seaplane tender *William B. Preston* in Davao Gulf. Then bombers hit Baguio and Tugogarao airfield in northern Luzon. A few hours later came the first big blow: the Japanese struck Clark and Nichols fields and knocked out most of the American B-17 bombers, lined up like pufferbellies on the airfield, and the fighter planes neatly beside them. Cavite naval base and Manila were first hit just after noon on December 9.[5] The smoke from burning Cavite was visible in Manila that night, but for that next week, Rosario Heights, where the Wilkinsons lived, was not a military target and was not bombed. The bombers came over, and Lorna and the children went to the dugout bomb-shelter as ordered. Two other families had come in to stay with the Wilkinsons, and they all trouped down, with Mary June and little Rupert leading the singing to keep up morale.

Wilkinson's position in British intelligence was known to General MacArthur, and as soon as the Japanese attacked, he asked Wilkinson to become his British liaison officer, to keep contact with General Wavell, the British commander in the Far East. Wilkinson cabled London and was informed that he had just been commissioned a major in His Majesty's forces. He scouted about and found the requisite uniform and crowns for the shoulders, and appeared in Sam Browne belt at the fortress where MacArthur had his headquarters. He formed a relationship with the American commander that became closer than he expected, for MacArthur was "*not* a spontaneous Anglophile."[6]

Wilkinson's job was to keep London posted on events. Every day he conferred with General MacArthur, and every night he sent a message to London. As the weeks went by the messages grew ever grimmer. The Japanese landed troops on Luzon and began working their way toward Manila. The Americans and Philippine constabulary were unable to stem the advance. On December 23 MacArthur had decided to abandon Manila, making it an open city to preserve the lives of the civilians and the city itself, and Wilkinson had to leave Lorna and the children and go with him to Bataan and Corregidor where MacArthur would hole up in the tunnels of the old fortress. There was no way, now that Wilkinson was called to active duty, that he could abandon his post and stay with his family.

The Japanese moved into Manila. The enemy nationals (Japan was at war with Britain as well as the United States) were taken to Santo Tomas, the university with large buildings and some 25 acres of enclosed land. There they were to be interned. From that moment on, Gerald Wilkinson was out of contact with his family.[7]

Wilkinson stayed near MacArthur, and when they were surrounded on Bataan and Corregidor, MacArthur decided to send his British liaison officer on a mission to General Wavell, in Java, who had just been made commander in chief of all allied forces in the Southwest Pacific. MacArthur gave instructions that his senior pilot was to fly Wilkinson over and back. One night in the middle of January 1942, they took off from the little hidden airfield in MacArthur's last remaining two-seater aircraft. The plan called for them to make three hops to reach Wavell in the Dutch East Indies; they would fly at night, lie up by day, and fly again the next night. It was a fine plan, but on the first leg, they reached a point about 70 miles from Corregidor and the plane's oil pressure suddenly dropped. The pilot turned around, flew back over Manila, and began circling over Bataan, waiting for daylight so they might make a safe landing. The circling annoyed the American anti-aircraft gunners, and they began shooting at what they thought was a Japanese airplane. The pilot decided this was dangerous, and when he saw a shadow that he thought was the field, he landed. It was the field, but in landing, they hit the ground hard, the plane bounced, came down on its left wing, and turned turtle, coming apart in three pieces. Neither man was more than scratched. They picked their way out of the wreckage, and the airfield crew found transportation to take them back to Corregidor.[8]

Like everyone else on "the Rock" Wilkinson seemed to be stuck. But three weeks later, several submarines arrived. There was gold to be shipped out of Corregidor (the Philippine government treasury) and there were code experts to be sent out so they would not be captured by the Japanese. Also a few nurses and other lucky ones were to go. Wilkinson was ordered aboard one of these submarines, which set out for Java. Nine days later the submarine arrived, having traveled on the surface by night and submerging to avoid Japanese aircraft during the days.[9] Wilkinson found a plane to take him across the Java hills to Wavell's headquarters, where he presented MacArthur's requests for weapons. But there were no weapons; Singapore had just fallen, and the Japanese were on the move everywhere in the Pacific. Wilkinson spent two weeks at Wavell's headquarters, answering messages from MacArthur, and then was ordered by the American commander to Washington to present MacArthur's case for fighting back. He flew to Australia in a Dutch plane and then went to Melbourne. He waited 10 days for a flying boat to take him to San Francisco but it never came. So he took a freighter, and arrived there on March 31. Then he hurried to Washington to report to Field Marshall Dill at the British Embassy. He returned to Australia and when MacArthur came out of Corregidor, Wilkinson rejoined his staff. But after a short time, the British decided they preferred a regular line officer as liaison between their forces and the American commander, and Wilkinson was reassigned. He ended up working for "Little Bill" Stephenson, the head of political intelligence operations in the United States, out of an office in Rockefeller Center, New York. The work was most secret; for Wilkinson it involved making as many contacts with Far Eastern experts as possible, and learning what he could from people who came out of the Japanese sphere to the west. He traveled frequently from Washington to New York to London in these days, and in the course of the war he was to meet nearly every figure of major importance, from Churchill and Roosevelt down to the members of the War Cabinet of Britain. He worked from time to time with Harry Hopkins and represented Stephenson to General "Wild Bill" Donovan, the head of the American Office of Strategic Services.

Not long after reassignment to the west, Wilkinson had a chance to visit Hawkley Hurst. He arrived just as his father-in-law was completing the insertion into the churchyard wall of a plaque commemorating Harold Davies' life and death. They stood in the churchyard that gray day, and Clive was very quiet. Gerald touched his arm.

"With him went everything you had hoped for, did it not?"

The older man nodded and brushed away a tear. He had hoped that after the war Harold and Gerald would carry on the Davies companies and the family traditions, and hand them along to another generation. Now, no one could tell what was going to happen.[10]

From time to time they all had news of Lorna and the children. Lorna had not done well at first in Santo Tomas camp. She had fallen ill and her weight dropped to 89 pounds from a normal 120 or so. Friends feared she might have tuberculosis, and when that was found not to be the case, still they indicated the fears to the Japanese authorities, who let Lorna and the children move back to the Rosario Heights house and remain there for nearly a year under house arrest. During this period, and in the camp, the Filipino employees of Theo H. Davies & Co., Ltd. literally saved the lives and health of their friends who were imprisoned. The inventories of the company still existed, although written off by Honolulu, and the Japanese had not seized them. Thus there were supplies of Sherwin-Williams paint, and groceries and dry goods to be sold. This task was undertaken in behalf of the internees by Gustav Laurent, the merchandise manager who now turned out to be the Swiss consul, and the money obtained was used to buy food and medicines for the people of the Davies company and Honolulu Iron Works. The Iron Works itself—Earnshaw's Docks, was hard hit by bombers in the first weeks of the war and then, along with nearly all else on the waterfront and industrial sections of Manila, was taken over by the Japanese.

Meanwhile Wilkinson's duties gave him a carte blanche that was marvelous in learning about the future in Asia, and planning for it—assuming, of course, that the Allies were to win the war. In London he called on the Hongkong and Shanghai bank, and made friends with its important officials there. He called on the London agents of the Manila firm of Warner Barnes and Co., and dreamed (in his diary) of taking over some of Warner Barnes business at war's end.[11]

He went to call on the Butterly Company of London, which owned a whole group of coal and steel companies. He saw a new sort of bridge that could be easily shipped and assembled and thought about bringing those over to the Philippines after the war to replace the destroyed bridges. He looked into Butterly's capital and gave them a memo about the Davies company in Manila. He went about London leaving balance sheets and operating statements in useful places. All this, of course, took but a fraction of his time, and much of the effort was useful in his official work; for all these people had contacts in Asia, and that was Wilkinson's specific intelligence sphere.[12]

During the visits to England, Gerald Wilkinson almost always managed a night or a weekend at Hawkley Hurst. He and Clive Davies began to talk about the future. At first in the despair that followed Harold's death, Clive refused to consider anything past the war years. But soon Gerald had him talking about refinancing the Manila operation. They spoke of acquiring 100 percent of E. J. Nell company, and all of Hume Pipe and Asbestos companies. Wilkinson said he thought the future of Theo H. Davies & Co., Ltd. was bright but that of Honolulu Iron Works dim in a postwar world. Clive reminded him that the purpose of Honolulu Iron Works was primarily to serve as a "service station" to the sugar industry. That purpose must continue. And as they talked, Clive warmed to the discussion, until he was speaking of Gerald securing a million dollars from the Davies company in Honolulu and another million dollars from Honolulu Iron Works. He also warned Wilkinson not to let Honolulu Iron Works acquire any part of ownership of Davies, Manila. Somewhere in the past, from Clive Davies' point of view in the 1940s, a serious error had been made in diluting the control of Honolulu Iron Works, and the Davies interests demanded that it go no further.[13]

As they talked, and as Wilkinson traveled, and talked with others, his plans began to jell. C. V. Starr, the American who had made a fortune in Far Eastern insurance, gave him advice about ownership and management. Officials of Unilever, even then a huge multinational corporation, suggested he might want to join them after the war. He countered with an offer to take over Unilever's Philippine Refining Company on behalf of Theo H. Davies & Co., Ltd.

Once in a great while Wilkinson had news of Lorna. In December, 1944 in New York he met an American repatriate who had seen her not many weeks before, and learned that in May she and the children had been sent back to the camp, after Premier Tojo had objected to the large number of foreign nationals wandering in the city with their distinctive arm bands, and had ordered all, not too ill, to move into the camps. Three days after they moved back, somehow the house in Rosario Heights caught fire and burned to the ground. The incident seemed to wipe out a whole segment of the past.

Aircon, one of the successful Davies subsidiaries, was developed in the 1950s to supply air conditioning in the Philippines.

Chapter Forty

BRAVE NEW WORLD

The first *Clive Davies* had heard of the bombing of Pearl Harbor and the attack on Manila was over the wireless on that Sunday afternoon. But it was four days later before he had direct word. His sister, Alice Warner, had arrived at Hawkley Hurst for tea, and she was there when the cable came from Russell saying that there had been no damage, but there was no news yet from Manila, and in a way that was more important, for Lorna and Gerald were there.[1] It was January before they had heard from Lorna, a cheerful cable saying all was well in Manila, which everyone by then knew was not true. Meanwhile, Geoffrey announced his engagement to Joan Cooke, daughter of a retired naval officer who was bursar of the Royal Hospital School near Ipswich. The war had completely changed the course of romance in England: Joan and Geoffrey were married in the chapel of the school and the reception was held at her family's house in Holbrook.[2] Again it was a wartime marriage, with family visits hurried and foreshortened by duty. Geoffrey was transferred that spring to become first lieutenant of the *Cutty Sark,* the yacht of the Duke of Westminster, which had been converted to become a warship. Rather, she was reconverted, for *Cutty Sark* had begun life as a World War I destroyer, and had become a private yacht only after the end of the War to End All Wars. Later Geoffrey journeyed to Philadelphia to pick up a new destroyer escort.

In Honolulu business continued during the war, although not as usual. Every aspect of the business, including the sometimes troublesome Kukaiau ranch, was profitable. One problem was securing merchandise to sell, but that was not confined to the Davies company. Kukaiau could sell every bit of beef it could produce, and beef had become the basis of the ranch in the past few years, as the mules had been replaced by trucks on the sugar plantations. The ranch was typical of the Davies farming enterprises in its experience. The ranch staff were organized for defense; the *paniolos* (cowboys) were formed into a cavalry unit (Company 13, 2nd Battalion, Hawaii Rifles). John Holi was the first lieutenant. They rode patrols at night to be sure the Japanese did not sneak up on Hawaii in force. One boy, Dan Miranda, was drafted. All the others were deferred as essential workers — which they certainly were if Hawaii wanted to eat. Still, some of the young men insisted on going off to war. Foreman Joe Correia's sons, George and Louis, both enlisted in the Territorial Guard and went to active duty; Louis got a medical discharge not long afterward and came back to

Brynberian. This house was built by Clive Davies at the top of Tantalus peak on Oahu, and was given by him to his son Geoffrey.

Clive Davies, in Hawaii, March 1952.

the ranch. They needed him. The ranch had its troubles. It was not long before fence wire and staples ran out and they were stealing from one pasture to repair another. They got some second-hand railroad ties from Kaiwiki Sugar Company, which was converting much of its transport from rail to trucks.[3] But mostly they made their own fence posts in the old style, from *koa, ohia,* and *mamani* logs.

Many of Davies Company's employees and those of the subsidiaries joined the American armed forces, but sales and operations continued. Hawaii was living under martial law after December 7, and that meant many changes in Davies business: some lines of luxury goods had to be eliminated for the duration. The sales of Honolulu Iron Works in 1941 had come to $17,500,000, and were expected to go up in 1942.[4] Honolulu Iron Works' Kakaako shops were turned over almost entirely to defense work.

The Davies company's mercantile sales hit new levels during the war in spite of shortages and rationing. In Honolulu the wholesale store sold $4,300,000 worth of dry goods, as compared to $2,400,000 the year before. More groceries were sold, too, and one reason was an increase in the use of meat. The oriental population had lived primarily on fresh fish, but with the war, the Japanese fishermen were forbidden to take to the sea and the fresh fish supply dwindled to what could be raised in local ponds. Meat, more expensive, took a larger share of the food dollar. Hardware dropped off a bit in sales, largely because of shortages in all sorts of hard goods—nails and screws and anything needed in the defense effort. With virtually no building going on except at military installations, the lumber department suffered. The difficulty, where it existed, was almost entirely in procuring goods to sell.[5] The business flourished in every way. In 1943, the company earned nearly two million dollars before taxes, and had $425,000 available for dividends. The cash position was excellent; the year ended with $1,675,000 cash on hand. And HIW got out of the MacFarlane Foundry investment in Cuba, which had gone sour as the Cuban government taxed foreign earnings ever more heavily.[6]

Clive Davies continued to be extremely active, considering his age; in

1944 he was 74 years old, and he still journeyed regularly to London to work on company papers. At home at Hawkley Hurst, he spent many hours in his library, reading and annotating records of the company, its predecessors, and going through his father's papers.

As the war progressed it became apparent that the major problem of the Davies' interests would be to straighten out the affairs of Manila. During the war, all the company personnel were carried on the Davies payroll. Months before war's end, the lawyers were trying to assess the damages, and establish claims that would be several postwar years in settlement. But the immediate problem was to decide what was to be done. It was not easy without a timetable for Philippine independence, although that independence was guaranteed. In the summer of 1944, Wilkinson managed two days at Hawkley Hurst, and he had long talks with Clive, ending with one during the drive to Alton station the last day in Clive's little Morris auto. Wilkinson wanted to open a major China operation at the end of the war, to go into business with T. V. Soong and his family. Wilkinson had plans to bring new capital into the firm "which I can control"—he did not go further. Clive Davies had no objection. He did have one caveat: Wilkinson must put at the top of his list of "do's" the question of cementing relationships with John E. Russell. China, Manila, none of these were as important as that point. Russell must be made enthusiastic about the Wilkinson plans or there would be nothing but trouble in the future, as there had been too often in the past.

Given this condition, if Wilkinson could solve the Russell problem, there was no reason that in the future he could not count on becoming chairman of the entire firm, with personal interests in the Far East and freedom of action there—and do it all from England. That last statement was made by Clive Davies just as they reached Alton station and saw the engine coming, so Wilkinson jumped out, waved, and hurried to catch the train. *There* was something for him to think over on the journey back to London.[7]

In early September that year, Wilkinson was in Quebec for the Quebec conference of allied leaders and hurried down to Washington on September 12, carrying messages for Lord Beaverbrook and Brendan Bracken from Prime Minister Churchill. Then Wilkinson caught a train to New York, and that same night went to a party for John E. Russell. Wilkinson and Russell spent parts of several days together in New York and Washington and talked over many matters. They agreed that the Philippines offered enormous opportunity, and that China and other areas offered contingent opportunity. Russell said Theo H. Davies & Co., Ltd. would advance $500,000 in capital. Wilkinson was to be head of the new company (to be called Theo H. Davies—Far East) with more autonomy than before, and was to have 20 percent of the stock, which would be paid out from dividends. They agreed that Hawaiian-Philippine corporation would be up for sale, since the plantation stockholders would no longer have any political reason for investment in the islands after the Philippines became independent. The mill had been wrecked—an American bomber had neatly laid the smokestack across the whole mill one day. What was left had been looted thoroughly by Filipinos in need of corrugated roofing for houses and every sort of metal for a hundred purposes. One of the few assets (and they did not know it at the moment) was the fleet of steam locomotives that drew the cane cars on the railroad. The manager of Hawaiian-Philippine, by a stroke of genius, had laid tracks into the jungle, driven the "dragons" as they were called, deep into the green foliage and then picked up the tracks. The Japanese may have wondered what happened to the mill railroad's motive power, but no one bothered the locomotives, and they remained, rusting a bit but safe, all during the war in their green cocoon.[8]

Wilkinson moved around New York in the highest financial and social circles, dining at the 21 Club then the rage of Manhattan, lunching at the Oak Room of the Plaza Hotel, meeting brokers and financial men at the Bankers Club, and night clubbing at the Stork Club and Cafe Society uptown. He particularly cultivated Konrad Hsu, a Chinese who was close to the Soong family, perhaps the most powerful family in China. The Soongs and their associates were busily putting together business connections for the future, hedging every bet. Much of their money had been transferred to New York and San Francisco, since China's situation fluctuated between uncertain and desperate. They were even ready to move their holdings to South America, if the Chiang Kai-shek government fell and the Americans recognized a new regime. Konrad Hsu, Wilkinson believed, was his key to the opening of China for the postwar years. They talked of a three-way partnership, involving Chinese-British-American capital and management (with Wilkinson apparently supplying the management), and the names of Kuhn-Loeb, Ladenburg & Thalman, I.T.T. were bandied about, as they planned long railways and vast industrial projects.[9] But not all Wilkinson's plans were quite so "blue sky." Harold Weidig, head of the Theo H. Davies New York office took him to lunch with Mervyn Brown, head of the export division of General Foods corporation, and at the end of it, Wilkinson had a commitment for the General Foods agency in the Philippines.

Late in April 1945, Wilkinson took the train to San Francisco and on May 2 he met Lorna and the children, who arrived on the SS. *Admiral Eberle* after three and a half years of confinement in the Philippines. The ship also carried nearly a dozen employees and associates from the pre-war days, and it was necessary to have at least a few words with each of them. The reunited family stayed on in California for a few days and then went east to Yonkers, N.Y., where Gerald had been loaned a house called Catercorner.* Russell came to New York and more details of the new company were thrashed out. Russell met Konrad Hsu and assented to creation of an agency for China that would handle several lines of heavy machinery, such as Allis Chalmers, on a 50/50 basis with the Chinese. Wilkinson was also abubble with plans for a consortium of British and American capital to further his Philippine enterprises. He was definite in his decision to return to the Philippines. Edith Davies had suggested one day at Hawkley Hurst that he might consider a political career at the end of the war. His contacts with important figures, from Churchill on down, were invaluable. Sir George could certainly help him within the Conservative party. And Wilkinson's mother had also suggested the same. But he had written her a

---

*Catercorner belonged to T. Chrystie, a friend of the Davies family and New York attorney for Theo H. Davies & Co., Ltd.

long philosophical letter that made his position clear: he was a merchant venturer, not a politician, and he would so remain. He felt that Britain, emerging from the war badly in debt, would need all her merchant venturers, and so it was in a combination of altruism and desire for personal gain that he would return to Manila.[10] He told much of this to Russell, and they discussed the future animatedly; the old animosities seemed to have been wiped away by the war. Wilkinson said he felt his future lay in development of a new business in the Far East, but he did have the responsibility, laid upon him during the war years by Clive Davies, of looking after the family interests in the future. What were to be their relations? Russell said that was just what he was waiting to talk to Clive Davies about. He, Russell, was 57 years old and Ted Guard, who was his principal assistant, was 63, Bennett, his other standby, was 60. New blood was needed in the company on the "inner circle" level. Russell was thinking about bringing Harold Weidig from New York to be his executive assistant and future president of the company.[11]

Sir George Frederick Davies

In August, Clive Davies came to New York to see the Wilkinsons and Russell. Clive had aged heavily in the past six years since he had visited America; he was an old man now and much concerned about passing the business into younger hands. A year earlier, he had mentioned Honolulu to Geoffrey and Joan at Hawkley Hurst, and Geoffrey had responded favorably. Geoffrey had said that when he was "demobbed" he would be prepared to go to Honolulu and dig in to learn the business.[12] Now, in the new domesticity of the Wilkinson household, Clive Davies was pleased to see how Lorna had been tempered by her gruelling years in Manila under the Japanese. She was quiet but seemed to exude a new strength of character. Clive was pleased to see that she took three games from Gerald at tennis one afternoon (she playing the doubles court). She seemed to him a different person, stronger, and totally admirable,[13] although she never did learn to spell properly.

Clive Davies soon went to San Francisco, where he met Russell and Bennett and they talked more about the future. They agreed that the company was to be made 51 percent American. That did not mean that outsiders were to be brought in. Indeed, Russell was considering ways in which they could recover the 25 percent of the stock that had so unwisely fallen into the hands of Castle & Cooke and Matson. No, the 51 percent would be attained by trading on the dual citizenship of a number of the Davies family. Lorna, for example, was an American. So were all of Clive's children but Geoffrey, and several of George F.'s children. By this device, the Theo H. Davies management would be able to claim that theirs was "an American company" and avoid renewal of past criticisms. Further, it would help with war damage compensation in the Philippines and foreign trading guarantees of the federal government, from which Davies was then excluded. Lorna, Gwendolen, and Harold's estate could certainly be counted on right away. There were also 1800 shares available for sale, and these could go to Americans who were members of the "inner circle"— meaning Russell, Bennett, Guard, Weidig, Angus, and McCorriston of merchandising, and the Davies family. It had to be agreed, however, that non-family members of the the "inner circle" would sell to other members at a fair market price.[14] Since there were 26,886 shares outstanding, the American participation had to be brought to 13,712. All this was planned out, and the total "inner circle" participation came to 20,128 shares, or 74.86 percent, a very comfortable margin of control. The future was also discussed coolly. Clive Davies was to be succeeded on his death as chairman by Sir George, and the principle of maintaining an "elder statesman" as chairman was to be carried on. The chairman would be president of all Theo H. Davies & Co., Ltd. subsidiaries. Retirement for executives was to be at 65, and with a new employee retirement program, plus the stock availability, this should work no hardships. With Russell, Clive Davies made a special point of emphasizing the need to keep Gerald Wilkinson properly informed about Honolulu affairs, since Clive had chosen Wilkinson to be the leader and spokesman of the English stockholders after he was gone. The two of them talked a little about Geoffrey Davies, too, who would soon be coming to Honolulu to learn the business. Russell said he had the spot picked out: Geoffrey would be brought along to be treasurer of the company. That was well enough, cautioned Clive, but let Russell remember that Geoffrey was totally untried, although he had his father's confidence as a man.[15]

There was no reason for Clive to go on to Honolulu. His personal associations there were limited after all these years, and he had accomplished his mission in New York and San Francisco. He returned to New York without visiting the islands. Gerald was still in the service and had been called to London, but Clive stayed a few nights with Lorna at Cater-corner. Gerald returned in midweek and had several more conversations with Clive Davies about the future. Then Clive went home to Hawkley Hurst, a happy man. The line of succession had been resolved, and the future seemed clear.

Chapter Forty-One
CHINA DREAM

C*olonel Gerald Wilkinson* was released from His Majesty's service in the fall of 1945 and immediately went to England with Lorna and the children to stay at Hawkley Hurst. They remained there through Christmas, taking long walks in the country, enjoying the crisp autumn and winter countryside—such a change for Lorna and the children after those dreadful months in Santo Tomas! Gerald had many talks with Clive Davies about the business.[1] As the talks continued, Gerald's confidence and perhaps his self-importance grew. He suggested on Boxing Day (December 26) that he ought to "demand" from Russell a seat on the board of directors of the Honolulu firm. Clive Davies, who was not as sanguine about the Wilkinson-Russell relationship as either of the principals appeared to be, suggested that such a course would be premature. In the first place Gerald could talk to Russell about the matter in 1946 on his way through Honolulu. In the second place, when either Clive or Sir George died, his selection to the board was inevitable. Clive knew, too, that "demanding" never did sit very well with John E. Russell.

All this time, Wilkinson was preparing for his return to Manila. He bought a 1942 Studebaker Champion, which was shipped to the Philippines. He employed a young naval officer, Emory Bronte, as assistant and sent him on to Manila to build housing for the various executives of the company. Most of Manila was destroyed, G. G. Gordon had written, and apparently even the company's records.[2] Gordon, after his release from the prison camp, began pulling pieces together as best he could given the difficult state of life in the Philippines. E.J. Nell had saved one *bodega* (warehouse) of goods, apparently unnoticed by the enemy; otherwise, nearly everything from the past was gone. And as for the future, nothing seemed secure. Before the war, Nell had the agency for Carrier Air Conditioning Co. in the Philippines, but he was not certain it would be given back to them. Just as Wilkinson was looking about to take over various agencies of the U.S. and British manufacturers, so were others.[3]

Wilkinson was eager to begin the China operations soon, and General Manager Taddiken of Honolulu Iron Works sold Russell on the plan. HIW had built six of the large Japanese factories in Formosa; that island was now to be returned to China, and the proposed Sino-Hawaiian Corporation should be able to guarantee the Iron Works the business of rebuilding them, since the Chinese involved were so well placed. Konrad Hsu (Hsu Chang) held a Ph.D. in science from Columbia University and had gained favor with the Nationalist government by installing radio facilities in Kweilin during the war. He was still closely connected with T. V. Soong and his family. A second man was Michel Li (Li Teng Quien), co-director of the Chinese Ministry of Communications and a man close to Generalissimo Chiang Kai-shek.

The third Chinese principal was C.S. Liu (Liu Chin-san), a banker, right-hand man for the Soong interests in Washington, who had been high in government and banking councils for ten years. It was a formidable group, representing strong influence with the sources of power in Nationalist China. The fourth member, Frank Szto (Sze To-fun), had been head of the Kwangtung Sugar administration in the years when Honolulu Iron Works built four of their eight sugar mills. He was Dr. Hsu's brother-in-law and probable appointee to a high position in Canton.[4]

Faced with such an array, and the support of Taddiken and Wilkinson, John E. Russell acceded to establishment of a corporation to be funded by Theo H. Davies & Co., Ltd. to a total of $50,000 if necessary. The purpose of the company, of course, was to secure agencies and contracts for Davies and Honolulu Iron Works. Before much more could be done, however, Wilkinson had to get back to Manila and start work.

Before he could get there, he was drawn into a nasty controversy by Major General Charles Willoughby, one of MacArthur's staff members, who had charged in testimony before the Pearl Harbor investigating commission that Wilkinson had behaved with loyalty to England alone—meaning that he had not given the Americans benefit of military information he possessed in time to alert them about the Pearl Harbor attack, but he had informed Theo H. Davies & Co., Ltd. of Honolulu, a British firm. Wilkinson was furious. He prepared a press statement which quoted the message he had sent to Honolulu on December 2, 1941, alerting the Americans to the Japanese military buildup in Indo-China and the opinion that the Japanese were preparing a blow against Britain and the U.S. for the very near future.[5] The story was given publicity in the press. Willoughby, from Tokyo, charged that Wilkinson had deserted his wife and children. Wilkinson then cabled MacArthur for a retraction and reminded him that the general had ordered Wilkinson to accompany him to Bataan on December 24, 1941. Whatever MacArthur did, Willoughby issued no more charges. Wilkinson finally had a left-handed apology—and denial of making remarks—from Willoughby. (That arrived in July.)

While Wilkinson was in Honolulu he arranged for Manila to represent Hawaiian Philippines Sugar Company and San Carlos Sugar Company, and Bogo-Medellin and Cebu companies in addition. During the war years he had encountered the Fords, who owned a large part of Asturias Milling Company. Now they asked him to represent them as well, which was a distinct business victory for Theo H. Davies & Co., Ltd.

Wilkinson arrived in Manila on March 20 and got down to work, in an office on the sixth floor of the Ayala building. Then the problems began to come in. As friends learned that he was back he was asked to do a hundred chores, from looking into George Fairchild's* property in Pasay to worrying about competition from new firms coming into being.[6] He was offered one chance to make a killing: a huge supply of American Navy surplus beer had been stored in Guam and could be bought for ten cents on the

---

*The Fairchilds were "fathers" of the sugar industry in Manila and friends of Wilkinson.

dollar, and probably sold in thirsty Manila for two hundred percent profit. But Wilkinson remembered something Clive Davies had said once, and cabled Russell for a policy decision.

Russell remembered an incident of 1933. American prohibition was repealed that year by Constitutional amendment. The Rainier Bottling Company of the state of Washington had been supplying Davies with various soft drinks, including "near-beer." The restriction off, Rainier began shipping beer to Hawaii. When Clive Davies discovered this, he ordered the practice ended, and the inventory of beer disposed of to Davies employees. So when Wilkinson's cable arrived, Russell knew the answer without asking. Russell lost no time in cabling back: FIRM'S ESTABLISHED POLICY PROHIBITS HANDLING LIQUOR INCLUDING BEER.[7] So the long arm of Theo H. Davies had made itself felt, again, nearly a half century after his death!

The business moved ahead. Gustav Laurant returned to the merchandising department and soon had the Chinese merchants eating out of his hand, so to speak. But Manila was flooded with luxury goods by slick promoters: combs, pens, pomades, hair lotion, and all sorts of cosmetics. There were shortages in basic supplies, and the usual sources were not producing enough. Even when the shipments came, the capacity of the docks, after the war damage, had dropped from 3000 tons of goods a day to one tenth that amount. The important task was to get the goods into the Philippines, and Wilkinson's staff turned their attention to it, with help from Harold Weidig in New York, Bennett in San Francisco, and Ted Guard in Honolulu.

The Sino-Hawaiian corporation came into being in the spring of 1946 and signed a contract with Honolulu Iron Works to do its construction. Konrad Hsu came to Manila for a short visit and then went to Hong Kong, where he established an office. Hsu in Hong Kong soon discovered that of the six old Kwangtung mills built before the war only the Shuntak factory (built by Skoda, HIW's major competitor) was still in operation. Frank Szto, at this point a major general in the Chinese nationalist forces, took Hsu up to Canton. Soon Konrad Hsu was talking about 50 factories, each with a 1000-ton capacity. Formosa, he found, was "ticklish" because T. V. Soong seemed to have a sugar monopoly there.[8]

Konrad Hsu and Sino-Hawaiian had many big plans. Honolulu informed them of a 600-ton sugar factory for sale in the islands, and Hsu said the Kwangsi government wanted it. Well, perhaps they wanted it; at least it seemed as though they might want it. But when asked to put up a $25,000 deposit to hold the factory, Kwangsi's governor suddenly left town, and in the end the factory was sold in South America.[9] Then there was the case of two surplus LCI's that the Kwangsi bank was going to buy for $60,000. By the winter of 1947, John E. Russell was so disgusted he wrote Wilkinson suggesting that the connection really ought to be dropped in spite of "the glimpses of great things to be in China presented to you by Dr. Hsu."[10] Russell pointed to the countless hours of time spent in New York, San Francisco, Honolulu and Manila on Sino-Hawaiian affairs that involved enormous volumes of correspondence and no sales. The sale of the two LCIs finally did come through, and Davies-Far East (as the new company was known) collected ₱15,000, or about $7500. They had invested nearly that much in Sino-Hawaiian in the beginning. G. G. Gordon also carried the burden of correspondence and suffered the deleterious effects of Dr. Hsu's proclivities for night life in Manila. In the fall of 1947, the Waimanalo sugar mill came up for sale for about $50,000 when the company stopped grinding. Dr. Hsu and his associates began a furious round of negotiation and came to Hawaii to inspect the mill on behalf of the "buyers", but the sale finally collapsed in October. That was enough even for Wilkinson. In March 1948, Sino-Hawaiian closed down its Hong Kong office and for all practical purposes was out of business — although Dr. Hsu could spin off pages and pages of plans for sure-fire profits. In truth, Sino-Hawaiian was as dead as a dodo. Through it all, Russell and Bennett, watching the maneuvers of Dr. Hsu, were very much concerned because of Wilkinson's firm backing of his friend. Russell exhibited a statesmanlike forbearance: when another chief executive might have ordered Wilkinson to disengage the company from this crawling disaster, Russell let the farce play out to the end, until even Gerald Wilkinson could not support it longer. Bennett took the position that everyone was entitled to a mistake or two, and Gerald was certainly having his.[11] So the experiment came to an end, although even at the last Dr. Hsu was still writing Gerald about the enormous potential just before Peking fell to the communists, and then Shanghai, and all the rest of mainland China, and Chiang Kai-shek moved into Formosa and called it China. Wilkinson finally recognized the real truth of the matter: that nothing was going to halt the head long collapse of the Nationalists. But by this time it did not seem so important; Lorna was back in Manila, and Gerald was deeply involved in a dozen other affairs, all of them far more profitable than the Sino-Hawaiian venture.

Hilo Iron Works after 1946 tsunami.

Chapter Forty-Two

GEOFFREY BEGINS

In the spring of 1946, Geoffrey Davies was demobilized from the Royal Navy and prepared to go out to Honolulu to settle in and learn the business. There was a considerable difficulty about his visa to the United States; application was made in February, and the State Department lost it. Such behavior was not unusual in those days in Washington; the enormous pressure of many nationals from a hundred countries deluged the system until it was overworked, and the natural arrogance of bureaucrats grew as Washington realized that America was once more "the promised land." It took much effort by Clive Davies, Russell, and others to resolve the problem. Finally, by his own wish, Geoffrey entered on an immigrant's visa. If all went well, he was prepared to raise his family in Honolulu and make his home there. The alternative, seen from a cottage in Hampshire, was a life of endless queuing for goods that never seemed in adequate supply, and hard times in a cold climate.[1] Clive arranged for Craigside to be made ready for Geoffrey. The understanding was that eventually the property would be transferred to him if he wanted it, down to Harold's white suits, riding breeches, and other clothing left behind, and a large supply of wine and liqueurs about which Clive Davies knew nothing.[2]

Geoffrey's coming to Honolulu raised a problem that the Davies company had not faced before. He was married, and a daughter, Susan, had been born. He was also a member of the British upper middle class. How could Russell pay this untried young man a salary on which he could support himself at Craigside, which demanded a gardener? Russell wrote Clive an anguished letter on the subject. He wanted to pay Geoffrey at $350 a month, although this was a hundred dollars more than he was paying Francis Swanzy Morgan, grandson of another partner, who had joined the firm after attending Stanford University and serving a wartime stint in the United States Navy. The difference was bound to become known. "We used to be able to keep such things private, but now, with all the returns that have to be filed, that has become impossible."[3] He would try to give Geoffrey an "entertainment allowance" of perhaps $100 a month, but that was the best he could do. But Clive Davies was wiser. Harold had started at the going wage for apprentices. If Geoffrey came in under special circumstances, it would not be quite as it ought to have been, through no fault of his own. He said Geoffrey should have $250; he would have his stock dividends to live on.

Many changes had come to Hawaii and the Davies' interests since Harold's day, just six years earlier. Ted Guard had conducted the merchandise department so skillfully in the difficult war period that he had neither too much nor too little inventory at the end of 1945.

During the war years the local merchants had been inclined to buy heavily and maintain large inventories. They had experienced various shortages and never knew what course the war might take. But as the war ended, they relaxed and cut back sharply on inventory in the last half of the year. It took the skill of a tightrope walker for Guard to keep up with them and not end up with 10,000 extra cases of toilet paper. (That commodity, however, would soon enough prove to be worth nearly its weight in gold.) In 1944, the merchandising end of the business had totalled nearly $26 million. A year later it was off $1.5 million but this was still double the figure for 1940.[4]

One problem had been a series of strikes in Hawaii. The American Federation of Labor and the Congress of Industrial Organizations were both trying to organize workers in the islands. The CIO, through the

International Longshoremen's and Warehousemen's Unions, had by far the strongest position. Theo Davies, and other planters, had stored up some future trouble by signing contracts with some AFL unions. In September, 1945, a strike had hurt business badly. By the end of the year Russell had a hunch that there was going to be a far worse strike in the coming year, and he and Guard agreed that inventories would have to be increased, even though it might mean a costly incursion into their cash balance.[5]

Generally speaking, the plantations were doing well. Laupahoehoe had made a profit of $114,000 in 1945; Hamakua had earned nearly $157,000, and all the other investments seemed satisfactory enough. Waiakea mill was the problem these days. The company had lost $170,000 in 1945, and the reason for it was not hard to discover. The land was steep and difficult. The islands were suffering a severe labor shortage, and every planter was praying for Filipinos—a new wave of immigration had been promised, but by the spring of 1946 virtually none had arrived. The threat of labor organization (ILWU local 142 had organized Waiakea) had brought the labor costs up. To counteract them, Davies and other planters had brought in new machinery, a mechanical harvester, and trucks. But the trucks did not work on Waiakea's rough ground, and they were sold to Kaiwiki sugar company. Payroll continued to be the big problem. In 1940 it had been $408,000 and in 1945 it was $551,000 a year. In 1940 Waiakea had produced 6.05 tons of sugar per acre. In 1945 it produced 5.63 tons.

The Waiakea loss of 1945 had caused John E. Russell to hire John Midkiff and John Sanderson, a pair of sugar experts, to survey Waiakea and bring him some answers for the future. The mill was bound in by homesteaders, who would not grant right of way, so arterial roads could not be built to bring cane to the mills. The land did not lend itself to mechanization. The soil was so sticky and the rocks so thick the cane could not be cleaned by conventional methods; special washing processes would have to be developed. The yield was 10,000 tons; the company should produce 15,000 tons. To achieve that would require an increase of employ-

Geoffrey C. Davies, his wife Joan, and their daughter Susan,
just after arrival in Hawaii in December 1946.

ees to 650 and a payroll of $700,000 at the 1945 rates. Even with federal
government compliance payments, the net loss would be $60,000 a year.[6]
The surveyors, in other words, could offer no hope except to cut back
Waiakea Mill's operations by half, which would net about $8500 in profit,

based on a subsidy payable by the Commodity Credit Corporation. The problem was complicated by the filing of a suit against all the sugar plantations on Hawaii. The AFL, struggling for membership, sued the planters for underpayment of wages under the National Labor Relations Board's rulings, and so did the CIO; Waiakea's liability would be another $25,000 or so, to add to the difficulties.

The difficulties of Waiakea mill were overshadowed temporarily early on Monday morning, April 1, 1946, when a series of tidal waves or *tsunamis* struck Hilo and the Hamakua coast of Hawaii island. In Hilo, where the Hilo Iron Works factory on the bank of the Wailoa River began operations at 7 o'clock in the morning, the men watched in awe as the water came in. They had time to climb to the tops of the buildings and so no lives were lost (although many of the men lost their homes down by the waterfront, and some of them lost members of their families). Scores were killed in Hilo and up the coast. Laupahoehoe school and village were destroyed, and twenty children and teachers were swept away. When the tidal waves had subsided, most of Hilo *makai* (seaward) of the Kamehameha Highway had disappeared. The railroad was washed out in many places, and the rolling stock, which happened to be in Hilo, had been wrecked. One whole train simply disappeared!

The damage was so extensive that the railroad went out of business, which meant the plantations and mills would hereafter have to find their own transportation. The Davies plantations turned to Kukuihaele, which took sugar from Laupahoehoe, Hamakua, Kaiwiki, Paauhau, and Honokaa mills. The Matson company put four Liberty ships on the run, and the sugar began to go out—much as it had in the old days when each mill shipped its own sugar by high line onto the sailing ships. The storage facilities at Hilo were also gone. The Davies losses were estimated at about $300,000, including 1340 tons of sugar on the dock at Hilo, which was covered by insurance.[7]

But the natural disaster of the *tsunami* was overshadowed when the ILWU struck the sugar plantations. The strike was a part of ILWU leader Harry Bridges' campaign to take over total union control of the Hawaiian

Islands. The natural situation of the islands lent itself to just such maneuver, and the logistics of the sugar plantations made it impossible for them to fight back effectively. The strike began on September 1, after the union had rejected the offer of the Hawaiian Sugar Planters Association. At Waiakea, both CIO and AFL were represented, and the CIO's ILWU men went on strike—then the AFL men refused to cross the picket line. The strike affected all 33 plantations in the islands, and 21,000 workers. Some plantations were hurt more than others. Castle & Cooke's Ewa plantation on Oahu suffered severely from the drought when the workers were no longer there to turn on the irrigation pumps. But Waiakea, in spite of all its other difficulties, had at least shipped 7,800 tons of sugar and had only 158 tons unharvested. Laupahoehoe had shipped 11,500 tons, Kaiwiki 9,400 tons, Hamakua 11,000 tons. Ship movement to the islands stopped. The Davies inventories, like those of all wholesale houses, began to go down.

After 79 days the strike ended, largely through the insistence of Castle & Cooke, which seemed to be worst hurt of all the sugar companies.[8] The ILWU had won a victory; the sugar workers had achieved significant raises in pay, betterment of working conditions and shortening of hours, and the union had cemented its strength throughout the islands.

Geoffrey Davies and his family arrived in Honolulu shortly after the settlement of the strike. They moved to Craigside and he went to the office on Bishop Street every weekday. Russell put him up for the Pacific Club, but he preferred to go out with other young men of the office.[9] He was thoroughly independent and wanted very much to "make it on his own" without reference to the family name. He began talking to Russell about doing a specific job. What he did not want was to have the post of treasurer or any other simply opened up so he could slide into it because his name was Geoffrey Davies.[10] Within a month Russell sent him over to Kukaiau ranch, for a short stint on the plantations. Russell, in a way, should have been grateful for Geoffrey Davies' attitude, for the family could be quite a trial to him. For example, Sir George had been to the photographic studio and had his portrait taken in his court uniform with all his medals. In a grand gesture he had sent the portrait to Honolulu "for the board room." Dutifully Russell had hung it, a grim reminder to all who sat there that Theo H. Davies & Co., Ltd. was a *very* British organization. When Clive visited Honolulu in the summer of 1946, he had seen the portrait and demanded its removal. It was to be taken down and stored in his private office. And so it was; Sir George was coming to Honolulu in 1947, and Russell promised that when Sir George arrived and occupied Clive's office the portrait would greet him from the wall.[11]

As so often happened these later years, Russell was deeply occupied with personnel problems. The departure of C.J. Henderson in 1937 had left a void never filled, particularly after Harold's going. Cal Hunter, the secretary of the company, resigned in 1947 to go and live in California, and Russell promoted Charles Holt, a young man whose family had been in the heavy implement business. (The Holt company was one component of Caterpillar Tractor Company.) E.M. Nash was to be made comptroller, after many years service as assistant treasurer, and Alan Stewart, a younger man, to be his assistant. The treasurer's post was held for Geoffrey. Among the other young men who seemed to be comers were Francis Morgan, who had interested himself in labor problems on the plantations (a welcome interest indeed!) and F.A. Schaefer, III, son of the family that owned Honokaa Sugar Company, on which the Davies had long had an eye.[12]

Geoffrey Davies continued to advance well in the eyes of the Honolulu community and of Russell, who gave excellent reports on his "progress" to Clive Davies. There was one little family incident that indicated Geoffrey's basic independence of spirit: Sir George and Lady Davies arrived in splendor on the *Matsonia*, surrounded by photographers who did not see many of Britain's upper crust. Sir George had ordered a half dozen shirts made for him. They were not ready when he left and were delivered to Geoffrey later. Geoffrey sent them, stating on the customs declaration that they were shirts for Sir George Davies. British customs stopped the parcel and demanded a king's ransom in duty. Sir George wrote Geoffrey asking that he write the customs saying the shirts were a gift. Geoffrey refused to do so. So much for close family ties![13]

This same independence of spirit crept into Geoffrey's relationships with Russell and the other older officials of Theo H. Davies & Co. He was determined not to be a "yes man" and so he often found himself in argument. Such a state of affairs was not unknown at the Davies company. Hunter and Ted Guard were notorious for not getting along; Hunter had what Russell called a "take it or leave it attitude" which was amplified by memoranda stating facts and arguments (often correct) which he slammed down on the desk of the recipient. Russell overlooked the brusqueness because of Hunter's other qualities. Guard, Russell said, was so jealous of his own prerogatives that he would not listen to Hunter on personnel matters, although Hunter was personnel officer and had been trained in the subject. Guard was a great trial to Russell because of his attitude. "Half the time Ted had been wrong, but because of his position and value to the firm I have overlooked it and supported him."[14]

Geoffrey went to work for Ted Guard. He sold John Deere tractors and cultivators to farmers in Waialae and along the north shore of Oahu. He served a stint in the retail establishment. He had charge of E. O. Hall, the retail hardware store. By the end of 1947, Russell thought he was coming along very nicely but had put back the time that he would be ready to take over the treasurer's job. Geoffrey had started in business late (at 30) but there were still fundamentals to be learned.[15] Then Sir George threw a monkey wrench across the sea into the Honolulu machinery.

Chapter Forty-Three

GEOFFREY DAVIES' DILEMMA

If one were to understand John E. Russell and the dilemma he faced in Honolulu, one would have to realize that Russell was as loyal an American as the Davies were Britons and that at the same time Russell was as loyal to his employers as a man could be. That latter trait of personal loyalty caused him to yield in almost every case to requests of members of the Davies family for anything at all. It had been proved in the case of the dividends in the past; when Russell and the other executives in Honolulu decided against paying dividends, and the Davies family insisted, they got the dividends. And so it was, too, with the employment of members of the family. The Davieses had seesawed on this matter during Russel's years with the company, and he never quite knew when the company might be sold from under him. But in the 1940s, with Gerald and Geoffrey coming into the company, he had began to feel a bit more stability, and the decision to increase the "American" ownership had been welcome as well.

Sir George's visit to Honolulu, and the princely welcome he had received, had endeared nearly everything about Hawaii to Sir George (except Geoffrey Davies) and he thought more kindly of the place than he ever had before. Going home, he had the bright idea that perhaps young George Theophilus Davies, commonly called George, Jr., might join the firm. He mentioned it tentatively to Russell, who never denied a Davies anything, and then he went home. In November, 1947, he dined with

Clive at one of their clubs in London and mentioned the matter to Clive.

Clive wrote to Russell, giving the details. Young George had read law at Cambridge and trained in a solicitor's office. He had taken a war job in the government and had directed a large staff. He had joined the Royal Air Force and worked his way up to a commission.* Most recently he had been secretary of a London finance company.

This letter upset Russell because there really was no place for a man of George T. Davies' experience except as an officer of the company. And that would be hard for many, including Geoffrey Davies, to take. Russell had heard from Bennett that Clive had been writing about Geoffrey's future. Just then that future seemed to be up in the air. Russell was not sure about the treasury job, for Geoffrey seemed more competent "as a money-maker" than at accounting. But what did Clive Davies want? The interjection of George T. Davies raised many issues. Russell's solution was to fob him off to the New York office, where he would not disturb the course of Honolulu business. After that they would see.[1]

By the end of 1947, Geoffrey Davies had gotten his feet good and wet in Honolulu, but he was totally unable to escape the consequences of being a Davies. He was working in merchandising that fall and, being inquisitive mind, he looked at what he was doing. One of his tasks was to sell yard goods to Oahu clothing manufacturers. He made the rounds of the small garment industry in Honolulu, and the "rag trade" laughed at him. He discovered that while he was offering units of 15,000 yards at a markup of 25 percent, these manufacturers could buy direct from the mainland and buy 60,000 yards at a time, at a much lower price. Why didn't Davies cut their markup to ten percent? Then he could sell. He took this information back to Guard in a confidential conversation. Guard immediately rushed down to the dry goods department and upbraided William Koch, the manager, for "putting ideas into Geoffrey's head about smaller markups."[2] As Geoffrey soon enough learned, he had put his finger on the basic weakness of the Davies mercantile position of the postwar era.

---

*He served in RAF intelligence.

For years Davies had operated primarily as a wholesale mercantile house. The firm secured a number of agencies, for spice companies, grocery houses such as General Foods, patent medicines, and over-the-counter drugstore items. Davies brought the merchandise in by ship at its own expense, marked up the price to make a profit, and sold to the trade. All this worked well in "Mom and Pop" grocery stores and small drugstores. The dry goods department sold to the small dry goods stores, and the hardware department to hardware stores. In the 1930s, Davies had acquired the Hawaii franchise of Western States Groceries, which operated the Piggly Wiggly chain. These Piggly Wiggly stores were small shops. For example, in 1937 Davies bought a lot at 10th and Waialae avenue for $10,000 and put up a Piggly Wiggly store there. But, in these postwar years, Hawaii's merchandising pattern began to change. The islands were invaded by chain stores: Woolworth's and Long's Drugs, Thrifty Drugs, and local chain operations. These chains grew along with another development: the shopping center; whole sections of a community were carved out and made into thirty or forty shops. The concept was staggering to the imagination of the 1940s, but it was already beginning. Geoffrey, coming from outside, found it easier to see the change than Ted Guard or nearly anyone else in the organization. But Ted Guard, who had been with the company for more than 40 years and had worked his way up from assistant manager of the Hilo store, would hardly listen to a young man from England with no previous experience in business.

But the trouble, from Geoffrey's point of view, was that while Russell spoke of a "training program" there was no program. When Clive Davies had gone to Honolulu in 1896, almost immediately he had been thrown into the cashier's job, which was hard work. But Geoffrey was given no job (nor had Harold before him until Henderson quit). When Geoffrey was in Guard's department each day he would go to Guard and say: "Mr. Guard, have you something for me to do today?"

Each day Guard would answer: "No, Geoffrey." So Geoffrey Davies got the idea that the firm was moving all around him, and that Russell and the others expected him to stay for a few years, and then go back to England and write letters to Honolulu.[3]

The coming of George T. distressed Geoffrey because he wondered if too many Davieses were not being thrust down the company's throat. He felt that his father underestimated the feudal characteristics of the Honolulu firm and the willingness of Russell to do anything to keep the Davies family happy. And Geoffrey was far from that, wandering from dry goods to lumber, after which he was supposed to go to Hilo.

When George T. Davies did come to Hawaii, the cousins were not particularly drawn to one another. Soon George was off to New York, where he was to learn the financial end of the business, given his particular background. (Harold Weidig was distressed to have another member of the family thrust upon him.)[4] Geoffrey continued to move about in the organization without any sense of belonging. Clive came to Hawaii in the spring of 1948, and he and Geoffrey had a long talk about the business. Clive spoke of Russell's having picked Geoffrey out to become treasurer of the company. But the fact was that Russell had already tried to indicate that Geoffrey really ought to be in another position, in one letter, and then, when Clive did not take the hint, the cause was lost. The relationship of Clive Davies and John E. Russell was indeed "feudal" in the sense that Russell never wanted to gainsay his main principal, Clive Davies. Clive went into many matters and made a memorandum of the discussion.[5] Three days later he met with Russell and showed him the memo. Russell promised to straighten out matters with Geoffrey. Clive soon left for New York, to soothe Weidig's ruffled feathers over having been saddled with George T. Davies.[6]

As Geoffrey Davies learned, he saw the company changing around him. In 1948 the decision was made to liquidate Waiakea Mill Company. The increased cost of labor following the strike of 1946 was the last straw. The employees were discharged and the lands with clear title were sold off. The machinery was sold outside or absorbed into the other Davies properties. The net loss was $135,000. At the end, the mill was all that was left, and this was not worth much. They tried to sell it in Colombia, Jamaica, Mexico, and Siam. There were no takers. They had one offer of $25,000 for its scrap value. Finally they took it.[7] One of the Davies' most successful sugar companies of Theo H. Davies' day was out of business.

In May, 1949 the ILWU decided to show its muscle in Hawaii and struck the docks. This meant no shipping and no inventories. Ted Guard must have yearned then for those 10,000 cases of toilet paper for, in the months that passed, this item, like all disposable necessities, fell into short supply. The Territorial Government promised to keep necessities moving, in naval vessels if necessary, but Davies and the other mercantile companies were hard pressed. Sugar, of course, could not be shipped at all. The strike dominated Hawaiian life for the next 177 days until it was settled on October 23.

After the strike was cleared away, Russell did what he had promised to do and brought Geoffrey Davies into the financial management of the company. For a time Geoffrey had charge of E. O. Hall but he also worked with the books. In this activity he came across an $8000 expense item for establishing George T. Davies in New York and exploded in a letter to his father.[8] He was particularly irate because a few months earlier he had asked the firm to advance money to its younger executive-type employees. The housing situation in Honolulu was so desperate that Roy Bennett (son of the San Francisco manager and old-line Davies man) had been forced to live in two rooms with his wife and baby, because they could not find decent accommodation. That request of Geoffrey's had been ignored, and now he was furious at George's misuse of the company and said so. This complaint, made to his father, got back to Russell, who did not like it, and to George T. Davies, who could not have liked it much either. Geoffrey must have inherited, along with the Fox countenance, a good share of the Calvinism that had stiffened the soul of the Rev. Theo Davies and his son, that young sideburned merchant who had come to the Sandwich Islands in 1857. But aside from this evidence of scruple (which Geoffrey said was occasioned by talk he heard within the company), Geoffrey was getting on very well. Arthur Smith, one of the firm's senior directors, wrote glowingly of Geoffrey, and Smith's main sources of information were John E. Russell and Ted Guard. Russell brought Geoffrey into the directors meetings of all the companies, so he could see how the wheels worked. And in the spring of 1949, just as Geoffrey was getting ready to make a triennial trip home with his family (transatlantic fare at his own expense, mind you, unlike George T.), Russell sent him on a mission to the Big Island to write a report on the plantations. He wrote an excellent report that was full of ideas for change and better ways of operating.[9]

When Geoffrey Davies and his family arrived in England they divided their time between the Cooke house in Suffolk and Hawkley Hurst. Clive had some important personal matters to discuss with Geoffrey. British taxation had grown so stringent by 1949 that Sir George Davies had sold Leigh House, his estate with its 800 acres of land, because he could no longer maintain it properly. Clive was beginning to feel the pinch in the 38 rooms of Hawkley Hurst, with its high level of expense, and he wondered what were Geoffrey's plans for the future? Did he feel that his future rested with the company? Geoffrey said he wanted to remain in Honolulu, and Clive offered to transfer Craigside to him, which Geoffrey accepted. But Hawkley Hurst? The house was so large that no one could afford to maintain it given the English tax structure. Geoffrey might want some day to come and farm part of the land, but the house, no; he would never take it.[10]

Clive asked Geoffrey how he felt about the company, would he want to be president of Theo H. Davies & Co., Ltd? No, said Geoffrey, that would mean tying himself to Honolulu. And like his father and his grandfather, at some point, perhaps not too far away, he would want to return to live in England.

Chapter Forty-Four

THE PROMOTION OF GEOFFREY DAVIES

When *Geoffrey Davies* returned to Honolulu in the last weeks of 1949, Clive Davies settled down to the quiet life again. He was worried about Edith for her heart had been acting up, and at one point earlier in the year he thought he was going to lose her. She suffered from *angina pectoris* and had bad spells from time to time. But all in all Clive Davies could contemplate life with some satisfaction. Geoffrey seemed to be doing well in Honolulu. Gerald and Lorna had made a place for themselves in Manila, and that company was progressing in spite of the doubts of Director Arthur Smith, who now announced to Clive's surprise that he had always been opposed to the formation of the Theo H. Davies-Far East and predicted that it would come to a bad end.[1] Clive Davies was particularly impressed by a report on merchandising that Geoffrey had done; it pointed out that several warehousemen at the Davies nine-story building could handle 200 tons of goods a day, while a man with a fork lift at the Amfac warehouse could handle five times as much. Unfortunately for Geoffrey, Ted Guard had been doing things his own way for so many years that he was not prepared to deal with this sort of recommendation or even discuss so major a change in operating procedures. This was Geoffrey Davies' major complaint against the upper management of Theo H. Davies

& Co., Ltd. Russell and Guard would not listen to new ideas, and they were backed by a supine board of directors who were under Russell's thumb. Geoffrey also had the feeling that Russell did not take him seriously. To be sure he was in his third year with the company, but he had six and a half years of naval experience behind him, which meant dealing with men, and in wartime in which decisions could mean life or death.[2] Guard and Russell continued to treat him as an outsider.

Guard had passed the age of 65, and it was time for him to retire under the company's new policy. After much soul-searching, Russell agreed to bring Harold Weidig out from New York for a six months' trial in the position, but it would be some time before Weidig began to function.

Russell began the education of Geoffrey Davies at the board level with a seat on the family's subsidiary holding, Laupahoehoe sugar company. Early in 1950, Geoffrey picked up the *Advertiser* one morning and learned that Laupahoehoe was selling its fleet of trucks used to haul sugar to the point of shipment. After the *tsunami* of 1946 and the decision of the Hilo railroad not to build, each sugar mill had to make its own arrangements for shipment. Russell had decided to start his own trucking company, Hawaii Trucking Corp., and then when it became expensive, he decided to sell it off to a Japanese family which had gone into the trucking business. All this became clearer that same afternoon, when Geoffrey Davies went to a meeting of the Laupahoehoe board of directors, and Russell brought the matter up and asked for a vote. One by one, the directors voted yes — except one. That one was Geoffrey Davies, who said that he understood that the company had $100,000 invested in this equipment and he was not going to agree to the sale of an asset of that size with ten minutes of discussion and no position papers. Russell said he was willing to hold off the vote until Geoffrey had a chance to examine the facts. But Russell had stated that he had transferred the assets and the trucks were already working for the Japanese company. In other words it had all been done by the administration, and the board of directors was being asked to approve, after the fact. He would not vote at all, said Geoffrey.[3] He recalled that three years earlier he had visited the plantations when this trucking problem came up. The managers of the mills favored giving the Japanese the job then, but Russell had told Geoffrey it would give the Japanese too much power in the sugar industry, and he had insisted on starting his own company. Now Geoffrey did not know how much the trucks had been sold for, what was happening to the employees, what guarantees Laupahoehoe had about the maintenance of rates, and how much of the profit would go to pay off the mortgage on the equipment. He did not get the answers, either.

What Geoffrey objected to, he said, was the unbusinesslike air of the entire operation. Again, referring to the trucking fiasco, he told the story of the purchase of the first truck. Charlie Holt, the new secretary of the parent company, had then been working in the plantation department. Holt had been told to order a truck, so he called Honolulu Iron Works and ordered them to build a truck to carry 15 tons. Since he was dealing with Honolulu Iron Works, a Davies company, he did not follow up with a written order; that was not the custom. When the truck was built, it was discovered that Honolulu Iron Works had made the wheelbase too short to conform to territorial highway regulations. Thus, 13.5 tons was the maximum load the truck could carry. Nor could Hawaii Trucking (the Laupahoehoe firm) make an insurance claim because there had been no written order.

Geoffrey's raising of these points created a stir at the Laupahoehoe board meeting. It was not usual for anyone to object to what Mr. Russell did. Geoffrey offered to resign from the board. If they wanted him as a director, they would have to keep him informed and listen to his views. Russell ended the meeting saying he wanted Geoffrey to remain on the board. He said nothing about Geoffrey's demands.

Geoffrey Davies wrote all this to his father, seeking his advice.[4] Clive wrote back that Geoffrey must face the facts: Laupahoehoe was wholly owned by the Davies family, and they put the management in the hands of Theo H. Davies & Co., Ltd. Thus the general manager of the Davies company was the boss of Laupahoehoe and would make the decisions. The directors of Laupahoehoe were really puppets with an important qualification.

"Mr. Russell comes to the board with the definite advice on a matter of policy which the shareholders hold him responsible for giving. I think that a director, who may have misgivings as to the wisdom of that advice, should make it plain in casting his vote to support of the agents' recommendation, that he is voting to endorse that recommendation, without thereby expressing an opinion as to the wisdom of that recommendation.[5]"

To Geoffrey, his father's devious thinking represented a distinction without a difference. In his own logic, either a director was a director and functioned as a thinking member of a board of directors who set policy for a company, or why have such directors? Geoffrey did not then understand that the establishment under which the Davies interests operated in Hawaii was created by Hawaii law, and that much of what happened in the captive corporations was no more than subterfuge. His entire approach was anathema to the orderly conduct of business, as Russell had always conducted it, and as Wodehouse, Clive Davies, and Swanzy had conducted it before him. The management made the decisions and they were ratified by the boards.

Geoffrey, like his father and grandfather before him, was made British consul. He had contacts then with Canadian cruiser captains, the chief of staff of the New Zealand army, the chairman of the British cotton board, and various ministers, subministers, and peers who passed through Honolulu on their way east and west.[6] This social life he enjoyed. He did not mix very well in the rarified society of Honolulu's *kamaaina* families, many of them the children of missionaries who had come to do good and done well (as the old island saw has it). The Pacific Club and the Oahu Golf & Country Club and Waialae Country Club tended to bore him. He joined the newer Outrigger Canoe Club and entertained there mostly. Because he did not mix much in the normal activities of wealthy Honolulu he saw little of the others of the Big Five, and not much more of the Davies company's top officialdom. When he had parties a number of the younger Davies people were likely to be invited, but almost never were any of the officers asked. This standoffishness did not help Geoffrey Davies' relationships with the senior staff. He seemed to be somewhat schizophrenic in his company relationships. No man in the company was more popular with the mail clerks and stenographers. He was kindly, always had a smile and a wry remark which often brought inordinate laughter. But with his superiors he was inclined to be brusque to the point of rudeness, and that was the reputation he acquired.

The fact was, of course, that Geoffrey Davies and John E. Russell were not only of different generations, different nationalities, and different social positions, they were also operating at cross purposes. Geoffrey had hoped to come to Hawaii and use his abilities and energy to make a reputation for himself in some aspect of company life. Then he would be content to function as a director's director, representing capital, with others handling the management. Russell never understood this attitude. What he wanted from the British shareholders was "support"—it was a term he used constantly, and what it implied was backup of Russell's decisions. It was nice to have a member of the family around giving approval of what he did, so that no one at home in England would suddenly descend upon Honolulu and tear up the organization. Geoffrey did not understand that years earlier Clive Davies had established this relationship. As long as John E. Russell produced the dividends, protected the investments, and did not rock the boat, all was well in Hawkley Hurst, and that sense of well being radiated out to London, Dorset, and wherever Davies heirs lived.

From Russell's point of view, Geoffrey was more difficult at the moment than Gerald Wilkinson, for even though Wilkinson had a foothold in company management, having been granted that seat on the board of Theo H. Davies & Co., Ltd., Wilkinson was five thousand miles away in Manila. Geoffrey seemed to be under foot no matter where Russell stepped.

The point of Geoffrey's concern was the merchandising department of the company. Hawaii was changing rapidly in these postwar years. The beauty of the islands had been discovered by thousands of young Americans who had come here from the mainland in military service, and many of them came back to find employment, and establish businesses. Where there had been only a few hotels along Waikiki Beach, new ones began to spring up. Houses were built up the hills of St. Louis Heights, Wilhelmina Rise, and near the Waialae Country Club, and enormous shopping centers were in the planning. The orientals particularly the Japanese, who had been held back all these past years, began to hold their heads up high as their sons came back from the famous 442nd Regimental Combat Team which had distinguished itself in the war in Europe, and from smaller units in the Pacific. Federal legislation regarding equality in housing and other matters made discrimination uncomfortable and would soon bring about its end. Geoffrey Davies wondered why no oriental had ever risen in the Davies company; that was another indication of his different approach to life. His grandfather would have been shocked at the idea of an oriental in high position, particularly a Japanese; his father would have been nearly as shocked. The current management of the Davies company had never considered such an idea, any more than had the general *haole* community.

Orientals, of course, had always been part of the Hawaii market for the Davies company; but they had never truly catered to it and they did not now. Since orientals were the major part of the population, this position did not help merchandising.

After insisting for months that Guard and Russell give him some area in which to try his management abilities, Geoffrey finally persuaded them to put him in charge of E.O. Hall, the retail hardware store Davies had operated for many years; or Geoffrey thought he had persuaded them. When he appeared at E. O. Hall he discovered that Guard had never told Mr. Cronin, the manager, that Geoffrey was to be in charge. Geoffrey had to force Guard to put it in writing.[7]

Geoffrey was distressed because E. O. Hall company was losing $3,000 a month. Nobody blamed him; the losses had begun years before; the company was antiquated and its storefront looked like a 1920 Sears Roebuck catalogue. Geoffrey took a trip to San Francisco to study west coast hardware merchandising and came back to refurbish the store. All these changes helped business but they could not resolve problems of ten years standing. Meanwhile Geoffrey moved into E.O. Hall like a new broom; he conducted a sale, which took tennis rackets and other goods off the shelf, some of them items that had been gathering dust for six years. There seemed to be something of that quality about the whole merchandising operation, but each time Geoffrey came up with a new general idea for improvement, he was patted on the head, so to speak, and ignored. The old merchandising methods were not working in the postwar world but no one in Theo H. Davies management but Geoffrey Davies seemed to realize it.

Geoffrey was made assistant treasurer of Theo H. Davies & Co., Ltd., but this elevation did not change him from a critic into a member of Russell's "team." Geoffrey kept nagging about the merchandising department. Russell and Guard explained away much of the difficulty in terms of the shipping strike, and there was certainly merit in that argument. But merchandising lost money in 1948, and the estimates were off by $1,250,000—which distressed Clive Davies as much as anything had in years.[8] Russell's answer to losses was to cut inventories and reduce the lines.[9]

The next year, 1950, the merchandising department did show a little improvement but it was in no way keeping up with the development of the Hawaiian Islands. Theo H. Davies & Co, Ltd. was falling behind the others of the Big Five.

Net Profits[10]

	1940	1950
Theo H. Davies & Co., Ltd.	$ 298,000	$ 365,000
Amfac, Inc.	777,000	1,330,000
Castle & Cooke, Inc.	1,079,000	1,816,000
C. Brewer and Co., Ltd.	771,000	1,651,000
Alexander & Baldwin, Inc.	996,000	1,993,000

Obviously, something was very wrong in the Theo H. Davies & Co., Ltd. operations. To be sure, it could be argued that all these were larger companies than Davies company but they had not always been. Clive Davies' concern was real and all the more so because in the summer of 1950, Sir George died. He had been most improvident in arranging his personal affairs, and the tax laws had caught up with him. The death duties of 65 percent were invoked even against some stock gifts he had made to his children. In the end, he left an estate of £262,860, of which the British government took £209,360. Clive took the warning seriously; he made plans to unload Hawkley Hurst and put his investments in order. He made gifts to his children and grandchildren and disposed of as much of his fortune as he believed wise. These transfers helped strengthen Geoffrey's personal position with the Russell management, which by the end of 1950 regarded Geoffrey with mixed emotions. He was a likable man, but he did have a dreadful way of upsetting apple carts. For several months Clive had been hoping that Geoffrey would be put on the board of directors of Theo H. Davies & Co., Ltd., but Russell had stalled. Clive attributed this delay to Geoffrey's habit of speaking out. His suggestion was that Geoffrey curb it.[11] Geoffrey's response was to have a "showdown" with Russell, at which he demanded to be taken seriously or he would leave.

But meanwhile, events were in progress that would change Geoffrey's career and the course of Theo H. Davies & Co., Ltd.

Chapter Forty-Five

THE BANISHMENT OF
GERALD WILKINSON

O*n September 16, 1950,* Clive Davies' world fell apart. Gerald and Lorna Wilkinson had come back to England on the usual triennial leave. This time, however, it was all different. They came to luncheon at Hawkley Hurst, and Gerald had no sooner entered the house than he asked Clive for an interview. When luncheon was over and after they had settled down in the study, Gerald dropped his bombshell: he and Lorna had reached a point of no return in their relations, and he felt they should both be freed to go their own ways. He was talking divorce. He asked Clive's views.[1] He must have known what they would be, but Clive gave them anyhow: according to his appreciation of God's laws, he said, divorce was incompatible with the allegiance of a Christian. Gerald, he knew, was a Christian and a member of the Church of England. Separation was another matter —but that meant enormous self-sacrifice for a man.

Gerald was noncommittal. But now that he had raised the subject, if they did separate, or even divorce, what would the effect be on Gerald's career with Theo H. Davies & Co., Ltd.?

Clive was not prepared to answer that question. He was not the managing director of the company any more, with power of hiring and firing. What would happen to Gerald's career remained to be seen; that was all he could say.

Wilkinson was moved to tears, and he expressed sadness that the relationship had come to such a pass and the fondest affection for Clive and Edith Davies. That was the end of the discussion. Next morning was Sunday. Clive went to church twice that morning and read the lessons. Gerald and Lorna went to the second service with him and stayed to communion. Edith, apparently overcome by the news from Lorna, did not come to the morning service but did come to Evensong.

Nothing more was said on Sunday, but on Monday Clive sought an interview and told Gerald bluntly what he had decided. As a Christian Gerald had the responsibility to abstain from divorce or any ground for separation. Clive suggested that if Gerald followed the course he indicated, he would be guilty of cruelty, selfishness, and a "funking of the responsibilities of the marriage vow." Clive had learned that it was not just a question of personality, but another woman was involved. It would be a fundamental sin to involve himself with another woman, said Clive.

When the interview was ended, Clive knew ruefully that he had not made an impression on Gerald. Lorna had certainly not helped much, she had sat all weekend complacently, and when she sought an interview with Clive, she indicated it really did not make much difference to her. Certainly there were deep personal reasons involved in the matter, some of them obviously stemming from Lorna's character change during the Japanese imprisonment. But there was nothing more to be done or said in so civilized a household as that of Clive Davies, so the matter was not mentioned again until Saturday, September 23, when Gerald left for Manila and came in to say goodbye. He and Lorna left for London at four o'clock that afternoon. Edith's parting words to Gerald Wilkinson were that if he and Lorna divorced, this would be "his final farewell to our home."

The issue was resolved quickly enough. The plans of Gerald and Lorna Wilkinson for divorce had already been made; within a month it was all settled. John E. Russell came to London that fall, and Clive told him the story. They agreed that Gerald would be ejected from the "inner circle" and the board of directors of Theo H. Davies & Co., Ltd. at the annual meeting in March. But the months went by and Clive Davies heard no more on the subject from Russell. The departure of Gerald Wilkinson from the board of Theo H. Davies & Co., Ltd. would leave only himself as a family member. He almost never attended meetings, which meant family control was exercised only through his letters, and he was in his eightieth year, which meant that unless action were taken family control would possibly soon cease. So in February, Clive wrote the most insistent letter he had ever sent Russell, in essence demanding that Geoffrey be placed on the board. It was done with all Clive's usual tact, and he suggested that both he and Russell talk to Geoffrey about being a disruptive member.[2] But no matter what he said, what it came down to was that Clive Davies was wielding the Davies votes which still controlled Theo H. Davies & Co., Ltd.

Russell yielded, but he did lay out for Clive Davies his precise opinions. He had misgivings about bringing Geoffrey to the board. He knew Geoffrey was independent, and would rebel if not given his right to express his views as a director. At the same time he was an employee, and as such he had to accept decisions of management.

> I admit this may be difficult. Geoffrey wants authority. My considered opinion is that he is not ready to be given wide authority. This is a large business which makes money because we have carefully chosen men in charge of our departments. These men are sensitive and proud of their positions and of their achievements. To be quite outspoken, Geoffrey has a somewhat difficult personality along with his courage, energy and intelligence.[3]

Geoffrey had demanded authority in that "showdown" meeting earlier in the year. He wanted a post of "inspector general" in which he would travel through the company visiting branches, subsidiaries, and departments, and discovering their anomalies. The idea so frightened Russell that he summoned his favorite "outside" director to his assistance in the argument: Arthur G. Smith, attorney for the company and a member of the firm of Smith, Wild, Beebe & Cades. If Russell was conservative, then Lawyer Smith would have to be placed on the right side of Calvin Coolidge.

Smith obliged Russell with a memorandum:

I assume that eventually as one of the representatives of the family in Hawaii, Geoffrey *will have to be given* [author's italics] a position different from that which he now holds, but . . . I would be quite worried if Geoffrey were to be given in the too near future . . . the post . . . or any similar position where he could make more or less authoritative suggestions . . . [4] I am very fond of Geoffrey and have a high regard for his ability, character and integrity, but he is *not* diplomatic, and from what I have heard he has a tendency to pick out minor details, especially with regard to expenses, and I am afraid he would, as things are now, unintentionally antagonize some of your best men.

Russell had asked for a show letter, and he had gotten it. He sent it on to Clive, who replied with a long letter, indicating that he knew what was going on in the company, that Geoffrey had obviously done a fine job at E.O. Hall, and in his plantation report, and his report on warehousing (which showed conclusively that the Davies company was 20 years behind the times). He suggested that Geoffrey was not the only one without tact ("a word of encouragement, if it is merited as to his administration of E.O. Hall's and as to his report on Warehouses and Transport, might have a considerable effect. . . ."[5]). The letter ended on the note that Geoffrey *was to be appointed*.

Having no recourse at the moment, Russell acceded, and at the annual meeting on March 27, Geoffrey was appointed a director to succeed Gerald Wilkinson. Harold Weidig, the new merchandise manager, was appointed a director to succeed Sir George Davies. Geoffrey was not to be inspector general, but "operations analyst" — which Russell obviously considered to be a nice way of dealing with the problem. Geoffrey could analyze to his heart's content and the reports could be filed in the round file.

For one simple fact had become apparent in 1951. John E. Russell trusted no one in the younger generation. His confidants were Ted Guard, who was still hanging about the premises in a small office, preparing notes for a corporate history and getting in Weidig's way, and C.V. Bennett in San Francisco, who was already semi-retired. Weidig had been touted by Clive Davies as a comer and was brought to Honolulu at Clive's insistence, over Russell's objections. Clive considered Weidig to be presidential material. Russell said he was strictly a merchandising man, and not capable of seeing the total operation of the company.

Russell's real problem was obvious enough; he did not want to retire, and he was 63 years old, just two years away from the day set at the insistence of Clive Davies some years earlier. For twenty years outsiders had been pressing Russell to take on an assistant who would have real responsibility and be prepared to take over. Russell had always resisted; C. J. Henderson had resigned to go to better opportunity, and no other American had ever been selected. Clive and Russell had agreed that the president of the company ought to be an American—in halcyon days the one exception mentioned had been Gerald Wilkinson. But Russell had quietly resisted with every fiber the development of that man. Closest to it at the moment, he said, was James D. Brown, director of the plantation department, but he gave no real indication of preparing to turn over the reins of power even to Brown.[6]

One of Russell's strong points was his ability to adjust to any situation, once it had been forced upon him. He apparently welcomed Geoffrey to the "inner circle" with open arms and said no more to Clive about his son's deficiencies. In the summer Davies Company opened serious negotiations for the acquisition of F. A. Schaefer & Co. Geoffrey did most of the work and Russell wrote complimentary letters to Clive about Geoffrey's efforts. He would make Geoffrey his "right hand" on his return.[7] Clive was truly pleased with what he saw as the reconciliation of the two: "What you write about Geoffrey is the best news I have had of him since he went out to you in 1946."[8] Russell said further that he wanted to appoint Geoffrey treasurer of the company in 1953, if all went well.

So it seemed that Geoffrey Davies was on his way to authority in the company and that the management problems would be resolved by Russell's yielding to the wishes of the family. Gerald Wilkinson's name was seldom mentioned in Honolulu or at Hawkley Hurst. The power of Theo H. Davies & Co., Ltd. in Honolulu could have been involved to force him out in Manila, because Honolulu owned 75 percent of the stock, but Davies was a business and Gerald Wilkinson was its most valuable asset in the Far East.

In 1948 Theo H. Davies-Far East had begun to burgeon. The net profit that year was more than ₱300,000. In 1951 it reached ₱560,000 (at two pesos on the dollar) while the parent company's profits were only $412,000, including the ₱187,500 that Manila paid over that year in dividends. And Wilkinson had run the assets of the Philippine company up to ₱4,000,000. One did not kill the goose that laid the golden egg, no matter how one disagreed on moral values. Wilkinson brought his new wife, Mariana, to Honolulu that summer of 1951. Russell wrote Clive in a flurry[9] that he would have the erring couple to tea only for business reasons and would call on them at the Halekulani Hotel, but have no other social intercourse. Clive quite approved this bizarre behavior. Geoffrey wrote in some pride that he had spoken brusquely to Gerald in the building but had no other communication, and Clive approved heartily of that behavior.[10] He was totally unforgiving, and yet, when Gerald came to England and wrote him out of courtesy, Clive took him to lunch at the City of London Club. It was a strained affair, both men trying to keep the conversation on neutral ground. All the old intimacy had gone and it could never return. What remained was the business they shared in common, for in that sense Gerald was still a vital member of the Davies family.

Mrs. Clive Davies in front of Hawkley Hurst, probably in 1950.

Chapter Forty-Six

THE DEATH OF CLIVE DAVIES

G*eoffrey Davies'* scathing criticisms of the Davies merchandising program had been greeted with deep resentment by Ted Guard, who was responsible for the decay. Guard had remained adamant for twenty years as the world moved beyond him; Russell had always supported Guard because they were making money but in 1951 they were losing. Clive Davies wanted $1,500,000 in investment taken out of merchandising; that's how bad it was. They had lost dozens of eager young men over these years: Alan Davis, for example, went off to run C. Brewer and Co. when they got into management difficulty. But in 1951, change could no longer be avoided. A new merchandise accounting system was devised, and new controls were put into effect. There were terrible times as the card-punch system and the old way overlapped, conflicted, and became confused; one could not modernize an old-fashioned business overnight.

In February 1952, Russell and his wife went to Manila. They were entertained by the Wilkinsons and by others of the staff. Russell wrote glowingly of Stewart Jamieson, Wilkinson's right hand man, and in so doing Russell exposed his real feelings about the Honolulu company. He had been telling Clive that he planned to bring Geoffrey up as his "right hand" but in this letter he revealed that he already regarded J. D. Brown as occupying that position.[1]

What Russell saw in Manila was so impressive that he had to agree with Clive that the Manila operation "was in able hands."[2] Earnshaw's Docks was in good shape. E. J. Nell, the engineering company was "happy" and profitable. The Wilkinsons took them down to Bacalod on the island of Negros, and they visited various installations of Theo H. Davies-Far East, Earnshaw's and Hawaiian-Philippine Sugar *Central* (mill) at Silay, where they stayed with manager Ned Herkes. Russell met the district planters, who then were led by Arsenio Jison, an implacable enemy of Theo H. Davies-Far East and of Wilkinson. But Russell learned, too, that the planters of the district did not all think alike and that some of them at least, had been happy with the split of sugar arranged at the end of World War II as a price of rebuilding the mill: 60 – 40. The planters were demanding 62.5 percent of the sugar, and it seemed that they might get it, although the matter was being taken up by the legislature just then. They visited San Carlos mill, a much happier place, although in need of rebuilding. They visited Bogo-Medellin, which also impressed them favorably. The only thing that did not impress them favorably was their propinquity to the Wilkinsons. Gerald was the soul of tact and courtesy, but Russell came back and told Clive the Russells had been miserable every moment.[3]

No one who did not understand the nature of Honolulu society could understand the depth of emotion brought on by the Wilkinson divorce among people who scarcely knew Lorna and Gerald Wilkinson. The *kamaaina* crowd were a close-knit and even incestuous group; they stoutly resisted outsiders, but once they were accepted they were treated as though they were members of an extended family. Over the years from 1934 to 1950, the Wilkinsons had been regarded as part of the Davies family, and when Honolulu mentioned the names of the Big Five, Honolulu curtsied. That attitude, as much as any loyalty of the Russells to Clive Davies, accounted for the bitterness Wilkinson faced in Honolulu. But the Russell trip put the final seal on Gerald Wilkinson's position: to try to dislodge him would obviously be fatal to the Davies company in the Far East.

In Honolulu, Geoffrey seemed to be digging in well. He had been assigned a study of fertilizers for the plantations, which he had carried out.

He was handling negotiations with Lincoln National Life Insurance company for builders' mortgage loans that would help the Davies building supply division, he was still supervising E. O. Hall, while Russell agonized over the choice between modernizing and closing down that retail hardware business, and Geoffrey was pressing for modernization of the Piggly Wiggly chain.[4]

The company had serious financial problems again, because of the losses of the merchandise department and the general low level of profitability over a long period. As far as the family was concerned, this was somewhat misleading. For the structure of the Davies holdings in Hawaii made many people see the Davies enterprises as less significant than they were. One could adjust the comparative profit figures significantly if one added up all the Davies enterprises:

Net Profits[5]

	1940	1959
Theo H. Davies & Co., Ltd.	$298,000	365,000
Hamakua Mill (51 percent)	42,000	285,000
Honolulu Iron Works	438,000	470,000
Laupahoehoe Sugar Co.	50,000	121,000
Amfac, Inc.	298,000	365,000
Castle & Cooke, Inc.	777,000	1,330,000
C. Brewer and Co., Ltd.	771,000	1,816,000
Alexander & Baldwin, Inc.	996,000	1,993,000
Total Davies Enterprises	*828,000*	*1,241,000*

The major reason for the difference — and the underestimation of the Davies interests in Hawaii — was largely through the comparison of incomparables. The other companies of the Big Five had long since ceased to be family-held. Indeed, just then, 1952, C. Brewer and Co. was undergoing a reorganization in the face of three separate and divided factions of stock-holders. The Brewer figures represented the company's holdings, but the Davies position was far more complex. The family, of course, had no wish to advertise their importance, for tax reasons as well as British diffidence, and for years Russell had been telling various authorities that Theo H. Davies & Co., Ltd. was only the agent for these other companies. In the literal sense, this analysis was accurate; in reality the men who ran Theo H. Davies & Co., Ltd. ran the entire enterprise under Clive Davies' close super-vision.

In the spring of 1952, Clive Davies became concerned again about the financial stability of the company. The debt to banks had gone above $3,000,000 and that troubled him. So although Clive Davies was nearly 81 years old, he traveled to Honolulu again to straighten matters out, stop-ping in New York, Chicago, and San Francisco for conferences with bankers as he had done so many times in the past forty years. In May he was in Honolulu, assessing the situation. They had just bought F. A. Schaefer & Company to secure control of Honokaa Sugar Company on the Big Island, and paid $450,000 for it. Honokaa was a bright feather in John E. Russell's cap, for he had worked hard and long to get this company for Davies. In 1944, when the Schaefers still controlled Honokaa, Russell had found them Leslie Wishard as manager, and Wishard had taken a moribund mill and plantation and rehabilitated it into an extremely valu-able property. They had added $650,000 to the assets and increased in-vestments by $600,000 to acquire control of Honokaa and strengthen the position in Honolulu Iron Works, which had been diluted years before. So far they had cut the investment in merchandise by nearly a quarter of a million dollars.[6]

Clive directed Russell to sell two pieces of land, one a lumberyard site on Oahu and the other a warehouse site at Hilo, for which they ought to get $600,000. Like his father Clive believed in lease rather than purchase, and directed Russell to put together figures so that they could go to the bankers at the end of the year and fund their short-term debt on a longer basis. They were moving away from merchandising and should not need the same sort of cash flow in the future.

Clive Davies was back in England by the beginning of summer. He was pleased because of the progress that Geoffrey had made in Honolulu. On his recent visit, many people had spoken of Geoffrey's flair for business. Harold Weidig had been strong in his praise of Geoffrey's warehouse report. Johnston, the Piggly Wiggly manager, had told Clive that he was surprised that a comparative novice in the business had been able to put his finger on so many of the salient problems of the grocery business.[7] Clive settled down to his usual routine, watching the business affairs of Honolulu carefully. Then, one day he discovered a spot of blood on his underwear. He had not been feeling very well, and as always when something ailed him, he went up to London to see his Harley Street specialists. Eight years earlier he had a lump in the groin, which the doctors called a femoral hernia and more or less disregarded. It began to grow, and this year the doctors decided he should have an operation.[8] On October 5, he entered the King's College hospital for thorough examination.

The doctors operated, and on October 25 he sent Russell a cheery note enclosing clippings from the *Times* about a new breed of Australian cattle that might be suitable for Kukaiau ranch. He was looking forward to getting out of the hospital, but he had no appetite, he said. He did not mention the operation.

The doctors kept him in the hospital for they had discovered the cancer that was killing him. He grew weaker every day but continued to write in his diary, almost until the end, on November 16, 1952.

After Clive's death, the family discovered that the government had grown greedier even than it was at Sir George's death. The estate in England was valued at £236,000 and the tax collector demanded £207,000 of it. Fortunately, Clive Davies had profited by Sir George's sad experience, and he had transferred or placed in trust the bulk of the fortune, so the government could not get at it. The future of the Davies interests in Hawaii seemed secure. One question did remain; now that Clive was gone, who was to be the senior officer of the company and leader of the family?

Chapter Forty-Seven

MORE TROUBLE IN PARADISE

Ｉf *Gerald Wilkinson was not* very popular in Honolulu and
Hampshire, England, after 1950, he more than made up for it in Manila,
where he was easily one of the best-liked of all foreigners. He drove himself unmercifully and often had to take off a few days and bed down to
recover from dengue or some other fever. But he built a strong organization of Europeans and Filipinos, in spite of concern from Honolulu that he
was putting too much authority into local hands. The first post-war years
were spent getting together the materials for expansion. With the exception of the Sino-Hawaiian fiasco, Wilkinson's investment sense was sound,
and after 1950 he was more or less let alone by Clive Davies and Russell,
who did not know quite how to deal with him. The proof of his abilities was
shown again at the end of 1952, when the net profit of Theo H. Davies-Far
East was ₱511,000, or 40 percent on capital.[4] Since the net profit of the Davies
company in Honolulu was just under $117,000, one might say (as many
people did) that the tail was wagging the dog. If one subtracted the
$93,000 in dividends from the Far East company stock from the Honolulu
company's operating statement, then the result was indeed shocking.[2]

What had brought about this serious decline in the fortunes of the
Honolulu company? In a word: merchandising. The income from merchandising dropped half a million dollars that year. One need look no
further than the composition of the board of directors to see why.

The president of the company was John E. Russell, 63, who had grown ever more conservative over the years. The vice-president and treasurer was Ted Guard, well over 65, who had been retired as merchandising manager just in time to escape the debacle he had never understood. The second vice-president was C. V. Bennett, former San Francisco manager, also retired. The other senior directors were E. H. Wodehouse, who had been moved out as managing director 23 years earlier, D. F. McCorriston, formerly manager of the dry goods department, who was also retired, and Arthur G. Smith, the ultra-conservative lawyer. They were joined in their general attitude by H. W. B. White, the only really "outside" director in the company, who was vice-president of the Hawaiian Trust Company. Also on the board of directors were Geoffrey Davies, Harold Weidig, and James D. Brown, the manager of the plantations department, who was the only one of the younger men that Russell would really listen to.[3] Missing from the board was the head of the most profitable operating portion of the Davies' interest, Wilkinson.

Russell felt impelled to apologize and explain the company's sad performance to the stockholders in the annual report. He noted that the company had purchased a majority interest in the Hawaii Builders Supply Company; the indication was that Theo H. Davies was going to join the general boom of the construction industry. So badly was John E. Russell smarting from the merchandising losses that he warned Wilkinson about the Philippine merchandising department. It was true that in 1952, merchandising in the Manila company had lost money—but the reasons were entirely different from those that caused the losses in Honolulu. A slump in the Manila textile market and drastic changes in the Philippine government's import controls had brought the Manila loss—and even as Russell warned, Wilkinson had already taken steps to change operations to fit the times.

Before the war, the Davies company had been agents for Hume Pipe, which was a branch of an Australian firm. The factory in the Philippines was bombed out, and the Hume company and Hughes, its former manager, had disagreed, so Wilkinson had put together Hume Pipe and Asbestos Company. Four years later he had merged it into a new company, pulling together the Eternit corporation of Belgium, Johns-Manville of the U.S., Hume Pipe, and his friends Aurelio Montinola and Cesar de Zulueta, who had formed the Amon Trading Corporation in Manila. Eternit began to produce roofing, sidings, and various other construction materials of pressed concrete. This was the answer to government controls on foreign merchandise: manufacture in the Philippines.[4]

This was Wilkinson's new direction. In London he had secured the agency for Mayon Metal Windows, a leading British product. He was just then negotiating to change over from selling Sherwin-Williams paints made in America, to manufacturing paints in Manila. Davies-Far East were agents for Union Oil (which had a bad year). The general insurance business was doing very well, and so was the life insurance agency. The company sold sugar for the four sugar mills: Asturias, Bogo-Medellin, Hawaiian Philippine (which the Davies company had acquired in the rebuilding at the end of World War II), and San Carlos Milling Company.

E.J. Nell Company had made a ₱500,000 profit, and its subsidiary, Diesel Injection and Magneto Service Company, had been spun off by Wilkinson into a new company in which Davies-Far East had thirty-six percent interest. Earnshaw's Docks and Honolulu Iron Works were still going strong, providing support for the sugar mills and making other heavy equipment.[5]

Wilkinson simply never stopped. In the spring of 1953 he organized Aircon, because E.J. Nell Company, which had been agent for Carrier Corporation, was having too much trouble getting import licenses for the air-conditioning units. After a dozen years' residence in the Philippines, Wilkinson had a keen sense of Filipino pride and nationalism, and he saw where it was taking the government and business. Aircon, he told Russell, was to be "an experiment in Filipino leadership." All the officers would be Filipinos. Wilkinson and his associates would take a back seat. He expected "teething troubles" and no immediate profit from the investment—but he did not ask John E. Russell, chairman of the board of Theo H. Davies-Far East for permission to do these things; he told him he had done them.[6]

Sherwin-Williams Philippines (Sherphil) would cost Davies company an investment of ₱300,000. Wilkinson was going into business with the Montinolas and the Roxas brothers, who would subscribe most of the rest of the ₱500,000 necessary to set up the company.

When John E. Russell got these reports, he scribbled little notes on the margins, and in his letters to Manila he tried to show himself on top of the business, as a board chairman should certainly be. He thought the merchandise results "ominous" and was "sorry to see" that the insurance department profits were off. He was disturbed because new contracts had not been signed in August for the next year with the difficult planters of Hawaiian-Philippines *Central* district.[7] But it was mostly sham; Russell could not possibly keep up with the three-ring circus Wilkinson was running in Manila.

One of the secrets of Wilkinson's success was his real friendship with the Filipino people. He knew all the major political figures and got on well with them. His war record—the retreat with MacArthur to Corregidor and his subsequent journey to Java by submarine—gave him an heroic aura much appreciated in Manila. He had been decorated by the Americans, and King George VI had made him a Commander of the British Empire for his wartime service. He was also the master of the grand gesture. He was a fine horseman and loved to ride and to play polo. Several of his Filipino friends also liked to play, but they were denied membership in the Manila Polo Club, whereupon Wilkinson resigned and joined the Filipinos in forming Los Tamaros, named for a peculiarly ferocious carabao found in Mindanao. Such gestures appealed to the sense of drama of the Filipinos, and Wilkinson's popularity grew.[8]

If Wilkinson off in Manila was out from under the pressures of Honolulu, one could not say that of the board of directors and officers of the company in Honolulu. The year 1953 was another disaster in spite of another $200,000 in profit in Manila. The Honolulu books showed a profit of $289,000, but there were several major problems. First was the $7,400,000 tied up in a merchandising business that was going nowhere. This lack of progress could no longer be blamed entirely on the past. In spite of the recommendations of some of the younger members of the company, the top management simply would not recognize the major changes in Hawaii. When the chain stores came in and located in the shopping centers, the Mom and Pop stores all over Hawaii began to suffer. Then why not follow suit? They had Piggly Wiggly, a respectable chain grocery operation. But Russell was reluctant to spend the money to build the buildings or assume the rental cost of operations in the new shopping centers.* So Piggly Wiggly declined along with other operations. The Davies company had the agency for Harley Davidson motorcycles, and motorcycles began to catch on as they never had before. But the trouble was that young people wanted small motorcycles, Kawasakis and Hondas, not Harley Davidsons. All that saved the Davies company in 1953 was an enormously successful sugar crop, which brought a revenue of $101 per ton.[9] John E. Russell's purchase of Honokaa was certainly vindicated: that company produced earnings of $14.75 per ton.

Another factor that was causing constant difficulty was the high cost of the pension plan that Clive Davies had authorized before his death. More than $1.5 million had already gone into the fund; not a big factor if the company was doing well but looming very large in 1953. The company's debt was worrisome. Notes to banks came to $3.4 million, with another $1.2 million in accounts payable. The bond issue was down to $825,000, but whether or not a new bond issue could be floated in view of the company's miserable performance was a problem.

President Russell did not know quite what to do about the management problem of the company. Theo M. Davies, and Arthur Davies in England qualified as "senior" members of the family, who might replace Clive Davies as chairman of the board. But Theo M. Davies and Arthur Davies knew practically nothing about the company. Clive had tried to provide for such an eventuality.[10] He had suggested that after he was gone, to succeed Sir George Davies, the next candidate for chairman must be

---

*Geoffrey Davies notes that Russell did spend money expanding in Kailua, on Keeaumoku Street, and on Nuuanu but on too small a scale. They did build the supermarket in Waialae Kahala shopping center that was later bought by Star Markets.

Russell himself. But in that case Russell would have to appoint a president of the company so that he could step up. In 1953, Russell had no one to appoint. James D. Brown had been elevated to executive vice-president, and he was at that time heir-apparent, but Brown suddenly discovered he had a bad heart. So that was out. Weidig had already been rejected by Russell as not of presidential timber, and Geoffrey Davies, who was appointed treasurer that year, maintained his habit of raising unpleasant issues at board meetings. Whatever confidence Russell had built up vanished rapidly as Geoffrey Davies kept reminding him of past statements and actions that were at variance with the present. As Russell was grasping for straws, he thought of George T. Davies, who had been made manager of the New York office when Weidig came back to Honolulu. George T. Davies would serve admirably, if he proved to be adequate to the job and of less rasping personality than his cousin. Besides this, George T. Davies had become a U.S. citizen, which was important to the company. So he was brought to Honolulu to become President of Honolulu Iron Works. Clive Davies had approved that a long time ago, and in 1953 the Iron Works had made a profit of $526,000. It seemed unlikely that anything would go wrong. George Davies came to Honolulu, where he was appointed to the board of directors of Theo H. Davies & Co, Ltd., too. John E. Russell could keep an eye on him and see what developed.

In 1954 the depression of Theo H. Davies & Co., Ltd. continued. Manila was making money. Kaiwiki, Hamakua, and Honokaa sugar companies made money. Even Hawaii Builders Supply made money. But with all this, the Davies company managed only to show a profit of $316,000, and that, by writing off the cost of closing down the whole grocery division against reserves. Yes, they closed down the grocery division; and Geoffrey Davies made himself even more unpopular by criticizing the operations of the dry goods department.[11] He suggested that they also close down the drug department.

What was Theo H. Davies to do if it was going out of merchandising in the old sense? One avenue for profit was mortgage loans, but it was an extremely competitive market, with a number of insurance companies loaning in the new Waialae Kahala development on the Bishop Estate lands. Geoffrey Davies was interested enough in this proposition to join with several other men and form a company servicing loans in Hawaii.[12]

In the fall of 1954, Russell's thinking about the company began to show a change. Hitherto he had not concerned himself with matters of control; that had always been Clive Davies' department. But now Russell wanted to bring control of all the Davies investments under Theo H. Davies & Co., Ltd. (and thus under himself). It was true that the Davies company was agent for the sugar companies, but that was not quite the same as owning them outright. Russell discussed this matter with Geoffrey Davies, but Geoffrey Davies may have seen the move for what it was, a change in policy, and he demurred. Russell had hoped that Geoffrey would go and sell the idea to the family stockholders; he refused. So Russell turned to George T. Davies, who acquiesced and thus increased his position in Russell's eyes.

Geoffrey argued that Russell would be better off increasing the Davies influence in Honolulu Iron Works, which had fallen to 18 percent. They also argued about the grocery business. Geoffrey wanted to get back in with Piggly Wiggly and go the supermarket route. Russell did not like the idea. Geoffrey wanted to go into the automotive business. Russell was not enthusiastic. Geoffrey also wanted to go to long term financing; Russell did not.[13] All these matters stood between Geoffrey and Russell. When his uncle Theo M. wrote Geoffrey later in the year, after George T. had been to England to sell Russell's point of view, Geoffrey advised against the move.[14] So the Davies family balked, and Russell was furious with Geoffrey.

Geoffrey Davies made a serious effort to promote new avenues of income for the Davies company. He tried to get Lincoln National Life Insurance to increase its commitments for home loans in Hawaii, but without success. What was needed was an insurance company to support the Davies mortgage loan department and make it prosperous. But there was little interest in this program in Russell's office, and nothing happened. Lincoln cut back in fact. Geoffrey tried to find other insurance companies, Massachusetts Mutual, for one. He pointed to the large investments of Prudential Insurance Co. and John Hancock in Hawaii. But he got nowhere.

At the end of 1954, Geoffrey Davies was dispatched by John E. Russell on a trip to Manila, to continue his "analysis" work. The relationships between Manila and Honolulu being what they were, Gerald Wilkinson was not aware that Geoffrey really had no specific job but was trying to find a niche for himself, with Russell and Guard still holding the reins of power.

Geoffrey spent several weeks in the Philippines and came back to write reports on Davies-Far East, Earnshaw's Docks, and Honolulu Iron Works that were generally very complimentary but mildly critical in spots. He sent a copy to Wilkinson, who erupted and wrote a strong denunciation of most of what Geoffrey Davies said, which he sent to Russell. Such an outburst must have been just what John E. Russell was waiting for. Geoffrey Davies went off on leave to England that summer with Joan and the children. He returned in late summer to Honolulu.

At the airport, he picked up a copy of the *Advertiser,* and thus learned that Geoffrey C. Davies, treasurer of Theo H. Davies & Co., Ltd. had resigned as treasurer to become vice-president in charge of new business development of the company. His jaw dropped.[15] But soon it all became clear. James Brown's heart condition had effectively ruled him out as president of the corporation (he died that year), and Russell, who must retire as president because of age, wanted to continue to control the company as chairman of the board of directors. To do so he must have a president who was willing to take administrative responsibility, but allow Russell to remain as chief executive of the company. Geoffrey Davies obviously would not be that man. But the new executive vice-president, George T. Davies, seemed to be the man. And if Geoffrey Davies did not like it, the board of directors still consisted of Russell and his old allies Bennett, Guard, Smith, White, and Wodehouse.* George Davies could be

---

*Since 1952, Russell had held the stock proxies of the family stockholders, giving him full authority. Their concern was investment, not operations, and since Clive Davies' day they had been content to let Russell run the company as long as he protected that investment.

expected to vote with Russell under the circumstances. Only Harold Weidig might take Geoffrey's side, and there was no point in testing it. The excuse given was that as future president of the company, George T. Davies did not feel himself adequate in the realm of finance and wanted someone better versed in that department than his cousin. So they went to San Francisco and brought over O. B. Hammond from that office. Hammond was a former stock analyst and then manager of the San Francisco office of Davies, who had been hired by C. V. Bennett. He had Russell's confidence where Geoffrey Davies did not. So Geoffrey Davies was out as treasurer and Hammond was in. Geoffrey had been "kicked upstairs" to become Vice-President of Nearly Nothing At All.

If the circumstances seemed hurried, that was not at all the case. Hammond had already been in Honolulu before Geoffrey left for his vacation. It was quite obvious that John E. Russell had planned the change all the way along.

Chapter Forty-Eight

ENTER GEORGE T. DAVIES;

EXIT GEORGE T. DAVIES

President John E. Russell in Honolulu concentrated on bringing the Davies sugar enterprises together and cutting the cost of increasing mechanization. That was his great contribution to the health of the Davies companies in the 1950s. But it was no substitute for the sort of planning and expansion that were going on elsewhere in Honolulu. Castle & Cooke expanded their pineapple operations into the Philippines. C. Brewer began searching the Pacific for agricultural enterprises. Amfac bought companies on the mainland and diversified so greatly that it was hard to remember that company had once been "H. H. Hackfeld, Honolulu merchants." But Theo H. Davies & Co., Ltd., under Russell's management, missed one opportunity after another. The Dillingham corporation showed their heels in building and community development, putting up the Ala Moana shopping center. Amfac went into consumer finance while Davies fiddled around the edges, dickering with Lincoln National Life Insurance Company, which was too timid to take the big leap into the Honolulu mortgage loan market.

Geoffrey Davies did try, as vice-president in charge of new business, to find some new business. One of his tasks was to see if he could do something with the Davies building. Since the company had gone out of the grocery business and was eliminating much of its merchandise, Theo H.

Davies & Co., Ltd. was rattling around in the nine-story structure. Russell would have liked to have sold it if he could, to recuperate cash. Russell was remembering what Clive Davies had told him shortly before he died: lease, don't buy. So Geoffrey scoured the hustings for renters or buyers. He even looked into the possibility of turning the building into a parking garage. But the Davies building, in all its 1921 splendor, had been constructed pimarily as a warehouse and was not really suitable for much else.[1] To prepare the building for another use meant spending a million dollars or more. Russell balked. Nothing happened. Geoffrey Davies also tried to rejuvenate the mortgage-loan department and tried to get an agency for Vickers-Armstrong aircraft. He tried to build up the steamship and travel departments, but he was too late for the one and too early for the other. He tried to persuade Russell to go into real estate development.

Out of all this came virtually nothing. What Davies needed was a real new enterprise of the multi-million dollar kind, and John E. Russell was not about to "gamble." So Geoffrey Davies and his secretary, Chiko Noda, had days, weeks, and months in which to devote themselves to nothing at all. With her assistance, Geoffrey set about translating his grandfather's papers in that spidery hand, into typewritten English, carrying on a task begun by his father—preparation for a company history—and furthered to a certain degree by Ted Guard and Geoffrey's Uncle Arthur.

The Davies company ran its business right around this grandson of the founder. As a member of the board of directors he did have one voice and he did not hesitate to use it, but he was a very small minority of one. In 1956, Russell put his plan of buying up the sugar shares into effect; George Davies having persuaded the majority of stockholders to that end. Over Geoffrey Davies' objections, shares were exchanged on the basis of $\frac{1}{4}$ Laupahoehoe for 1 Kaiwiki sugar company share, and then 93 percent of the Laupahoehoe shares were acquired by the Davies company. The outstanding shares represented the holdings of Geoffrey, his personal family, and his trusts and his uncles, who were as conservative as John E. Russell.[2]

In 1956 the company showed a slight improvement in business profit, much of it due to the $155,000 contributed in dividends by Davies Far

The old Davies Building on Bishop Street,

Honolulu, completed on December 14, 1921.

East. Four quarterly dividends adding up to six percent were paid on the common stock. A twenty percent stock dividend was declared to equalize a surplus that had developed over the years, and the stock was split five for one, to cut the unit share value and make the stock more readily salable. All this activity, as Geoffrey Davies and Harold Weidig ascertained, was Russell's preparation to try to sell the company.[3]

The real progress in Davies was being made in the Philippines. Gradually Davies-Far East was buying up control of Hawaiian-Philippine Sugar *Central.* Everything Wilkinson touched seemed to turn into gold. One reason was that he sensed and accepted the Filipino need for association with foreign companies on a level of strict equality and perhaps just a touch of superiority. After Ramon Magsaysay was elected president in 1954, the new president began doubling efforts to rebuild the Filipino economy. One problem was a shortage of cement. Four cement factories existed in the Philippines, but they did not turn out enough product to meet the need. Magsaysay put the problem to Gerald Wilkinson. That was all that was needed; with government backing, Wilkinson put together a consortium (mostly Filipino) and organized Republic Cement Corporation. Davies-Far East and Hume Pipe together held about 20 percent of the stock. One might think that Wilkinson worked by pulling strings, but it was not true. For example: Earnshaw Docks and Honolulu Iron Works might have been expected to get the contract to build the cement plant; but no, it was put up for bids, and a German company won the award. The main reason was not even price but the mistake that Earnshaw's, who represented Allis-Chalmers, made in including Japanese subcontracts in their bid. The Filipino directors of Republic Cement balked at that.[4] But such events, and Wilkinson's graceful acceptance of the will of his Filipino associates, won him a growing respect and more business than ever.

In Honolulu, Geoffrey Davies tried to put Davies company in the subdivision business. But Russell would not go along. Lincoln National Life Insurance Company wanted more business in Hawaii, and Geoffrey was given this task, too. It was a difficult task, for John Hancock and Sun Life of Canada, and Manufacturers Life had strong positions among the *haoles.*

With the Orientals, the company was Occidental Life, and for a very simple reason: before World War II other life insurance companies would not write life insurance on Orientals (who were not considered to be people, apparently) but Occidental did, and even in the 1970s no company had been able to dislodge them from their leadership position.

Geoffrey Davies continued to be a gadfly to the Davies management. Although stripped of authority he had retained his analyst's role, and his analyses reflected Geoffrey's lack of respect for persons or positions. Russell was considering the liquidation of Kukaiau Ranch Company. Geoffrey told him it could be operated profitably and without the expenditure of the huge amounts of money the plantation department (which found Kukaiau a nuisance) had said it would cost. In looking over the situation of Kukaiau, Geoffrey raised some embarrassing questions. The ranch manager was not being consulted by the plantation department. Given all these signs, the company could proceed with liquidation only at the risk of embarrassment, so Kukaiau was saved.[5]

In 1957, Russell proceeded with his plan of action to retain control of the company while appearing to step down. He appointed George T. Davies as President of Theo H. Davies & Co., Ltd. as well as Honolulu Iron Works.[6] In terms of the annual report, Russell had achieved all he had attempted: total assets could now be shown as nearly $20,000,000. And profits were up — *consolidated* net earnings were shown as $1,100,000. But *consolidated* was the operative word: the Philippine company this year had profits to equal the Honolulu company, and the result was so embarrassing that the Davies company changed over to a consolidated approach without emphasizing Honolulu's share.[7]

This was the year in which Geoffrey Davies' discontent finally broke through. Warren Titus, who had been under his supervision in the odds and ends department, was appointed a vice-president as soon as Geoffrey had convinced Russell that there was a future in the steamship department. James H. Tabor, a recruit from Hawaiian Pineapple, was brought in to take over Honolulu Iron Works and made a Davies executive vice-president. And still Geoffrey was given nothing to do by Russell or his cousin, George T. Davies. Geoffrey also objected to the sale of Western States Grocery (Piggly Wiggly) to Western Star Markets. All this added up to nothing in his estimation, and so in October, 1957, he announced that he was about to resign. He was so much out of step with Russell and the others that he could see no alternative course.[8]

Keeping a recalcitrant member of the Davies family under wraps was one thing, but letting that member resign in anger and move back to England where the stockholders lived was quite another. So George Davies wrote a placating letter to Geoffrey, outlining an executive committee and advisory and research functions that looked excellent on paper, until one began thinking of how they would translate: all study, no action.[9] Still, Geoffrey Davies did not resign.

George Davies and Russell saw the need for new business if the Davies company was ever to catch up to the others of the Big Five, but their efforts to achieve it were anything but dynamic. They organized a small San Francisco marine agency, Marine Chartering Co. Geoffrey Davies was very high on this project and had nursed it along under his steamship department; Russell was opposed but went along. In the end, however, the project sickened through malnutrition. It did not solve their problems.

In the winter of 1957–58, a new element entered the Davies ambience. The mainland investment firm of Butcher & Sherrerd began picking up odd lots of stock in Theo H. Davies & Co., Ltd. It was not hard to buy Davies stock then because the deaths of Sir George and the Janions had thrown considerable amounts of stock onto the market and a number of other holders had begun to sell as performance declined. There were about 150 different stockholders. Inevitably some of this stock found its way into the Honolulu market, although there was no listing or general trading in the company's securities.[10] By February Butcher held nearly 11 percent of the stock or 17,500 shares, and Russell and George T. Davies became a bit nervous. The reason for Butcher's interest was obvious: the company had excellent assets but a very bad profit record over the past half dozen years. Cannibalization, a sell-off of the assets, could bring a

profit on the stock, which was selling at around $30 a share. To head off
Butcher, Russell and George T. Davies asked Geoffrey, who was in England
on leave, to see what he could do. In London, he arranged with Baring
Brothers and the Hong Kong and Shanghai Bank to take 18,000 shares of
Theo H. Davies & Co., Ltd. at $30.[11]

Davies' profitability was again threatened in 1958 by a strike of the
ILWU. The union wanted 25 cents an hour increase in pay, and the
planters offered five cents. The union struck. The strike lasted four
months, and Davies profits dropped from $468,000 to $365,000 for the
year. Even the Philippine company could not save them that year, because
currency restrictions prevented the transfer of much of the Far East company dividends, although the company earned nearly a million pesos after
taxes.[12]

After a year as president of the company, by the spring of 1958,
George T. Davies had discovered that running the company under the
aegis of John E. Russell was not his dish of tea. His wife did not like
Honolulu and her health suffered. He decided to quit. James H. Tabor, the
executive vice-president, was chosen to take over the No. 2 role in the
company. Tabor was an American, which was a plus from the Davies point
of view. He was an Oklahoman, who had gone to college at the University
of the South and then to Harvard College and Columbia Law School. He
seemed in every way a proper choice for an executive, at least to John E.
Russell. He had only one major problem: he knew virtually nothing about
the Davies business and had not had the time to learn. The most knowledgeable of the company officers—after eleven years in Honolulu—was Geoffrey Davies. But Geoffrey Davies was the last man in Honolulu that Russell
would have let sit in the president's chair.

Chapter Forty-Nine

THE REBELLION OF

GEOFFREY DAVIES

I*n 1958 John E. Russell was not a happy man.* The departure of George T. Davies had once more upset his plans, and now a new unknown quantity had become his right hand man. Russell was suffering from diabetes, although he managed for years to avoid the insulin stage. He was suffering from attack by Howard Butcher, who had acquired a large block of Theo H. Davies Co., Ltd. stock. Butcher was a power to be reckoned with; he also had 150,000 of 547,000 shares of C. Brewer stock and 50,000 of 490,000 shares of Amfac stock.[1] He wanted a seat on the Davies board.

Butcher had approached Gerald Wilkinson with an eye to their joining forces and taking over Davies. Wilkinson had refused, for reasons of his own. He had a gentleman's agreement with John E. Russell that no sales of Theo H. Davies-Far East stock would be made without first offering them to Wilkinson.[2] His first loyalty was to the company he had built, and he had hopes of spending the rest of his life in the Philippines and continuing to build Davies-Far East into a mammoth power in Asia. He had already had some talks along this line with Tony Keswick, an old school friend from Winchester and his brother John Keswick (later Sir John), managing director of Jardine, Matheson & Co., Ltd. in Hong Kong. They had mentioned the topic of merger, and Gerald had thoughts of one day thus taking over Jardine, Matheson.[3] The Butcher incursion had alerted Gerald, and

Geoffrey Davies too, to the problem of dissipation of control of the Davies company. They exchanged letters and agreed to try between them to buy up all shares that came on the market.[4] Russell's reaction was to try to persuade the English stockholders to allow him to issue another stock dividend and more treasury stock, to dilute the Butcher investment.[5] Butcher, who had attained seats on the boards of Brewer and on Amfac, wanted to put his brother Keene Butcher on the board of Davies. He suggested that course to John E. Russell. Russell agreed, and here Russell made a vital error. Earlier, he had wanted the Davies family, represented by Theo M. Davies, Arthur, and Stephen Young (an attorney, and son of Violet Mary) to sell their sugar stocks, although Geoffrey had told them that this was the first step in destruction of the family interests. Now, Russell wanted to bring onto the board of directors a representative of a family that was trying to take over the company. To say that Russell's attitude was "a shock" to Theo and Arthur Davies and Stephen Young (as Russell did) was understatement; it was a revelation.[6] The Davies family in England now began to have an inkling of what Geoffrey had been saying for some time: Russell could easily destroy Davies and their investment if he continued on his course. The family was certain that John E. Russell's major concern was protection of the family investment; and his various attempts to preserve or to sell out were, they believed, aimed at that preservation. Still, their attitude began to change.

By 1959 Geoffrey Davies had decided there was no future for him in Honolulu, and despite his appointment to head all the plantations and Kukaiau Ranch, he had decided to go home to England and seek employment. He told Russell that in two years he planned to quit. Before he left Hawaii, he wanted some barriers set up against Russell's outright control. The only person left with any family connection was Gerald Wilkinson. Geoffrey had never gotten over the divorce, but Wilkinson had always comported himself sympathetically to the family even under their deepest disapproval. Geoffrey allied himself firmly with Wilkinson. He sold 4000 shares of his Theo H. Davies stock to Gerald Wilkinson, and he told Russell that Gerald ought to be brought back onto the Theo H. Davies board of

The Very Reverend Arthur W. Davies. He eschewed
active interest in the family business to take a leading
role in education and the church.

directors. Russell did not like that idea. He wanted to bring Keene Butcher
onto the board, and to retain his old guard: Charles Bennett, who was 75,
Attorney Smith, who was almost as old, Ted Guard, who was 77, and himself
at 70. When written in a letter, as he did to Stephen Young in London, the
suggestion appeared as ludicrous as it looks in cold type.[7]

Although Geoffrey was planning to follow the family tradition of
early retirement from the Honolulu scene, he was busier than ever, particularly with the plantations, because Tabor knew nothing about sugar. At
Geoffrey's request, Leslie Wishard had been employed to make an overall
report and plan for the plantations with an eye to increasing their effi-

ciency. When it came in, Russell found it too expensive. Wishard wanted to put up a big factory, capable of handling 300 tons of cane per day, to produce sugar for the three plantations into which the Davies interests had been organized: Kaiwiki, Hamakua, and Laupahoehoe. To do so, Russell would have to raise $10,000,000. Russell did not want to make the commitment. But Geoffrey, who was in charge of plantations, did persuade Russell that they could not sit back and simply repair and maintain their aging sugar mills. They would leave Hamakua mill alone for 10–15 years, except to provide a new cleaning plant in a year or two, and additions to the boiling house.[8] They would concentrate Laupahoehoe milling at Ookala, and eventually build the 300-ton mill there. By these changes they hoped to secure a shorter harvest season and allow for automation.

Something certainly had to be done to bring the Davies company off dead center. Profits were rising, but slowly, largely through consolidations and cutback of expenses and the constant infusion of cash from Manila. But debt was increasing again. While others of the Big Five were striding forward into new fields, Davies company continued to limp along without leadership. More and more fortune hunters were beginning to realize just that. On November 27, 1959, Harry Stonehill, a rich investor, met with Russell to propose a takeover of Davies company at $65 a share. He would pay more if necessary.[9] Russell realized what a dangerous position this offer put him in. Davies Company was paying $1.20 a share on earnings of $4. Shareholders could sell out at $65 with no capital gains tax and invest their money in England to earn $3 easily. The stock was selling on the local market at $42. And just then Russell was negotiating for a $6,000,000 insurance loan to try to solve the unending problem of cash shortage and bank overdrafts.[10]

For a time Theo M. Davies had succeeded Clive as the coordinator of the family stockholders in England. Russell wrote quarterly—not monthly—reports to Theo M. But in 1959, Attorney Stephen Young succeeded to the mantle as age got the better of Theo Davies. There was another reason; in following the lead of Russell in the sugar stock purchase quarrel, Arthur Davies and Theo Davies had created a rift with the younger generation members who agreed with Geoffrey Davies. Theo M. said that he had always followed the advice of the chief executive of the company; now perhaps he was not so sure.

Stephen Young planned a trip to America in December to familiarize himself with the business, about which he really did not know much. He intended to follow the old route Clive had taken; George T., who had taken a job with Bankers Trust Company in New York, wanted to see him. When Russell learned that Stephen Young planned to stop in New York, he sent him a cable insisting that he come to Honolulu first, and followed with a letter in which he explained that only *he* could tell Young what was happening. Perhaps there was something he did not want George to say first.[11]

The matter of control of the company had not yet reached a serious stage, but by 1959, the Davies family no longer owned absolute control. Altogether they owned 44 percent of the stock; Baring Brothers— Hong Kong and Shanghai Bank had eleven percent, and the directors and officers owned twelve percent, which did give control to the management. Other British stockholders held eight percent, which could be regarded as fairly safe; Butcher held eleven percent, and the rest was split among smaller holders: the Swanzys had five percent, Standard Oil had 3.5 percent.[12]

Various lots of Theo H. Davies stock were traded from time to time; Russell himself bought and sold just to test the market. Then in January, 125 shares were bought by J.C. Earle, another speculator. Given the tax situation and the proclivities of the Davies family, more and larger sales might be expected. Clive Davies' daughter, Elizabeth, now Mrs. Pierre Beguin, wanted to buy a house in Switzerland, but to do so would have to dispose of some of her stock in Davies, the Iron Works, Kukaiau Ranch, or Laupahoehoe Sugar Company. She sold Iron Works stock and bought her house.[13] Since she, like most of the family stockholders, depended on the Davies investments for income and capital outlay, more attrition could be expected.

Barracudas of Wall Street were looking for just such opportunity. In February 1960, George Murphy, a capitalist who had just bought 50 percent of Pacific Chemical & Fertilizer Company, wanted to buy control of

Theo H. Davies & Co., Ltd. He might be doing it, said Russell, to liquidate the company,[14] in which case Russell's estimate was that the shares would be worth about $100 each in terms of the assets. This move was fended off—but with the assets so high in relationship to earnings and stock prices, one could see that more efforts would be made. Scarcely had the Murphy bid been turned down when Boyd MacNaughton, president of C. Brewer, in which Howard Butcher had a large interest, came to Russell with a proposition to exchange the Davies common stock for Brewer preferred—the idea being to give the English shareholders an ironclad investment that would appeal to them.

Murphy came back with an offer for less than control, but a seat on the board. Russell wanted to give it to him. Geoffrey and others did not. Geoffrey, having sold 4000 shares of Theo H. Davies stock to Gerald Wilkinson, continued to buy other shares for himself, until he and Wilkinson had become the largest stockholders in Theo H. Davies & Co., Ltd. He and Gerald kept buying as they could manage it.

Butcher tired of the game when he discovered he was getting nowhere and wanted to sell his 20,000 shares in Davies & Co. Geoffrey and Gerald decided to take 4000 shares each, but Butcher offered Earle an option on the rest at $65 a share. These negotiations dragged on.

On July 26, at a meeting of the board of directors, Russell suggested that the management buy the 22,000 Butcher shares (which had been advertised in the newspapers for sale at $33) and finance the purchase with a $1,000,000 loan from J.C. Earle. On his part, Earle would have the privilege of converting the loan to common shares at any time (at $37.50).

Geoffrey Davies saw this as a wedge by which Earle could push into the Davies directorate and perhaps, with Russell's assistance, take over the company. Further, the buyback at more than 10 percent over the market price would give Earle an enormous profit. Geoffrey was certain by this time that Russell was trying to do something of the sort. Russell forced through a weak resolution. Gerald Wilkinson, the Baring brothers, and others protested, but the loan was taken and the shares were purchased.[15]

By autumn Geoffrey and Gerald Wilkinson were certain that Russell was seeking an avenue to sell out the company. He had already closed down E. O. Hall, a failure in Davies hands, sold Piggly Wiggly, a failure too because of bad management, and he was trying to spin off Kukaiau Ranch to the Parker Ranch interests. Davies had acquired a macadamia nut business with Honokaa sugar company, but it gave them nothing but trouble. They could not find anyone to manage it properly and they had not the imagination to promote it.

Geoffrey Davies felt that if much more of this continued the company would be irretrievably wrecked. He and Gerald Wilkinson were made alert by the Earle note.[16]

Later that autumn Russell began dealing with Alexander & Baldwin, who offered $35 a share in a takeover bid. When Geoffrey Davies learned of these negotiations, he put some figures together. He wrote Stephen Young, his cousin, who represented a considerable body of stock, and who had become the spokesman for the English stockholders, that the investment was in danger. The profitability of Theo H. Davies & Co. was hardly improving. The consolidated profit was $900,000 as compared to Castle & Cooke's $2,900,000 for the year (1959), nearly half the profit of Davies came from the Philippine company. Also the Davies debt was increasing alarmingly. The new $6,000,000 loan had been made at extremely high interest rates, and the general picture appeared dimmer each year than the year before. But all that could be rectified, and the difficulty of the Alexander & Baldwin sellout was that it was extremely cheap in relation to the assets.[17]

That written, Geoffrey went to England to see various shareholders of the family, and Baring brothers, to secure support if possible. He knew he had little chance with the Rev. Arthur W. Davies, who considered the Davies investment as no more important than any other, and who had no family feeling about it, as he had told George F. and Clive years earlier. The Dean was totally sold on Russell. But with the younger generation, who owned 31 percent of the stock, it was a different story. Geoffrey's appeal to family pride, his warnings coupled with those of Gerald about the poor management of Russell and Tabor, and above all, the miserable showing of return on investment, had their effects.[18] Geoffrey saw 18 people in 21 days, covering 2000 miles. He also saw Baring Brothers, who told him that their principal reason for investing was to support the Davies family and himself in particular, and if Geoffrey resigned and Chairman Russell managed to secure a merger with Alexander & Baldwin (as he had suggested to them that year he would try to do), they would sell their shares and have no further interest in the company.

Stephen Young, perhaps because he was a lawyer, tended to support the Russell management and told Geoffrey in a letter that he would have to do so if it came to that.[19]

Geoffrey made this trip to England in December 1960, returning in January, 1961. Russell, just then, was talking to Alexander & Baldwin's Neale Cadogan about the sale. He said he could control 75 percent of the common stock in favor of the merger.[20] He was that confident of family support. He did not know that Geoffrey's trip to Europe had changed several minds. When Geoffrey reappeared in Honolulu, Russell called him to the office and with all confidence in his own position, charged Geoffrey with disloyalty to the company. Geoffrey agreed. He was, he said, disloyal to the *management* of the company. That had been his dilemma for several years; he disagreed with much that management was doing, yet he remained a part of management. He had told Tabor in the spring of 1959 that he would resign in two years. The two years would end in March, 1961, at which point Geoffrey definitely would leave the company.[21]

Following that confrontation, Russell decided that he must secure Geoffrey's removal from the board of directors, and he began a campaign to that effect with the English stockholders. Geoffrey soon had wind of this move and consulted an outside attorney, prepared for a nasty fight if necessary. Director Smith, the Davies lawyer, soon learned of this move and so did Russell.[22]

The meeting came on April 6, 1961. Gerald Wilkinson came in from Manila on the Saturday before, and George T. Davies came the following Monday. Gerald came to support Geoffrey, but George T. came full of John E. Russell's stories about Geoffrey's recalcitrance, with the opinion that

Geoffrey was an irresponsible troublemaker. But George had a few days to think, and he began talking to business people in Honolulu. The executive vice-president of the First National Bank of Hawaii told him the bank was worried about Davies management and particularly about the declining merchandising department, about which Geoffrey had complained so much.[23]

On Wednesday of that meeting week, after talking to a number of people, George T. Davies came to Geoffrey's office and apologized to him for what he had done to Geoffrey when he was in Honolulu as president of Theo H. Davies & Co., Ltd. He had learned, he said, that Davies management was worse than Geoffrey had painted it in the meetings of the board. George T. Davies was thoroughly familiar with the Honolulu Iron Works, for he had first come to Hawaii with that company. Now, he had just discovered that the Iron Works was on the edge of bankruptcy. Under the circumstances, he certainly would support Geoffrey's re-election to the board.

For weeks Geoffrey had been soliciting proxies from English stockholders to assure his retention of the board seat. John E. Russell could add well enough, and just before the meeting he called Geoffrey into his office again and told him the re-election would be unopposed. Then, with a twinkle in his eye, he asked Geoffrey if by any chance he had secured some legal advice.

The meeting was held on schedule, and Geoffrey C. Davies was re-elected to the board without discussion. He then went back to his office in the Davies building and tidied up his affairs. True to his promise he had terminated his employment as of March 31 and took no further part in operational activities. But he was determined to stand between the management and an unsatisfactory sellout. George T., who said he rued the day he had appointed James Tabor to be his successor (Geoffrey had opposed this appointment on the basis that Tabor was too inexperienced) promised to return to New York and write Uncle Theo, Uncle Arthur, and Stephen Young to acquaint them with the danger into which the company had fallen. And to underline that change in feeling, before George and Gerald

Wilkinson left Honolulu, they asked John E. Russell, James Tabor, and Harold Weidig to agree in writing that they would not try to merge or amalgamate the company without first consulting Gerald Wilkinson. Nor could Russell and Tabor sell any treasury stock or put out a new issue, or borrow above the seven million dollars already agreed upon, without such consultation. The reason for this move was that Wilkinson's Far East Company had a legal right to demand such treatment because of the consequence of a sale to its operations. Also excessive debt or stock dilution could be inimical to the Manila company.[24]

Gerald Wilkinson, in his turn, agreed in writing that he would make no attempt to take control of the Davies company in Hawaii. Russell insisted on this condition; one could see what his real fears were.

Having negotiated this instrument of mutual distrust, George T. Davies, Wilkinson, Russell, Tabor, and Weidig all signed. The sparring was over, but the fight was just beginning. James Tabor and Harold Weidig were dispatched to England by Russell to secure renewed support from the English shareholders and restore control of the company to Russell and Tabor. What would happen remained to be seen.

Chapter Fifty

CHANGE IN LEADERSHIP

A*fter the annual meeting of 1961*, there was no question about the situation that existed in the Davies company management. It was a battle to the finish between Gerald Wilkinson and Geoffrey Davies on the one hand, and John E. Russell and James Tabor on the other, with the English stockholders and the bankers in the middle and able to sway the decision. By July 19, the holdings and proxies of Geoffrey and Gerald Wilkinson came to 67,800 shares of 183,000. Russell had 5600 shares, Guard had 4950, Bennett had 1650, Tabor had 1200. They could claim also the support of the Arthur Davies group, with about 10,000 shares, Uncle Theo with 6600, and some other Honolulu shareholders. The battle was neck and neck, they thought. Gerald arranged for the purchase by Lincoln Life of 7000 shares which he could control and bought another 1000 for himself. Further, Stephen Young had finally decided to support Geoffrey Davies and Gerald Wilkinson.[1] This meant several thousand more shares. So by August, Geoffrey was drawing up a plan for the future.

Russell was to retire or be ousted as chairman before the next annual meeting, although he could remain as a director if he wished. Treasurer O. B. Hammond was to leave. The board of directors was to be cleared of the old dead wood—Guard and White. Gerald Wilkinson was to become chairman of the board *and* chief executive officer, with full authority to pick his own organization.

All this depended on securing 51 percent of the votes. They needed George T. Davies and the bankers and insurance companies. Geoffrey would undertake to get them.[2]

In a matter of weeks, Geoffrey had the support of all these factions, and George T. was writing Uncle Arthur, the Dean, to plead the case for change. He suggested a meeting. The meeting was held on October 10 in London among George Davies, Stephen Young, Rev. Dr. Arthur Davies, and Theo M. Davies. The uncles were completely brought around and agreed that Russell must retire, Tabor must go, and Gerald Wilkinson should take over the management of the company in all their interests.

In the interim, perhaps even occasioned by concern over the developments in England, John E. Russell suffered a severe heart attack. The uncles hoped this would bring him to the point of resignation of his own volition, but Geoffrey did not believe it. He expected a fight but also believed Russell and Tabor ought to be informed that he had the votes. He wanted them to know before he returned to Honolulu early in 1962 to prepare for the annual meeting.[3]

Geoffrey Davies was right in that Russell was not going to give the company to Gerald and Geoffrey without a fight. Russell wrote Stephen Young that he believed the post of chairman ought to be abolished, and that Tabor should be given executive responsibility for all the Davies companies. Young then wrote all members of the family, calling a meeting in London to see if they would support Geoffrey's position.[4] The result was that Geoffrey gained voting rights of 75 percent of the common stock. Learning this, on November 16 John E. Russell resigned. James Tabor made a quick trip to England but, when he saw how firmly Geoffrey was in control he too, resigned. All that remained was to settle the terms.

So an era had come to an end, as surely as had happened with the death of Theo H. Davies in 1898. John E. Russell had many letters of appreciation from within the company and in the Hawaii community, and they were well-deserved. Russell had served Theo H. Davies & Co., Ltd. well for more than 40 years. In the 1920s, when the company was faltering on the edge of a financial abyss, Russell had persuaded Clive Davies to a policy of long-term finance that saved the day. He had restored the finances again in the difficult years of the 1930s. His foresight in sugar operations had been known well in the Hawaii community. Theo H. Davies had established the policy of hiring the best managers, and letting them alone to run the plantations and the mills, where other factors tended to interfere with their people. Clive Davies had continued that program, and so had Russell, although he was faced with the most difficult times of any of them. When unionization came, he was quick to see the implications and to plan ahead for a highly mechanized sugar industry. The intensive mechanization program at Honokaa was his idea and his responsibility, and it made of a very poor plantation one of the most profitable in the islands. Russell's encouragement of the Davies sugar operations in the Philippines made all the difference, and he showed here a shrewd eye for the potentially successful properties. It was ironic that his career should come to an end in financial quarrels, for in the earlier years this had been his area of strength.

But what was done was done. John E. Russell disengaged gracefully and retired from the company. Soon Tabor also left. To fill the void, Gerald Wilkinson hurried to Honolulu early in December, 1961.[5]

In January, at a special stockholders meeting, Geoffrey Davies' program for the company was put into effect. Gerald Wilkinson became the new chairman of the board and chief operating officer. He had already started to bring the company back from the edge of disaster. His first small coup was to sign Dillingham International Company to an agency agreement for Davies-Far East in Manila.[6] But then came the difficult task of total rebuilding. The figures for 1961 came all too soon: the net earnings of Honolulu had dropped from $926,000 in 1960 to $561,000, payroll was up, long-term debt was virtually undiminished, and net working capital was down. At the same time the report showed that the Philippine company's consolidated net profit for 1961, reflecting Davies-Far East's equity in the earnings of the subsidiaries Gerald Wilkinson had developed, was 3,450,000, or more than twice the earnings of the Honolulu end of the business.[7] Wilkinson obviously had an enormous job to do.

The first task he faced was to reorganize. Geoffrey Davies had considered returning to the company in some capacity under the new management. Wilkinson offered him the post of executive vice-president. At the same time Wilkinson appointed Harold Weidig as president. Weidig was 62 years old, and the retirement policy of Davies still called for executives to retire at 65. So this offer to Geoffrey meant that under optimal conditions he could expect to be president of the company in three years; Geoffrey Davies decided in the end not to take the job,[8] but to remain outside.*

Wilkinson's next step was to bring together a group of executives whose judgment he trusted and give them their heads. In the spring O. B. Hammond (whom Geoffrey Davies held responsible for much that was wrong with the company finances) was asked to resign as vice-president and treasurer, and Alan Stewart, the controller, was appointed to be treasurer. Francis Swanzy Morgan was appointed vice-president for agriculture and industrial relations. Once a week Wilkinson met with these three key executives, Weidig, Morgan, and Stewart, with Secretary Charles Holt keeping minutes. He explained the policies he was following and discussed them. For the first time in 20 years the executives of the Davies company were given a feeling of total participation.[9] Competent department heads were given pay raises and encouragement, and incompetents were swiftly moved out. Chiko Noda, formerly secretary to Geoffrey Davies, who began to work for Wilkinson, spoke to him one day about the "blood bath." He agreed that it was uncomfortable, "But isn't it better," he said, "to do it quick than to let them live on in torture?"[10]

All the executives soon knew what *must* happen in the next two or three years: Wilkinson was committed to bettering the position of the stockholders, and that could be accomplished only by a reduction in debt and an increase in net profit after taxes, or both. Assembling the figures took very little time; they had been there all the while but top management had not looked at them. The figures showed that unless profits could

---

*Geoffrey Davies took the position that if he joined management he might once again face the same problems of loyalties divided between management and the stockholders interests.

be raised the dry goods department must go, and the hardware department would probably follow shortly afterward. These two departments employed $3,750,000 in company funds, and Davies could be better off investing its money in government bonds than in pursuing business in arenas that had been taken over by others in Hawaii.[11]

Hawaii Builders' Supply, for which Geoffrey Davies had such high hopes years before, had proved to be a loser. Its bad debts were high; profits were just over three percent, without charging interest for the $4.5 million of the company's money it used. It was slated for liquidation.

The insurance, shipping and travel departments were let alone as either profitable or inconsequential. The plantations were put under a study to see where money could be saved by consolidating factories.

Within six months after his arrival, Wilkinson had come to one basic conclusion about the future, which seemed as true at the beginning of the 1980s as it did nearly twenty years before:

> For the development of sound new industries, Hawaii seems to me to be most badly placed. It lacks diversity of raw materials and its labour costs are among the highest in the world without proportionate increase in efficiency. U.S. coast-wise shipping laws between here and the mainland impose a freight disadvantage upon imports and exports compared with transportation costs between many U.S. industries on the mainland and their customers. These disadvantages and extreme unionism seem to me to be likely to perpetuate a squeeze on the margin of net profit, after taxes, that can be earned in Hawaii except in fringe businesses such as tourism (which lacks stability and is vulnerable to competition in every Tom, Dick, and Harry) and real estate development in which enormous profits have been made by capitalists or entrepreneurs who foresaw the growth of Honolulu.
>
> I do not mean to say that reasonable profits cannot . . . be earned . . . but I think that several sections of our business are unlikely to produce good earnings in future and many have to be eliminated.[12]

Through the years, and particularly under James Tabor's management, Honolulu Iron Works had ceased to be an asset to the Davies company. Davies control had passed away years before, when Sir George pushed for broadening of the base as part of his plan to unload the whole Davies business. Wilkinson planned to unload Honolulu Iron Works as soon as the Davies company could do so profitably.

The results of Wilkinson's new-broom treatment at Theo H. Davies & Co., Ltd. was quickly observed in the Honolulu financial community. When O. B. Hammond learned that he was fired, he unloaded his 762 shares of Davies stock, and Pacific Insurance Company bought them immediately at $65 a share. Davies was staging a comeback in the marketplace after only five months.

Wilkinson looked up the market value of Hawaiian shares:

Company	January 2, 1962	May 24, 1962
Alexander & Baldwin, Inc.	$39\frac{1}{2}$	$29\frac{1}{8}$
Amfac, Inc.	$33\frac{1}{2}$	32
Castle & Cooke, Inc.	$49\frac{1}{2}$	34
C. Brewer and Co., Ltd.	$43\frac{1}{2}$	$39\frac{1}{2}$
Dillingham Corp.	33	$23\frac{1}{8}$
Theo H. Davies & Co., Ltd.	$63\frac{1}{2}$	65

Honolulu, then, was getting under control it seemed, although Wilkinson did not relish the prospect of that first annual report under his management, having had to break down the old structure before he could build the new. But he had one powerful asset: when Wilkinson left Manila, he put in charge of the company Milton H. Pickup, an old friend who had come to the Philippines at just about the same time as Wilkinson. Pickup was a chartered accountant who had built a successful accounting business in Manila and became the outside auditor for Davies Far East. Several years earlier when Gerald was left with a management crisis in the departure of his No. 2 man, he asked Milton Pickup to join his firm, and Pickup sold his business to a Filipino firm and came to Davies. The two were close, and Pickup seemed to sense what Wilkinson wanted and needed; he also had a certain solidity that complemented Wilkinson's dashing character. Davies-Far East, then, was in good hands. Further, Wilkinson did not for a moment take his eye off events in Manila and the islands. He would alternate between Manila and Honolulu about every three months, as soon as he got Honolulu under control.

Wilkinson had reorganized E. J. Nell, the machinery and engineering company, and Aircon, the air conditioning company, during a visit to Manila. He was just then organizing a small chemical company, which would manufacture the resins their Sherwin-Williams Philippines Company used to make paint. He expected Davies-Far East to break all records on its earnings in 1962 (and it did). He knew those profits would be needed to offset the continuing decline of Davies in Hawaii. The most serious problem Wilkinson faced was a financial mess left by the old management in connection with the refinancing of the company's debt. They had accepted convertible notes with New England Mutual and Massachusetts Mutual Life Insurance companies, in order to get the $6 million loan they needed to stave off disaster. They had been forced to do so because of the miserable showing of Davies over so long a time. But in 1962, if Wilkinson cleared the decks and began to pull the company out of the slough, that million dollars worth of notes held by J.C. Earle could be converted at $37.5 per share—even as the price hit $65. By straining resources and cutting back on the dead wood, Wilkinson found the money to pay off those notes. Next year he faced the same problem—$1.5 million in life insurance company notes would become convertible at the same price, and of course, the companies would convert them, thus increasing the cost to Davies by about 80 percent on the loan. Wilkinson persuaded the insurance companies to accept prepayment of the notes and to take Davies long-term notes in prepayment. The deal cost Davies $225,000 in penalty payment, but it was cheap compared to the alternative.

The merchandising business had changed so much since World War II that a whole new approach was essential. If the hardware and dry goods departments could not make profits, they would have to be abandoned. But what was really needed was new blood, and the company got it when William E. McCoy, an executive of Caterpillar Tractor, joined the company in 1963.[13] McCoy had just taken a new job with Caterpillar in Australia, but he saw an opportunity in Honolulu and was much taken with Wilkinson, so he moved again.[14]

But in Wilkinson's thinking about the future, he realized that having missed the first opportunities of the postwar boom in real estate, finance, and modern retail merchandising, Davies had to look afield for the sort of profit opportunity that would expand the company. Sugar was, and would be, very nearly on dead center: the increasing labor costs and technological improvements would offset each other. In good years sugar would make a large profit; in bad years sugar would lose money. And always over the shoulders of the planters loomed the U.S. government, with its habit of fiddling with agricultural policies and prices. The government subsidies of one sort or another were not an unmixed blessing, for what Congress could give Congress could also take away, and Hawaii, with the highest plantation labor cost in the sugar world, could not compete on the open world market. The opportunity must be found in some area where exploitation of resources or markets had not yet begun. Wilkinson found it in Spain, through an old friendship from the Philippines. Cesar de Zulueta, partner in Amon Trading Company of Manila, was forced into an awkward position by new nationalistic legislation. The old idea that foreigners ought to be excluded from retail trade (to drive out the Chinese merchants who had a stranglehold on retailing outside Manila) had borne fruit. Amon Trading Company was primarily a building -supplies firm, and Zulueta was faced with giving up his Spanish nationality or going out of business. He chose to sell his interests, leave the Philippines, and return to Madrid. There he joined forces with Eduardo Vega, a Spanish businessman, and they formed a trading company with Davies' backing, Theo H. Davies, Iberica, S. A. To accomplish this bold gesture, Wilkinson put up $250,000 in capital from Davies-Far East, with the understanding that Davies Iberica could not impose upon the credit of the parent company. For this, Davies got 60 percent of the stock in Davies Iberica.[15] The company would begin operating in 1963, to take on agencies and seek manufacturing opportunities, in just the way that Theo H. Davies had done in Hawaii in the 1870s, and Gerald Wilkinson had done in Manila in the 1940s and 1950s.

Chapter Fifty-One

THE UNTIMELY END OF
GERALD WILKINSON

In 1963 the Philippine company outstripped the parent company. Manila reported a profit of $1,400,000, and Hawaii's *consolidated* income was down to $792,000, because of the drought at Honokaa and Hamakua sugar companies. Two changes—the liquidation of Hawaii Builders' Supply and the sale of Honolulu Iron Works—were assisted unknowingly by the new state government. Attorney General S. Kashiwa called Wilkinson into his office to charge that the Davies company was involved in antitrust activity through various interlocking directorates and sale of competitive lines.[1] The matter was complicated by the gubernatorial election of that year, in which Republican Governor William Quinn was running against Democrat John Burns. If they did liquidate Hawaii Builders' Supply before the election, Quinn could be charged with putting 100 people out of work through his anti-trust division. Wilkinson had a talk with Governor Quinn, the purpose of which was to inform the governor of the Attorney General's attitude and the company's position, which was to deny wrongdoing. It also set up an obligation so that Quinn would have to remember the Davies company's forbearance when it came to the ticklish question of anti-trust with Honolulu Iron Works.[2] It was a good try, but Quinn was defeated by John Burns, who had made an alliance with the Nisei who came back from World War II to give them a strong position in the Democratic party. Suddenly, in 1962, Hawaii changed from being a Republican state, in which the Big Five seldom had difficulty in making themselves heard, to a Democratic state where anything might happen.

In 1963, to solve several problems the Davies interests managed a sale of Honolulu Iron Works to George Murphy and associates. The anti-trust talk ceased.

Geoffrey Davies had given serious consideration to joining the company in some capacity, but as time went on he decided against it. He was too lazy, he said at one point.[3] He had too many family commitments to take a full time job, he said in the spring of 1962 when he arrived in Honolulu. So it was left at that; Gerald Wilkinson saying that any time Geoffrey wanted to join he was welcome, but nothing coming of it. In fact, Geoffrey was beginning to function in the new management much as his father had functioned in the past, as a sounding board, element of support of management decisions, and sometimes as a brake.[4] But, unlike his father, he corresponded only with the chairman of the company.

By the summer of 1964 Davies' Hawaii operations had begun to show the effects of Wilkinson's new management. Net profit was up instead of down. Merchandise Director McCoy's division was beginning to pull up, and it appeared that the hardware and dry goods departments would be saved. Davies-Far East profits were increasing again, but the next year might be different. In August, Wilkinson went to Manila, at least partly to try to straighten out a most difficult situation that had developed with the planters of Silay district, who used the Hawaiian-Philippine Sugar *Central.* which by then was a 51 percent Davies operation. The planters of the Philippines had always been noted for their irascibility and general dislike of foreign influences. In 1940 a mill official named Addison Kinney had been shot and killed without provocation at the mill of the North Negros Sugar Company, in Manapia. The planter who fired the shot, Felix Vasquez, was released on bail, jumped bail, and was never brought to trial. In all this the planter was vigorously supported by other planters, who were willing to swear that their friend had killed the foreigner in "self-defense," although Kinney did not have a weapon and had died from half a dozen shots.[5] After World War II, there had been serious question whether or not it was worthwhile to rebuild the Hawaiian-Philippines Sugar *Central,* because the planters were demanding an ever larger share of the sugar milled. They owned the land, planted the crops, and delivered them to the mill or the mill's railroad; and then the mill ground the sugar and paid them according to results. The figure had begun at 60 percent for the planters and 40 percent for the mill. The planters believed it ought to be more nearly 70-30, but the Hawaii stockholders would not rebuild without a favorable split and a long term contract. The planters accepted that but resented it. By the 1960s the split was 65-35, and the planters were complaining again. In 1961 Gerald Wilkinson had negotiated endlessly, it seemed, with representatives of the planters. It was hard to come to grips with the problem, for the single biggest factor in the group was Oscar Ledesma, who always stayed in the background and told his associates what to do.[6] The planters refused to sign a new contract except at a rate Wilkinson believed ruinous. So the negotiations continued, with the contract expiring at the end of 1964.

The planters wanted Hawaii-Philippine Company to spend a large sum of money increasing its mill capacity. Wilkinson said there was no current need, and that the company could not afford to undertake so extensive a job without bettering its arrangements. He wanted a long term contract under more favorable terms. The negotiations continued in a growing air of acerbity. Oscar Ledesma was appointed Philippines' Ambassador to Washington, and Wilkinson went there to negotiate with him. John D' Authreau, the Davies Far East sugar-marketing man, and Milton Pickup negotiated in Manila and Bacolod on Negros and at the houses of the planters. But no agreement was reached. Wilkinson was usually a patient and forbearing man, and he had a reputation in the Philippines for friendship and understanding of the Filipino mind and aspirations. Yet, as everyone outside Silay District seemed to agree, the district planters would try the patience of a saint, and finally, perhaps bemused by more important negotiations in Honolulu and England in 1962, Wilkinson lost his aplomb. The planters were making many unfair and unfriendly charges against Hawaiian-Philippine and Davies Far East. Wilkinson decided to counteract them and prepared a full-page newspaper advertisement telling the Hawaiian-Philippine side of the story. Word of this plan got to several friends, including Wilkinson's legal advisor, Emmanuel Pelaez, a member of the Philippine Senate for a number of years, who had been elected vice-president. When Pelaez heard of the idea, he advised his friend Wilkinson to drop it. But Wilkinson insisted that there came a time when a man must stand on principle, and the planters had gone too far. The advertisement was published in the Manila *Bulletin.* It brought forth a full-page response from the planters, and the quarrel grew worse.[7] The planters decided to buy out Hawaiian-Philippine Company. They sent Joe Marie Locsin, son of a well-known planter family, to New York to raise money. But, having learned the price Davies wanted, they offered about 60 percent and that negotiation broke down. They sent Joe Marie Locsin to Cuba to buy a sugar mill. He did, but when it arrived it was too small to even bother erecting. They sold it. They decided to build a mill of their own and were persuaded by a Japanese manufacturer to buy an extremely expensive new one, which was erected in 1964. They began milling there, at a loss.

In all this period there were hints that the planters would have liked to reach an accommodation, so negotiations of a sort continued. But the planters demanded that the *extranjeros* give in on every point and made much of their *amor propio,* which sometimes in the Philippines covered other motives. As the competing mill continued to lose money, some of the planters came back, and Hawaiian-Philippine managed to secure cane from other districts in Negros. Joe Marie Locsin became one of their most implacable enemies and finally sued the company for running its railroad across his land—a right that had been granted, but not in perpetuity, when he was milling with Hawaiian-Philippine. Eventually he won the suit, but having done so, and his *amor propio* satisfied, he allowed Hawaiian-Philippine to continue to run its trains across his land to that of the other planters, and he continued to send sugar to the mill that was losing money.[8] Later they reached an accommodation.

But if doing business in the Philippines was difficult, doing business in Spain demanded an even thicker skin and more complex management and negotiation. Davies Iberica entered the Spanish market just after Generalissimo Franco had begun to open Spain to modern technology and new ideas. But the Spanish Code, the legal system, was a strange holdover from ancient days, with many aspects of feudalism intermixed with those of the national socialism developed by the Falange political organization and overlaid by Franco's own dicta as generalissimo and unchallenged ruler of the country. The net result, as Cesar de Zulueta and Theo H. Davies & Co., Ltd. discovered, was that any foreign company doing business in Spain had to keep two sets of books, one set that was used for official purposes and one which showed the actual profits of the company. Unfortunately for shareholders and others, the actual books could not be used to show profit and loss on the parent company statement; the legal set had to appear. For this reason, from the beginning, the Davies-Iberica's books gave little representation of the true affairs of the company.[9]

In January, 1965, Geoffrey Davies decided to go to Spain to see how Davies Iberica was progressing, in his role as member of the board of directors of the parent corporation. He spent several months taking a course in Spanish in Ipswich before he went, which was hardly necessary in terms of conversing with Cesar de Zulueta, who was as fluent as a native in French, Spanish, and English, but it might help Geoffrey learn to read a Spanish balance sheet. (He did not then know of the complexities of Spanish finance.)

In Honolulu, by mid-year the improvement in the Davies company's position was notable, and that also meant it was noticed by outsiders. The third generation of Davies was growing restless; they had been promised by Geoffrey and Wilkinson an improvement in the value of their investment, but income was not materializing rapidly enough and taxes and living costs were rising. Several of the third generation English stockholders sold off blocks of stock in 1964, and there was some grumbling about the prices received. Wilkinson suggested that it was time to find a friendly market for such stocks, preferably a banking institution, which would give the proxies to the right people.[10]

President Harold Weidig was concerned enough that he made an independent analysis of the Theo H. Davies stock performance over eight years. If a family member owned 1000 shares of stock in 1956 and kept it, with the stock dividends and splits, he would in 1964 have 1621 shares and would be receiving an income from them of $1945 a year.[11] He believed that was quite good. But some of the shareholders continued to complain, so in March, 1965, Gerald Wilkinson was a bit concerned when George Murphy made another pass at Theo H. Davies stock. (Murphy and his associates had bought Honolulu Iron Works in 1963, paying $804,000 for the Davies interests. Soon they would sell out to a Chicago company, and not long afterward Honolulu Iron Works would be sold off, piecemeal, to leave at the end only the empty shops in Kakaako on Ala Moana Boulevard.)

Geoffrey held a meeting with Stephen Young and Tony Davies to consider the threat. The three of them represented 60,000 shares of Davies stock. They turned down the Murphy offer, which meant Murphy would have a hard time getting control, so he went away. But the threat remained, and Geoffrey warned that the English shareholders must be soothed, preferably by money.[12] But Wilkinson was firm; the company must be brought up and its debt reduced and its profits increased. He went to London and talked confidently to the shareholders about the future — but he would not jump the dividends. For 1964, he could show total net profit for all holdings of $2,400,000, but the dividend was only $1.40 per share on stock worth around $65 on the market, a dividend of just over 2 percent. The shareholders could not be blamed for believing they could do better with their money elsewhere.[13] Early in 1965 some 7500 shares were suddenly offered by third generation descendants of Theo H. Davies.

By the spring of 1965, Davies Iberica was in trouble. Cesar de Zulueta had exceeded the capital limitation of $250,000 by far. The concern had agencies for Fedders air conditioning, for cement blocks, and they were going into the bathtub business. They were deeply involved in a real estate venture. They had gone into debt to about $800,000 — far beyond their ability to pay — and the Davies company had to bail them out with its credit, guaranteeing a large loan with The Chartered Bank of London. The matter could be concealed from the stockholders for a time (and was), but not forever. The situation was so serious that Wilkinson planned ten days in Madrid on a trip that coming summer, to see for himself precisely what the facts were and the prospects might be. As for the other parts of the Davies empire, they were doing very well and at the end of the year would show a net profit of nearly three and a quarter million dollars, which would be highest in the company's history.[14] The annual report would note casually that this did not include Davies Iberica's total "expenditure over income."[15]

Gerald Wilkinson had not been feeling quite himself for several months. In Manila, it had always been his habit to work late, until six or seven o'clock in the evening, but on his last stay there, Milton Pickup had noticed that many times Gerald disappeared about four o'clock in the afternoon and did not come back. As an old friend he asked about it, and Gerald replied that he found that he felt washed out, went home, relaxed, went to bed early and then felt fine the next morning.[16] When Wilkinson returned to Honolulu that spring, he put himself into the hands of the Straub clinic to discover what, if anything might be wrong. After a series of tests, Straub discovered a tumor of an adrenal gland, just above one kidney. The glands were malfunctioning and causing him to go from hyperactivity and pounding heart to listlessness without warning.[17]

It was a serious matter and the clinicians said it called for immediate surgery. Since Wilkinson and his wife Mariana were on their way to Europe, he decided to have a second opinion from a London specialist. In June he did go to Madrid, and then in July he was in London and entered the hospital there. The diagnosis was confirmed and the surgery ordered. He wrote a series of bright brave letters to friends and relatives on the day before the operation, but he wrote one sombre letter to Milton Pickup, his friend and executor of his estate, with a note that it must be destroyed immediately. In that letter Wilkinson said he had good reason to believe he would not survive the operation, and he gave instruction to Pickup about his estate. Then he went into surgery. As they had been so often in the past, Wilkinson's hunch was accurate. He died there on July 2, 1965.

Hilo Iron Works after 1960 *tsunami.*

Chapter Fifty-Two

PICKING UP THE PIECES

G*erald Wilkinson's death* left a void in the Davies interests that could not be allowed to remain, for Geoffrey Davies was sure that the Wall Street buccaneers would begin moving in on the company unless management confidence was restored immediately. Harold Weidig came to London for the funeral, and before he returned to Honolulu, he and Geoffrey had a long talk. Weidig expressed his confidence in the future and said he was willing to delay the retirement scheduled for the end of that year, and Davies said he would seek support of the family. In the next few weeks, Geoffrey Davies was in touch with holders of 97,500 shares of Davies stock, which, with the friendly banks, represented control, and they agreed to support the management against takeover bids.[1]

It was fortunate that Geoffrey had taken these precautions. Weidig had no sooner returned to Honolulu than the Murphy group at Honolulu Iron Works tried to reopen negotiations to purchase Davies. Weidig shucked them off immediately. There was no interest by the English shareholders group in selling, he said.[2] The expressed firmness of intent had an excellent effect on the market—within a month Davies shares, which had been selling at $55, went to $65 again.[3]

By the end of the first month it was apparent that Geoffrey Davies was functioning as a very active, although absentee, chairman of the board. That title had belonged to Wilkinson, who had taken over from Russell as chairman of both Theo H. Davies & Co., Ltd. and Theo H. Davies-Far East. The title was not immediately passed, and Geoffrey Davies told Weidig that he was now "senior executive of Davies & Co."

The problem of continuity also worried the men in Manila. Milton Pickup had been president of Davies Far East since 1962, but he had not been chief executive officer. Pickup and Weidig consulted and decided that Weidig should be made chairman of the overall company, but that Pickup had been president of Davies-Far East since 1962, but he had not enjoyed in the years before 1962.[4] But Geoffrey Davies and George T. Davies consulted and negated the plan. They discussed the idea of Geoffrey's returning to Honolulu and taking over as chief operating officer, but they negated that too. Geoffrey Davies would be in the wings, prepared to take over from Weidig if anything happened. They would discuss all that when next they met.[5] The annual meeting was held in April, and Geoffrey Davies was named chairman of the board.

The offers were coming fast. C. Brewer and Co. made a pass at Davies. H. M. Goss, George Murphy's partner, wrote Geoffrey Davies, pretending he did not know that Murphy had been in touch with Weidig. Eastman Dillon Company of New York sent their London correspondent to see an official of the Baring Brothers, Andrew Carnwath, and make a tentative and highly veiled offer from an undisclosed buyer for $120 a share.

In November, Geoffrey Davies went down to Madrid to look over Davies Iberica and was much impressed with the successes of Cesar de Zulueta and his staff. They had gone heavily into land development, and the lands had appreciated in value. But the time had come, they decided this fall, to concentrate on financing the trading operations which had grown so rapidly.[6] The problem with Davies Iberica was financial: the cash deficiency for the last quarter of 1965 was 30 million pesetas, or $500,000. Zulueta was talking about new loans again. In terms of sales he should certainly have them, for the gross business had gone from 13.5 million pesetas in November, 1964, to 58.5 million pesetas in November, 1965. The future looked bright, and there seemed to be good reason for their cash problem: for example, they had ordered a shipment of Toro lawn

Milton Pickup

mowers from the U.S., and they came so late in the year that Iberica decided to hold them over as inventory, which meant cash outlay and warehousing expenses.

Early in 1966, the Davies company was gratified when Dillingham Corporation bought 21,000 shares of Theo H. Davies & Co., Ltd. stock—the Earle stock, which had been floating around for a long time. It seemed good to have the stock in Honolulu hands once again.

Lowell Dillingham came to the Davies office for a talk with Harold Weidig, and offered all the help he could give. No, he said, he did not believe Dillingham was entitled to a directorship on the basis of their holdings.[8] It all seemed halcyon, yet Geoffrey had a suspicion or two; James Tabor had associated himself with Dillingham, and the company had a reputation for swallowing its associates. It was a problem they would have to watch, but having the stock where they could watch it was better than having it abroad.

Meanwhile, James Tabor was in touch with Mariana Wilkinson, trying to buy her stock for Dillingham, and Tabor also went to England to try to buy Lorna Wilkinson's stock. Harold Weidig went to London to confer with Geoffrey Davies and put up at Brown's, his usual hotel. There, in the lobby, who was the first person he encountered? James H. Tabor. They exchanged a few embarrassed words and parted. Tabor tried to see all the stockholders of the family. He telephoned Wilkinson's daughter Mary June, who declined even to talk. But the Dillinghams were not the only ones trying to take over Theo H. Davies & Co. A capitalist named Harold Hughes went to England to see Stephen Young and approach the family in that manner. He tried the bankers. He even went down to Madrid to try to involve Cesar de Zulueta, who was a director of Davies. By the spring of 1966 these two matters—Davies Iberica and the fending off of takeovers—had become the most important problems of the company. Scarcely a month went by without some new move being made somewhere. For example, on June 16, Walter Davies, the executive vice-president of the Morgan Guaranty Bank in New York, telephoned Weidig in Honolulu at 3:45 p.m. to tell him that the bank had an offer for 7000 shares of Davies stock that they held in a trust fund. The bank had been persuaded in 1964 to buy the stock by Gerald Wilkinson, who had spent a good deal of time seeking "friendly homes" for blocks of Davies stock unloaded by various family members. But with Wilkinson gone, the relationship was not the same, and on June 16, with the offer in hand, the bank gave Weidig five minutes to make a decision. Weidig had no power to make that sort of decision, nor was he rich enough to carry perhaps $40,000 on his own shoulders, so he had to let it pass. He could not discover the price at which the stock had been sold or the name of the purchaser. Nor was it probable that they would know the name of the purchaser when the stock shares were transferred officially, because some lawyer or dummy corporation would be used to hold the stock.[9]

As for the Hawaiian and Philippine companies, the prospects and performance were good. The profits of Davies-Far East for the first six months were nearly $600,000, up considerably over 1965.[10] The sniping of the takeover specialists was a growing matter of concern to Geoffrey Davies, and toward the end of July he held a luncheon at Brown's Hotel in London for 16 family shareholders, including Uncle Arthur and Uncle Theo. After they had counted noses and shares, he pointed out that Davies family holdings, excluding those of the Wilkinson estate, which could be considered to be friendly, had decreased in the past few years from 44 percent to 33 percent of the stock. Given the holdings by friendly banks and trusts, that 33 percent still meant control, but if the family continued to sell off bits and pieces, then all would suffer. The control bloc of the stock was by far the most valuable piece, and they should work together and not be picked off one at a time.[11]

Two weeks later, Weidig had a talk with George Wheaton of the Dillingham corporation, and innocently noted that he had learned Dillingham had bought another bloc of stock. So they had, said Wheaton—and Weidig knew then who had made that tricky purchase from Morgan Guaranty Bank.[12]

As 1966 ended, the Davies hopes were high. To be sure, consolidated profits were down from $3.2 million in 1965 to $2.9 million in 1966, but the big profit of '65 had been due largely to sugar. Davies-Far East broke records again. Davies Iberica made a small profit for the first time. Most important, merchandising was showing profits, the tractor and implement department was planning to put up a new building in Waipahu, and, although the quality of cane had been poor for 1966 grinding because of adverse weather, the cane for 1967 looked to be in excellent condition and sugar production was expected to be up. Improvements in the Ookala mill indicated that Laupahoehoe plantation might have a bumper year, as compared to a loss of $355,000 in 1966. Some years earlier, the company had acquired a small firm, Stubenberg Company Limited, which made— really invented—new sorts of machinery to save labor in the cane plantations and mills. Stubenberg was doing very well; its operations showed a money profit, but more important, its development of machinery was changing the face of the industry.[13] The 1966 annual report beamed with enthusiasm and indications of a strong future. The English shareholders must have been at least somewhat cheered by the increase in dividends to $1.85 a share, which was 35 cents more than in 1965. The company had several new directors, including the Chinese-American capitalist Chinn Ho, Milton Pickup of Davies-Far East, and Cesar de Zulueta.

But Davies still had management problems. Harold Weidig was more than a year past retirement. There was no one in Honolulu who could take his place. Geoffrey wanted Milton Pickup to move to Honolulu, but Pickup resisted; his whole life was built in the Philippines. In October of 1966, Geoffrey met Pickup in Spain and was so insistent that Pickup could not refuse.[14] The new president of Davies-Far East would be Gordon Fraser, who had been found by the executive search process and brought from the mainland. This solution was not a happy one, but Davies-Far East suffered, as did Davies Honolulu, from a shortage of management on the upper level. There were several good men of fine potential in each place, but none quite ready for the top job.[15]

As 1967 opened, the serious problem facing the Davies company seemed to be the Spanish company, for although Cesar de Zulueta was extremely effective as a salesman and executive, the company suffered in financial management. There was no one in Davies Iberica who had the American or British sense of financial controls. The problem was also one of expansion. The demand for foreign goods in Spain was so great and the cash position of Spaniards so poor in terms of foreign exchange, that the Spanish company must carry large debt, and that meant the parent company in Honolulu must finance it. This involvement had been growing year after year, as the Spanish company's capitalization rose to a million dollars and its debts commensurately, and finding the cash was a problem for a company that dealt heavily in sugar, a notoriously greedy cash-eating crop. But otherwise all looked well. The Dillingham Corporation had apparently subsided in its interest in Theo H. Davies & Co., Ltd. No further attempts had been made to persuade heirs to sell stock, and all was quiet on the Honolulu front.

On March 2, 1967, all this changed. Lowell Dillingham telephoned Harold Weidig and reminded him of that conversation in which Weidig had asked if they wanted a seat on the board. Now they did; Dillingham wanted to put George Wheaton, his executive vice president, on the board of Theo H. Davies & Co., Ltd. Weidig was quick to agree, and quick to put up a flare to Geoffrey Davies. For the first time, the inner council of the Davies company had been breached by an outsider. From the pleasant English country house in Suffolk, Geoffrey Davies sensed, that March day when he received Weidig's letter, that something new was in the air.[16]

Chapter Fifty-Three

"THE DILLINGHAM PARTY"

S*ummer of 1967* began gloomily for the Davies company. Milton Pickup had not yet arrived; he would not take over until 1968. And Harold Weidig had to send the bad news to England: the merchandising department was slipping again and, except for the Tractor and Implement division, was losing money. In fact, as Geoffrey Davies looked over the figures, he commented that these other departments seemed to have been losing money for three years, but that big machinery sales had pulled them out of it. This gloomy appraisal was not helped by an outside opinion, volunteered by Ed Auer of Lincoln National Life, to the effect that he did not believe Davies was making full use of its merchandising capital to achieve proper return.[1]

This sort of news played into the hands of the takeover adventurers; they were always interested when a company had strong assets and a weak earning position. For that reason, when James Stewart, the film actor, purchased 2000 shares of Davies treasury stock (at $68 a share) all concerned were pleased because Stewart was investing for the long haul, his manager said, and he might want more stock later.[2]

But Dillingham Corporation had already begun its attempt to move in and take over Davies in spite of the resistance of the management and family stockholders.

On April 26, the board of directors of Theo H. Davies & Co., Ltd. met, and Geoffrey Davies welcomed George Wheaton. He announced that Milton Pickup would come to Honolulu in one year, needing that time to break in the new man in Manila, Gordon Fraser. They talked about Davies Iberica and its problems, but cautiously, in view of the presence of the new director. George Wheaton had nothing to say.[3]

But when the board of directors of Davies company met again in June, Dillingham director Wheaton made a motion about the sale to Stewart. He wanted all stock to be offered generally in the future. Could the company not have gotten a higher price had they gone out looking for another buyer? Since the last previous sale had been at $63 and Weidig had crowed a bit to Geoffrey Davies about getting $68 from James Stewart, the question seemed to indicate that the other buyer could well have been Dillingham Corporation. The board voted, seven members present. Only Wheaton voted no. The matter was not pursued, but in the Davies camp, Director Wheaton was treated at arms' length.[4]

By the spring of 1967, Dillingham had acquired about 35,000 shares of Theo H. Davies stock, buying quietly, in any size lot. They owned slightly under 15 percent of the total stock, which at this time totalled some 230,000 shares.

Dillingham was ready to move. On July 25, Lowell Dillingham announced that Dillingham proposed to offer the shareholders $97.50 per share for Theo H. Davies & Co., Ltd. stock. Seeing that the last big sale had been made to James Stewart at $68, obviously Dillingham thought $97.50 would be a taking offer. But Executive Vice-President George Wheaton had not done his homework properly and apparently did not realize that the Davies management was seeking friendly stockholders and would sell low to them. Whether or not this was legal under strict interpretation of financial laws was another matter; but since Davies was not a public corporation, nor were the anti-trust laws in any way involved (except perhaps if Dillingham succeeded) there seemed no reason that Theo H. Davies & Co., Ltd. could not be operated in any manner that its officers pleased and its stockholders accepted.

Geoffrey Davies was quick to reply to Dillingham in the negative, and to send a letter to stockholders advising them to take no action. More would be forthcoming he said, but for the moment "in the view of the board the offer is entirely inadequate."[5] Geoffrey Davies meant precisely that, at this point, it seemed impossible to avoid a sale of some sort soon, for the performance of the company could not possibly compete with a stock offer that represented the assets of the company. His objection to the Dillingham offer was that it was a "steal" of the assets. But some of the stockholders were certainly going to wonder why they had been told to sell their stock at $60 and $65 recently when the assets were so high. That was going to be Geoffrey Davies' big problem.

The issue was not long in arising. At a board meeting on August 3, well-briefed by his attorneys,[6] Wheaton appeared. He first attacked the language of the minutes of the last meeting and secured a change regarding his objection to the James Stewart sale. Then he claimed that the stock should be worth six times the earnings ratio. If the stock was worth what Davies directors said it was, it should be paying $17 a share.

Oh, asked Harold Weidig (who had also obviously been well-briefed by his attorneys), if that was the case, then why was Dillingham selling at $60 a share when its earnings were $2.83 in 1966? If Davies' stock were valued on the Dillingham basis it would be selling at $180 a share.

This sort of argument got them nowhere. Wheaton then began a new approach. He addressed himself to the in-house directors who had no important financial resources and told them that each director was taking a personal liability for his votes and that they had better understand that. It was a direct threat. Frederick Schutte, one of the directors, replied that the company guaranteed directors against personal suit unless they were "willfully negligent."

So that argument ended in impasse, and then the vote came, 7-1 against Wheaton. The meeting ended, but not the session. Weidig held them all for a few moments and told them that he had just heard from Geoffrey Davies in England and that the family was practically unanimous in turning down the offer. Wheaton's sense of pain and shock were evident, and before he left, he asked in surprise what would make the family turn down so good an offer?[7]

Dillingham's next step was to go public with the battle. They called a press conference and raised the issue of the sale to Jimmy Stewart—which the Dillingham public relations man knew would make a good press for them. If $68 was good enough for Jimmy Stewart, why wasn't $97.50 good enough for the Davies stockholders?[8]

It was an excellent move from a public relations point of view, but fortunately for the Davies company, the Davies family stockholders didn't read the American newspapers, and most of them were only vaguely aware of Jimmy Stewart. So while Dillingham had all the publicity it could want, the value of it seemed minimal.

Dillingham sent out its offer to the Davies stockholders and waited. The offer was to expire in August but, when no results were forthcoming, it was extended until September. Meanwhile Geoffrey Davies had come to Honolulu to shore up the defenses, and suddenly Davies stockholders were deluged with letters and facts and figures from both sides. The newspapers and radio stations made hay with the story. A caller to Aku, the early-morning Honolulu disc-jockey at KGMB, made a joke about Jimmy Stewart and Dillingham. The Waikiki journals ran Stewart's picture and made other jokes. But in the offices of Dillingham and Davies there was little joking. As time passed and the stock did not come in, Dillingham Corporation tried harder. They would not raise the offer, but they did guarantee that if by October 9 a better offer were received, Dillingham would return the shares. But the stockholders must act by September 8.[9] If that sounded interesting, it also had the disadvantage of being extremely complicated, and Geoffrey Davies' approach was much simpler: Hold out and you will get more. The family stockholders believed Geoffrey, and the banks and other "safe" holders stood firm. On September 8, Dillingham had only 6498 shares of new stock acquired as the result of its takeover bid. The move, with all its attendant publicity in the American press, had been a total failure.

That fall Geoffrey Davies was approached by several businessmen who were interested in Davies. One approach came from John Keswick, chairman of Jardine, Matheson & Co., Ltd. of Hong Kong. Jardine had grown since those days when Gerald Wilkinson was talking to the Keswicks and dreaming of absorbing their company. The Jardine, Matheson of 1967 wanted to establish itself in the whole of the Pacific Basin, which meant they must move into Australasia and toward America. They cared little for tourism but were interested in trade and manufacturing, for apparently they, like the Davies company had learned since World War II that the middleman's role, which had established the fortunes of both companies, was declining. Sir John Keswick spoke of a working partnership with Davies: he did not wish to buy the company, but he would be pleased to go into joint ventures, particularly anything that might be as successful as Davies-Far East had been. That dream, first seen by Clive Davies, and then brought to fruition by Gerald Wilkinson, had established the Davies company among worldwide or multinational companies, as a shrewd and successful operation.[10]

A few days after the Keswick meeting, Geoffrey Davies met G.I. Barty-King and G.R. Ridley of the Grosvenor estate, which had large property holdings in London. They wanted a joint venture with the Davies company because they believed the development of Hawaii would begin with the advent of the "jumbo-jets" which were just in the offing. They were interested in the Davies downtown property in Honolulu, which included the Davies building and another block across Queen Street between Alakea and Bishop. The idea appealed to Davies, particularly if it could be hooked up with a large tourist land deal. The reason for the appeal was that such an association could absorb all the loose Davies stock that might come on the market for twenty years. Where better to have stock held than in a trust with which they were in business?[11]

The question of protecting the company against continuing sale by family members seemed more urgent than ever, and Geoffrey Davies arranged for the sale of 7000 shares of stock to Jardine, Matheson at $100 a share. He hoped to sell another 3000 shares to the Grosvenor estate in a few months. That combination sale ought to take care of all the family shares that would come up for sale for the next ten years.[12] The Jardine sale meant more than that—John Keswick and Michael Herries (later Sir Michael) promised to vote their shares with the family, and arrangements were made for Harold Weidig to visit Hong Kong and spend a week or two with Jardines. This would come shortly before Weidig's retirement as president, scheduled to begin with the annual meeting on April 30, 1968.

With the end of 1967 came another difficult problem: Davies overall income was off again, this time the consolidated net profit was $1,728,000 as compared to $1,872,000 the year before, but the book value of the 236,000 shares was up from $134 to $140. Laupahoehoe Sugar Company had lost $253,000 that year, but Hamakua had made a profit of $608,000 and Honokaa a profit of $555,000. Sugar, as always, was unpredictable, and two plantations next door to one another (as these were) could show entirely different results, depending on local weather for the most part. This year Laupahoehoe's problem was human; the consolidation of grinding at Ookala had cost dearly.

The company had expanded the macadamia nut business it inherited from F.A. Schaefer & Co. Macadamia Nuts of Hawaii was forming partnerships with growers of macadamia trees who agreed to process their nuts at the Davies factory. Around Honomalino 3500 acres of orchard were under cultivation, but this was almost all for the future; the nuts still came from the Honokaa orchards. Kukaiau ranch showed a small profit but was so heavily in debt to Davies for losses over the years that the profit seemed small indeed. Kawaihae Elevator Company, which had facilities for fattening cattle, was taken over by the Davies company this year with 80 percent ownership. The objective was to reduce the cost of fattening cattle for the Honolulu market. It lost money, as it had from the outset.

Stubenberg Manufacturing Company again led the field in the manufacture of specialized sugar field equipment, which Davies hoped to expand into a world business. The Spanish company lost money again. No one wanted to talk about how much ($200,000 loss) or to discuss the enormous investment ($2,000,000 debt) that was building up in Madrid, nor could one explain to American stockholders that the book figures were meaningless anyhow. Spain was very vexing.

One could only crow so much about Davies-Far East, but its profits were up again and, in spite of the competing sugar mill put up by the planters of Silay, the profits of Hawaiian-Philippine Company were up 39 percent.[13]

Milton Pickup, the new president, who was in Hawaii for the meeting of January 25, 1968, predicted that the profits for 1968 would be better, although Iberica would still lose $100,000. For their loyalty (it could not have been because of company performance) the stockholders received dividends of $2.25 for the year.[14] Not even George Wheaton objected at that meeting, which was to be his last. The next week Lowell Dillingham wrote Geoffrey Davies a letter offering Davies all the 35,167 shares that had been acquired by Dillingham at such heavy expense, for $110 a share. Having refused the $97.50, Geoffrey Davies could scarcely demur at the price.

Milton Pickup then had much of the responsibility for scurrying about to find the money, $3,868,000. He had to secure a release from New England Mutual Life Insurance company, which was the long-term creditor of the company on that $6,000,000 loan of Russell's, and find $3,000,000 from Bankers Trust Company and $1,000,000 from the Bank of California on short term. It had to be short term—it would never do for the year to roll around and the 1968 annual report to show that Davies had borrowed four million dollars to buy up its own shares.[15] Finally it was done. The Dillingham Corporation may have suffered in public relations perhaps, but Dillingham made a nice profit of about a million dollars on the exchange; but of course one had to subtract all the expense of sending a man around the East and England to try to buy up shares, and the cost of the takeover attempt itself. Theo H. Davies & Co., Ltd. had established a new price for the shares, $110, which would require some study as to implications. But at least the company had been saved from the most dangerous moment in its history.

The First and the Last: Geoffrey C. Davies, the last member of the Davies family to serve as chairman of the company (as of 1981), sitting at his desk with the portrait of his grandfather, Theo H. Davies, in the background.

Chapter Fifty-Four

ENTER JARDINE, MATHESON & CO., LTD

The more the directors of Theo H. Davies & Co., Ltd. contemplated the financial structure of the company, the more they realized that something had to be done about the stock. The price of shares had suddenly leaped to $110-$120. If they had wished a listing on the American Stock Exchange, as seemed to be the next proper step in the company's development, they must place 300,000 shares in the hands of the general public. So they decided on a change: the 300,000 outstanding shares were split 5 for 1, with dividends to be paid on the basis of one-fifth of the old. The capitalization limit was then increased to 10,000,000 shares.[1]

The problem of the Davies company now was to find a home for that Dillingham stock, and the split was a part of the attempt to turn a profit from it. This was done in a roundabout way in October 1968, when Davies traded 175,000 shares of its stock for 89,250 shares of Boise Cascade stock, and then sold the Boise Cascade stock for $5,926,200. The net result was to pay off the loans from Bankers Trust and Bank of California, give the Davies stockholders an increase in equity of nearly $2,000,000, and place Davies stock in safe hands. By year's end, Theo H. Davies & Co., Ltd. had outstanding 1,194,475 shares of stock, which had changed the nature of the company. But the working capital problem was solved. The big drain was still Davies Iberica, whose situation was so confused and so negative that Greg Floro, treasurer of Davies-Far East, was borrowed for several months to try to straighten out the tangle.[2] Consolidated net profits were up again, though only slightly, but total dividends were $633,000 as compared to $528,000 in 1967.[3]

In 1969 the profit picture was still not as it ought to be in terms of the assets of the Davies enterprises. The Spanish company lost money again. The sugar companies were all profitable, Hamakua and Honokaa each made half a million dollars, and Laupahoehoe made $173,000. The net profit of Davies Far East was $2,650,000. Then why was Davies consolidated net income so low — $2,183,000? Spain had part of the answer. The loss again this year was $218,000. Here Fedders Iberica, a subsidiary making and selling air conditioners, made $400,000, but Facosa, another subsidiary that made concrete products, lost $350,000, and the trading company lost the rest.[4] Kukaiau ranch lost a little money. Hawaiian Holiday, Inc., the macadamia nut business, lost more. The old tractor and implement department had been so successful that it was reorganized into two companies, Pacific Machinery and Interisland Equipment, the one selling heavy machinery and the other light. Interest charges were very heavy because the company was again using enormous amounts of cash. The interest expense of $1,293,000, plus $332,000 in accumulated deficits of subsidiaries written off, showed where the money went.[5]

In all this the problem was largely managerial. Gordon Fraser turned out to be totally unsuitable as president of Davies Far East and left the company. He was succeeded by Gregolioa Floro, the Filipino who had been brought along by Gerald Wilkinson from a bookkeeper's job, but within a year Floro's health failed and he had to resign. In Spain there was no one to put a financial curb on the exuberant salesman and creative thinker, Cesar de Zulueta. In Honolulu there was no one who seemed obvious as successor to Milton Pickup. The management problem affected operations everywhere, from Hilo to Agana, Guam, from the Western Visayas, to Edificio Davies in Madrid. The Davies company was a truly multi-national corporation with but one thin level of management, and that cracking on two ends and held up only in the middle in Honolulu. Davies was marketing everywhere, in the Middle East, in the Far East, in Europe and America, and Stubenberg's machine genius was in demand all over the world. Yet the company limped along with little improvement in its income, year after year.

After some months of consideration, Davies and the Grosvenor Estate announced a plan for development of the Davies block in Honolulu. They would put up a skyscraper, Davies Pacific Center, which would cost $24,000,000, at the corner of Bishop and Merchant streets. The old building would be torn down and Davies executives moved into offices in Castle & Cooke's building in the Financial Plaza of the Pacific. The other departments were spread around Honolulu, with a new 140,000 square-foot warehouse out by the Honolulu International Airport. Dillingham Corporation got the construction job; in business there was little place for hard feelings.

The company also went into business with Jardine, Matheson & Co., Ltd. in the first of the sort of ventures foreseen by Geoffrey Davies and John Keswick and Michael Herries. Davies-Far East, Jardine, Matheson & Co., Ltd. and several Thai investors formed a company to manufacture Fedders air conditioners and market them in Southeast Asia.

No one could say that Davies was not trying new avenues. They looked into use of bagasse as a building material; they bought a 25 percent interest in a small trading company in Fiji; they entered a joint venture to build an apartment house on Punchbowl in Honolulu. But 1970 saw a fall in income. It was merchandising again, in Honolulu and Madrid. Sales were up, but expenses were up higher, and the net was loss. Davies had gone into furniture for hotels, restaurant equipment, bowling alley construction and equipment (most of Honolulu's bowling alleys were built by Davies), school supplies, toys, and back into sporting goods. They went out again. There was a wistful little note in the Davies annual report for 1970 to the effect that 1,586,273 visitors came to Hawaii in 1970, and that the population of the state had increased 21 percent in ten years. To look at the Davies figures, one would never know it. The company had missed the boat on tourism and on real-estate exploitation and on the new consumerism—the big profit makers in Hawaii. It was enough to give Milton Pickup ulcers, and it did.[6]

This year, 1970, they did not have the Philippine company to bail them out because the Philippine government had decided to float the peso, and it dropped from P3.90 to the dollar to P6.50 to the dollar. The result was that though Davies-Far East continued to make excellent profits, they were peso profits and the loss came in foreign exchange. It did not do much good to earn 49 percent more income than Davies-Far East had in 1969; that consolidated balance sheet in Honolulu was figured in dollars. The company's net income was $350,000. If it had not been for Davies-Far East, it would have been a loss, however.

In 1970, Milton Pickup tried many remedies. He hired a new controller for Davies Iberica and made him directly responsible to the controller of Theo H. Davies & Co., Ltd. in Honolulu.[7] He sold off the new warehouse and paid off $2,000,000 of the long-term borrowing. And, in Spain, they liquidated the merchandising department of Davies Iberica, and Caesar de Zulueta resigned from the Davies board of directors. Each of the three sugar companies made profits in excess of $600,000, Davies-Far East's income was nearly double, at $1,735,000, and so the Davies company was able to show a net consolidated income of $1,604,000 in 1971. Of course the stockholders might say to themselves: consider the profit if we had only the sugar companies, making $1,800,000 and Davies-Far East: the profit would have been over $3.5 million.

The stockholders had a right to be concerned. They would have been even more concerned had they considered the comparative positions of Davies and the other companies of the old Big Five.

Profits

	1960	1970
Theo H. Davies & Co., Ltd. (consolidated)	$ 900,000	$ 315,000
C. Brewer and Co., Ltd.	359,000	7,491,000
Alexander & Baldwin, Inc.	2,958,000	10,421,000
Castle & Cooke, Inc.	2,991,000	20,368,000
Amfac, Inc.	2,183,000	14,160,000

Accepting the fact that 1970 had been a bad year for Davies, just as 1960 had been for Brewer, still Davies was not recovering the way Brewer had. The profits of the others were in eight figures in 1971, but Davies' profit of $1,604,000 would have been a loss without Davies-Far East. [8]

When Greg Floro's health failed, he resigned and Erwin G. Vorster, Milton Pickup's brother-in-law, was chosen to become the new president of Davies-Far East. This succession of managerial musical chairs could hardly help but hurt the Far East company, and it was not long before the management began to loosen at the seams. Also differences began to show themselves in the relationships between Geoffrey Davies and Milton Pickup. In the days when Clive Davies functioned as chairman of the board, he had insisted on hearing regularly from all his key executives, and John E. Russell had never been able to sway Clive Davies from acting as chief executive of the company in many ways. Geoffrey Davies and Gerald Wilkinson had kept in remarkably close touch during Wilkinson's brief career as chairman and chief executive officer. But Milton Pickup did not keep Geoffrey Davies informed in the same detailed fashion, and by the end of 1971 their relations had grown distinctly cool. President Pickup did not always tell chairman Davies where he was and what he was doing, and the chairman fretted.[9] The management problems at Davies-Far East showed in an alarming increase in expenses, but its earnings were fine: nearly $2.2 million for 1972. Davies' future was addressed in a "five-year plan" which projected healthy increases in profits. At the end of the year, the management could boast in the annual report that consolidated net income was $3,028,000—but if one took away the income of Davies-Far East and $451,000 recovered in the closing out of Davies Iberica as an "extraordinary gain," there was still something wrong at Davies.[10]

Many efforts were still being made to find a road to increased profitability. Davies bought the Paauhau Sugar Company from C. Brewer and added its assets to Honokaa. This purchase would mean big capital expenditures to improve efficiency in the next few years and would be financed by big loans at low interest from the federal land bank, which agreed to lend Honokaa $8.5 million and Laupahoehoe and Hamakua $9 million. The remainder of the old $6 million loan negotiated by John E. Russell was paid off, but Davies had borrowed $17 million to build the Davies Pacific

Center, which was to be converted to a new long-term loan. The general merchandise operation had been discontinued almost completely and what was left was still losing money, but at least most of that dead wood had finally been cut away. A new acquisition had been made in Australia with the purchase of a controlling interest in Toft Brothers Industries, a sugarcane equipment manufacturer.

There was nothing particularly ominous about the operating statements and balance sheets of 1971 and 1972, except that the company did not seem to be going anywhere, even yet. The five-year plan was supposed to be a means of remedying this difficulty. A decision was taken to remove all the subordinate Davies employees from the board of directors. In effect, this meant that Milton Pickup was the only director left in Davies who was a company employee. Francis Swanzy Morgan, and W. E. McCoy were made group vice-presidents, and A.V. Stewart continued as treasurer and vice-president, but they were no longer involved in board-level policy making of the company. Yet another move to efficiency and savings was to buy up all the outstanding stock of the sugar companies (most of this held by members of the Davies family) to minimize such problems as concern for dividends.

A new problem arose in 1972. Boise Cascade had hopes of acquiring or going into partnership with the Davies company, but its own difficulties became such in 1972 that the company put its 175,000 Davies shares up for sale. Lincoln National Life wanted to bail out (probably to seek more lucrative investment), and that meant another 38,500 shares were going on the block.[11] The directors decided to buy up the shares for the treasury if they could, and they agreed on an offer of $17 a share for the 213,500 shares. If successful it would cost Davies $3,629,500 to protect the company from outside purchase. For at this point, Davies had 1,203,442 shares outstanding. Someone determined on a takeover, with the bases of these shares, would have a very strong position. And the Davies company was still suffering from the same disease that had attracted Dillingham: high assets in the U.S., an exciting prospect in the Philippines, but poor operating performance.

Lazard Freres, who had the Boise Cascade shares, rejected the Davies offer and came back with an offer to sell at $26. Baring Brothers offered to buy half the shares at $22. In the end, Baring Brothers bought the 213,500 shares of Boise Cascade and Lincoln Life, kept 100,000 shares, and sold off the rest. Jardine, Matheson & Co., Ltd. bought 45,000 shares, and very soon D. W. N. Landale, a Jardine director, joined the Davies board.[12] Cesar de Zulueta bought what remained of the Davies interests in Spain, and they parted company amicably, Davies having eaten its enormous losses in the investment over a period of years. The Spanish company continued, and Zulueta later sold off his interests, but the successors profited, largely by reaping harvest from ground tilled at enormous expense by the Davies company over a decade.

That fall of 1972, the decision was made to stop trying to make a success of the macadamia nut business and to sell off Hawaiian Holiday. For four years they had tried to make it go, and in 1972 the advances out to planters came to $1,700,000 which would increase by $300,000 for several years. Davies, trying to refund long-term debt, was in no position to carry an investment for which no one on the board could see the light—and there was just behind them the searing experience of the company's failure in Spain. The next year the macadamia orchards at Honomalino were separated from the Honokaa sugar company. It would not be long before the whole Hawaiian Holiday operation was sold to Paul DeDomenico on deferred purchase terms, who would succeed in revolutionizing the marketing of the macadamia nut but who would also find profits from this venture elusive.

Theo H. Davies & Co., Ltd. had settled down to more or less solid and predictable ventures in Hawaii but was really not doing very well at them. Once again, in 1973 the big profits were in sugar and from the Philippines. Laupahoehoe and Honokaa each earned more than $1,000,000 this year. Davies Far East earned $2.6 million, but some of the management weaknesses were beginning to show. The insurance business there faltered, and Aircon came up with a financial scandal: auditing incompetence had overstated profits for the past two years, thus confusing the total picture more than a little. Republic Cement was losing money — as it had in 1972. The salvation of Far East profits was sugar, with Hawaiian-Philippines, Bogo-Medellin, and San Carlos all making enormous profits.

At Jardine, Matheson & Co., Ltd. Henry Keswick and David Newbigging looked over the Theo H. Davies balance sheet and operating statement. Here was a company that in 1972 had $108,000,000 in assets, and whose current and long-term liabilities were each less than a quarter of that amount. The stockholders' equity was nearly 40 percent of the total liabilities, so it was a sound enough company on paper. Further, Jardine's director, D.W.N. Landale, reported on the series of meetings that indicated profits would be up in 1973 (and they were: the Davies company in 1973 set a new record for itself of earnings of $3,681,000). There were no more Davies family members in view as far as the company was concerned; Geoffrey Davies was nearly sixty, and, although he had a son, young Peter was not yet in his teens. One could say then, that the family interests in Davies had changed enormously in the past decade' and that the company very soon must be delivered into other hands.

As far as the family was concerned, the prospects of going on as they had been were not encouraging. Taxes and life in Britain were becoming constantly more expensive, and the Davies investment still was not a very rewarding one: Theo H. Davies cash dividends in 1972 amounted to 70 cents per share, which if valued at $20 a share (as they had been when split a few years earlier), meant less than a three and a half percent return on investment. A savings bank paid much better. [13]

Nor did there seem to be much real hope for change in the future. The company in Honolulu was stuck in a rut from which it seemed to be unable to emerge. Sugar was an excellent investment, but a troublesome one that demanded constant attention, excellent management, and large infusions of capital. One year a sugar investor was on top of the world, and the next year he could be deep in the dumps. Spain had appeared to Gerald Wilkinson to offer that needed new spurt of excitement and profitability. The excitement had come, but the profitability had not—management problems again, on the fiscal side. As for the future, there were ominous signs in Manila of weakening, and Manila was the bastion of Theo H. Davies & Co., Ltd. and had been for a dozen years.

Geoffrey Davies had really already made his choice. When he fomented the upheaval that unseated John E. Russell, he might have gone back into active management. When Gerald Wilkinson died, Geoffrey Davies might have returned to Honolulu and taken over as chief executive. But secretly he had felt incapable of assuming that responsibility. There was even more to it than that; the scars of his twelve years of conflict with John E. Russell ran deep. In 1959, when Geoffrey Davies decided to leave the company, he wrote a long letter from his house in Tantalus overlooking Honolulu, to James Tabor, the president of the company. He detailed all his quarrels and spoke of his blasted hopes, and he was insistent on his course of withdrawal from management.

"Frankly," Geoffrey Davies wrote, "my experience of recent years has had the effect of killing my enthusiasm and interest in the company. It would be difficult to revive it. As someone once wrote, the fires of youth can be banked for so long that they are put out altogether."[14]

All the questions that upset him in 1959 still faced the Davies company: profitability, management, and vulnerability to takeover attempts. The new management had not resolved the problems, and Geoffrey Davies had not resolved them either.

On September 10, 1973 Geoffrey Davies called by arrangement at the office of Matheson & Co., Ltd. in London. He was met by Michael Herries and Henry Keswick, who offered to purchase 100 percent of the Davies company stock. They would pay cash to U.S. shareholders at a rate of $40.50 per share. United Kingdom shareholders would receive equivalent value in Jardine, Matheson stock (which would save them from an enormous tax bite from Inland Revenue). Within a few days that offer was accepted by the family and by Baring brothers. In the fall of 1973, then, Jardine, Matheson bought all the shares outstanding of the Davies company. All the Davies family and all their adherents profited handsomely in the transaction. For Geoffrey Davies, the load of maintaining the family company was removed. He remained as chairman of the board of directors, but the ultimate power was in the hands of the stockholders. Milton Pickup remained as president, but soon moved to Hong Kong, as Jardine, Matheson realized that Davies-Far East was as important to them as Theo H. Davies & Co., Ltd., and they soon split Far East off as a separate company, Jardine Davies Inc.

With the sale to Jardine, Matheson & Co., Ltd, a whole new dimension of support and opportunity became available to Theo H. Davies & Co., Ltd. This Jardine company was the same with which Robert Janion had dealt so many years earlier, when Hawaii was still "the Sandwich Islands," and Theo H. Davies was yet an untried clerk in a Manchester counting house. Jardine, Matheson & Co., Ltd. had grown and profited, with an enormous expansion in the years after World War II. Gerald Wilkinson had once dreamed of absorbing Jardine under the Davies roof. Now the amalgamation had come about, although the other way around. The Davies family had always felt the importance of their English-ness and had been proud of the record of their company. Now, although the company was passing out of family hands, it was to remain British, which somehow seemed just right, but it was apparent that Davies would continue to be an important part of the Hawaii community.

The Davies family had been something of a mystery in Hawaii since the day when Theo H. Davies moved back to England to stay. Hawaii had done well by them, and so had the Philippines, and in their way, they had done well by Hawaii and the Philippines, too. Old Theo H. Davies had been a good friend to Hawaii if not, perhaps, to the United States. Without Theo Davies, St. Andrews Cathedral might never have been built. Clive Davies was a supporter of many charities, St. Andrews and The Seaman's Institute large among them. Geoffrey Davies took a particular interest in the Hawaii Preparatory Academy at Waimea, on the Big Island of Hawaii, and assisted that school for years. Their company more than they was an essential part of Hawaiian life and had been for a century. In the nineteenth century Theo H. Davies set a standard for honesty and responsibility among merchants. He was also an innovative man in terms of finance, although he never claimed much in that department. His manner of raising money through agents in San Francisco was soon copied by other factors in Honolulu. In terms of technical progress, too, Davies and his associates were often far ahead of their times. Alexander Young of Honolulu Iron Works built the finest sugar mills in the islands, and he invented the maceration process which is still used to extract sugar and molasses from cane. Francis Swanzy was responsible for much of the attention paid to Hawaiian pineapple, although Davies did not fare well in that business. Swanzy was also a forward looking man. Theo Davies had welcomed and backed experiments in plantation mechanization with the steam-driven plow, and his plantations on Hawaii were the first to use them extensively. Swanzy was taken by the mechanical tractor, and he brought the first tractors into use on Davies plantations. John E. Russell was a forward looking sugar man too, and he developed the use of cane trucks rather than the railroad to deliver cane to mills. He also backed other experiments, including the bulldozer method of harvesting cane, with its subsequent washing processes. Under Russell's management, Theo H. Davies & Co., Ltd. became a leading user and seller of heavy equipment.

In the 1920s, the Davies building on Bishop and Merchant streets was the wonder of Hawaii merchandising, with its many elevators and chutes from upper floors to street. In the 1970s, the new building became a wonder of another sort, one of the set-back, high-rise developments that has helped in establishing the atmosphere that exists in the downtown area of Honolulu.

The major change in 1973 was, that under the Jardine, Matheson umbrella Theo H. Davies & Co., Ltd. was able to break out of the constantly recurring cycle of problems associated with family shareholding and management succession. Davies had moved into a diversified organization whose operations and interests reached from London to the Far East.

The Davies company also retained its leadership in the manufacture of sugar, emerging as one of the lowest-cost producers of sugar in Hawaii.

In Manila, Gerald Wilkinson had played a major role in the economic development and independence of the Philippines. Very early in his stay, he had recognized that the Filipinos would be independent, and they would resent buying goods from outside that could be manufactured at home. He had adapted quickly to local conditions and prejudices and had managed to make successes because he trusted the Filipinos and they trusted him.

In Hawaii the new chief executive officer was Robert Sutton, a young Australian who had made his mark with Jardine, Matheson & Co., Ltd in Singapore. Sutton was transferred to Davies in 1976 and moved swiftly and quietly into the Honolulu community. He joined the major clubs, he became a Bank of Hawaii director. Under Sutton's management the company's operations were consolidated and improved. The company began functioning as a subsidiary of a major international enterprise.

In the Philippines, the Davies company was cut loose from the Hawaiian parent and recast as a separate subsidiary, Jardine Davies Inc. The change went virtually unnoticed in Honolulu, where the Philippine company was nothing more than a name. In Manila the change recreated the sense of independence that had passed with the departure of Gerald Wilkinson and then Milton Pickup for Honolulu.

But if the change was subtle, it was still definite. A few months after the takeover Geoffrey Davies encountered Milton Pickup at a board meeting of Theo H. Davies & Co., Ltd. in Honolulu. They disagreed, as they so often did, on a matter of policy.

"Why, Milton, you sound like a Jardine man," said Geoffrey Davies.

"I am," replied Milton Pickup. "Remember, Geoffrey. You sold the company. I'm a professional."

Davies Pacific Center on Bishop Street, 1981.

Notes

A number of sets of correspondence and collections of papers have been available to me for preparation of this book. Theo H. Davies saved the press copies of much of his correspondence after 1868 when he returned to Honolulu to straighten out the affairs of Janion, Green & Co. Most of these were transcribed and edited by Geoffrey C. Davies and Miss Chiko Noda. One of Robert C. Janion's old press books is also available. Mrs. Rosamond Morgan, daughter of Francis M. Swanzy, has retained a collection of her father's correspondence. Since she was in the process of preparing a book about her father at this writing, she did not wish his letters used but was most generous in giving access to the letters of others addressed to Mr. Swanzy. T. Clive Davies kept a diary for almost all the years of his adult life, which was made available to me by Geoffrey Davies, his son. He also kept other papers relating to the Davies Company and other family companies. Geoffrey Davies made available his own correspondence for the years he was with the company, and some of the correspondence of Gerald H. Wilkinson, his brother-in-law, who was chairman of the company from 1961–65. Other Wilkinson papers were available in the Davies Company files, and from his son, Rupert Wilkinson. The Wilkinson war diaries at the library of Churchill College, Cambridge University, England, were helpful. T. Guard, longtime merchandising manager of Theo H. Davies, began compiling materials for a company history in the 1950s. These included clippings from Hawaii newspapers and scores of letters to persons connected with the Davies Companies. Mrs. Rosamond Morgan at one time began a similar collection of research materials. Over the years all of the company managing directors made monthly reports to Theo H. Davies, and later to his son T. Clive Davies. These are available in the Davies Company files. The corporate records (board meetings and stockholders' meetings) of the various companies are also in the Davies files, save those of the Honolulu Iron Works, which were delivered to the new owners when they purchased the company in 1973. I am indebted to Bud Cunha for files and materials about Honolulu Iron Works.

Theo H. Davies also compiled several special records, one of his journey to Hawaii in 1856–57 aboard the Dutch bark, *Quatre Bras,* and others of his trips around Oahu, Maui, and Hawaii islands, and a recollection of his early years in Hawaii. I have adopted shorthand terms for these various collections as follows:

Theo H. Davies	THD
Theo Davies Account of the Voyage in *Quatre Bras*	*Quatre Bras*
Theo Davies Account of the walk around Oahu	Oahu
Theo Davies Account of the trip around Kauai	Kauai
Theo Davies Account of the trip around Hawaii	Hawaii
Theo Davies recollections of the early years in Hawaii	Recollections
Geoffrey C. Davies	GCD
George F. Davies	GFD
George T. Davies	GTD
T. Clive Davies	TCD
Harold F. Davies	HFD
William L. Green	WLG
T. Guard	TG
Honolulu Iron Works	HIW
Robert C. Janion	RCJ

Rosamond Swanzy Morgan	RSM
Milton H. Pickup	MHP
John E. Russell	JER
Francis M. Swanzy	FMS
James H. Tabor	JHT
Thomas Rain Walker	TRW
Harold D. Weidig	HDW
Gerald H. Wilkinson	GHW
Ernest H. Wodehouse	EHW
Stephen N. Young	SNY

Notes
Chapter One
The Voyage of the *Quatre Bras*

1. The voyage of the *Quatre Bras*, Nov. 19, 1856 to Sep. 16, 1857, unpublished manuscript by THD.
2. THD to his father, a series of letters, 1860–61, in possession of Geoffrey C. Davies. Theo Davies was extremely sensitive about his early failure and alluded to it often in his letters to his father.
3. Theophilus Harris Davies, a biographical sketch by T. Clive Davies, Honolulu, 1946.
4. THD to his father, GCD collection. TCD sketch p.4.
5. THD to his father, Jun. 15, 1857.
6. TCD sketch, p.4.
7. Ibid.
8. *Quatre Bras,* Nov. 14, 1856.
9. Ibid.
10. *Quatre Bras,* Nov. 16, 1856.
11. *Quatre Bras,* Nov. 20, 1856.
12. *Quatre Bras,* Dec. 1, 1856.
13. *Quatre Bras,* Dec. 6, 1856.
14. *Quatre Bras,* Dec. 7, 1856.

Notes
Chapter Two
The New World Beckons

1. *Quatre Bras,* Dec. 10, 1856. Davies was an enthusiastic diarist and reported at great length on every aspect of his voyage. In this, one can see gradual change in attitudes.
2. *Quatre Bras,* Dec. 22, 1856.
3. *Quatre Bras,* Jan. 9, 1857.
4. *Quatre Bras,* Mar. 3, 1857.
5. *Quatre Bras,* Apr. 20, 1857.
6. *Quatre Bras,* Apr. 29, 1857.
7. Ibid. Davies set out on his voyage heavily prejudiced against all foreigners; he seemed to remain that way, too.
8. *Quatre Bras,* Jun. 26, 1857.

Notes
Chapter Three
Janion, Green & Co. I

1. *The Hawaiian Kingdom,* Ralph S. Kuykendall, U of Hawaii Press, 1967. TCD's notes on early history of Theo H. Davies Company compiled in 1941–45.
2. History of the Hawaiian Flag.
3. RCJ to William Miller, Dec. 6, 1845.
4. Ibid.
5. Ibid. The history of the Charlton land dispute, RCJ to Richard Charlton, Mar. 29, 1847, is complex and of interest in the Davies story largely because the Davies Company came to occupy some of that land.
6. TCD early history of Theo H. Davies Co.
7. Notes of RSM. Also RCJ to T.H. Stevens, Nov. 18, 1846.
8. Notes of RSM.
9. RCJ to Charlton, Mar. 29, 1847.
10. RCJ to Starkey, THD early history of Theo H. Davies Co., Ltd.
11. Morgan notes, TCD early history.
12. Early history.
13. RCJ to John Starkey, Jan. 20, 1847.
14. TCD notebook on the early history of the company, business in the middle east.
15. *Shoal of Time,* Gavin Daws, Macmillan, 1968, pp.124–128.
16. Ibid.
17. TCD notes on early history. RCJ to Mr. Faulkner, Jun. 7, 1849.
18. *Shoal of Time,* p.133.
19. RCJ to Charlton, Jun. 4, 1849. This typical English attitude was shared by Theo H. Davies when he came along.
20. James Starkey to RCJ, Dec. 31, 1849.
21. TCD notes on early history.
22. TCD notes on early history.
23. TCD notes and drawing of downtown Honolulu.

Notes
Chapter Four
Janion, Green & Co. II

1. *Quatre Bras,* Jul. 2, 1857. Davies gives an excellent picture of the social life of the foreign community of gentlefolk in Honolulu.
2. *Quatre Bras,* Jun. 30, 1857.
3. *Quatre Bras,* Jul. 2, 1857.
4. Ibid.
5. Ibid.
6. *Quater Bras,* Jul. 18, 1857. Theo Davies was popular with the missionary community because his mores were more like theirs than most businessmen's.

7. Kuykendall, Vol. II. *The Hawaiian Kingdom.*
8. Letter of David Gregg, U.S. Commissioner to Hawaii, to Department of State, Jul. 1857. National Archives.
9. *Quatre Bras,* Jun. 26, 1857.
10. *Quatre Bras,* Aug. 4, 1857.
11. *Quatre Bras,* Jul. 18, 1857.
12. U.S. State Department papers, 1857. National Archives. Consular record. The records show that from the beginning, American representatives were bent on annexation of Hawaii.
13. *Quatre Bras,* Jun. 26, 1857.
14. THD, Journey around Oahu, 1857.
15. Letter of U.S. Vice Consul George Laythrop to State Department, Sept. 8, 1856.
16. Letters of William L. Green to the Earl of Malmesbury, 1859.
    Public Records Office, London.
17. Ibid.
18. THD Early Recollection of Honolulu, written in 1885, unpublished.
19. Recollections.
20. TG memo on Honolulu Iron Works.
21. THD Recollections.
22. *Quatre Bras,* Jun. 26, 1857.
23. TCD Sketch of life of THD.
24. Recollections.
25. THD journey to Hawaii, 1859, unpublished.
26. Recollections.
27. TG notebook on Honolulu Iron Works.
28. RSM notes on Hawaiian Steam Navigation Company, culled from records of the Hawaii Archives.
29. RSM notes.
30. THD to his father, Jul. 24, 1863.

Notes
Chapter Five
Invitation to Disaster

1. THD, to his father, Apr. 1863.
2. THD to his father, Jan. 26, 1861.
3. THD Recollections of early Honolulu, unpublished.
4. Ibid.
5. Hawaii Dept. of Interior letters, Vol. 7 p. 479. Letter to Janion, Green & Co., May 14, 1863.
6. Hawaii Dept. of Interior letters, Vol. 7 pp. 491 - 493. Letters to Janion, Green & Co. Sep. 1863, regarding Hawaiian Steam Navigation Company.
7. TG notes on Honolulu Iron Works.
8. THD to his father, Apr. 1864.
9. THD to his father, Dec. 1865.

10. THD to WLG, Jan. 4, 1865.
11. Ibid.
12. TG notes on Honolulu Iron Works.
13. THD to WLG, Jun. 30, 1865.
14. *Hawaiian Gazette,* Jan. 1865, advertisements.
15. *Hawaiian Gazette,* Jan. 20, 1866.
16. *Hawaiian Gazette,* issues of Feb. 1866.
17. *Hawaiian Gazette, Apr. 7, 1866, May 26, 1866.*
18. *Hawaiian Gazette,* Jul. 14, 1866.
19. RCJ to WLG Jul. 1866.
20. *Hawaiian Gazette,* Jan. 31, 1867.
21. *Hawaiian Gazette,* Apr. 3, 1867.
22. *Hawaiian Gazette,* Jun. 10, 1867.
23. Henry Beecroft Jackson to RCJ, Mar. 20, 1867.

Notes
Chapter Six
Salvage Operation

1. *Hawaiian Gazette,* Sep. 4, 1867.
2. THD to RCJ, Jul. 4, 1871.
3. *Hawaiian Gazette,* Jan. 1868.
4. THD Recollections of early Honolulu, unpublished.
5. THD Voyage to Kauai, 1860, unpublished.
6. THD Recollections.
7. *Kuykendal, Vol. II.*
8. *Hawaiian Gazette,* Feb. 1868.
9. *Hawaiian Gazette,* Apr. 1868.
10. THD to creditors of Janion, Green, Jul. 31, 1873.
11. Ibid.
12. Daws, *Shoal of Time.*
13. *Hawaiian Gazette,* Oct. 31, 1869.
14. TG notes on the Honolulu Iron Works.
15. Ibid.
16. Ibid.
17. THD's marriage settlement on Mary Ellen Cocking, 1871, in THD papers. It is interesting to note that George MacFarlane was a witness to this private act and MacFarlane was also an executor named in Davies' will of the period, a sure indication of the close friendship that existed between them then.
18. *Hawaiian Gazette,* Nov. 26, 1871.

Notes
Chapter Seven
Fortune

1. Files of *Hawaiian Gazette* for Jan. and Feb. 1870.
2. THD letter to creditors of RCJ, Jul. 31, 1873.
3. THD to RCJ, Jul. 4, 1871.
4. THD to Mrs. James Wodehouse, in a series of letters written in the spring of 1886, revealing their quarrels and the history of Davies' appointment to the vice-consulate.
5. THD to RCJ, Jul. 4, 1871.
6. THD to RCJ, Oct. 31, 1871.
7. THD to RCJ, Oct. 23, 1871. Davies' antipathy to Rhodes obviously stemmed back to his visit to Victoria in 1865. It appears constantly in the correspondence.
8. THD to W.D. Bickerton, Nov. 10, 1871.
9. TCD to RCJ, Jan. and Feb. 1873. The affairs of Janion, Green & Co. were coming to a close this winter, and Davies was very close-mouthed about the profitability and prospects of the Honolulu Iron Works, obviously recognizing its supreme importance with the burgeoning of the sugar plantations.
10. THD to RCJ, Jul. 4, 1871.
11. THD letters in files of Public Records Office, London. From time to time Davies carried the correspondence of the British Foreign Office. He was an acute and knowledgable observer of the Hawaii government scene.
12. Ibid.
13. THD to Janion, Green & Co. creditors, Jul. 31, 1873.
14. Ibid.
15. THD letterbook, Mar. 1874. Various letters, instructions to George MacFarlane and Thomas Rain Walker, and references to his departure appear here.
16. THD to George MacFarlane, Jun. 8, 1875.

Notes
Chapter Eight
Trouble in Paradise

1. THD to Wilder, Jan. 31, 1876.
2. THD to Joseph Dredge (his brother-in-law), Apr. 7, 1876.
3. Letters of Henry Peirce to Dept. of State, 1874. U.S. National Archives.
4. In the 1950s, TG made an historical study of the sugar industry in connection with his collection of materials for a history of the Theo H. Davies Company. This material is from the TG report.
5. Ibid.
6. THD letterbook, fall of 1876. Several letters refer obliquely to the MacFarlane departure. Davies' bitterness is evident, but also his insensitivity to his employees shows through.

7. THD to TRW, Oct. 8, 1876.
8. Recollections of R.R. Hind, from John Hind's memoirs, as reported to TG by Leslie Wishard.
9. Recollection of C.F. Hart by his daughter, Mae H. Jordan, in a letter to TG Feb. 27, 1957.
10. TG memo on early history of sugar in Hawaii; T. Guard's correspondence with the Rev. Arthur Davies, 1957.
11. Leslie Wishard's correspondence with T. Guard on Union Mill and related subjects, 1957.
12. Ibid.
13. Ibid.
14. TG study of the history of the sugar industry, made in 1957.
15. TG memo on the history of Laupahoehoe Sugar Company, 1957.
16. TG memo on the history of Hamakua Plantation and Hamakua Mill, 1957.
17. TG memo on the history of the Hawaiian sugar industry, 1957.
18. THD to RCJ and TRW in the winter of 1876 - 77, when TRW was on leave in England.
19. TG memo on the history of the Laupahoehoe Sugar Company, 1957.

Notes
Chapter Nine
Man of Affairs

1. *Hawaiian Gazette,* Jul. 26, 1875.
2. THD to RCJ
3. *Hawaiian Gazette,* Dec. 26, 1878.
4. THD to RCJ, a series of letters in the spring of 1878, in THD letterbook.
5. THD to RCJ, Sep. 17, 1879.
6. Ibid.
7. TG notebook on history of Honolulu Iron Works.
8. THD to RCJ, Jun. 8, 1880.
9. THD to Messrs. Walker, Janion and Luce, Jul. 19, 1880.

Notes
Chapter Ten
The End of the Old Firm

1. THD to TRW, Sep. 1880. THD letterbook.
2. Ibid.
3. THD to Williams, Dimond Company, Aug. 24, 1880.
4. Ibid.
5. THD to TRW, Oct. 16, 1880.
6. Biographical sketch of Francis Mills Swanzy from files of Theo H. Davies Company.
7. The account of visit to Hawaii from England, by Theo H. Davies, Nov. 20, 1880, unpublished.
8. Account.

9. Account.
10. THD to TRW, Feb. 8, 1881. The erosion of Davies' confidence in Thomas Rain Walker's ability to handle delicate financial affairs was steady after 1877. He valued Walker and made him a partner in 1882, but he had no illusions as to Walker's abilities as an entrepreneur.
11. Account, and THD to TRW, and THD to Henry Dimond, Feb. 1881.
12. THD to Williams, Dimond & Co., May 24, 1881.
13. THD to Williams, Dimond & Co., Jul. 30, 1881, THD to HD, Aug. 20, 1881. The Davies/Spreckels quarrel waxed and waned, but the essence of it was that Spreckels attempted to control the whole sugar industry of Hawaii and very nearly succeeded. Had it not been for Davies and Hackfeld & Co., he probably would have done so.

Notes
Chapter Eleven
The Spreckels Affair

1. THD to TRW, Aug. 11, 1881.
2. THD letter to editor of San Francisco *Chronicle*, published Dec. 1, 1881.
3. THD to THD Co., Dec. 14, 1881.
4. THD to Paul Isenberg, Mar. 10, 1882.
5. THD series of letters to planters, Apr. 1882.
6. THD to James Woods, Apr. 6, 1882.
7. THD to Thomas Hughes, Apr. 7, 1882. Apparently Theo H. Davies had suffered several changes of mind in the late 1870s and early 1880s. He had planned to go home and stay there as early as 1879, but it simply did not work out for him. Then when he did get home, expecting to come back only occasionally, Janion died, and the partnership ceased on the day of his death. All the financial skein had to be untangled. At the same time, the sugar industry was in difficulties, and the quarrel with Spreckels was waxing, and Davies did not feel that his staff was adequate to manage all these difficulties without himself at the helm. When he returned in 1882, it would seem that he expected to make his life in Hawaii. Nellie had been found fit by her doctors, and there seemed to be no other way of life. What was to happen in the next three years, to Nellie, to the business, and in Hawaiian social and political life, would bring another change in Davies' attitude.

Notes
Chapter Twelve
The Sugar Boom

1. All the information regarding the status of the Davies sugar interests in the 1880s comes from T. Guard's compilation of statistics and the narrative he constructed after correspondence with scores of people, some of them children of contemporaries who recalled Theo H. Davies himself.

2. THD memo to staff, Feb. 1881.
3. TG sugar book.
4. Ibid.
5. Ibid.

Notes
Chapter Thirteen
The Evils of Drink

1. *Hawaiian Gazette,* Dec. 6, 1882.
2. TG to Arthur W. Davies, Apr. 3, 1957.
3. THD to W.W. Armstrong, Jun. 22, 1881.
4. THD to Lady Brassey, Jul. 7, 1881.
5. THD to RWJ, Feb. 23, 1883.
6. THD to Harold Janion, Nov. 18, 1882.
7. THD to Charles Notley, Mar. 6, 1883.
8. THD to Harry Luce, May 23, 1883.
9. THD to J.T. Arundel, Jun. 10, 1883.
10. THD letterbook, Sep. and Oct. 1883. Letters to various persons about Davies' staff problems.
11. THD to James Wodehouse, Nov. 30, 1883.
12. THD to A.S. Cleghorn, Dec. 4, 1883.
13. THD to J.T. Arundel, Nov. 27, 1883.
14. THD to TRW, Nov. 1, 1883.

Notes
Chapter Fourteen
Business As Usual

1. THD letterbook, Oct. 1883.
2. THD to Tatham & Co., Jan. 3, 1882.
3. THD to W. Christopherson, May 19, 1882.
4. THD to Tatham & Co., Oct. 19, 1882.
5. THD to Charles Bishop, Mar. 20, Mar. 25, 1883.
6. Daws, pp. 230 - 231. Kuykendall Vol. III, 267,8.
7. Memo on maceration, T. Guard sugar book.
8. THD to Williams, Dimond, Jul. 14, 1884.
9. THD to Williams, Dimond, Jul. 31, 1884.
10. THD to Henry Dimond, Oct. 28, 1884.
11. Ibid.

Notes
Chapter Fifteen
Home Again, Home Again

1. THD to Mrs. Butcher, Mar. 12, 1885.
2. TG to Arthur W. Davies, Mar. 22, 1957.
3. THD letterbook, summer and fall of 1885. Various correspondence outlines the THD plans.
4. The entire later correspondence with Bishop Willis was printed by the Honolulu newspapers and Davies had it compiled into a booklet for presentation to those interested in the strange quarrel.
5. THD to TRW, several letters in the fall of 1883, in THD letterbook.
6. THD letters to the Rev. Alexander Mackintosh, 1885, 1886.

The story of the Davies family's last days in Honolulu and their return to England is told in the THD letterbook for the summer and fall of 1886 and in the TG notes on THD.

Notes
Chapter Sixteen
The Trials of '86

1. Thomas Hamilton to author, Dec. 1978. *Hawaiian Gazette,* Oct. 1884.
2. TG sugar book.
3. THD to Harold Janion, Apr. 2, 1886.
4 THD plantation notes, May 6, 1886.
5. THD to William Lidgate, May 31, 1886.
6. William Lidgate to THD, Jun. 3, 1886.
7. William Lidgate to THD, Jul. 12, 1886.
8. William Lidgate to THD, Aug. 12, 1886.
9. THD to William Lidgate, Aug. 27, 1886.
10. THD to TRW, Sept. 9, 1886.
11. TRW to THD, Oct. 22, 1886.
12. Ibid.
13. Ibid.
14. THD to James Wodehouse, Dec. 2, 1886.
15. THD to Sir James Fergusson, Aug. 13, 1887.
16. Kuykendall, Vol. III, pp. 298 - 9.
17. THD-*Swanzy* correspondence, THD letterbook, Sep. 1886.
18. THD to FMS, Oct. 15, 1886.
19. The entire story of the farce of the *Dunnotar Castle* rescue, and the Hawaiian government seizure of Ocean Island was reported by FMS to THD in a series of letters in September, October and November 1886.

Notes
Chapter Seventeen
The Growing Unrest

1. Daws, p. 253.
2. See accounts of Wilcox revolution, in Daws, Kuykendall Vol. III, and U.S. diplomatic correspondence, Hawaii, 1887 - 88.
3. THD letterbook, 1887-88.
4. U.S. Diplomatic and consular correspondence, 1887 - 88.
5. U.S. Minister Merrill's report to Secretary of State, Jul. 1, 1887.
6. British Foreign Office papers, Public Records Office, 1887; THD to T.W. Gladstone, Dec. 31, 1886.
7. THD to FMS, Jul. 1, 1887.
8. THD to TRW, Jul. 29, 1887.
9. THD to James Hay Wodehouse, Oct. 14, 1887.
10. THD to Lord Salisbury, Nov. 17, 1887.
11. THD to J.H. Wodehouse, Feb. 27, 1888.
12. THD to TRW, Mar. 2, 1888.
13. THD to James Hay Wodehouse, exchange of correspondence, May, Jun. 1886.
14. THD to JHW, Feb. 20, 1883.
15. THD to TRW, Sep. 10, 1883.
16. THD to TRW, Apr. 18, 1882.
17. TRW undated letter in possession of Mrs. Rosamond Morgan.
18. FMS to THD, Aug. 21, 1886.
19. THD plantation notes, May 6, 1886.
20. *Hawaiian Gazette,* Feb. 21, 1888.
21. THD letterbooks, 1888 - 89.

Notes
Chapter Eighteen
The Coming of Ka'iulani

1. THD letterbook, winter 1888.
2. *The Times,* Jun. 22, 1888.
3. THD Co. Articles of Partnership, Oct. 1889.
4. THD ledger balance, May 30, 1888.
5. TG sugar book.
6. Ibid.
7. THD to Alexander Young, Jun. 2, 1888.
8. Biography of THD in *Southpost Visitor,* May 16, 1898.
9. THD account of voyage to Germany in THD papers.
10. THD account of trip to India and Hawaii, 1889–90.
11. THD account of visit to Hawaii, 1890.
12. Ibid.

13. Ibid.
14. Ibid.

Notes
Chapter Nineteen
The Hawaiian Revolution

1. THD letterbook, 1889.
2. Minister Stevens' reports to Washington, U.S. Diplomatic correspondence, Hawaii, U.S. National Archives, Washington D.C.
3. THD to Sir James Fergusson, Jun. 29, 1891, British Public Records Office, London.
4. Letter, James G. Blaine to President Benjamin Harrison, Aug. 10, 1891. Harrison presidential correspondence.
5. Minister Stevens correspondence, op cit.
6. Ibid.
7. Ibid.
8. Memoirs of Lorrin A. Thurston, pp. 231–232.
9. THD to the Rev. Sereno Bishop, printed in Hawaii newspapers in Oct. 1892, from clippings in TG collection.
10. Lord Rosebery to J.H. Wodehouse, Dec. 5, 1892, British Public Records Office.
11. A.S. Cleghorn collection, Hawaii National Archives.
12. The story of the Davies trip to the U.S. with Princess Ka'iulani is carefully documented in a scrapbook retained by the Davies family. The Davies papers include various drafts (in the hand of THD) of speeches Ka'iulani made in Washington, New York and Boston.
13. Kuykendall Vol III, pp. 618–20. The Hawaiian Kingdom.
14. TCD papers.
15. THD letterbooks, 1893–94. Davies was constantly writing Ka'iulani about her woeful finances and giving advice on all sorts of matters, from scholarship to marriage.
16. Blount Commission report.
17. THD to Ka'iulani, Dec. 18, 1893.
18. THD to Ka'iulani, Apr. 25, 1894.

Notes
Chapter Twenty
The Corporation

1. *Honolulu Star,* Feb. 8, 1894.
2. *Pacific Advertiser,* Feb. and Mar. 1894.
3. Undated clipping, San Francisco *Chronicle,* THD papers.
4. THD to TRW, Jul. 12, 1894.
5. THD & Co. Ltd. minutes book, 1894.
6. TG notes on the collection, Honolulu Iron Works notebook.
7. Ibid.
8. Ibid.

9. TG sugar book.
10. Laupahoehoe minutes book, 1892.
11. TG sugar book.
12. Ibid.
13. In the 1930s, Jared Smith, a public relations man, began an historical pamphlet dealing with the early days of Theo H. Davies & Co., Ltd. This work was never finished, since John E. Russell and Clive Davies agreed that it might be embarrassing to the descendents of some and survivors of other persons who had connections with the Davies Company. This material is extracted from the Smith work.
14. *Southport Visitor,* May 29, 1898.
15. THD letterbook, 1893–94.
16. Ibid.

Notes
Chapter Twenty-one
Clive

1. TCD diary, Jan. 20, 1896.
2. TCD diary, Jan. 24, 1896.
3. TCD diary, Jan. 21, 1896, Feb. 22, 1896.
4. Leslie Wishard, Jr. to author, Nov. 1978.
5. TCD diary, Mar. 1896.
6. TCD diary, Jun. 1896.
7. Ibid.
8. THD to FMS, Dec. 4, 1896.
9. THD to FMS, Dec. 4, 1896.
10. TCD diaries Jul – Aug. 1897.
11. THD letterbooks, 1896–1910.
12. Interview, Mrs. Rosamond Swanzy Morgan, May, 1978.
13. THD to FMS, Dec. 1897
14. THD to FMS, Feb. 2, 1897.
15. During World War II, when there was plenty of time, Clive Davies spent many hours in his study at Hawkley Hurst working on various aspects of the history of the family and the Davies enterprises. At that time he prepared a number of capsule biographies: Thomas Rain Walker, Francis Mills Swanzy, etc. This note is from his biography of Walker.
16. THD to FMS, Oct., 1897.
17. GFD to FMS, May 4, 1898.
18. THD autopsy report, Davies family papers.

Notes
Chapter Twenty-two
The Emergence of Swanzy

1. THD will probated, Aug. 4, 1898.
2. THD will, clause 22.
3. No corporate balance sheet exists prior to 1902.
4. TRW biography by T. Clive Davies.
5. TG papers on Honolulu Iron Works.
6. Charles Hedemann to FMS, Aug. 15, 1899.
7. TG papers on Honolulu Iron Works.
8. TCD to FMS, October correspondence 1899.
9. TCD to FMS, May–Sep. 1898 correspondence.
10. W.G. Irwin to A. Hoffnung, Sep. 15, 1899.
11. Correspondence between FMS, TCD and W.G. Irwin, fall of 1899.

Notes
Chapter Twenty-Three
Subtle Change

1. TCD diaries, 1905, 1906.
2. Laupahoehoe minute book, 1902.
3. Laupahoehoe minutes book, 1903–1905.
4. Correspondence, George H. Rolph, FMS, summer 1905.
5. BE, *History of California and Hawaii Sugar Company* by Boris Emmet.
6. TCD to FMS, May 29, 1905.
7. TCD to FMS, May 23, 1905.
8. TCD correspondence, 1906–1907.
9. TCD to FMS correspondence, 1906–1907.
10. TCD to FMS, Jun. 25, 1909.
11. TCD to FMS correspondence, spring 1909.

Notes
Chapter Twenty-Four
Clive Davies Goes Home

1. Charles Hedemann to FMS, Oct. 5–25, 1907.
2. FMS to TCD correspondence, and FMS to GFD correspondence, 1909.
3. Daws, pp. 304–306; GFD to FMS, Jun. 23, 1909.
4. TCD to FMS, Jun. 25, 1909.
5. Laupahoehoe minutes book, 1908.
6. TCD to FMS, Jun. 6, 1909.
7. Report of James Wakefield, merchandise manager, Theo H. Davies & Co., Ltd., Nov. 21, 1910, to TCD.
8. George M. Rolph to Sugar Factors, May 7, 1909.
9. TCD to FMS, Jan. 13, 1911.

Notes
Chapter Twenty-Five
Management Troubles

1. Francis Mills Swanzy wrote an account of the life of Thomas Rain Walker and included his story of their last meeting. This must have been done very shortly after Walker's death, for the shock is evident.
2. TCD diaries, 1913.
3. Ibid.
4. TCD diaries, Sep. 1913.
5. THD Co. minutes book, 1912.
6. TG prepared a layout of the THD Co. office as it was in 1912.
7. Hamakua Mill minutes book, 1913.
8. TCD to FMS, Jan. 12, 1910.
9. TCD family records.
10. TCD to FMS, Jan. 12, 1910.
11. Kukaiau minutes book, 1913.

Notes
Chapter Twenty-Six
War for the Davies

1. Letters, Major John Ollivant and Captain Finlayson to Barbara Davies, Oct. 1914.
2. TCD to FMS, Nov. 14, 1914.
3. Laupahoehoe minutes book, 1913.
4. FMS to C. Lancaster, Nov. 1915.
5. Ibid.
6. TCD diaries 1914–15.
7. Clive Davies' habit was to sum up the year at the end of his diary, concentrating on the aspects of life that concerned him most at the moment. Sometimes it was the Honolulu business, sometimes it was the problems of Hawkley Hurst. In 1914, TCD seemed relatively pleased, given the war and the tragedy it brought.
8. TCD diary, Jul. 1916.
9. TCD diary, Dec. 1916.
10. THD Co. minutes book, 1916.
11. TCD diary, Feb. 9, 1917.
12. TCD diary, Apr. 27, 1917.
13. TCD diary, May 1917.

Notes
Chapter Twenty-Seven
The Mazes of Finance

1. TCD diaries, 1917–18.
2. THD Co. minutes book, 1914–18.
3. EHW to TCD correspondence re merchandising department, 1920.
4. TCD to FMS, May 3, 1915.
5. THD to TCD, Aug. 15, 1920.
6. Kukaiau Ranch minutes book, 1915–20.
7. Correspondence, EHW to TCD regarding Philippine problems, 1919–20.
8. Charles Hedemann correspondence with EHW, 1919.
9. TCD diary, Nov. 1919.
10. TCD diary, Dec. 15, 1919.
11. TCD diary, Jan.–Feb. 1920.
12. TCD diary, Apr. 1920.
13. TCD diary, May 1920.
14. TCD diary, Aug. 1920.
15. TCD diary, Dec. 1920.

Notes
Chapter Twenty-Eight
The Break in the Dike

1. TCD notes, Feb. 1921.
2. EHW to TCD, May 1920.
3. TCD gives a detailed account of the journey in his diaries of 1921. He never had the literary pretensions of his father, but he put down all the salient facts, including the concern he and Edith felt when young men kept keeping Muriel out half the night.
4. TCD memos, Oct. 1921.
6. *Honolulu Star-Bulletin,* Nov. 21, 1921.
7. TCD diaries, Dec. 1921.
8. TCD notes on family conference. Usually, Clive Davies did not write about family affairs in his large notebook, which was reserved for business matters. But he obviously believed this conference important enought to put down in detail. He was right. It represented the beginning of the end of Davies family control of Theo H. Davies & Co., Ltd. and the other interests in Hawaii.
9. TCD memo, Jan. 9, 1922.

Notes
Chapter-Twenty-Nine
Expansion in Manila

1. EHW letters to TCD, spring 1920.

2. TCD notes, Nov. 1921.
3. TCD diary, Aug. 8, 1922.
4. TCD diary, Sep. 28, 1922.
5. TCD diary, fall 1922, winter 1923.
6. TCD notes, fall 1922.
7. TCD diary, Dec. 31, 1922.
8. TCD diary, 1923.
9. EHW correspondence, with TCD, winter of 1923–24.
10. EHW to W.B. Craig, Apr. 19, 1924.
11. TCD diary, Jun. 1925.
12. EHW to TCD, Dec. letters, 1924.
13. EHW to E.D. Tenney, Mar. 25, 1925.
14. EHW to TCD, Feb. 2, 1926.
15. EHW to TCD, Oct. 28, 1926.
16. EHW to S.M. Simpson, Jul. 28, 1927.
17. EHW to W.G. Hall, Oct. letters, 1927.

Notes
Chapter Thirty
The Big Change of 1929

1. TCD diaries, Jan., Feb., Mar., 1927.
2. TCD report on meeting with Frank Atherton, Mar. 1927.
3. TCD diaries, Jul, Aug., Sep. 1927.
4. TCD diary, Oct. 17–19, 1927.
5. TCD diaries, summer 1928.
6. TCD to EHW, Apr. 16, 1929.
7. EHW to W.G. Hall, Jul. 19, 1928.
8. EHW to W.G. Hall, Aug. 31, 1928.
9. EHW letter to TCD and others, Oct., Nov. 1928.
10. EHW to W.G. Hall, Dec. 20, 1928.
11. EHW to C.J. Hedemann, Feb. 26, 1929.
12. TCD to W.G. Hall, Mar. 19, 1929.
13. TCD diary, Mar. 21, 1929.
14. TCD notes, Mar. 27, 1929.
15. Ibid.
16. Ibid.

Notes
Chapter Thirty-One
Crash in America

1. TCD diary, Jul. 24, 1929.

2. Ibid., Aug. 9, 1929.
3. Ibid., Jan. 31, 1930.
4. THD Co. minutes book, 1929.
5. Laupahoehoe, Hamakua, Waiakea minutes book, 1929.
6. TCD diary, Jan.–Feb. 1930.
7. Ibid., Feb. 4, 1930.
8 Ibid., Feb., Mar. 1930.
9. TCD diary, May 20, 1930.
10. TCD notes, May 19, 1930.
11. TCD diary, Jul. 29, 1930.
12. Interview with Milton Pickup, Dec. 1978.
13. TCD diary, Aug. 5, 1930.
14. Ibid., Aug. 20, 1930.
15. Ibid., Aug. 26, 1930.
16. Ibid., Aug. 29, 1930.
17. Ibid., Dec. 18, 1930.
18. TCD to HIW, Aug. 12, 1930.
19. JER to TCD, Sep. 3, 1930.
20. Ibid.
21. Ibid.
22. GC Hunter to TCD, Oct. 22, 1930.
23. JER to TCD, Oct. 1, 1930.
24. JER to TCD, Nov. 25, 1930.
25. TCD to JER correspondence, Dec. 1930.
26. THD & Co. minutes book, 1931–32.
27. TCD diary, Apr. 14, 1931.
28. Ibid.
29. TCD analysis, TCD papers, May 26, 1927.
30. TCD notes, May 13, 1931.
31. Ibid.
32. TCD diary, Oct. 1, 1931.

Notes
Chapter Thirty-Two
The Conscience of Clive Davies

1. TCD diary, Mar. 9, 1932.
2. Ibid., Mar. 25, 1932.
3. C.J. Henderson to GFD, Mar. 23, 1932.
4. JER to TCD, Aug. 16, 1932.
5. TCD to JER, Oct. 3, 1932.
6. C.J. Henderson report of Philippine trip, Dec. 1932. Henderson was enthusiastic about Hunter; and since Henderson was John E. Russell's chief assistant, Russell was also enthusiastic. Clive Davies had reservations after one meeting.
7. Ibid.

8. JER letters to TCD, Dec. 1932.
9. TCD notes, May 1931.
10. TCD notes, Jan. 24, 1933.
11. TCD notes, Jan. 24, 1933.
12. Ibid.
13. Ibid.
14. TCD to JER, Dec. 18, 1932.
15. TCD notes, Aug. 1, 1933.

Notes
Chapter Thirty-Three
Dissension in the Ranks

1. TCD diary, Jan. 10, 1934.
2. Ibid., Jan. 12, 1934.
3 TCD to JER, Mar. 21, 1934.
5. Francis S. Morgan to author, Sep. 1978.
6. JER to TCD, Apr. 1934. Two changes seem apparent in this period: (1) For the first time Russell had begun to consider the company as much belonging to him as to the ownership, and (2) the seeds of his distrust of Gerald Wilkinson were sown in Gerald's exhibition of unshielded ambition.
7. JER to TCD, Jun. 29, 1934.
8. C.J. Henderson report to JER, 1933.
9. GHW to JER, Sep. 24, 1934.
10. Ibid.
11. TCD to JER, Nov. 1, 1934.
12. GHW to JER, Oct. 5, 1934.
13. Interview with Milton Pickup, Dec. 29, 1978.
14. GHW to his mother, Nov. 1934.
15. GHW to JER, Oct. 5, 1934.
16. GHW to JER, Dec. 10, 1934.
17. TCD diary, Jan. 29, 1935.
18. TCD notes on conversation with C.A. DeWitt, Jan. 30, 1935.
19. Ibid.
20. TCD notes and diary, Feb. 4, 1935.

Notes
Chapter Thirty-Four
New Davies Blood

1. TCD diary, Dec. 1935.
2. TCD notes, Mar. 14, 1935.
3. TCD diary, Nov. 8, 1934; GCD to author, summer 1978.
4. TCD notes, Mar. 14, 1935.

5. TCD notes, Apr. 27, 1935.
6. TCD diary, Sep. 28, 1935.
7. TCD diary, Dec. 31, 1935.
8. JER–TCD correspondence, spring and summer 1934, in THD & Co., Ltd. files.
9. THD & Co., Ltd. minutes book, 1920–60.
10. TG sugar book.
11. HIW treasurer's report, 1934, in THD & Co., Ltd. files.
12. GHW to JER, Jan. 9, 1935.
13. GHW to JER, Feb. 20, 1935.
14. JER to GHW, May 8, 1935.
15. JER to GHW, Sep. 9, 1935.
16. TCD to JER, Oct 2, 1935.
17. TCD to JER, Aug. 9, 1935. John E. Russell's attitude toward the Davies family and company became more ambivalent all the time. On the surface he was the willing servant, but beneath the surface he was determined to retain control of the company, and he regarded all members of the family as threats, obviously. He worried about Wilkinson, and he kept Harold so unemployed that Harold was miserable.
18. TCD–JER correspondence, Aug.–Sep. 1935.
19. TCD to GFD, Apr. 12, 1935.
20. Ibid.

Notes
Chapter Thirty-Five
The Union Menace

1. THD & Co., Ltd. annual report, 1935.
2. C.J. Henderson to TCD, Jan. 10, 1936.
3. Ibid.
4. GHW to THD Co., Ltd., Jan. 20, 1936.
5. C.J. Henderson to TCD, Feb. 3, 1936. The espionage against the unions is clearly detailed in Henderson's papers.
6. Ibid.
7. Ibid.
8. Hawaiian Industrial Relations Bulletin No. 3, in Henderson papers.
9. L.M. Judd report to C.J. Henderson, Jan. 30, 1936.
10. Ibid.
11. TCD correspondence, summer and fall, 1935.
12. G.F. Murray to TCD, Mar. 14, 1936.
13.
13. File of confidential reports from agents of the Industrial Association of Hawaii, C.J. Henderson papers, 1936.
14. Confidential report of Industrial Association of Hawaii, Jan. 31, 1936.
15. S.O. Hall memorandum to HSPA, Mar. 12, 1936.

Notes
Chapter Thirty-Six
Wilkinson vs. Russell, Round One

1. THD & Co., Ltd. minutes book, 1936–7.
2. TCD correspondence, 1936.
3. JER–TCD correspondence, 1936.
4. TCD diaries, 1936, particularly May 18.
5. Shareholder list, THD & Co., Ltd., Jun. 30, 1936.
6. TCD notes, May 15, 1937.
7. TCD diary, Feb. 17, 1937.
8. TCD diary, Feb. 22–24, 1937.
9. TCD diary, Mar. 9, 1937.
10. TCD diary, May 1937.
11. TCD notes, May 15, 1937; TCD diary, May 17, 1937.
12. TCD diary, May 21, 1937.
13. TCD diary, May 1937.
14. TCD diary, May 27, 1937.

Notes
Chapter Thirty-Seven
A Sea Change

1. TCD to JER, Oct. 24, 1936.
2. JER to TCD, Dec. 4, 1936.
3. TCD diary, Dec. 1936.
4. Geoffrey Davies to author, summer 1978.
5. JER to TCD, Mar. 6, 1936.
6. JER–TCD correspondence, Jan.–May 1937.
7. JER to TCD, Jun. 15, 1937.
8. JER to TCD, Nov. 12, 1937.
9. TCD to JER, Dec. 12, 1937.
10. HDTD to AWD, Apr. 1937.
11. JER to GFD, Jun. 7, 1937.
12. JER to TCD, Dec. 15, 1937.
13. JER to TCD, Jun. 16, 1937.
14. JER to TCD, Nov. 13, 1937.
15. Figures supplied by Castle & Cooke.
16. TCD to JER, Dec. 12, 1937.
17. JER correspondence, Aug. 2, 1937.
18. TCD notes, May 9, 1939.
19. TCD diary, Mar. 20, 1939.
20. TCD notes, May 9, 1939.
21. TCD diary, Mar. 20, 1939.
22. Ibid.
23. TCD notes, May 9, 1939. op. cit.

Notes
Chapter Thirty-Eight
And then Came December . . .

1. TCD diary, Jun. 25, 1939.
2. TCD diary, Jul. 1939.
3. TCD diary, Jul. 27, 1939.
4. TCD diary, Jul. 27. 1939.
5. GCD to author, Feb. 1979.
6. HFD correspondence, summer 1939.
7. GHW to JER, Sep. 16, 1939.
8. TCD diaries, Sep. 1940.
9. TCD diary, May 14, 1941.
10. GHW diary, Jun. 28, 1941.
11. TCD diary, Sep. 9, 1941.
12. C.H. Hemenway to JER, Feb. 3, 1941.
13. JER to TCD and JER to Sir Edward Peacock, Feb. 13, 1941.
14. British loan papers, THD & Co., Ltd. papers, 1941.
15. THD Annual report, 1941.

Notes
Chapter Thirty-Nine
War in the Pacific

1. GHW to JER, Feb. 1, 1941.
2. JER to GHW, Aug. 26, 1941.
3. GHW to JER, Sep. 19, 1941.
4. JER to GHW, Mar. 17, 1941.
5. *The Lonely Ships,* by Edwin P. Hoyt, pp. 190–92.
6. GHW diary, 1941.
7. GHW letter to TCD, Mar. 17, 1942.
8. Ibid.
9. GHW diary, Mar. 10, 1942.
10. GHW diary, 1942–44.
11. GHW diary, Apr. 6, 1943.
12. GHW diary, spring 1943.
13. GHW diary, May 30, 1943.

Notes
Chapter Forty
Brave New World

1. TCD diary, Dec. 11, 1941.

2. TCD diary, Apr. 16, 1942.
3. Kukaiau Ranch minutes book, 1941–3.
4. JER to TCD, May 12, 1942.
5. TG monthly reports to TCD, 1942.
6. JER to TCD, Jan. 8, 1944.
7. GHW diary, Jul. 27, 1944.
8. George Gordon to author, Nov. 1978.
9. GHW diary, Jan. 1945.
10. GHW diary and TCD diaries, 1944–45.
11. GHW diary, Jul. 8–19, 1945.
12. TCD diary, Oct. 25, 1944.
13. TCD diary, Aug. 15, 1945.
14. TCD notes, Aug. 20, 1945.
15. Ibid.

Notes
Chapter Forty-One
China Dream

1. TCD diary, Nov.–Dec. 1945.
2. GG Gordon to GHW, Sep. 1945, undated.
3. GHW to EJ Nell, Oct. 18, 1945.
4. GHW to JER, Aug. 12, 1945.
5. GHW press release, Feb. 14, 1946.
6. GHW correspondence, Mar. 1945.
7. JER to GHW, May 3, 1946.
8. Konrad Hsu to GHW, Jun. 6, 1946.
9. Sino-Hawaiian Co. records, Jun.–Sep. 1946.
10. JER to GHW, Feb. 8, 1947.
11. JER to CV Bennett correspondence, 1946–48.

Notes
Chapter Forty-Two
Geoffrey Begins

1. GCD to author, summer 1978.
2. TCD to GCD, Nov. 25, 1946.
3. JER to TCD, Jan. 19, 1946.
4. TG monthly report to TCD, Jan. 1946.
5. JER to TCD, Dec. 18, 1945.
6. Waiakea Mill Co. books, 1945–47.
7. JER to TCD, Apr. 1946.
8. JER to TCD, Sep. 16, 1946; Daws, p. 363.

9. JER to TCD, Dec. 18, 1946.
10. JER to TCD, Jan. 30, 1947. ·
11. JER to TCD, Mar. 6, 1947.
12. JER to TCD, Jul. 16, 1947.
13. GCD to author, summer 1978.
14. JER to TCD, Jul. 16, 1947.
15. JER–TCD correspondence, summer, fall 1947.

Notes
Chapter Forty-Three
Geoffrey Davies' Dilemma

1. JER to TCD, Dec. 22, 1947.
2. GCD to TCD, Nov. 2, 1947.
3. GCD correspondence with TCD, Sep. 1947.
4. TCD notes, Mar. 26, 1948.
5. TCD memo of conversation with JER, Mar. 23, 1948.
6. TCD diary, May 1948.
7. Waiakea Mill Co. records, 1949.
8. GCD to TCD, Feb. 21, 1949.
9. GCD report on planations, May 1949.
10. TCD notes, Oct. 23, 1949.

Notes
Chapter Forty-Four
The Promotion of Geoffrey Davies

1. A.G. Smith letters to TCD, 1949.
2. GCD to TCD correspondence, 1947–48. Geoffrey Davies wrote to his father regularly. In the beginning he spoke his mind openly about the business, but ran into so much shocked opposition from Clive Davies that he stopped that by 1949. Thereafter, much of his correspondence was about Craigside, other property, and family affairs, but occasionally Geoffrey's feelings would get away from him and he would discuss his business troubles, mostly with John E. Russell.
3. GCD to TCD, May 7, 1950.
4. GCD to TCD, May 10, 1949.
5. TCD to GCD, May 18, 1950.
6. GCD to TCD, Dec. 1949.
7. GCD to TCD, Jan. 8, 1950.
8. JER to TCD, Mar. 31, 1949.
9. JER to TCD, Apr. 5, 1949.
10. This net-profit table is constructed from information received from the various companies, plus the Theo H. Davies & Co., Ltd. annual reports for 1940 and 1950.
11. TCD to GCD, Dec. 18, 1949.

Notes
Chapter Forty-Five
The Banishment of Gerald Wilkinson

1. TCD diary, Sep. 16, 1950.
2. TCD to JER, Feb. 24, 1951.
3. JER to TCD, Mar. 6, 1951.
4. A.G. Smith to JER, Mar. 6, 1951.
5. TCD to JER, Mar. 20, 1951.
6. Conversations between author and C.H. Holt, Mrs. H.D. Brown; JER correspondence, 1950.
7. JER letters to TCD, Aug. 28, 30, 1951.
8. TCD to JER, Sep. 7, 1951.
9. JER to TCD, Jul. 26, 1951.
10. GCD to TCD, Aug. 1951.

Notes
Chapter Forty-Six
The Death of Clive Davies

1. JER to TCD, Feb. 2, 1952.
2. TCD to JER, Jan. 15, 1952.
3. JER to TCD, Feb. 5, 1952.
4. JER to TCD, Aug. 4, 1952.
5. The profits of the various companies are from figures supplied the author in Jan. 1979.
6. TCD notes, May 2, 1952.
7. TCD diary, Oct. 6, 1952.
8. TCD to JER correspondence, Jul.–Aug. 1952.

Notes
Chapter Forty-Seven
More Trouble in Paradise

1. THD & Co., Ltd. annual report, 1952.
2. Ibid.
3. Ibid.
4. *Manila Chronicle,* Nov. 29, 1968.
5. GHW to JER, Feb. 19, 1953.
6. GHW to JER, May 19, 1953.
7. JER to GHW, Aug. 1, 1953.
8. Carlos Ledesma, Manila, to author, Nov. 1978.
9. THD & Co., Ltd. annual report, 1959.
10. TCD notes, Mar. 20, 1959.
11. GCD to JER, Feb. 11, 1954.

12. GCD to O.B. Hammond, Jan. 11, 1954.
13. GCD to GTD, Sep. 28, 1954.
14. GCD to TMD, Dec. 30, 1954.
15. GCD to author, spring 1978.

Notes
Chapter Forty-Eight
Enter George T. Davies; Exit George T. Davies

1. GCD correspondence, summer 1956.
2. GCD memo to JER, May 4, 1956.
3. Author's interview with Harold Weidig, Jan. 5, 1978.
4. GHW quarterly report to JER, Nov. 21, 1955.
5. GCD report to JER, May 31, 1957.
6. JER to GTD, Apr. 17, 1957.
7. THD & Co., Ltd. annual report, 1957.
8. GTD to GCD, Oct. 8, 1957.
9. Ibid.
10. GCD to GHW, Feb. 3, 1958.
11. Ibid.
12. THD & Co., Ltd. annual report, 1958.

Notes
Chapter Forty-Nine
The Rebellion of Geoffrey Davies

1. JER to T.W. Haynes, Dec. 20, 1957.
2. JER to GHW, Mar. 5, 1958.
3. Milton Pickup to author, Jan. 5, 1979.
4. GCD to author, summer 1978.
5. JER to AWD, Mar. 10, 1959.
6. JER to TG, Jun. 3, 1959.
7. JER to Stephen Young, Nov. 27, 1959.
8. GCD to Leslie Wishard, Dec. 10, 1959.
9. JER report of meeting with Harry Stonehill.
10. JER to Stephen Young, Dec. 31, 1959.
11. Ibid.
12. Shareholders analysis, C.H. Holt, 1959.
13. GCD correspondence, Feb. 1959.
14. JER to Stephen Young, Feb. 26, 1960.
15. Telegrams, GHW, Baring Brothers, in GCD files, Aug. 1960.
16. GCD to author, Feb. 1979.
17. Ibid.

18. GCD correspondence, Dec. 1960.
19. Stephen Young to GCD, Mar. 14, 1961.
20. GCD to GHW, Mar. 16, 1961.
21. GCD to author, summer 1978.
22. GCD to his sister Muriel, Apr. 11, 1961.
23. Ibid.
24. Ibid.

Notes
Chapter Fifty
Change in Leadership

1. Stephen Young to GCD, Aug. 24, 1961.
2. GCD memo on reorganization, Aug. 19, 1961.
3. GCD to GTD, Nov. 3, 1961.
4. SNY to stockholders, Nov. 9, 1961.
5. GCD to SNY, Dec. 12, 1961.
6. GHW to GCD, Jan. 10, 1962.
7. THD & Co., Ltd., annual report, 1961.
8. GHW to GCD, Jan. 15, 1962.
9. GHW to SNY, May 25, 1962.
10. Chiko Noda to author, Jan. 12, 1979.
11. GHW to SNY, May 25, 1962.
12. GHW memo, May 1962.
13. THD & Co., Ltd. annual report, 1962.
14. William McCoy to author, Jan. 12, 1979.
15. THD & Co., Ltd. annual report, 1962.

Notes
Chapter Fifty-One
The Untimely End of Gerald Wilkinson

1. GHW memo, Oct 23, 1962.
2. GHW to GCD, Nov. 2, 1962.
3. GCD to GHW, Jan. 10, 1962.
4. GCD to GHW correspondence, 1963–64.
5. A.W. Woods, Hawaiian-Philippine Co. to S.O. Halls, Dec. 31, 1940.
6. Author's interviews with Joe Marie Locsin, George Gordon, Oscar Ledesma, Carlos Ledesma, E.L. Westley, in Manila, Nov. 1978.
7. Emmanuel Pelaez to author, Dec. 1978. Carlos Ledesma to author, Nov. 1978.
8. Joe Marie Locsin to author, Nov. 1978.
9. Milton Pickup to author, Jan. 1979.
10. GHW to GCD, Jun. 15, 1964.
11. HDW to GHW, Mar. 22, 1965.

12. GCD to GHW, Mar. 15, 1965.
13. THD & Co., Ltd., annual report, 1965.
15. Ibid.
16. Milton Pickup to author, Jan. 1979.
17. Ibid.

Notes
Chapter Fifty-Two
Picking up th Pieces

1. GCD to HDW, Jul 19, 1965.
2. HDW to GCD, Jul. 22, 1965.
3. HDW to GCD, Aug. 4, 1965.
4. HDW to GCD, Aug. 1, 1965.
5. GCD to HDW, Aug. 20, 1965.
6. GCD to HDW, Nov. 19, 1965.
7. GCD to HDW, Nov. 23, 1965.
8. HDW to GCD, May 13, 1966.
9. GCD to HDW correspondence, Jun. 1966.
10. HDW to GCD, Jul. 25, 1966.
11. GCD to HDW, Jul. 30, 1966.
12. HDW to GCD, Aug. 12, 1966.
13. THD & Co., Ltd., annual report, 1966.
14. GCD to HDW, Dec. 30, 1966.
15. GCD to HDW, Dec. 31, 1966.
16. GCD to HDW, Mar. 19, 1967.
17. Milton Pickup to author, Jan. 1979.

Notes
Chapter Fifty-Three
The Dillingham Party

1. GCD to HDW correspondence, May 1967.
2. HDW to GCD, Jun. 13, 1967.
3. Minutes of THD & Co., Ltd. board meeting, Apr. 26, 1967.
4. HWD to GCD, Jun. 23, 1967.
5. GCD letter to shareholders, Jul. 31, 1967.
6. HDW to GCD, Aug. 2, 1967.
7. HDW to GCD, Aug. 3, 1967.
8. Honolulu *Star-Bulletin*, Aug. 4–5, 1967.
9. Lowell Dillingham to THD & Co., Ltd. stockholders, Aug. 24, 1967.
10. GCD to HDW, Sep. 27, 1967.
11. GCD to HDW, Oct. 9, 1967.
12. GCD to HDW, Dec. 6, 1967.

13. THD & Co., Ltd. annual report, 1967.
14. THD & Co., Ltd. annual report, 1967.
15. Milton Pickup to author, Jan. 12, 1979.

Notes
Chapter Fifty-Four
Enter Jardine, Matheson

1. THD & Co., Ltd. board meeting, Mar. 20, 1968.
2. MHP correspondence, Jan.–Jun. 1968.
3. THD & Co., Ltd. annual report, 1968.
4. THD & Co., Ltd. annual report, 1969. ·
5. Ibid.
6. MHP to Dracoman (Davies.–Far East), May 15, 1970.
7. MHP to J.G. Johnston, Apr. 24, 1970.
8. Figures were supplied by various companies mentioned.
9. MHP to GCD, Dec. 9, 1971.
10. THD & Co., Ltd. annual report, 1972.
11. THD & Co., Ltd. board meeting, May 25, 1972.
12. THD & Co., Ltd. board meeting, Aug. 10, 1972.
13. GCD to author, summer 1978.
14. GCD to JHT, Mar. 22, 1959.

IMPORTANT LANDMARKS

OAHU

1   Kaalaea

2   Waialua

3   La'a

6   Honolulu Iron Works

8   Kahuku Plantation Co.

MAUI

2   Kipahulu Mill

1   Lahaina Sugar Co.

KAUAI

1   McBryde Sugar Co.

THEO. H. DAVIES & Cº LTD
FOUNDED 1845

Companies on Oahu, Maui, Kauai, today

OAHU

3   Atlas Electric

3   TheoDavies Brokerage

5   TheoDavies corporate office

6   TheoDavies Euromotors

5   Jardine Insurance Services

5   TheoDavies Marine Agencies

5   TheoDavies Properties

3   TheoDavies Tire Company

3   Hawaiian Fluid Power

4   Pacific Machinery

7   Hilo Iron Works (Stubenberg Division)

MAUI

3   Pacific Machinery

3   TheoDavies Euromotors

KAUAI

2   Pacific Machinery